G000150782

"Many books have appeared on Thomas Merton
untimely death, but this illuminating interpretat
completely new ground. Readers who love Mert
before in this wise and balanced commentary. N
for the first time will discover why this passiona
considered one of the spiritual giants of our age. And best of all, in Christopher
Pramuk we encounter the spiritual depth, intellectual acuity, and compassionate
humanity of Merton himself."

Kevin F. Burke, SJ
Dean, Jesuit School of Theology
Santa Clara University, Berkeley Campus

"Christopher Pramuk's *Sophia: The Hidden Christ of Thomas Merton* is, dare it be
said, a gorgeous book. Its beautifully crafted pages are full of insight about Merton
and his 'sapiential' theological method, the poetical and mystical manner in which
he lived into the rich symbolic matrix of faith and drew from it living wisdom,
made luminous by his engagement with non-western religions, Eastern Orthodox
thought, and the kataphatic and apophatic modes of knowing of his own tradition.
Moreover, *Sophia* invites the reader into a compelling meditation on the doing
of theology in the contemporary world. It affirms the need for a bold theological
imagination and a faith intensely aware of Sophia, the divine presence alive in the
world."

Wendy M. Wright
Professor of Theology
John C. Kenefick Faculty Chair in the Humanities
Creighton University

"*Sophia: The Hidden Christ of Thomas Merton* is a luminous, even mesmerizing,
essay on the very nature of theology itself. Pramuk illuminates not only Merton's
profound Christological vision, but places that in thought-provoking conversation
with the great Russian theologians who—during a century of bitter strife—were
irradiated by the mysterious figure of Wisdom. This work will be of deep interest
to students of Christology, of Merton, of contemporary theology, and to all who
pause in wonder before the recovering encounter of theology and the mystical."

Mark A. McIntosh
Van Mildert Professor of Divinity
The University of Durham, United Kingdom

"Pramuk's work is, far and away, the most sophisticated theological study ever
done on the writings of Thomas Merton. It sets a very high bar for anyone else
who intends to comment on the writings of the monk whose writings, nearly a
half century after his death, still exert such a powerful influence on contemporary
religious seekers."

Lawrence S. Cunningham
John A. O'Brien Professor of Theology
The University of Notre Dame

Sophia

The Hidden Christ of Thomas Merton

Christopher Pramuk

A Michael Glazier Book

LITURGICAL PRESS

Collegeville, Minnesota

www.litpress.org

A Michael Glazier Book published by Liturgical Press

Cover design by David Manahan, OSB, with Ann Blattner. Cover drawing by Thomas Merton. Used with permission of the Merton Legacy Trust and the Thomas Merton Center, Bellarmine University.

Excerpts from documents of the Second Vatican Council are from *Vatican Council II: The Basic Sixteen Documents*, by Austin Flannery, OP © 1996 (Costello Publishing Company, Inc.). Used with permission.

Unless otherwise noted, Scripture texts in this work are taken from the *New Revised Standard Version Bible: Catholic Edition* © 1989, 1993, Division of Christian Education of the National Council of the Churches of Christ in the United States of America. Used by permission. All rights reserved.

© 2009 by Order of Saint Benedict, Collegeville, Minnesota. All rights reserved. No part of this book may be reproduced in any form, by print, microfilm, microfiche, mechanical recording, photocopying, translation, or by any other means, known or yet unknown, for any purpose except brief quotations in reviews, without the previous written permission of Liturgical Press, Saint John's Abbey, PO Box 7500, Collegeville, Minnesota 56321-7500. Printed in the United States of America.

ISBN 978-0-8146-8417-7 (paperback)

1	2	3	4	5	6	7	8	9

Library of Congress Cataloging-in-Publication Data

Pramuk, Christopher.
    Sophia : the hidden Christ of Thomas Merton / Christopher Pramuk.
      p. cm.
    "A Michael Glazier book."
    Includes bibliographical references and index.
    ISBN 978-0-8146-5390-6
    1. Merton, Thomas, 1915–1968.   2. God (Christianity)—Wisdom.   3. Jesus Christ—Person and offices.   I. Title.

BX4705.M542P73   2009
231'.6—dc22   2009024583

For my parents, Jack and Gladys Pramuk,
who immersed me in music, and Merton, from the very beginning.

And in loving memory of Vincent J. O'Flaherty, SJ

The waking have one common world,
but the sleeping turn aside each into a world of his own.
He that is awake lights up from sleeping.

—Herakleitos, 5th Century BCE

Awake, O sleeper,
and arise from the dead,
and Christ will give you light.

—Ephesians 5:14 (NAB)

The helpless one, abandoned to sweet sleep,
him the gentle one will awake: *Sophia*.

—Thomas Merton, 1962

Contents

Acknowledgments

If theology can be described as a lifelong conversation with wonder and mystery, then I have been blessed beyond merit or measure with the best conversation partners one could hope to find. First of these is my wife Lauri, whose companionship remains the greatest wonder of my life. Likewise I want to thank my two children, Isaiah and Grace, and my extended family near and far, who make me smile and laugh (and sing) a lot, and keep me rooted firmly to the earth.

Of the many mentors and colleagues who have given inspiration and encouragement along the way, special thanks go to Kevin Burke, SJ, whose friendship has sustained me immeasurably for nearly twenty years. It was in conversation with him that the seeds for this study were first planted. Likewise to Tom Esselman, CM, and Roger Haight, SJ, who together share at least some of the blame for igniting my love for the discipline of theology. During the writing of this book I was especially supported by Ernesto Valiente and Stephen Belt, two friends whose magnanimity and passion for life have taught me more than I can say, and by my wonderful colleagues in the Theology Department at Xavier University.

I will forever be grateful to Lawrence Cunningham of the University of Notre Dame, who generously guided my doctoral research on Thomas Merton, and without whose encouragement this book would have never seen the light of day. Like Merton, Larry's extraordinary facility with the written word continues to form, challenge, and inspire my own approach to theology. Less directly but no less significantly, I am indebted to the worldwide community of Merton scholars whose work precedes and informs my own everywhere in these pages. Among these I especially wish to thank Patrick O'Connell, Christine Bochen, and William Shannon, coauthors of *The Thomas Merton Encyclopedia*; Brother Patrick Hart; Christopher Nugent; Canon A. M. Allchin; and Paul Pearson, the director of The Thomas Merton Center at Bellarmine University.

Finally, I am immensely grateful to all at Liturgical Press who embraced this project and helped see it through to completion, not least my gifted editor Mary Stommes, and editorial director Hans Christoffersen. May God bless and sustain the remarkable work that religious publishers do, day in and day out, in service of the church, the theological community, and spiritual pilgrims everywhere.

* * * *

"Hagia Sophia." By Thomas Merton, from EMBLEMS OF A SEASON OF FURY, copyright © 1963 by The Abbey of Gethsemani. Reprinted by permission of New Directions Publishing Corp.

Thomas Merton, from BREAD IN THE WILDERNESS, copyright © 1953 by Our Lady of Gethsemani Monastery. Reprinted by permission of New Directions Publishing Corp.

"Seven Archaic Images." By Thomas Merton, from EMBLEMS OF A SEASON OF FURY, copyright © 1963 by The Abbey of Gethsemani. Reprinted by permission of New Directions Publishing Corp.

Thomas Merton, from NEW SEEDS OF CONTEMPLATION, copyright © 1961 by The Abbey of Gethsemani, Inc. Reprinted by permission of New Directions Publishing Corp.

Thomas Merton, from RAIDS ON THE UNSPEAKABLE, copyright © 1966 by The Abbey of Gethsemani, Inc. Reprinted by permission of New Directions Publishing Corp.

Thomas Merton, from THE ASIAN JOURNALS OF THOMAS MERTON, copyright © 1975 by The Trustees of the Merton Legacy Trust. Reprinted by permission of New Directions Publishing Corp.

Thomas Merton, from THE LITERARY ESSAYS OF THOMAS MERTON, copyright © 1960, 1966, 1967, 1968, 1973, 1975, 1978, 1981 by The Trustees of the Merton Legacy Trust, Copyright © 1959, 1961, 1963, 1964, 1965, 1981 by The Abbey of Gethsemani, Inc., Copyright © 1953 by Our Lady of Gethsemani Monastery. Reprinted by permission of New Directions Publishing Corp.

"Keng's Disciple." By Thomas Merton, from THE WAY OF CHUANG TZU, copyright © 1965 by The Abbey of Gethsemani. Reprinted by permission of New Directions Publishing Corp.

Thomas Merton, from ZEN AND THE BIRDS OF APPETITE, copyright © 1968 by The Abbey of Gethsemani, Inc. Reprinted by permission of New Directions Publishing Corp.

Thomas Merton, from CONJECTURES OF A GUILTY BYSTANDER, copyright © 1966 by the Abbey of Gethsemani. Used by permission of Doubleday, a division of Random House, Inc.

Thomas P. McDonnell, from A THOMAS MERTON READER, copyright © 1974 by the Trustees of the Merton Legacy Trust. Used by permission of Doubleday, a division of Random House, Inc.

Thomas Merton, from THE SIGN OF JONAS, copyright © 1953 by the Abbey of Our Lady of Gethsemani and renewed 1981 by the Trustees of the Merton Legacy Trust. Reprinted by permission of Houghton Mifflin Harcourt Publishing Company.

Thomas Merton, from THE BEHAVIOR OF TITANS, copyright © 1961 by the Abbey of Our Lady of Gethsemani. Reprinted by permission of Curtis Brown, Ltd.

Catherine Evtuhov, *The Cross and the Sickle: Sergei Bulgakov and the Fate of Russian Religious Philosophy, 1890–1920*. Copyright © 1997 by Cornell University Press. Used by permission of the publisher, Cornell University Press.

From A SEARCH FOR SOLITUDE: THE JOURNALS OF THOMAS MERTON, VOLUME THREE (1952–1960) by THOMAS MERTON and EDITED BY LAWRENCE S. CUN-NINGHAM. Copyright © 1996 by The Merton Legacy Trust. Reprinted by permission of HarperCollins Publishers.

From TURNING TOWARD THE WORLD: THE JOURNALS OF THOMAS MERTON, VOLUME FOUR (1960–1963) by THOMAS MERTON and EDITED BY VICTOR A. KRAMER. Copyright © 1996 by The Merton Legacy Trust. Reprinted by permission of HarperCollins Publishers.

From DANCING IN THE WATER OF LIFE: THE JOURNALS OF THOMAS MERTON, VOLUME FIVE (1963–1965) by THOMAS MERTON and EDITED BY ROBERT E. DAGGY. Copyright © 1997 by The Merton Legacy Trust. Reprinted by permission of HarperCollins Publishers.

From LEARNING TO LOVE: THE JOURNALS OF THOMAS MERTON, VOLUME SIX (1966–1967) by THOMAS MERTON and EDITED BY CHRISTINE M. BOCHEN. Copyright © 1997 by The Merton Legacy Trust. Reprinted by permission of HarperCollins Publishers.

Excerpts from AN INTRODUCTION TO CHRISTIAN MYSTICISM: INITIATION INTO THE MONASTIC TRADITION 3, copyright © 2008 by Cistercian Publications. Reprinted by permission.

Paul Evdokimov, WOMAN AND THE SALVATION OF THE WORLD, copyright © 1994. Reprinted by permission of St. Vladimir's Seminary Press.

Reprinted by permission of Farrar, Straus and Giroux, LLC: Excerpts from THE COURAGE FOR TRUTH: THE LETTERS OF THOMAS MERTON TO WRITERS by Thomas Merton, edited by Christine M. Bochen. Copyright © 1993 by the Merton Legacy Trust. Excerpts from DISPUTED QUESTIONS by Thomas Merton. Copyright © 1960 by The Abbey of Our Lady of Gethsemani. Copyright renewed © 1988 by Alan Hanson. Excerpts from THE HIDDEN GROUND OF LOVE: THE LETTERS OF THOMAS MERTON ON RELIGIOUS EXPERIENCE AND SOCIAL CONCERNS by Thomas Merton, edited by William H. Shannon. Copyright © 1985 by the Merton Legacy Trust. Excerpts from LOVE AND LIVING by Thomas Merton. Copyright © 1979 by The Merton Legacy Trust. Excerpts from MYSTICS AND ZEN MASTERS by Thomas Merton. Copyright © 1967 by the Abbey of Gethsemani. Copyright renewed 1995 by Robert Giroux, James Laughlin, and Tommy O'Callaghan as trustees of the Merton Legacy Trust. Excerpts from

THE NEW MAN by Thomas Merton. Copyright © 1961 by Thomas Merton. Copyright renewed 1989 by Farrar, Straus & Giroux, LLC.

*Permissions for the following works were still in process at the time of publication.

Edward K. Kaplan, HOLINESS IN WORDS: ABRAHAM JOSHUA HESCHEL'S POETICS OF PIETY, copyright © 1996, published by State University of New York Press.

Abraham Joshua Heschel, MAN'S QUEST FOR GOD, copyright © 1954, published by Scribner's.

Abbreviations

RU	*Raids on the Unspeakable* (1966)
SD	*Seeds of Destruction* (1964)
SFS	*A Search for Solitude* (1996)
SJ	*The Sign of Jonas* (1953)
SSM	*The Seven Storey Mountain* (1948)
TME	*The Thomas Merton Encyclopedia* (2002)
TTW	*Turning Toward the World* (1997)
WCT	*The Way of Chuang Tzu* (1965)
WF	*Witness to Freedom* (1994)
ZBA	*Zen and the Birds of Appetite* (1968)

Other Works

ED	*An Essay on the Development of Christian Doctrine* (John Henry Newman)
GA	*An Essay in Aid of a Grammar of Assent* (John Henry Newman)
HW	*Holiness in Words* (Edward K. Kaplan)
MRT	*Modern Russian Theology* (Paul Valliere)
OUS	*Fifteen Sermons Preached Before the University of Oxford* (John Henry Newman)

Drawing by Thomas Merton. Used with permission of the Merton Legacy Trust and the Thomas Merton Center, Bellarmine University.

Preface

In a recent volume of essays in constructive theology from around the world, Terrence Merrigan and Jacques Haers suggest that to survey the state of contemporary Christology is to be reminded of William Butler Yeats's celebrated poem, *The Second Coming*:

> Turning and turning in the widening gyre
> The falcon cannot hear the falconer;
> Things fall apart; the centre cannot hold;
> Mere anarchy is loosed upon the world,
> The blood-dimmed tide is loosed, and everywhere
> The ceremony of innocence is drowned;
> The best lack all conviction, while the worst
> Are full of passionate intensity.

What prompts Merrigan and Haers to cite Yeats's unsettling lines is the "multiplicity of portraits of Jesus which characterizes the contemporary theological landscape, and the challenges thrown up by this multiplicity." With a certain urgency and not a little polemic—"In an age such as ours when the discipline [of Christology] has been opened up to all comers"—the authors pose the following question: "Can properly Christian discourse survive if its traditional center, the God-man, Jesus Christ, is dissolved into a myriad of disparate and even conflicting images and notions?"[1]

The anxiety generating this question pertains not only to Christology, of course, but more generally to a perceived crisis of identity in Christian life in the postmodern world. On the one hand, this crisis is not, as Johann Baptist Metz insists, a crisis of faith *content* so much as a crisis of *praxis*, or discipleship. On the other hand, as Metz also insists, it is the language of dogmatic theology, as a form of ecclesial memory, which comprises the

---

1. Terrence Merrigan and Jacques Haers, *The Myriad Christ: Plurality and the Quest for Unity in Contemporary Christology* (Leuven: Leuven University Press, 2000), vii.

positive seedbed of Christian spirituality.[2] If Western Christians today appear to lack commitment to a life of faith, it may be because the terms of that faith have lost all purchase in their memory and imagination. It may be, as Yeats intimates, that even "the best" of their teachers "lack all conviction" or despair of passing on the received wisdom of an ancient tradition to a generation that seems increasingly spellbound by the glitter of technology, the lure of consumerism, and the surreal whirlwind of change in a global, media-saturated environment. What is more, that very environment seems daily to confirm that everywhere "the blood-dimmed tide" has been loosed, and this not in spite of religion but *because* of it, sanctioned by it, celebrated by it. If religion once awakened in human beings a sense of primordial innocence, its darker currents seem to whisper today, almost mockingly, that "the ceremony of innocence is drowned."

Nearly five decades ago the Roman Catholic bishops of the world at the Second Vatican Council committed themselves to the principle that Christianity is no Baroque museum but a living tradition, vibrantly responsive to the signs of the times. With open-eyed hope for the peoples of the modern world, the council urged us to learn anew from the lives of those women and men who have gone before us, those "companions of ours in the human condition" who have faithfully followed Christ (*Lumen gentium* 50). This book is predicated on the conviction that Thomas Merton is one of these faithful companions, indeed, one of our very best, who still has much to teach us, not only about the human condition but also about the mystery of God unveiled in Jesus Christ, the One who radically shapes our image of what it means to be truly human.

"The future of serious Catholic theology," writes David Tracy, "lies with its ability to recover [the] classic resources of the mystical tradition without forfeiting the need to retrieve them critically."[3] This book looks to Thomas Merton as a classic theologian of the mystical tradition from East to West, and offers a retrieval and interpretation of his mature Christology. While in no way presuming to provide a conclusive answer or solution to the myriad challenges confronting Christology today, this study will suggest, with Merton's life as witness, that the remembrance of Sophia holds significant promise for invigorating (I do not say "centering") christological and trinitarian discourse in response to these increasingly fractured, technological, industrialized, and militarized

---

2. See Johann Baptist Metz, *Faith in History and Society: Toward a Practical Fundamental Theology*, trans. and ed. J. Matthew Ashley (New York: Crossroad, 2007), especially pp. 182–85. Metz describes Christian creeds and dogmas as "formulas of *memoria*" which—in a society "that is becoming ever more devoid of history and memory"—"break the spell of the dominant consciousness" in a "redemptively dangerous way."

3. David Tracy, "The Uneasy Alliance Reconceived: Catholic Theological Method, Modernity, and Postmodernity," *Theological Studies* 50 (1989): 548–70, at 565.

times. Bound up closely with the biblical doctrine of creation and the patristic doctrines of incarnation, divinization, and grace, a Wisdom or Sophia-inspired Christology offers a compelling narrative and metaphysical framework for making old things new again in theological discourse, for reimagining God's vital presence in the natural world, and for reaffirming in boldest dogmatic terms the transcendent dignity of human persons everywhere.

No doubt the imaginative framework explored in these pages presses beyond the comfort zone of traditional fundamental or scholastic theology, with its circumscribed (and patriarchal) definitions, into the more fluid realm of biblical imagination, contemplative experience, and poetics. Awakening the memory of Sophia, in other words—whether in new kinds of God-language and symbols, new (but also ancient) forms of prayer, art, or liturgical praxis—will require *risk*, and therefore discernment, by the church and its theologians. It would be gratuitous to suggest here that such a discernment is soon forthcoming, despite an evident burgeoning of interest in Russian sophiology and in Wisdom Christology among Western specialists today.

Yet the life of Thomas Merton, and especially his sensitivity to Eastern sensibilities, still beckons to contemporary pilgrims like a supercharged magnet, pulsing with the energy of a life centered in Christ that is at once mystical and political, personal and ecclesial, sacrificial and life-giving. As longtime Merton scholar Jonathan Montaldo writes, "The effect of reading Merton's autobiographical works is a species of *metanoia*. Reading Merton threatens incidences of being changed, of wanting to lead a different, deeper kind of life."[4] Today I would add one point to this perceptive comment: reading Merton also awakens the desire to forge a different, deeper kind of *theology*. Why? Because, in the end, Merton succeeded in his desire to reunite in his own spiritual and intellectual life "the thought of the East and the West, of the Greek and Latin Fathers."[5] Such a witness gives at least preliminary credence to an intuition that may seem, to the uninitiated, frankly surprising: that Sophia, the same theological eros that animated Merton's religious imagination, might be capable of infusing new vitality into ours. And that her voice might awaken in the lives of ordinary Christians, ways both ancient and new, of bringing to birth the love and mercy of Christ in a stricken world.

She smiles, for though they have bound her, she cannot be a prisoner.[6]

---

4. Jonathan Montaldo, "A Gallery of Women's Faces and Dreams of Women from the Drawings and Journals of Thomas Merton," in *The Merton Annual* 14, ed. Victor A. Kramer (Sheffield, UK: Sheffield Academic Press, 2001), 155–72, at 155.

5. Thomas Merton, *A Search for Solitude: Pursuing the Monk's Life*, ed. Lawrence S. Cunningham (San Francisco: HarperSanFrancisco, 1996), 87; hereafter SFS.

6. Thomas Merton, *Hagia Sophia*, in *Emblems of a Season of Fury* (New York: New Directions, 1963), 63–64; hereafter ESF.

Introduction

My first encounter with Thomas Merton came some thirty years ago as a teenager, when I happened across an old copy of *The Sign of Jonas* on my mother's bookshelf. Whether by chance or providence, I picked it up and began to read, and some days later came to the book's stunning epilogue, "Fire Watch, July 4, 1952." Merton's dialogue with silence and mystery—*There is no leaf that is not in Your care. . . There is no water in the shales that was not hidden there by Your wisdom*—struck me deeply, and like many others before and since, I was hooked. Merton became a kind of spiritual guide and trusted companion throughout my young adulthood. It is curious, however, that when I began to drop roots in the field of systematic theology in my early thirties, Merton began to drift from my theological horizon. By my mid-thirties, his writings had all but faded from my imagination, like the beautiful, but dated, church of my childhood. Certainly the idea that I would write a book such as this would have seemed to me then a kind of category mistake: spirituality, yes, prophetic social criticism, yes, interreligious dialogue, certainly, but serious constructive Christology?

It wasn't until my late thirties—as it happens, around two years after September 11, 2001, and in the charged atmosphere surrounding the launch of the second Iraq War—that Merton reemerged with some force for me as a locus of real interest for the most pressing issues in contemporary Christology, above all, how to speak of Christ in an age of pluralism, and, to be sure, an age of increasing violence between cultures and nations. Curiously enough it was Newman, specifically, his forays into the realm of epistemology, that provided the interpretive key, opening my eyes to the pivotal role of the imagination both in the encounter with Jesus Christ and in structuring religious discourse through theology and doctrinal development. In short, Newman's spirited insistence on a theological method that takes account of the whole person, and not just the rational or empirical mind narrowly conceived, reminded me not a little of Thomas Merton, not only one of the twentieth century's most successful communicators of the faith, but also one of its foremost pioneers of interfaith dialogue. I began to revisit Merton's life and writings with fresh eyes, focusing especially on his Christology. If it is the imagination, as Newman so compellingly argues, which governs our experience of God, which assembles and makes sense of the whole, then I wanted to know: who is this Christ that centered Merton's capacious religious imagination during the extraordinary last decade of his life?

The question, I soon found, is a slippery one. For the moment one tries to say something too assuredly about "Merton's Christology," one finds right away—as Merton said of his own struggle to understand Zen—that *that* is assuredly "not it."[1] Obviously one solution is to say nothing, that is, to abandon any attempt to pin down Merton's Christology as either too unwieldy, given the sheer range and scope of his writings, or more skeptically, as a misguided confusion of "spiritual theology" and "mystical poetry" with the *real* thing, meaning the kinds of Christology usually formulated and debated in lecture halls. But gradually I came to see that there is another way to approach Merton's Christology, and that is to frame it not as an intellectual puzzle to be solved so much as a unifying thread to be discerned in the larger tapestry of his life, or, to switch metaphors, a harmonizing key rising from his mystical biography. Such an approach would recognize (again, as in his struggle to grasp Zen) that the problem is not first and foremost an intellectual problem so much as "a problem of 'realization'—something that has to break through."[2] To get inside Merton's Christology is to allow "something to break through," an inner music to be heard, indeed, to be *enjoyed*, in the wide-ranging symphony that comprises his life and writings.

At the same time, and not to overdraw the analogy with Zen, for Merton himself the task of theology as such involves *both* "realization" (contemplation; mystical experience) *and* intellectual struggle, the two movements circling and informing each other as perhaps in a fugue or carefully patterned dance. Just as good choreography is careful not to foreclose or rigidly confine the dance but aims rather to structure, support, and unleash its spontaneity, its surprise, its grace, just so theology at its Catholic (and literary) best aims to structure, support, and unleash the living experience of God, contempla-

---

1. Thomas Merton, *The Hidden Ground of Love*, ed. William H. Shannon (New York: Farrar, Straus and Giroux, 1985), 569; hereafter HGL. It is a curious fact that in the countless pages of Merton's writings "one would look in vain for a systematic presentation of Christology" (William H. Shannon, "Christology," in idem, Christine M. Bochen, and Patrick F. O'Connell, *The Thomas Merton Encyclopedia* [Maryknoll, NY: Orbis, 2002], 51–54, at 51; hereafter TME). For this reason any attempt to retrieve and interpret Merton's Christology will have to be done with an eye toward a wide range of texts and genres; no single study, not least this one, can aspire to be exhaustive.

2. HGL, 569.

tion, the inner dynamism of faith. At the very least, theology, even in its most academic or speculative mode, ought not to *foreclose* the possibility of grace, surprise, or resonance in the community for which it is intended. In short, to do Christology as Merton reflexively understood and practiced the term is not only to "become fully impregnated in our mystical tradition,"[3] it is also to "bring out clearly the mystical dimensions of our theology, hence to help us to do what we must really do: live our theology . . . , fully, deeply, in its totality."[4] This is perhaps the most enduring lesson I have learned from Merton, and which I have tried to bring to the writing of this book. For, indeed, the more I tried to force-fit Merton's Christology into preconceived or abstract conceptual categories, the more I found that *that* was assuredly "not it." Yet the more I listened, meditated, and pored over his writings, the more I discerned an unmistakable music, a kind of unifying harmonic key, awakening in me the remembrance of God, a sense of a real Presence, and stirring dormant seeds of hope.

This book traces the emergence of Sophia in Merton's life and writings as a Love and a Presence that breaks through into the world, a living symbol and Name through which he encountered the living God and with which he chose, at his poetic and prophetic best, to structure theological discourse. It responds to the question of Merton's mature Christology by advancing the following thesis: it was *Sophia,* the "unknown and unseen Christ" within all things, who both centered and in many respects catalyzed Merton's theological imagination in a period of tremendous social, political, and religious fragmentation. Drawing intuitively from sources in the Judeo-Christian tradition as well as from non-Christian sources, and inspired especially by the Sophia tradition of Russian Orthodoxy—or "sophiology," as known in its speculative form—the Wisdom tradition became Merton's most vivid means of expressing "a *living experience* of unity in Christ which far transcends all conceptual formulations."[5]

Above all it was the prose poem *Hagia Sophia* (1962), by far the most realized, lyrical, and daring of Merton's meditations on Sophia, which, like a kind of magnetic north, drew my imagination back into itself again and again. That sublime text, the flowering in Merton of years of study and medi-tation on the Bible, patristic and Russian theology, and Zen, seemed at once

---

3. Thomas Merton, *An Introduction to Christian Mysticism: Initiation into the Monastic Tradition 3,* ed. Patrick F. O'Connell (Kalamazoo, MI: Cistercian, 2008), 35; hereafter ICM.

4. Ibid., 16; see also Thomas Merton, *Contemplation in a World of Action* (Notre Dame, IN: University of Notre Dame Press, 1998), 175–76 (hereafter CWA), where Merton cites Vatican II's *Dei Verbum* 8 to accent the same point.

5. Thomas Merton, *Zen and the Birds of Appetite* (New York: New Directions, 1968), 39; hereafter ZBA.

to multiply, and silence, all my questions. Rather than succumbing to my preconceived christological and trinitarian categories, it broke them open; in so doing, it awakened me to the mystical dimensions of theology. This book looks especially to *Hagia Sophia* as the culmination of a mystical theology construed under the light of Wisdom, a classic marriage of Eastern and Western spirituality, and a bold rendering of the Catholic sacramental imagination. *Hagia Sophia* is Merton's consummate hymn to the theological dignity of humankind and of all creation. It is a hymn of awakening, a call to peace. The remembrance of Sophia, I will suggest here, with Merton's life as witness, opens onto an integral spirituality of engagement in the world.

While this study is set as an exploration in systematic theology, because its protagonist is Thomas Merton its logic is not neatly linear but unfolds as a kind of story-shaped Christology, a theology of God retrieved through the life of Merton, but haunted more and more by the mysterious figure of Sophia. Because she remains largely unknown to readers in the West, even close readers of Merton, it will be important to begin by recounting in broadest strokes the story of Merton's awakening to Sophia, a narrative that weaves like a golden thread through the last decade of his life. Chapter 1 takes up this introductory task and then attempts to situate Merton's writings within the broader horizon of modern (and postmodern) Catholic theology. The central question posed in chapter 1 is this: what is it in Merton's mystical or sapiential approach to theology, and especially in his reception of Russian sophiology, that merits sustained consideration by the church and its theologians today? Readers less familiar with the broad contours of Merton's life and writings should find here enough touchpoints to be on firm ground for the remainder of the book.

Chapter 2 builds a case for the validity of Merton's approach to theology through an analysis of the pivotal role of the imagination in religious epistemology and theological method. Here we look to the respective epistemologies and semantic strategies of Newman and the great philosopher-poet of Judaism, Abraham Joshua Heschel, to argue that theology today will remain much impoverished without "a poetic dimension of theological thinking or even a theological literature in search of a poetic form and voice."[6] Newman's balanced appeal to the imagination as the dynamic faculty that aids and enlarges reason gives considerable sanction to the tradition of monastic theology in which Merton stands; Heschel's philosophy of religion, or "depth theology," comprises one of the most profound defenses of revealed religion

---

6. Mark S. Burrows, "'Raiding the Articulate': Mysticism, Poetics, and the Unlanguageable," in *Minding the Spirit: The Study of Christian Spirituality*, ed. Elizabeth A. Dreyers and Mark S. Burrows (Baltimore: Johns Hopkins, 2005), 341–61, at 348.

in the modern period and bears striking affinities with Merton's mystical-prophetic approach to language.

Crucial to any understanding of Merton's mature period is its increasingly prophetic and global content, a turning to the world shaped not only by his friendship with Heschel but also by his living relationship, as a Trappist monk, with the revelatory word of the Bible. Chapter 3 explores a wide range of texts, seeking to get inside the "archaeology" of Merton's expansive religious imagination, and above all, to probe his basic confidence in, and fluency with, the sacramental power of language. This chapter sets the stage for the second half of the book by framing the breakthrough of Sophia into Merton's consciousness in terms of his desire to remember and name God anew on the other side of his revolutionary awakening to the world beyond the monastery.

Chapter 4 chronicles the dawn of Wisdom in Merton's theological consciousness, beginning with the pivotal influence of four key mentors during the late 1950s, D. T. Suzuki, Herakleitos the Obscure, Maximus Confessor, and Boris Pasternak, followed by his study of Russian Orthodox sophiology. From the much-discussed epiphany at Fourth and Walnut in March of 1958 to his climactic pilgrimage in Asia, Sophia emerges here as a kind of unifying presence and theological wellspring in Merton's life, both centering and catalyzing his outreach to others in friendship, dialogue, and peacemaking. We come to the christological heart of things in chapter 5, which offers an interpretation of three of Merton's most formally and brilliantly realized sophiological texts: *The New Man* (1961), *New Seeds of Contemplation* (1962), and *Hagia Sophia* (1962). A description of events surrounding the composition and publication of *Hagia Sophia* sets the stage for a close theological reading of the text.

Chapter 6 takes up questions of a more historical, systematic, and constructive nature, which is to say, questions that Merton himself never fully addressed. Not least of these is the contested place of Sophia in traditional Christology and trinitarian theology. Who *is* Sophia? Is Russian sophiology trustworthy? Is it orthodox? Is it possible, or even desirable, to translate mystical texts such as *Hagia Sophia* into the terms of systematic or fundamental theology? And most compelling to me: Why did Sophia capture the imaginations of this small (and subsequently marginalized) group of thinkers who lived amid the ashes of World War I, the Bolshevik revolution, Auschwitz, Hiroshima, the Watts race riots, and the Vietnam War—a century in which theology had every reason to lose its nerve? Might Sophia be grasped against this fractured horizon as a kind of *apocalyptic* figure? All these questions may be boiled down to one: why Sophia—and not simply a vigorous renewal of the more familiar terms of christological or trinitarian discourse?

Chapter 6 advances the case that Russian sophiology—or more broadly, the "sophiological tradition," from the Russians in the East to Merton in the West—represents a distinctive response to both the profound challenges of modernity and a century of unspeakable violence, breaking open and potentially revitalizing theology and spirituality in four areas: (1) Christology (or theological anthropology), (2) Trinity (or cosmic theology), (3) Earth (or environmental theology), and (4) eros and the feminine in God (sexuality, feminist theology). Drawing from striking resonances in the spiritual biographies of Merton and the Russian theologians, the chapter concludes by exploring what amounts to a fifth area: apocalyptic, or the sanctification of time. Indeed, the apocalyptic tenor of both Russian theology and Merton's mature period suggest that sophiology is in many respects a theology of *crisis*, a bold attempt to retrieve the biblical vision of manifold creation and the diverse human community as essentially one, bound together in the life story of God from the beginning.

The conclusion briefly looks back to reprise the book's major arguments and then attempts to broadly assess the shape of the whole, considering how the sophiological perspective casts new light on some of the most pressing theological and spiritual questions of our time. Here we shall ask whether, and in what ways, the remembrance of Sophia might be brought to bear in Christian theology, liturgical life, and spirituality today. Indeed, with respect to Merton's central concern for everyday Christian spirituality, it will be emphasized throughout this book that the sophiological tradition implies not the embrace of an elaborate theology so much as a *way of life*: a commitment to prayer, community, simplicity, solitude, artistic and vocational creativity, asceticism—all tested means in the Christian tradition for cultivating a wider love in relation to the world, or what monastic spirituality calls purity of heart, poverty of spirit. For Merton the Trappist monk (or Father Louis, as he was known at Gethsemani), poverty of spirit is the a priori disposition required for realizing, in a holistic and transformative way, the sacramental presence of God in all people and things; it is the prayerful ground of sanity, of peace.

This brings me to a final introductory point about the central theological symbol at play in the following pages. As I understand her presence in Merton's writings and in the Russian theologians before him, Sophia is more, really, than a sustained metaphor for the universal presence of God, a kind of "anonymous Christology" in a feminine key. While that description would not be inaccurate, it tells only half of the story. For Merton and the Russians, Sophia is also a kind of real symbol and revealed Name for what Orthodox theology calls "divinization," meaning the *fullness of participation in the life of God*. In Bulgakov's favored expression, she is "the Humanity of God, the

Body of God . . . , the Divine World existing in God 'before' the creation."[7] Sophiology responds to the dehumanization of a blood-soaked century by daring to speak, with Chalcedon as its starting point, of the *humanization of God*, a certain humanness *in* God, made possible by God's free act of love-humility in the incarnation. Sophia is the eros of God become one with creation. And here the Russian theologians, with Merton close behind, take their cues from the haunting invocation of Wisdom in the Bible, especially Proverbs 8, where she emerges as a kind of "go-between" in creation.[8]

> Before the mountains had been shaped,
>   before the hills, I was brought forth—
> when he had not yet made earth and fields,
>   or the world's first bits of soil.
> When he established the heavens, I was there,
>   when he drew a circle on the face of the deep,
> when he made firm the skies above,
>   when he established the fountains of the deep,
> when he assigned to the sea its limit,
>   so that the waters might not transgress his command,
> when he marked out the foundations of the earth,
>   then I was beside him, like a master worker;
> and I was daily his delight,
>   rejoicing before him always,
> rejoicing in his inhabited world
>   and delighting in the human race. (Prov 8:25-31)

I was brought forth, I was there, I was beside him—from Soloviev and Bulgakov in the East to Merton in the West, the sophiological tradition hears in these lines the music of an expansive divine-human mystery, a dual hymn evoking not only the presence of Christ, the uncreated Wisdom of God who orders and plays in the universe, but also, through Christ's humanity, as it were, the primordial presence of the human race, created Sophia, in whom God rejoices and delights always.

At play in the following chapters, then, is not just a traditionally conceived Wisdom Christology but also a daring cosmology and theological anthropology, a vision of all things caught up in the life story of God "from the beginning." To say it another way, the remembrance of Sophia as described

7. Cited in Paul Valliere, *Modern Russian Theology: Bukharev, Soloviev, Bulgakov: Orthodox Theology in a New Key* (Grand Rapids, MI: Eerdmans, 2000), 336.

8. Andrew Louth, "Wisdom and the Russians: The Sophiology of Fr. Sergei Bulgakov," in *Where Shall Wisdom Be Found? Wisdom in the Bible, the Church, and the Contemporary World,* ed. Stephen C. Barton (Edinburgh: T and T Clark, 1999), 169–81, at 173.

in this book is a distinctively modern case of *dogmatic searching* or discernment in response to the signs of the times, a lucid case of what Newman calls the "illative sense" in theological method: the process of growing into the truth about the mystery of God. But this also means, for the robustly analogical imagination, growing into the truth about *the mystery of the human person.*[9] While the irruption of Sophia into Merton's consciousness was just one thread woven into a much larger fabric of his awakening to the world beyond the monastery, it was, I believe, the *golden* thread that helped him to hold the fabric together, ever more centered in Christ and forging in his life and theology the kind of Christ-centered humanism that Vatican II would envision for all the pilgrim people of God: to "recognize Christ . . . in the persons of all men and women and [to] love them with an active love, in word and deed" (*Gaudium et spes* 93).

As I hope is clear from these prefatory remarks, my approach in this study accords broadly with Anselm's description of theology as "faith seeking understanding," a method Merton once described as "experiencing theologically with the Church."[10] I presuppose an understanding of theology as a public conversation that always involves the questions, commitments, and prejudgments of the theologian. In my case these include a commitment to Roman Catholic faith and to the vocation of theology in communion with that tradition. Born in 1964 to parents of East European and Irish Catholic descent, and raised more or less in a post–Vatican II church, I belong to that generation of American Catholics (and dutiful altar boys) caught somewhere between the best of two distinct worlds: the High Tradition, with its wondrous cathedrals, icons, and "smells and bells," and the Low Tradition, with its thoroughly (and beautifully) human Jesus, concern for social justice, and intimate house church aesthetic. Were Merton alive today, I believe he would *still* say that the best way forward, the way of wisdom, will allow ample room for both theological trajectories and worship styles in the mosaic body of faith.

Finally, while this book is set as an academic study, its writing is also an act of gratitude and commitment. Though I first came to Merton's writings as a teenager, trying simply to understand the world and my place in it, it has been enormously invigorating to return to him later in life with all the questions and methods of a systematic theologian. It is remarkable, to say

---

9. This insight, as we shall see in chapter 6, lay at the heart of Russian sophiology's "positive Chalcedonianism," the idea that theology, through open and mutually enriching dialogue with other disciplines (natural science, sociology, economics, literature, anthropology, politics, and so on), must continually seek to "fill out" the content of Christology as articulated at the Council of Chalcedon (AD 451), in both its divine *and* its fully human dimensions.

10. ZBA, 46.

the least, that his writings are so responsive to both kinds of readers, the nonspecialist and the specialist, the spiritual seeker and the so-called expert, who nevertheless is, and will always remain, a seeker. No matter what else this book may or may not accomplish, I hope its pages reflect something of Merton's own spirit of intellectual openness and inquiry, a "way of seeing" that has left an immeasurable impact on my own imagination.[11]

11. While much literature has focused on Merton's witness as a Christian humanist, ecumenist, poet, interfaith pioneer, and peacemaker, there have been few systematic treatments of his Christology as such, and no sustained study to date of his relationship to Russian sophiology. Yet the potential fruitfulness of examining this relationship has been suggested, explicitly or implicitly, by a number of scholars.

Lawrence Cunningham identifies Wisdom or Sophia as the unifying thread in Merton's religious imagination during his pivotal years of "crossing over" to other traditions ("Introduction," in SFS, xii; idem, *Thomas Merton and the Monastic Vision* [Grand Rapids, MI: Eerdmans, 1999], 54, 62–63, 120). Sri Lankan theologian Aloysius Pieris looks to Merton as an exemplary model of East-West spirituality and asks whether Sophia might be the key to an "all-embracing, comprehensive and holistic" approach to Christology (*Fire and Water: Basic Issues in Asian Buddhism and Christianity* [Maryknoll, NY: Orbis, 1996], 146; idem, *Love Meets Wisdom: A Christian Experience of Buddhism* [Maryknoll, NY: Orbis, 1988], 9–13). Matthew Zyniewicz has examined the myriad sources contributing to Merton's complex understanding of wisdom and poses the question for future research, "What would a close reading of the Russian mystics' texts suggest about Merton's understanding of wisdom and doctrine?" ("The Interreligious Dialogue Between Thomas Merton and D. T. Suzuki" [PhD diss., University of Notre Dame, 2000], 262). Gerald O'Collins—citing not Merton, but Elizabeth Johnson—concludes his survey of contemporary Christology by gesturing toward a "Christology of presence," a variation on Karl Rahner's anonymously graced world but proceeding from "the image of Lady Wisdom." O'Collins asks, "At the end of three millennia of a strongly masculine consciousness reflected in the Bible, what might this feminine, nurturing image convey about Christ's salvific function for all people?" (*Christology: A Biblical, Historical, and Systematic Study of Jesus* [New York: Oxford University Press, 1995], 304; citing Elizabeth Johnson, "Jesus the Wisdom of God: A Biblical Basis for a Non-androcentric Christology," *Ephemerides theologicae Lovanienses* 41 [1985]: 261–94).

The broad impact of Eastern Orthodoxy on Merton's thought is chronicled in *Merton and Hesychasm: The Prayer of the Heart*, ed. Bernadette Dieker and Jonathan Montaldo (Louisville: Fons Vitae, 2003); hereafter MHPH. Of special note here are several studies by Anglican scholar A. M. Allchin, unparalleled in highlighting Merton's theology as a bridge between Eastern and Western Christianity, and the lucid commentary on *Hagia Sophia* by the poet Susan McCaslin. Christopher Nugent has written two penetrating studies of Merton's "way of seeing," with special attention to *Hagia Sophia* ("Merton, the Coincidence of Opposites and the Archeology of Catholicity," *Cistercian Studies* 26 [1991]: 257–70; idem, "*Pax Heraclitus*: A Perspective on Merton's Healing Wholeness," unpublished, 2005).

The most thorough study of Merton's Christology as such is that of George Kilcourse, *Ace of Freedoms: Thomas Merton's Christ* (Notre Dame, IN: University of Notre Dame Press, 1993). Taking his cues from what he calls Merton's "sapiential method," Kilcourse draws on a staggering range of texts (including chapters dedicated to Merton's poetry and literary criticism) to demonstrate his thesis that Merton's Christ is the "hidden Christ of kenosis." Most compelling is his association of Merton's mature theology with Karl Rahner, suggesting that as Merton opened his heart to the world, his lens shifted from a descending to a more historically conscious ascending Christology from below. Against the notion suggested by some scholars that Merton gravitated toward "a universalist, theocentric spirituality" in his last years, Kilcourse defends a "christocentric" reading of Merton's theology, citing *Hagia Sophia* as Merton's paradigmatic "hymn to celebrate God as Trinity" (cited in "Review Symposium on *Ace of Freedoms: Thomas Merton's Christ*," with Douglas Burton-Christie, Anthony Padovana, and Christine Bochen, *Horizons* 21 [1994]: 332–47, at 345). While this study also advances christocentric and kenotic reading of Merton's theology, I will suggest a somewhat more fluid reading of *Hagia Sophia*, one not too quick to reject a theocentric or universalist metaphysic at play in the poem's polysemic imagery. It is important not to draw too sharp a dichotomy between a christocentric and theocentric spirituality, as if the latter term can *only* mean a spirituality "sans Christ," which the debate surrounding Kilcourse's book intimates. Both a christocentric and theocentric dynamic come into play in Christian theology and spirituality, and this is especially so, it seems to me, in the case of Merton and the Russian theologians.

Finally, Michael Mott, Anne Carr, William Shannon, Bonnie Thurston, and Jim Forest have each authored (or edited) masterful studies of Merton's life and thought with wisdom more or less as a unifying theme. See Michael Mott, *The Seven Mountains of Thomas Merton* (Boston: Houghton Mifflin, 1984); Anne Carr, *A Search for Wisdom and Spirit: Thomas Merton's Theology of the Self* (University of Notre Dame Press, 1988); William H. Shannon, *Silent Lamp: The Thomas Merton Story* (New York: Crossroad, 1992); Bonnie Thurston, ed., *Merton and Buddhism: Realizing the Self* (Louisville, KY: Fons Vitae, 2007); Jim Forest, *Living with Wisdom: A Life of Thomas Merton* (Maryknoll, NY: Orbis, 2008).

Drawing by Thomas Merton. Used with permission of the Merton Legacy Trust and the Thomas Merton Center, Bellarmine University.

1

Turning toward the World:
The Birth of a Mystical-Prophetic
Theology

> The more I am able to affirm others, to say "yes" to them in myself, by
> discovering them in myself and myself in them, the more real I am. I
> am fully real if my own heart says *yes* to *everyone*.[1]

Biographers and scholars alike have long identified the late 1950s as a
pivotal period of transformation in Thomas Merton's life, the first stirrings of
his radical "turn toward the world," even as the world itself, and the Roman
Catholic Church, turned into a revolutionary new decade. Indeed, in the
decade prior to the Second Vatican Council, well before that extraordinary
event would turn the minds and hearts of Roman Catholics toward both
the ecumenical and non-Christian worlds, Merton was already engaged in
a serious study not only of the Christian East but of all the major religious
traditions of humankind. From the late 1950s to his sudden death while on
pilgrimage in Asia in December of 1968, he was reaching out, as Anglican
scholar A. M. Allchin has noted, with "an almost frightening intensity of
purpose" to practitioners of Eastern Orthodoxy, Hinduism, Buddhism, Islam,
and Judaism; the notebooks and private journals of this period reveal "an
explosion of activity going on in Merton's heart and mind."[2] Add to this his
vast correspondence with poets, artists, intellectuals, religious leaders, and
social activists from around the globe, and it seems that, indeed, Merton was
trying to say "*yes to everyone.*"

This "explosion," however, as Allchin poignantly observes, was "a special
kind of explosion, one which has no exact equivalent in the physical world.
It was a *non-disintegrating explosion*, and hence [its] effects were constructive
and not destructive."[3] In other words, "The center did hold. He did not fall

---

1. Thomas Merton, *Conjectures of a Guilty Bystander* (Garden City, NY: Doubleday, 1966),
144; hereafter CGB.
2. A. M. Allchin, "The Worship of the Whole Creation," in MHPH, 103–20, at 113.
3. Ibid.; emphasis added.

apart. Anyone less well integrated than he was might have done so."[4] If we keep in mind the social and intellectual fragmentation of the 1960s, irruptions never far from Merton's view, it is enough to truly wonder, how did the center hold for Merton? What kept him from falling apart?

Christ the Center

While even the most casual readers can be dazzled (or scandalized) by the universal scope of Merton's vision, what is not always appreciated is the *christocentric* character of his catholicity, that is, his "personal communion with Christ at the center and heart of all reality."[5] In other words, the center held for Merton because he never ceased deepening his understanding of Jesus Christ at the heart of the Christian tradition, nor did he compromise his daily adherence as a monk to Christian faith, prayer, and praxis. The primary aim of this book is to draw out the features of Merton's mature Christology, especially its fruition in his view of Christ as Wisdom of God, the unknown and unseen Sophia, in whom the cosmos is created and sustained. It was in no small part due to this Christology that Merton was able to affirm the other *as other*, that is, to say yes to them, and to do so well ahead of mainstream Christian or Catholic "inclusivism."[6] But before examining the contours of Merton's awakening to Sophia, a narrative that weaves from about 1957 through the remainder of his life, it is necessary to say a few words about the monastic context of Merton's thought and the mystical orientation of the Christology arising from that context.

As many scholars have noted, Merton voiced his yes to the world not as a systematic theologian but as a contemplative, that is, as one who sought communion "with other seekers on a one-to-one basis, seeking out those

4. Ibid.

5. Thomas Merton, *Dancing in the Water of Life: Seeking Peace in the Hermitage*, ed. Robert E. Daggy (San Francisco: HarperSanFrancisco, 1997), 259; hereafter DWL. See also Lawrence S. Cunningham, *Thomas Merton and the Monastic Vision* (Grand Rapids, MI: Eerdmans, 1999), 119–20.

6. The term "inclusivism" refers to the regnant paradigm in the Christian theology of religions that maintains the constitutive role of Christ in the salvation of all. In a word, all revelatory or salvific contact with God, all grace, is the grace of Christ. Though its manner of expression varies widely among theologians, christocentric inclusivism represents the basic position of the Roman Catholic Church at Vatican II and in the more recent declaration *Dominus Iesus* (2000), and in a range of Catholic thinkers as diverse as Merton, Karl Rahner, Hans Urs von Balthasar, Jacques Dupuis, Gavin D'Acosta, and Terrence Merrigan. The position may be broadly distinguished from both "exclusivism," which maintains that only persons who confess explicit faith in Christ (and accept membership in his church) may be saved, and "pluralism," which affirms non-Christian religions as "ways of salvation" or revelation in their own right.

commonalities that all who pursued the truth found."[7] In many respects this made all the difference. Merton's attention to religious *experience* more than doctrinal formulas, to divine *presence* and *light* more than revealed names, to personal *transformation* or awakening to the "true self" more than conceptual frameworks such as "salvation"—all of these facilitated his uncanny ability to connect deeply with persons of enormously varied backgrounds, that rare gift for allowing "the mystery of faith to be named and heard in a great many places where it is not usually named and heard."[8] It was the Dalai Lama who said of Merton, some twenty years after their meeting in Dharamsala: "This was the first time that I had been struck by such a feeling of spirituality in anyone who professed Christianity. . . . It was Merton who introduced me to the real meaning of the word 'Christian.'"[9]

While it is true, then, that dogmatic rigor was not for Merton the first criteria of Christian authenticity, it does not follow that he marginalized theology beneath the primacy of mystical experience, or that he had little or no formal Christology in place. Much less can it be plausibly argued that his long dialogue with the East and final Asian journey were emblematic of his passing into a vague theism or religious indifferentism. William Shannon gets it right when he observes to the contrary: "If [Merton's] understanding of God was strongly apophatic, it might be said that his Christology was clearly cataphatic: Christ is the revealer and manifestation of the hidden God. Merton's Christology is one of light."[10] It is telling that the posthumously published *Asian Journal*, the record of Merton's final pilgrimage, is punctuated with fragments of the New Testament—"*In ipso omnia constant . . .* All is in Him, from Him, for Him, for the Father through Him."[11] These are, as

7. Cunningham, *Monastic Vision*, 63. "[One] simply cannot understand Thomas Merton," Cunningham observes, "if one does not understand him as a monk" (17).

8. A. M. Allchin, "Worship of the Whole Creation," in MHPH, 118.

9. *Freedom in Exile: The Autobiography of the Dalai Lama* (New York: HarperCollins, 1990), 189.

10. William Shannon, "Christology," in TME, 51–54, at 51. The apophatic or negative way is a way of approaching and speaking about God that stresses God's radical dissimilarity from creation, God's ineffability and unknowability, and thus is characterized by leaving behind all concepts, thoughts, images, and symbols. The cataphatic or affirmative way emphasizes the similarity between God and creation, or more precisely, the conviction that God truly manifests Godself in the world and can really be experienced and known, at least analogically, in and through concepts, images, and symbols. Both the apophatic and cataphatic ways are firmly rooted in biblical spirituality and the Christian mystical tradition, and both come to play more or less in any authentically Christian spiritual path and in Catholic theology. See Harvey Egan, "Negative Way," in *The New Dictionary of Catholic Spirituality*, ed. Michael Downey (Collegeville, MN: Liturgical Press, 1993), 700–704; and idem, "Affirmative Way," ibid., 14–17).

11. Thomas Merton, *The Asian Journal of Thomas Merton*, ed. Naomi Burton, Patrick Hart, and James Laughlin (New York: New Directions, 1973), 38; hereafter AJ.

Lawrence Cunningham notes, the "Christian mantras" that bore Merton's crossing over into the world of Asian religions.[12] More significant, as will be seen in the chapters below, much of the explicitly theological content of his corpus reflects a high trinitarian doctrine drawn from a constellation of biblical, patristic, monastic, and modern sources.[13]

Yet the aim of this study is not to defend the orthodoxy of Merton's life or of his Christology. Without question, Merton's crossing over to other cultures and traditions was fraught with considerable risk, just as it is for Christian and Catholic theology today. That risk, because Jesus Christ dwells at its very center, is never merely theological but always deeply personal. While many pluralist theologians argue today, with not a little credibility, that true conversion to the non-Christian other requires theology to move Christ out of the center, Merton's theology, and to be sure, the witness of a whole life bound up with it, suggests a very different kind of risk. In many respects this book will unfold as a sustained examination of that risk in its elemental biographical and theological dimensions. Who is this Christ at the center of Merton's capacious theological imagination?

Historical Jesus/Mystical Christ

One way to begin is by distinction and contrast, that is, by clarifying who Merton's Christ is not. As even a cursory study of his more popular works will make clear, Merton shows little interest in the figure of the historical Jesus, at least by the standards of modern Christology and biblical studies. The first question one may be inclined to ask is, *why not*? And more to the point: will Merton's seeming lack of attention to Jesus of Nazareth be fatal to the intelligibility of his Christology today? Obviously we shall be much better able to address this question at the end of this study, but I raise it here simply to acknowledge from the outset how difficult it is for many Christians today, at least those outside a monastery, to share fully the experience of the monk or mystic, to "taste and see" the hidden Christ as *real*, as (in Newman's sense) a "fact of the imagination." Must not Christology today, for the sake of intelligibility (or inculturation, if one prefers) in a thoroughly secular,

---

12. Lawrence S. Cunningham, "Crossing Over in the Late Writings of Thomas Merton," in *Toward an Integrated Humanity: Thomas Merton's Journey*, ed. M. Basil Pennington (Kalamazoo, MI: Cistercian, 1988), 192–201, at 198.

13. On Merton's disavowal of indifferentism, see DWL, 259; CGB, 144; also Thomas Merton, *Turning Toward the World: The Pivotal Years*, ed. Victor A. Kramer (San Francisco: HarperSan-Francisco, 1997), 122–23 (hereafter TTW); and Cunningham, *Monastic Vision*, 119–20.

pluralistic, and historically conscious world, keep its eyes firmly on the Jesus of history, and less so, the risen Christ of faith?[14]

An initial explanation for Merton's seeming inattention to "Jesus" is relatively benign. As Shannon observes: like many Catholics prior to Vatican II, "Merton used the name 'Jesus' somewhat sparingly, preferring the title (seemingly turned into a name) 'Christ' or 'Jesus Christ.'"[15] Yet for Merton the issues at stake in modern Christology were far deeper than semantic. In those relatively few instances where he offers comment on the "quest" for the historical Jesus, it is clear that Merton was far from sanguine about the prospect of scholars somehow alighting on a "real Jesus" who does not turn out to be, after all, a reflection of "images and ideas of Christ that are creations and projections" of a "certain sector of society, a certain group, a certain class, a certain culture."[16] Significantly, Merton recognized that the danger of such "creations and projections" is by no means limited to efforts to retrieve a fully human portrait of Jesus; historically, the danger has been even graver with respect to triumphal, cosmic, or otherwise high Christologies, conceptions of Christ, for example, "as a ruler of history in which the Basileus has a central and decisive 'Christian' role."[17] In any case, whether creeping in "from above" or "from below," the danger of fashioning our image of Christ or even Jesus of Nazareth into an idol, a projection of our own "consciously fabricated social self," Merton describes in one word: "Fatal."[18]

In an uncommonly revealing letter of March 29, 1968, to his friend June Yungblut, Merton takes pains to distinguish his own conception of Christ from, on the one hand, the triumphal Christ of "theocratic imperialism," and on the other, the Jesus of historical criticism, whom he had described in an earlier letter (if somewhat flippantly) as "a mystic among others . . . just receiving a little flash of the light like the rest of them."[19] Distancing himself from both ends of the christological spectrum, Merton describes his Christ

---

14. Few have put a finer point on this question than American Jesuit scholar Roger Haight, whose landmark work in Christology lays down a serious challenge to the traditional trinitarian or Christ-centered hermeneutic (Roger Haight, *Jesus, Symbol of God* [Maryknoll, NY: Orbis, 1999]; idem, *The Future of Christology* [New York: Continuum, 2005]). At the very least, Haight's cogent analysis of the *lack* of intelligibility of traditional dogmatic language in a postmodern cultural milieu makes it clear that it is not enough to simply describe Merton's (or any theologian's) vision as "christocentric" or "trinitarian" and be done with it, as if such descriptors could secure the viability or even orthodoxy of a particular approach today. We shall revisit the most cogent questions raised by Haight's work in the conclusion.

15. Shannon, "Christology," in TME, 51.

16. HGL, 564.

17. Ibid., 643.

18. Ibid., 564.

19. Ibid., 637.

as the "Christ of the ikons," "the Christ of immediate experience all down through the mystical tradition, but in each case detached from special historical and cultural residues."[20] Merton's struggle to explain himself to his friend in this late letter, not trying to prove anything in formal theological terms, but speaking rather from heart to heart, is both poignant and illuminating. His words serve well to introduce this study as forthrightly as possible in terms of a struggle that still reverberates in christological discourse today:

> I don't know if you get what I mean. The point is that I don't think the historical Christ can be known in a way that is as relevant as this, and this is the kind of knowledge of Christ that St. John talks about in the Gospel and in his Epistles. In comparison with this "knowledge" of Christ, the knowledge of Jesus as a man who "was" a Jewish mystic is to me somewhat irrelevant. That is knowledge "about" Christ, not knowledge "of" Christ, and not (what interests me more) knowledge "in" Christ. Christ not as object of seeing or study, but Christ as center in whom and by whom one is illuminated. I will be the first to admit that all this may be extremely ambiguous. And I am questioning it much more now than I would have, say, ten years ago. The ambiguities are of course those of monasticism itself, and the Christ I am talking about is essentially the "monastic" Christ. The real problem comes in when early monasticism lost its truly kenotic and eschatological character, and became imperial shock troops in the service of a Christian social order (so called). To what extent is the Christ of monastic worship, with all the purity and refinement of ikon painting, Greek liturgy, theology of light, Hesychasm, etc., the justification of a certain "order"? To what extent is the experience of that Christ the experience of an inner security that came from supporting a "divine" social order? Hm. That calls for some thinking.[21]

Clearly Merton recognizes the dangers on all sides of the christological spectrum, and the need to admit, even embrace, considerable ambiguities. Significantly, he concludes the letter by describing his Christ as "the apophatic" Christ—"light that is not light, and not confinable within any known category of light, and not communicable in any light that is not no-light: yet in all things, in their ground, not by nature but by gift, grace, death and resurrection." He admits to his friend: "All this is very provisional. I have more thinking to do, and perhaps some revising. Certainly some revising."[22] The admission is important, for not only does it serve as a caution against any temptation to overly "systematize" Merton's thought, it also opens a window

---

20. Ibid., 643.
21. Ibid.
22. Ibid., 644.

onto a basic disposition in Merton, a *method of catholicity*, from which the church and its theologians could learn much today, and which will be highlighted throughout this book. We always "have more thinking to do, and perhaps some revising. Certainly some revising."[23]

But there are more constructive markers to highlight in the letter, especially in Merton's appeal to the iconic and apophatic Christ, which can help us to distinguish his mystical orientation from modern theology's emphasis on the historical Jesus. For Merton, the contemplative, if we can *know* Jesus today it is above all because Jesus *is risen*, because the light of his victory over sin and death shines in and through history, and comes to birth—really, experientially, transformatively—in us. We know Jesus, in a word, because he is the Christ, and because we have come to live in him, because he is the "center in whom and by whom one is illuminated." For Merton, to do Christology without substantive reference to the mystical or liturgical dimensions of Christian faith, creed, and praxis—that is, without becoming "fully impregnated in our mystical tradition"[24]—is to succumb from the outset to a seriously crippled notion of Christology.

Does this mean that only monks can "do" Christology, or understand and live it properly? Merton would respond with an emphatic no. In fact his whole inclination as a writer and theologian was to convince his fellow Christian seekers that really the opposite is the case. The hidden or apophatic Christ is not the abstract, esoteric, or ahistorical Christ; nor is mysticism or contemplation the sole province of monks. As he wrote to Zen scholar D. T. Suzuki, "The Christ we seek is within us, in our inmost self, *is* our inmost self, and yet infinitely transcends ourselves."[25] Every Christian, Merton believed, is a pilgrim on the road to Emmaus: "We follow Him, we find Him . . . and then He must vanish and we must go along without Him at our side. Why? Because He is even closer than that. He is *ourself*."[26] For Merton, the incarnate and risen Christ is both hidden and revealed in the world, the difference being largely a function *on our side* of awareness, or better, of "realization." This is not to suggest that Merton was uninterested in the historical "career" of Jesus or his full humanity as it comes to meet us in the gospels—far from it, as we shall see later. It is to suggest that for him a living and empowering faith in Jesus hinges on our awakening to the seeds of incarnation and resurrection

---

23. Or as Newman stated in the year he was made a cardinal: "Theology makes progress by being always alive to its own fundamental uncertainties" (cited in John Coulson, "Belief and Imagination," *The Downside Review* 90 [1972]: 1–14, at 14).

24. ICM, 35.

25. HGL, 564.

26. Ibid.

already planted in the world, in our true self, in every new moment. "The secret of my identity is hidden in the love and mercy of God."[27]

The question of intelligibility, of course, is closely related to the problem of starting points, or first principles, in Christology, one of the most contentious issues today. Unfortunately, the very terms of the debate tend to take Jesus' question to his disciples, "Who do you say that I am?" (Mark 8:29), and steer it headlong onto the narrow road of identification, forcing theologians and the faithful alike into camps: are you with *us*, or are you with *them*? Whatever the conflicts between Christology from below and Christology from above—a dichotomy perhaps much-too-sharply drawn today—it is possible that both trajectories meet more or less in the middle, to the degree that they conceive of Jesus Christ as the "real symbol" or living sacrament of God's self-communication in history. If this is the case, then Christologies that put their emphasis decidedly on Jesus of Nazareth might be seen as the front side of a multicolored, densely woven tapestry, while from the other side we find the same luminous threads yielding the Christ-centered mysticism of Teresa of Avila or Thomas Merton. This is how, in any case, one might interpret Sri Lankan theologian Aloysius Pieris, when he observes: "Teresa of Avila seems to have wondered why Jesus the man tends to disappear in the process of her gradual union with God. Merton suggests the answer: Jesus is not the goal but only the way to it. To be one with Christ is to be fully in the path, and therefore goal-consciousness must gradually supersede the path-consciousness."[28]

Whereas Christologies from below orient the Christian imagination squarely on "the path" with Jesus, Merton's Christology—in the pattern of forebears such as Cassian, Maximus Confessor, and Bernard of Clairvaux—does not hesitate to narrate a lyrical foretaste of "the goal," namely, the sweetness of living in the light of the resurrection, even while walking on this earth. The point is that Merton believed the latter is the inheritance of every Christian, not only the monk. Insofar as our faith remains a vibrantly eschatological faith, the Christian community lives in the liminal space between the "present and future, moving back and forth between them, tasting here and now 'in this body . . . in this vessel' some piece of heaven, a foretaste, 'a pledge.'"[29] Few modern theologians have done more to persuade seekers

27. Thomas Merton, *New Seeds of Contemplation* (New York: New Directions, 1962), 35; hereafter NSC.

28. Aloysius Pieris, *Fire and Water: Basic Issues in Asian Buddhism and Christianity* (Maryknoll, NY: Orbis, 1996), 144 (commenting on Merton's essay, "The Humanity of Christ in Monastic Prayer" [noted below in chap. 5, n. 33]).

29. William Harmless, *Desert Christians: An Introduction to the Literature of Early Monasticism* (New York: Oxford University Press, 2004), 392. The influence of Cassian on Merton

everywhere that this foretaste of heavenly life is not only possible "here below" but also positively asked of us, and made ever possible by the Spirit in whom "we live and move and have our being" (Acts 17:28).[30]

No matter whether a particular Christology places its emphasis on this or that side of the tapestry, the critical questions to ask, from the (sapiential) perspective that will be taken here, pertain to the shape of the whole: Does this portrait ring true with the biblical witness to Jesus and the memory of salvation from God in and through Jesus Christ? Does it adequately reflect not only the historical dimensions of the Bible and the humanity of Jesus but also the eschatological and doxological sensibilities of the faith community? Do its primary images and symbols find resonance in the Bible, the theological tradition, and in the *sensus fidei*, even where its central images and symbols may profoundly stretch, challenge, and purify that very tradition and those sensibilities?

As the church has well learned over two millennia, imaginative systems that have become corrupt or ossified in the midst of radical cultural change (and corresponding shifts in the *sensus fidei*) must be interrupted, questioned, and broken open. The leading internal mechanism for doing so, of course, is *change*, or the development of doctrine. In this respect, theologians like Edward Schillebeeckx, Elizabeth Johnson, and Jon Sobrino, who approach Jesus decidedly from below, may share more with thinkers like Merton than is evident at first glance, even if their approaches to Christology appear radically different. Aloysius Pieris, Jacques Dupuis, Paul Knitter, Raymundo Pannikar, Sarah Coakley, Michael Amaladoss, Peter Phan, Elisabeth Schüssler Fiorenza, Roger Haight—all of these theologians are engaged in "the search for the right theological form"; they are, so to speak, walking around the tapestry, now this way, now that, trying to find the right images and words to interpret Jesus Christ anew in view of seismic shifts in human consciousness.

In this never-ceasing process of discernment, the task of the theological community is, as Gordon Laycock notes, "a task of polarity: make the center strong, the symbols large, the words of Christ clear, and make that center

---

probably cannot be overstated. Where Cassian's whole program is directed toward the "divinization" (*theosis*) of the individual monk, with "purity of heart" as the proximate goal (*skopos*) to the ultimate joy (*telos*) of the kingdom of heaven, Merton's theology dramatically broadens the contemplative way to include all Christians, potentially all human beings in the world community. See ZBA, 130–33; also Thomas Merton, *Cassian and the Fathers: Initiation into the Monastic Tradition*, ed. Patrick F. O'Connell (Kalamazoo, MI: Cistercian, 2005).

30. Thus Merton laments that the "obsession with doctrinal formulas, juridical order and ritual exactitude has often made people forget that the heart of Catholicism, too, is a *living experience* of unity in Christ which far transcends all conceptual formulations. What too often has been overlooked, in consequence, is that Catholicism is the taste and experience of eternal life" (ZBA, 39).

accessible, the circle large, the periphery permeable."[31] Pieris, for his part, seeks after "an all-embracing Christology" that would weave together all of these luminous threads of Christian discourse into a single tapestry: "Jesus as the *word* that interprets reality, the *medium* that transforms history, and the *way* that leads to the cessation of all discourse. Sophia?"[32] Some three decades earlier, in a text that could easily be overlooked by systematic theologians, Merton too invoked her name and memory, and with it, perhaps, her living presence: "But she remains unseen, glimpsed only by a few. Sometimes there are none who know her at all."[33]

The problem of intelligibility, that is, of how to communicate the Christian faith in such a way that it can find real purchase in the experience and imagination of people today, will be addressed at least implicitly throughout this study, not least because it was a major concern of Merton himself. But it should not cause us to overlook what he identified as an equally critical threat to the vitality of Christian spirituality through the ages, whether inflated by triumphalism (as in the "theocratic imperialism" of Byzantium) or, much more likely today, despairing of real contact with God (as in the "death of God" theology of the 1960s). For Merton, a critical tipping point occurs when Christian spirituality, and the Christology supporting it, loses "its truly kenotic and eschatological character."

Perhaps the question becomes this: can we envision a Christology infused with both historical and eschatological sensibilities, a Christology that does not despair of the possibility of "living as resurrected beings"[34] even now, on this side of the heavenly banquet, but also a Christology which, by its very catholicity, refuses to privilege "special historical and cultural residues" and breaks itself open over and over again—*kenotically*, we might say—to the wisdom and presence of God wherever it may be found?[35] That Pieris would gesture to both Merton and Sophia in reference to the quest for an

31. Gordon Laycock, *Holy Things: A Liturgical Theology* (Minneapolis: Fortress, 1993), 192.

32. Pieris, *Fire and Water*, 146.

33. *Hagia Sophia*, ESF, 67.

34. See Jon Sobrino, *Christ the Liberator: A View from the Victims*, trans. Paul Burns (Maryknoll, NY: Orbis, 2001), 12–14, 35–53.

35. One of the qualities that I suspect drew Merton intuitively to the Russian Sophia tradition is its role as a "mediating discipline," a "both/and" conceptuality that respects both the high and low elements of the gospels, which takes Chalcedon as a revered starting point but also refuses to regard christological dogma as a finished thing (see Paul Valliere, "Sophiology as the Dialogue of Orthodoxy with the Modern World," in *Russian Religious Thought*, ed. Judith Kornblatt and Richard Gustafson [Madison, WI: University of Wisconsin Press, 1996], 176–92, at 187). I shall return to this important point in chap. 6 and the conclusion.

"all-embracing" Christology is no accident. It is to her irruption into Merton's life and theological consciousness that we now turn.

Merton and Sophia: A Narrative Overview

During the late 1950s Merton's religious imagination was especially shaped by two experiences of "crossing over": his dialogue with Zen and his close study of modern Russian Orthodox theology, a convergence that will be detailed closely in chapter 4. Our task here is simply to introduce in broadest strokes the breakthrough of Wisdom-Sophia into Merton's consciousness during the last decade of his life due principally to his immersion in the Russian Sophia tradition, or sophiology, which he encountered in the writings of Vladimir Soloviev (d. 1900), Sergius Bulgakov (d. 1944), Nicholas Berdyaev (d. 1944), Paul Evdokimov (d. 1970), and others. What attracted Merton to the Russians was their recasting of the narrative of salvation in the boldest imaginative and metaphysical terms. From biblical, patristic, and modern philosophical sources they had fashioned a "positive theology," a theology brimming with content. Though Merton himself never developed a formal sophiology, his internalization of Russian imagery is amply evidenced in journals, letters, and lecture notes of the period, as well as in more formally crafted works such as *The Behavior of Titans*, *The New Man*, and *New Seeds of Contemplation*. The prose poem *Hagia Sophia* is by far the most realized, lyrical, and daring of his meditations on the Wisdom figure of Sophia.

One of the earliest clues to the impact of the Russian theologians appears in Merton's journal of April 25, 1957:

> Bulgakov and Berdyaev are writers of great, great attention. They are great men who will not admit the defeat of Christ who has conquered by His resurrection. In their pages . . . shines the light of the resurrection and theirs is a theology of triumph. . . . These two men have dared to make mistakes and were to be condemned by every church, in order to say something great and worthy of God in the midst of all their wrong statements. They have dared to accept the challenge of the sapiential books, the challenge of the image of Proverbs where Wisdom is "playing in the world" before the face of the Creator.[36]

The passage crescendos to almost ecstatic pitch, as Merton begins to draw out the implications of the Russians' "daring" theology centered in Wisdom:

36. SFS, 85–86.

Most important of all—man's creative vocation to prepare, consciously, the ultimate triumph of Divine Wisdom. Man, the microcosm, the heart of the universe, is the one who is called to bring about the fusion of cosmic and historic process in the final invocation of God's wisdom and love. In the name of Christ and by his power, man has a work to accomplish. . . . Our life is a powerful Pentecost in which the Holy Spirit, ever active in us, seeks to reach through our inspired hands and tongues into the very heart of the material world created to be spiritualized through the work of the Church, the Mystical Body of the Incarnate Word of God.[37]

Several days later, Merton comments at length on what he judges to be a number of Berdyaev's "greatest mistakes," yet he continues to express admiration for his theological boldness, especially with respect to the cosmic vocation of humanity: "Berdyaev is demanding—as Blake demanded—that man should truly find his liberty in Christ. He is aware that this indeed is the message of Christ."[38] Some days later, Merton again juxtaposes criticism of Berdyaev (whose statements are, "as they stand, heretical") with effusive praise, noting his "profound insights into the real meaning of Christianity—insights which we cannot simply ignore."[39]

If there is a clear thread running through these early notes on the Russians, it is Merton's admiration for their theological creativity, their willingness to make mistakes "in order to say something great and worthy of God." "One wonders," Merton muses, "if our theological cautiousness is not after all the sign of a fatal coldness of heart, an awful sterility born of fear, or of despair."[40] But there is also a clear enthusiasm for the Russians' willingness to say something great and worthy about *humanity*. "Reading such things," he confesses, "one is struck with compunction. Look at us! What are we doing? What have I done?"[41] Made in the image and likeness of God, insists Berdyaev, humanity is called to witness to the creative work of God, with no less than a cosmic work to accomplish. The key to this "powerful Pentecost" in our lives is the union between God and humanity in Jesus Christ. As Merton observes, "The *Incarnation* is absolutely crucial here (and here [Berdyaev] is a real descendent of the Greek fathers)."[42]

While it is not unusual to find Merton rhapsodizing over new ideas, these passages convey something more than the joy (and labor) of intellectual discovery. What we find is rather the ecstasy of revelatory insight, as if the Rus-

37. Ibid., 86.
38. Ibid., 86–87; the details of Merton's critique of Berdyaev will be examined in chap. 4.
39. Ibid., 88.
40. Ibid., 86.
41. Ibid., 89.
42. Ibid.

sians had unlocked a door deep inside of Merton that had always been there but had never been fully opened, at least not in such a radically personal way. Interrupting his notes on Berdyaev there comes a sudden flash of insight and the birthing of a personal creed: "If I can unite in *myself*, in my own spiritual life, the thought of the East and the West of the Greek and Latin Fathers, I will create in myself a reunion of the divided church and from that unity in myself can come the exterior and visible unity of the church. For if we want to bring together East and West we cannot do it by imposing one upon the other. We must contain both in ourselves and transcend both in Christ."[43] This was, as Cunningham notes, "a critical moment in Merton's intellectual and spiritual maturity,"[44] a revelatory moment that would spill forth vividly in the years to follow. With the spirits of Soloviev, Berdyaev, and Bulgakov now awakened, the image of Christ as Wisdom of God, as Sophia, began to haunt Merton's religious imagination.

First, there was a dream (February 28, 1958) in which a young Jewish girl named "Proverb" came to embrace him,[45] a dream Merton later confessed to the Russian poet and novelist Boris Pasternak (October 23, 1958).[46] She then came to him in the crossroads of a great city (March 18, 1958), the much-celebrated epiphany at the crossroads of Fourth and Walnut in Louisville, Kentucky.[47] She found him again in the burning woods near Gethsemani (March 19, 1959), this time in the faces of local farm children, "poor little Christs with holes in their pants and . . . sweet, sweet voices."[48] Over a year later (July 2, 1960), on the Feast of Visitation, she came in the guise of a nurse, whose gentle whispers awakened him early one morning as he lay in the hospital. The experience strangely prefigured Merton's encounter with "M.," the student nurse with whom he would fall in love in the spring of 1966: "At 5:30, as I was dreaming, in a very quiet hospital, the soft voice of the nurse awoke me gently from my dream—and it was like awakening for the first time from all the dreams of my life—as if the Blessed Virgin herself, as if Wisdom had awakened me. We do not hear the soft voice, the gentle voice, the feminine voice, the voice of the Mother: yet she speaks everywhere and in everything. Wisdom cries out in the market place—'if anyone is little let him come to me.'"[49]

43. Ibid., 87; the revised, more expansive, passage appears in CGB, 21.
44. Cunningham, *Monastic Vision*, 55.
45. SFS, 176.
46. Thomas Merton, *The Courage for Truth: The Letters of Thomas Merton to Writers*, ed. Christine M. Bochen (New York: Farrar, Straus and Giroux, 1993), 90; hereafter CT.
47. SFS, 181–82; also CGB, 156–57.
48. SFS, 270.
49 TTW, 17.

Two years later Merton recast the hospital experience in the wondrous prose poem *Hagia Sophia*, now weaving a complex of feminine, biblical, and patristic archetypes into his gentle "awakening" by the nurse:

> At five-thirty in the morning I am dreaming in a very quiet room when a soft voice awakens me from my dream. I am like all mankind awakening from all the dreams that ever were dreamed in all the nights of the world. It is like the One Christ awakening in all the separate selves that ever were separate and isolated and alone in all the lands of the earth. It is like all the minds coming back together into awareness from all distractions, cross-purposes and confusions, into unity of love. It is like the first morning of the world (when Adam, at the sweet voice of Wisdom awoke from nonentity and knew her), and like the Last morning of the world when all the fragments of Adam will return from death at the voice of Hagia Sophia, and will know where they stand. . . .
>
> When the helpless one awakens strong at the voice of mercy, it is as if Life his Sister, as if the Blessed Virgin, (his own flesh, his own sister), as if nature made wise by God's Art and Incarnation were to stand over him and invite him with unutterable sweetness to be awake and live. This is what it means to recognize Hagia Sophia.[50]

In the deep winter of 1965, Merton penned two passages in his journal that must be mentioned here, not because they explicitly refer to Sophia (the first does, the second does not), but, more important, because they illustrate the way in which her merciful presence is repeatedly evoked in Merton's experience of the world and events around him, even in the midst of a radically broken world. The first passage in question Merton wrote on his fiftieth birthday, January 31, 1965, opening his journal on the auspicious occasion by citing from Wisdom 8:16: *Intrans in domum meam, conquiescam cum illa: non enim habet amaritudinem conversatio illius, sed laetitiam et gaudium* ["When I go home I shall take my ease with her, for nothing is bitter in her company, when life is shared with her there is no pain, nothing but pleasure and joy"].[51] Though he complains of suffering bitterly from the "fierce cold all night, certainly down to zero," he expresses joy in the fact that "I woke up in a hermitage!" Then hearkening to the Wisdom text, Merton wonders: "But what more do I seek than this silence, this simplicity, this 'living together with wisdom?' For me there is nothing else. . . . I have nothing to justify and nothing to defend: I need only defend this vast simple emptiness from my own self, and the rest is clear. (Through the cold and darkness I hear the

---

50. ESF, 61–62.
51. DWL, 200.

angelus ringing at the monastery.) The beautiful jeweled shining of honey in the lamplight. Festival!"[52]

There follows immediately a "thought that came to me during meditation," which turns out to be a devastating indictment of racism, and the dehumanization of persons generally, which Merton sees poisoning the atmosphere of modern mass society:

> The error of racism is the logical consequence of an essentialist style of thought. Finding out what a man is and then nailing him to a definition so that there can be no change. A White Man is a White Man, and that is it. A Negro, even though he is three parts white is "A Negro" with all that our rigid definition predicates of a Negro. And so the logical machine can devour him because of his essence. Do you think that in an era of existentialism this will get better? On the contrary: definitions, more and more schematic, are fed into computers. The machines are meditating on the most arbitrary and rudimentary of essences, punched into IBM cards, and defining you and me forever without appeal. "A priest," "A Negro," "A Jew," "A Socialist," etc.[53]

The striking juxtaposition of the "Festival!" flashing off an ordinary honey jar in the lamplight with the specter of wholesale racism, exploding in cities across America in 1965, illustrates almost perfectly the dynamic of Merton's thinking (and praying) throughout the tumultuous decade. To "live together with wisdom" is to live fully awake in the center of such contradictions, yet refusing to be defined by them, like an "essence" fed into a computer. For when I am "home with her," Merton reminds himself, I can "take my ease," for nothing is bitter in her company.

But there is a second remarkable passage to consider, coming just four days (February 4, 1965) after Merton had lamented "all that our rigid definition predicates of a Negro":

> Last night I had a curious and moving dream about a "Black Mother." I was in a place (where? Somewhere I had been as a child, but there also seemed to be some connection with the valley over at Edelin's) and I realized that I had come there for a reunion with a Negro foster mother whom I had loved in my childhood. Indeed, I owed, it seemed, my life to her love so that it was she really, and not my natural mother, who had given me life. As if from her hand had come a new *life* and there she was. Her face was ugly and severe, yet a great warmth came from her to me, and we embraced with great love (and I with much gratitude). What I

52. Ibid.
53. Ibid., 200–201.

recognized was not her face but *the warmth of her embrace and of her heart*, so to speak. We danced a little together, I and my Black Mother, and then I had to continue the journey I was on. I cannot remember more about this journey and many incidents connected with it. Comings and goings, and turning back, etc.[54]

What Merton "recognized" in this dream, it seems, was the very same "presence" he strived to recognize in everyone, namely, "the warmth of her embrace and of her heart." No matter that "her face was ugly and severe," what most moves Merton is that "a great warmth came from her to me," "as if from her hand had come a new *life*." Indeed, one of the most striking themes in all of these encounters is Merton's experience of himself as the object of Wisdom's friendship and intimate attention. Her embrace is transitive, so to speak, breaking in "from her to me," yet coming in the form of this concrete person or thing before him right now: the flight of an escaping dove, a lone deer feeding among the trees outside the hermitage, the faces of passersby on a busy street corner. For she "is playing in the world, obvious and unseen, playing at all times before the Creator."[55]

If there is a coda to this sequence of Wisdom passages in the journals, it comes, as Jonathan Montaldo suggests, in Merton's relationship with M., the student nurse with whom he fell ecstatically and painfully in love in the spring of 1966—the irreducibly "deep, mysterious, personal, unique" woman "in the depths of my heart [who] is not symbolic," who "is trying to become free in my love and is clinging to me for love and help."[56] Following an affectionate phone call with M. from a phone booth near Bardstown (September 10, 1966), Merton struggles to reconcile all of these "strange connections" with the feminine, this "secret child" in his "deepest heart": "I forgot to ask the exact date of M.'s birthday. (She was born just about two months before I came through Cincinnati on my way to Gethsemani! I had walked through Cincinnati station with the words of Proverbs 8 in my mind: 'And my delights were to be with the children of men!'—I have never

54. Ibid., 202.

55. From *Hagia Sophia*, ESF, 66.

56. Thomas Merton, *Learning to Love: Exploring Solitude and Freedom*, ed. Christine M. Bochen (San Francisco: HarperSanFrancisco, 1997), 328; hereafter LTL. See also Jonathan Montaldo, "A Gallery of Women's Faces and Dreams of Women from the Drawings and Journals of Thomas Merton," *The Merton Annual* 14, ed. Victor A. Kramer (Sheffield, UK: Sheffield Academic Press, 2001), 172. "M." is the initial used to refer to the woman by Christine Bochen, editor of the sixth volume of Merton's journals. It is important to note that these passages were not written for publication and give us only Merton's interpretation of the events. Merton stipulated that the private journals could not be published until twenty-five years after his death, a decision he authorized the Merton Legacy Trust to handle.

forgotten this, it struck me forcibly then! Strange connection in my deepest heart—between M. and the 'Wisdom' figure—and Mary—and the Feminine in the Bible—Eve, etc.—Paradise—Most mysterious, haunting, deep, lovely, moving, transforming!)"[57]

When the relationship had finally been "amputated just when it was about to begin," and done so by Merton, he struggles to reconcile the contradictions of his situation, "the awful loneliness, deprivation, desolation of being without each other, even though in our hearts we continue to love each other deeply." On the one hand, "it is merely what I have chosen and the choice is ratified over and over each day"; on the other, "I so vividly remember her body and long for her love."[58] Surely the real coda was yet to come, in the sheer rupture and cost to Merton of moving into an altogether new, and now more ambiguous, commitment to chastity and solitude on the other side of such a love. "I cannot regard this as 'just an episode.' It is a profound event in my life and one which will have entered deeply into my heart to alter and transform my whole climate of thought and experience: for in her I now realize I had found something, someone, that I had been looking for all my life. I know too that she feels the same about me. . . . I think we will both always feel that this was and is something too deep and too real to be essentially changed."[59]

Wisdom: The Theological Nexus

For anyone even a little familiar with the Song of Songs and the ancient Christian tradition of biblical interpretation known as "bridal mysticism," it is not hard to discern echoes of this tradition in Merton's decade-long dance with Sophia, and surely also in his love affair with M. With roots in the Christian East and in monasticism going back to Origen, bridal mysticism is more than a distinctive way of reading the Hebrew Bible typologically "in Christ"; from this daily practice it infuses the monk's whole way of seeing to become an integral *way of life*, a spirituality deeply ingrained both in Western monasticism and in Eastern Orthodoxy. As a Cistercian monk and gifted writer, Merton was both an heir of this rich tradition and its expositor for a whole generation of Western Christians. Even where the Song of Songs is not explicit in his writings, the regular reader of Merton expects to find spontaneous, canticle-like verses of praise and yearning for

---

57. LTL, 130–31.
58. Ibid., 329.
59. Ibid., 328.

"one whom my heart loves" shimmering like a veil between the lines of his poetry and prose.

Not too far from this line of thought, numerous commentators have seen evidence of a deep-seated "psychological nexus" at play in the above journals and in *Hagia Sophia*, which is to say, such texts reveal Merton's desire for intimacy and wholeness with respect to relationships with women in his life, whether past or present. It is important to neither ignore nor caricature the psychological aspects of Merton's spiritual journey, whether by venerating him (the porcelain saint, the lone prophet) or by demonizing him (the faithless priest, the free-loving Yogi). Not only was Merton thoroughly human, he was that rare religious figure with enough humility, courage, and, to be sure, self-deprecating humor not to hide his integral humanness from others.

Yet the very complexity of his life, of any human life, recommends caution and balance with respect to the psychological nexus; or better, it recommends that the psychological data be interpreted expansively and not reductively.[60] In other words, one can affirm the validity of a psychological reading of Sophia's appearances in Merton's consciousness and still insist that this is not the only or even the preeminent line of interpretation. To make it so would be to overlook the degree to which Merton's imagination was steeped in a distinctively Christian and monastic way of reading the Bible; indeed, it would overlook the way Merton himself read the world and his life, his whole life, allegorically in Christ, Wisdom, Sophia.[61] In short, a strong current in the Christian tradition has always understood that eros pertains to more than erotic love genitally expressed, or thwarted, as the case may be.[62] And

60. An appreciation for the complexity of myriad influences—biblical, theological, psychological, iconic, literary—rising to the surface in *Hagia Sophia* is partly what makes Susan McCaslin's reading of the poem so impressive (see "Merton and 'Hagia Sophia,'" in MHPH, 235–54).

61. While Edward Kaplan is generally a trustworthy commentator on Merton, his psychosexual reading of the journals is sometimes excessive, as when he identifies "Proverb" with Merton's "unmistakable erotic drives—all symbolized by the forbidden religion, Judaism, still 'rejected and cursed' by the Roman Catholic Church" (Edward K. Kaplan, "Under My Catholic Skin: Thomas Merton's Opening to Judaism and to the World," in *Merton and Judaism: Recognition, Repentance, and Renewal Holiness in Words*, ed. Beatrice Bruteau [Louisville, KY: Fons Vitae, 2003], 109–25, at 114). It is not a question of acknowledging the erotic component of these dreams, which Merton himself does (John Cassian did the same in the 4th century). Kaplan is more on target when he writes: "Whoever she is—and her identity is multiple—Proverb's 'touch' made of Thomas Merton another person. . . . more able to change, and more able to give and to receive love" (121).

62. See, for example, Denys Turner, *Eros and Allegory: Medieval Exegesis of the Song of Songs* (Kalamazoo, MI: Cistercian, 1995); Gillian T. Ahlgren, "Julian of Norwich's Theology of *Eros*," *Spiritus* 5, no. 1 (2005): 37–53; George Kilcourse, "Spirituality as the Freedom to Channel Eros," *The Merton Annual* 13 (2000): 7–15.

in the case of Merton, as with few other modern Catholic thinkers, there is a strong social, political, and theological nexus to be explored when love—yes, even love *as eros*—is grasped through the lens of a biblical, prophetic, and sacramental imagination.

If this is not the case, then what are we to make of Merton's haunting dream in the tumultuous year of 1965, his "reunion" with a Black Mother "whom I had lost in my childhood"? Note that this is the same year he would indict himself as a "guilty bystander," even while taking on (and taking on theologically) some of the most explosive issues of the age, including racism. In his "Letters to a White Liberal," for example, Merton had pointedly asked the rhetorical subject of the letter's title, "How, then, do we treat this other Christ, this person, who happens to be black?"[63] Throughout the 1960s Merton seemed bent on posing this question in myriad ways to his readers. No matter the literary genre in which he wrote (and there were many), his "answer" to the race issue, just as with the Vietnam War or nuclear proliferation, was always both mystical and political: "If we believe in the Incarnation of the Son of God, there is no one on earth in whom we are not prepared to see, in mystery, the presence of Christ."[64] *We danced a little together, I and my Black Mother.*

By way of summary, there are two points to underscore with respect to this overview of Merton's encounters with Proverb/Wisdom/Sophia in the last decade of his life, a narrative we will revisit in considerably greater detail in chapter 4. First, by the turn of the 1960s, the "Festival!" of life, all of it, had become of one piece for Merton. Merton refused to separate mysticism from politics, or any other area of life. In this sense, Sophia, like his beloved M., is not symbolic, she is "not abstract, disconnected, fleshless"—and here Merton shows himself to be not only a complex and integral human being like the rest of us but also, as we shall see, a legitimate Western heir of Russian sophiology.[65] Second, the journals bring us face-to-face with the central dynamic of Merton's personalist spirituality and Christology, namely, the transformative experience or event of being embraced by love and mercy, *the warmth of her embrace and of her heart.*

We have already seen how in describing this experience Merton reaches reflexively for biblical and patristic archetypes: the fall from paradise, the parable of the prodigal son, the *Confessions* of St. Augustine. Love for Merton

---

63. Thomas Merton, *Seeds of Destruction* (New York: Farrar, Straus and Giroux, 1964), 17; hereafter SD.

64. NSC, 296.

65. It will become clearer in later chapters the sense in which Sophia both is and is not symbolic (or "merely" symbolic) for Merton and the Russians, the difference being a function of the person or community in front of the text at hand.

is a reunion, a coming back "to somewhere I had been as a child." While utterly gratuitous and unexpected—"As if from her hand had come a new *life*"—love's embrace is also felt as a remembering, an awakening from sleep, a homecoming and rediscovery of one's true self, already resting, paradoxically, in the loving mercy of God. Once Merton woke up, that is, once he fully embraced this love for himself, and once he had tasted its boundlessness for all the world, it seems he could no longer regard any encounter with the world as "just an episode." The world had become for him an epiphany of God.

This, then, is the unmistakably theological nexus of Sophia, who is the eros of God become one with creation, and the lyrical subject of Merton's sacramental imagination most awakened by the Russian theologians. From his first encounters with Sophia in the late 1950s to the day of his death in Bangkok in 1968, Merton lived as a man possessed by Bulgakov's conviction that "one can seek to discover and will discover that 'God is all in all.'"[66]

"Here is an unspeakable secret: paradise is all around us and we do not understand. It is wide open. The sword is taken away, but we do not know it: we are off 'one to his farm and another to his merchandise.' Lights on. Clocks ticking. Thermostats working. Stoves cooking. Electric shavers filling radios with static. 'Wisdom,' cries the dawn deacon, but we do not attend."[67]

Merton as Mystical (or Sapiential) Theologian: Reclaiming the Whole Person

Why is Thomas Merton a vital, indeed a classic, resource for theology today? Where does his legacy fit into the broader historical and theological landscape of the twentieth century? While Merton's massive literary output is famously difficult to categorize or pin down, some attempt to contextualize his place as a theologian and spiritual writer in the modern (and postmodern) Catholic theological landscape—and with him, the place of the Russian theologians—is crucial in framing as clearly as possible from the outset the chapters that follow. In a word: *Why Merton? Why Sophia?* Again, we will be much better prepared to answer such a question at the conclusion of this study, but it is important here to offer some initial reasons why Merton, and this particular trajectory of Christology, might be worth a closer look today.

One way to broadly contextualize Merton's place in the modern theological landscape is to describe him, as I have already done to some extent, as a "mystical" or "sapiential" theologian, that is, a theologian whose primary

---

66. Cited in SFS, 104.
67. CGB, 132.

concern is not seeking after doctrinal precision so much as exploring the terrain of deep religious experience. Merton is a theologian primarily "in the sense that Evagrius uses that word, one whose prayer is true, one who sees deeply into the mysteries of God."[68] To identify Merton as a mystical or sapiential theologian is to place him in the orbit of another towering theologian of the twentieth century, Karl Rahner. Like Rahner, Merton "resolutely refused to divorce theology and spirituality into separate disciplines because of his conviction that one cannot exist without the other."[69] As has been said of Rahner, Merton's theology, too, is a "type of existential biography . . . a mystical biography of religious experience, of the history of a life before the veiled face of God, in the doxology of faith."[70]

In a course on Christian mysticism given to young monks at Gethsemani in the summer of 1961, Merton opens with the principle that the mystical tradition "is not separated from the dogmatic and moral tradition but *forms one whole* with it."[71] Drawing from Vladimir Lossky, one of the most creative thinkers of the Russian emigration, Merton defines both "mysticism" and "theology" in terms of an *experience* accessible not only to monks, but to all Christians: "By mysticism we mean the personal experience of what is revealed to all and realized in all in the mystery of Christ. And by theology we mean the common revelation of the mystery which is to be lived by all. The two belong together, there is no theology without mysticism (for it would have no relation to the real life of God in us) and there is no mysticism without theology (because it would be at the mercy of individual and subjective fantasy)."[72] Here Merton echoes Rahner's insistence that there must be no divorce between theology and spirituality. Without a firm grounding in theology, spirituality becomes psychological solipsism, "experience of experience," "the death of contemplation."[73] Theology keeps spirituality tied to a community, the church, the body of Christ.

68. Allchin, in MHPH, 118; cf. ICM, 107. Kilcourse prefers the term "sapiential," while Allchin prefers "mystical." I tend to favor the latter, since it locates Merton more readily alongside his sources in the tradition.

69. Harvey D. Egan, "Theology and Spirituality," in *The Cambridge Companion to Karl Rahner*, ed. Declan Marmion and Mary E. Hines (New York: Cambridge University Press, 2005), 13–28, at 14.

70. Johann B. Metz, "*Karl Rahner—ein theologisches Leben*," cited in ibid., 14.

71. ICM, 15–16. The introduction to ICM by Patrick O'Connell is invaluable, as are several studies based on the lectures by A. M. Allchin ("The Prayer of the Heart and Natural Contemplation," in MHPH, 419–29; idem, "The Worship of the Whole Creation," in MHPH, 103–20).

72. ICM, 65; and O'Connell's commentary, xxvi.

73. ICM, 36.

Lest Merton's ruminations on mysticism seem abstract, esoteric, or simply out of touch with historical reality, we should remember that these lectures were prepared in the same year he wrote the first "Cold War Letters" and began drafting *Peace in a Post-Christian Era*, a book that his own abbot general would forbid him to publish. As his friend and *Catholic Worker* correspondent Jim Forest reminds us:

> It was ten years since the first hydrogen bomb had been exploded, seventeen years since the destruction of Hiroshima and Nagasaki by much less powerful atom bombs. Americans were spending hundreds of millions of dollars on fallout shelters as a means of surviving nuclear war. . . . Both the United States and the Soviet Union had large programs for the development and stockpiling of chemical and biological weapons. "Peace" was a suspect word. Those who used it risked being regarded as "reds" or "pinkos." . . . The Roman Catholic Church in America in 1962, after many years of struggle with anti-Catholic prejudice, could be relied on to have a supportive attitude regarding America's economic system and foreign policy. Over many a Catholic parish or school entrance were carved the words, *Pro Deo et Patria*—for God and country. Many Catholics had made a career in the military, the FBI and the CIA. For the first time, there was a Catholic in the White House.[74]

It is precisely in this context—in a "season of fury," a "reign of numbers"—that Merton describes the "mystical tradition of the Church [as] a collective memory and experience of Christ living and present within her. This tradition *forms and affects the whole man*: intellect, memory, will, emotions, body, skills (arts)—all must be under the sway of the Holy Spirit. . . . Note especially the memory."[75] This view of tradition as a *collective memory and experience of Christ*, a belonging-to that shapes and defends the whole person, will be pivotal throughout this study. Yet the principle already aligns him, and quite self-consciously, "with a school of thought which was particularly active in continental Catholicism in the middle of this century, and whose outstanding representatives were men like Henri de Lubac, Hans Urs von Balthasar, Yves Congar, Louis Bouyer, and amongst monastic writers, Jean Leclercq."[76] To these we may add the theologians of the Russian emigration in Paris, whose

---

74. Jim Forest, "Foreword," in Thomas Merton, *Peace in the Post-Christian Era*, ed. Patricia A. Burton (Maryknoll, NY: Orbis, 2004), vii–xxiv, at vii–viii. There are many reasons why Merton's Cold War writings remain so prescient and prophetic today. As not a few cultural observers have noted, it is no stretch to discern strong parallels between the "threat of communism" in Merton's era and the "threat of terrorism" in our own—and the degree to which these "realities" (divinities?) haunt, shape, and drive public discourse, foreign and domestic policy.

75. ICM, 35–36.

76. Allchin, "Worship of the Whole Creation," in MHPH, 106.

translation of Orthodoxy into the West during the 1930s and 1940s—for the first time in ten centuries—greatly stimulated these Western thinkers.

All of these theologians made it their project, albeit each in highly distinctive ways, "to recover the theological vision of the first ten centuries, the centuries before the division between East and West, and before the rise of scholasticism in the West" and in so doing to overcome the aridity, rigidity, and formalism of neoscholastic theology. Like Rahner, they were committed to a manner of doing theology that rises out of prayer, communal life, and the doxology of faith. For each it might be said that "the heart of the matter lies in an appropriation of the tradition which is at once mystical and theological, subjective and objective, experiential and yet more than experiential." And while their work "involved a great deal of historical study and investigation," their "aims were anything but antiquarian."[77] Arising from the wreckage of the Russian revolution and two devastating world wars, it was a vision of theology that sought to retrieve, as Merton put it, the tradition's "human dimension," its "*incarnate* character," its capacity to form "the *whole* man."[78]

But note also that for Merton, no less than Rahner, the relationship between theology and spirituality, tradition and mysticism, is reciprocal. There is a very real sense in which lived Christian experience, that is, the insights of the prophet, theologian, mystic, or the people of God (the *sensus fidei*), can and must inform the body of faith. The faith experience of the body can and does give rise to the development of doctrine. What we must really do is "*live our theology . . .* fully, deeply, in its totality."[79] In this way theology is not simply retrieval, as if we could simply import the theological vision of the first ten centuries, or that of any other century for that matter, into the present situation. No—theology always involves a living and creative component, a searching for resonant theological forms that will speak from and for a faith community immersed in history, journeying in hope, and ever responsive to the signs of the times. For the Russian theologians, this would mean not only a striking development of the biblical Wisdom tradition, but also a recovery of the apocalyptic dimensions of New Testament faith, a retrieval Merton would make his own.[80]

---

77. Ibid.

78. ICM, 35–36.

79. Ibid., 16.

80. In his first lecture on Christian mysticism, Merton interjects quotes from Fr. Georges Florovsky that forecast the apocalyptic tenor of his own writings: "In this time of temptation and judgment *theology becomes again a public matter, a universal and catholic mission. . . .* Already we have reached a point where theological silence, embarrassment, incertitude, lack of articulation in our witness are equal to temptation, to flight before the enemy. *. . . . It is precisely because we are thrown into the apocalyptic battle that we are called upon to do the job*

In sum, it is not just *what* the tradition says (its faith content) that matters but also *how* it is said (its particular form) that determines whether the Gospel will be received vitally in any particular historical context. In the task of joining content with form not only did Merton have a firm grasp "of the entire Christian tradition as a living resource" but he also was "that rare thing, a great poet . . . who is also a great theologian." Merton is rightly celebrated as "one of the great theologians of the twentieth century,"[81] partly for his gift for communicating the Christian faith so vividly to others. And unlike most of his theological peers, known today almost solely among the elite "keepers of the mystery" in the academy and church, Merton is still sought out in great numbers by both ordinary seekers in the pews and "strangers" alike, that is, those outside or alienated from the Catholic Church and its sacramental life. This is what makes Merton, if not "a theologian's theologian," then certainly "a people's theologian, a theologian of the people of God."[82]

Yet despite Merton's staggering fluency with respect to the tradition, there remains a lingering perception in the academy that Merton studies pertain more to psychology or popular spirituality than to the dense theological tradition of the church. The result has been a certain neglect of his writings with respect to constructive theological discourse as such. No doubt the problem is exacerbated by the flood of new books churned out every year by the "Merton industry," some of questionable quality. But one may ask whether the fact that millions of spiritual seekers from around the world, Christian and non-Christian, still look to Merton as a spiritual mentor and Christian thinker of signal importance should disqualify him from consideration as a serious theologian. It seems, quite to the contrary, that Catholic theology might learn a great deal from this rare theologian who allowed, and still allows, "the mystery of faith to be named and heard in a great many places where it is not usually named and heard."[83]

---

of theologians. . . . Theology is called not only to judge *. . . but to heal*" (ICM, 37); see also Allchin, "Worship of the Whole Creation," in MHPH, 107.

81. Allchin, "Worship of the Whole Creation," in MHPH, 118.

82. Ibid. It is easy today to forget the impact of Merton's *The Seven Storey Mountain* when it was first published in 1948 and for a generation of Catholics thereafter. Coming from nowhere, as it were, from an unknown monk in an obscure monastery in Kentucky, the book almost immediately became an international best seller. Though Merton himself later lamented the book's youthful, world-denying piety, one can see in its popularity a momentous turn toward a new kind of Catholic spiritual writing, or rather *return*—to recall Augustine and Merton's Cistercian forebear, Bernard of Clairvaux—to a theological form in which the revelatory word was found in the particulars of one person's sincere quest for God. It was a style that drew instinctively from what Bernard called "the book of experience." On the parallels between Merton's "confessional" style and that of St. Augustine, see Cunningham, *Monastic Vision*, 1–4.

83. Allchin, "Worship of the Whole Creation," in MHPH, 118.

Sophia and the Search for Theological Form

But to frame Merton's contribution solely in terms of his remarkable gifts for communicating the Christian message is to tell only half the story. For in truth, the distinction between form and content in theology is itself questionable, and must not be drawn too sharply. As David Tracy suggests, "one of the fatal separations that modern Western intellectualism brings about is the separation between form and content."[84] Theologians such as Karl Barth and Hans Urs von Balthasar (and here we may add Merton) teach us "that the question of form is a vital issue in theology: 'form not as some extra aesthetic addition to content but form as that which renders the content so that *the search for the right theological form is at the very same time the search for the right theological content.*'"[85] "In other words, content obtains its meaning from form. In short, the problem of modern discourses on God is associated not only with their totalitarian rationality and self-present subjectivity, but also their *forms* for articulating God's reality."[86] In responding to this disjunction between form and content in modern theology, what Tracy attempts to do is not "to invent brand-new forms, but to retrieve or recover the *fragmentary forms* in the Christian tradition that have been forgotten, repressed, and neglected by modernity. Tracy suggests recovering two traditional theological *fragmentary* forms . . . for today: the apophatic and the apocalyptic forms."[87]

Why is Merton a vital resource for contemporary theology? Three points follow from Tracy's postmodern reflections on God. First, theology today must move beyond a method in which "totalitarian rationality and self-present subjectivity" have held sway, and this means opening itself to a plurality of forms, including the *poetic* and the *autobiographical*. But the search for the right form, insists Tracy, is not only about sign making or aesthetics, the creation or narration of new symbols, rituals, or stories. As a servant of the Christian community, the theologian's task is also (and this is the second point) about *memory*, the reforging of Christian identity anew through the retrieval and purification of communal symbols, memories, and narratives. But *which* symbols, memories, and narratives? For Tracy (and this is the third

---

84. Younhee Kim, "David Tracy's Postmodern Reflection on God," *Louvain Studies* 30 (2005):159–79, at 168, citing Tracy, "Traditions of Spiritual Practice and the Practice of Theology," *Theology Today* 55 (1998).

85. Kim, 168, citing Tracy, "Form and Fragment: The Recovery of the Hidden and Incomprehensible God," a lecture delivered at Princeton in 1999; emphasis added.

86. Kim, 168.

87. Ibid., 170, citing Tracy, "Fragments: The Spiritual Situation of Our Times," in *God, the Gift, and Postmodernism*, ed. J. D. Caputo and M. J. Scanlon (Bloomington, IN: Indiana University Press, 1999).

point) it is the "fragmentary" forms "that have been forgotten, repressed, and neglected" that must be retrieved and correlated with the present.

It is clear even at the beginning of this study that in their remembrance of Sophia, the Russian theologians in the East and Merton in the West were bringing to the surface a "forgotten, repressed, and neglected" aspect of the Judeo-Christian tradition, a narrative that associated God's very life and presence with eros and the feminine, with play and delight, with the natural world.[88] Not only this, some of Merton's best writings come to us in an *apophatic* and *apocalyptic* key. With respect to the second point, note how Tracy's insistence on the constitutive role of memory in theology echoes Merton's notion of the mystical tradition as "a collective memory and experience of Christ living and present within her." As Christopher Nugent observes, "Merton's guiding instinct, conscious or not, is that when one has lost one's way, the way out is the way back."[89] With respect to Tracy's insistence on the relationship between form and content in theology, if Merton's mystical and poetic approach to theology illumines anything, it is the integral role of the imagination, biblical and liturgical *anamnesis*, and poetics in giving voice to the tensive mystery, the *coincidentia oppositorum*, which lay at the heart of the Christian experience of God from the beginning.

In sum, if the search for the right theological form were to be gauged primarily by the conviction that, in the words of Dostoyevsky, "Beauty will save the world," then Merton's theology might be justly compared to the aesthetic project of another enormously creative Western thinker noted above, Hans Urs von Balthasar. Both men drank deeply from the well of Eastern and Neoplatonic thought, especially from the great theological synthesis of Maximus Confessor. Like von Balthasar, Merton's aesthetic arose not only from the biblical and Eastern patristic tradition (with its Johannine accent on realized eschatology) but also from a wide range of literary, ecumenical, and nontraditional sources. But rather unlike von Balthasar, Merton and the Russians made it the center of their projects to correlate their sophianic vision with historical events in the modern world, that is, to forge a thoroughgoing Christian humanism.

Thus where von Balthasar's "Theo-Drama" seems bent on unburdening the New Testament of all reference to horizontal time, worldly fulfillment, and apocalyptic expectation—all "unimportant and incidental vestiges of Jew-

---

88. See Patrick O'Connell, "Wisdom," in TME, 533–35; also for the same themes, Sandra M. Schneiders, *Women and the Word: The Gender of God in the New Testament and the Spirituality of Women* (New York: Paulist, 1986).

89. Christopher Nugent, "Merton, the Coincidence of Opposites and the Archeology of Catholicity," *Cistercian Studies* 26 (1991): 257–70, at 265.

ish eschatology"[90]—Merton follows the Russians (and others, like Abraham Joshua Heschel) in advancing a theandric vision in which history matters, a theology that views every aspect of human life, creativity, and wisdom (culture) as holding a privileged place in the life of God, as it were, from the beginning. In this respect Merton's mature focus shares more with the everyday mysticism of Rahner and the dialogical thrust of Vatican II's *Gaudium et spes* and *Nostra aetate* than with von Balthasar's "law of the ever more," which sees the real drama taking place not within human subjectivity or transcendence, but in the intra-divine, supra-temporal realm.[91] Or better, Merton more explicitly, and arguably more successfully, brings these two realms integrally together. Indeed, in his most penetrating social criticism Merton foreshadows in striking ways the concerns of contemporary liberation theologies and the apocalyptic horizon of Johann Baptist Metz.[92]

Concluding Remarks

> My ideas are always changing, always moving around one center, and I'm always seeing that center from somewhere else. Hence I will always be accused of inconsistency. But I will no longer be there to hear the accusation.[93]

Without question Merton's theology is difficult to categorize, and to try to do so is to risk doing violence to his very distinctiveness. Yet if we begin this study with respect for the inherent risks involved and a commitment to try, as much as possible, to "let Merton be Merton," we are more than justified to look to this extraordinary Trappist monk for signs of direction and hope in the current theological milieu, and not only in the West. For ours is an era in which a thousand voices proclaim, many quite credibly, that there really is *no center*, and that to posit one center into which all things converge is to perpetuate a foundational or totalizing myth that can only lead to more religiously sanctioned violence. Merton was keenly aware of the dangers

90. Hans Urs von Balthasar, *Theo-Drama: Theological Dramatic Theory (Volume V): The Last Act*, trans. Graham Harrison (San Francisco: Ignatius Press, 1998), 48.

91. Ibid., 30. It is unjust, of course, to paint von Balthasar's enormously mosaic thought with so few brush strokes. As is generally the case with all of these thinkers, what Merton and von Balthasar share on the whole is much greater than what divides them. To distinguish their approaches, as I do only tentatively here, is in no way to oppose them as mutually exclusive.

92. Not incidentally, Metz views the apocalyptic form as crucial for recovering the sense of historical urgency that is characteristic of Jewish eschatology—this over against the Platonizing, idealist, "bourgeois," or evolutionary perspectives endemic to much of the Catholic theology surrounding Vatican II (Teilhard de Chardin, de Lubac, von Balthasar, Rahner).

93. DWL, 67.

of religious idolatry. And although it is true that his cosmic view of Christ frequently shimmers with cataphatic light and presence, we shall see that *as Sophia* it makes ample room for the apophatic paradox of darkness and hiddenness, of ironic "raids" on the disturbing world of *the Unspeakable.*

To my mind, this is what makes Merton's mature theology not only mystical but prophetic, not only rhetorically haunting and beautiful but epistemologically and ontologically credible, perhaps even—dare I say it?—*true.* What draws me back to Merton is his rare capacity to affirm the intrinsic eschatological goodness of creation—"If it is stricken, it is also healed in Christ"[94]—which at once "turns into an accusation of the age in which [we] live, and into a command to be human in this most inhuman of ages, *to guard the image of man for it is the image of God.*"[95]

Perhaps above all in the following chapters we must try to keep in view Merton's insistence that when the mystical tradition is properly understood—that is, when it is integrally *lived*—that tradition is far from abstract, divorced from history, or alien to the body. At its best the mystical tradition forms and affects the *whole person*: "intellect, memory, will, emotions, body, skills (arts)—all must be under the sway of the Holy Spirit."[96] To do theology under the light of Wisdom is to open oneself to the whole of reality and allow something to break through, an inner music to be heard in the breathtaking overture that is the whole world, and not just the Catholic tradition. Whether or not this theological subtext can offer an adequate answer to the epistemological quandary of our times, I do not know. What I believe, however, is that Merton's most compelling response to the modern epistemological problem may be his witness to a different kind of knowledge and rationality, a way of seeing and knowing that is accessible to all through contemplation—and for Christians, through the full range of the church's sacramental life.

But this also implies the frank recognition that Merton's theology will not, and probably cannot, resonate intelligibly with everyone. (What theologian's can?) To the degree readers today, for example, have little meaningful contact with the liturgical or artistic traditions of the church—or still more, the poetic and prophetic landscape of the Bible—Merton's theology, not least his awakening to Sophia, may indeed sound like so much dreaming. "It is beautiful, to be sure, but *really . . .* ?" On the other hand, connecting with an audience steeped in doubt and skepticism, yet still yearning for something

94. Thomas Merton, *Raids on the Unspeakable* (New York: New Directions, 1966), 5; hereafter RU.

95. Ibid., 6, citing Berdyaev; emphasis added.

96. See note 75. One of the more stunning examples of this mysticism of the whole person (body, spirit, senses) is Merton's "Prayer to God the Father on the Vigil of Pentecost," in CGB, 177–78.

beyond what society today packages (and sells) as "reality," is one of Merton's most enduring gifts as a spiritual writer and mystical theologian.

The task before us then is to begin laying down markers for an approach to theology in which "totalitarian rationality and self-present subjectivity" are not the sole or preeminent indicators of truth or intelligibility. Indeed, as this first chapter has sought to elucidate, part of Merton's enormous appeal as a writer, poet, *and* theologian worthy of serious attention lies in his extraordinary facility with words and images: his theology "makes old things new through the transforming power of the imagination."[97] With the help of thinkers as diverse as Newman, Coleridge, and Heschel, chapter 2 aims to ground the epistemological claim at the heart of our study: it is through the imagination that Merton leads the reader through mediating images and symbols into the realm of mercy, communion, and presence.

97. McCaslin, in MHPH, 253.

Drawing by Thomas Merton. Used with permission of the Merton Legacy Trust and the Thomas Merton Center, Bellarmine University.

2

Making Old Things New: Imagination and Poetics in Theological Method

The heart is commonly reached, not through the reason, but through
the imagination, by means of direct impressions, by the testimony of
facts and events, by history, by description. Persons influence us, voices
melt us, looks subdue us, deeds inflame us. Many a man will live and die
upon a dogma: no man will be a martyr for a conclusion. . . . No one,
I say, will die for his own calculations: he dies for realities.[1]

In many respects the problem for theology after Kant, after Auschwitz,
after post-structuralism, perhaps after every "post"-something-or-other yet
to come, is the problem of *revelation*: whether or not revealed religion, with
its claim of privileged access to an unseen divine reality, is still defensible.
The theologian faces a twin dilemma: not only how to speak about the very
idea of revelation but, further, how to correlate its inheritance in a particular
tradition with the present historical moment. Every act of theology involves
basic epistemological commitments with respect to revelation: What is it?
Can it be experienced? In what sense does it belong, as Newman avers in the
passage above, to the realm of "facts and events," of "history," of "realities"?
Still more, every act of theology requires a linguistic or semantic strategy for
joining epistemology with method: What form or genre best communicates
the meaning and salvific content of revelation in a particular cultural milieu?
What resources in the tradition speak urgently to the historical moment?

When Thomas Merton describes the "real presence" of Christ in the
Psalms, the "logos of a barn," or the "dance of Sophia" in the beauty of nature, clearly he is drawing from traditional Christian imagery as well as his
own prayer life to communicate elemental beliefs and (above all) experiences
with respect to revelation. Yet how are we to understand such language?

1. John Henry Newman, *An Essay in Aid of a Grammar of Assent* (Notre Dame, IN: University of Notre Dame Press), 89; hereafter GA.

Here the modern concern for intelligibility and verification interjects, "Yes, it's certainly beautiful, but is it *true*?" Or the close corollary, "Did it *really happen*?" And if it did not really happen, can it still be true? Here one has to discern to what degree historical consciousness should operate as a first principle in theology; in Christology, to what degree does the intelligibility of a particular approach depend on a starting point in the historical Jesus? Moreover, at what point does such a starting point become, simply by remaining true to itself, the decisive hermeneutic? If historical-critical scholarship determines with reasonable confidence that certain textual memories or narratives from the tradition (e.g., the birth stories of Jesus) are not true in a strictly literal, empirical, or historical sense, do such texts nevertheless still ring true or resonate deeply with human experience as such, such that we can still reasonably make revelatory truth claims about them?

The latter question indicates the high degree to which religious epistemology yields to theological anthropology: Is the mind a blank slate upon which revelation, coming wholly from outside or above, as it were, makes (or does not make) its impression? Or is there, in fact, some connecting principle within the human person that joins us already, as it were, more or less intrinsically, with God, such that when the categorical objects of revelation (e.g., Jesus) come before us, as Newman suggests, something within us "actually vibrates and responds"—the object somehow resonates within us, even if empirically we are encountering it for the first time?

This is the stuff of epistemology: to critically examine our ways of seeing, knowing, and claiming insight into that which is real. Because the questions of epistemology are inherently self-critical, often ruthlessly so—think of the Zen *koan*, or black theology's critique of white theology—asking such questions can be a laborious and never-ending task. It is tempting to deflect all such problems, as Merton himself sometimes did, by taking refuge in religious experience—and casting a suspicious eye on language itself, discursive theology, and doctrine as inadequate and inherently distorting, at best, strictly second-order concerns. "The monk," as Merton once sardonically stated, "is not a man of answers."[2] Like the wise man of the Tao, we might prefer to take our stand "in the center of circle . . . while 'Yes' and 'No' pursue each other around the circumference."[3] Yet how sanguine can we be about finding that center where language ends and "pure" reality begins?

2. "Orthodoxy and the World," in MHPH, 473–84, at 483.

3. The image is borrowed from Merton's *The Way of Chuang Tzu* (New York: New Directions, 1965), 43 (hereafter WCT): "When the wise man grasps [the pivot of Tao], he is in the center of the circle, and there he stands while 'Yes' and 'No' pursue each other around the circumference. . . . What use is this struggle to set up 'No' against 'Yes,' and 'Yes' against 'No'? Better to abandon this hopeless effort and seek the true light!"

Revelation: Toward a Sapiential Framework

In the first place, as theology after Wittgenstein has taught us, the distinction between the experience of God's own reality and human words about God is too crude. Thus Philip Endean, in his study of Rahner, writes: "It is not that we have experience and then clothe it, so to speak, in words: language is a necessary condition of our being able, at least in one sense of the word 'experience,' to have an experience at all."[4] Nicholas Lash puts the matter this way: "the accounts that we give, the interpretations that we offer, *make a difference* to the experience itself, constitute an internally constitutive feature of that experience."[5] What Endean and Lash observe of Rahner is surely also true for Merton: to experience Christ mystically at all, "he must have been socialized into the Church—the Church of which Scripture is the foundational document."[6]

To extend the metaphor from the Tao, Merton's theology embraces a paradox. On the one hand, we are already resting in God, that is, the center of the circle; on the other hand, we have lost our way, and the way home, paradoxically, is through "Yes" and "No," that is, through language—in Merton's case, the images and symbols of Christian revelation. To say it in linguistic terms, Merton's mystical theology mines the spaces between the revealed word and silence, saying and unsaying, positive and negative theology, seeking to discover, in the words of David Tracy, "some ordered relationships for understanding the similarities-in-difference in the whole."[7] Sometimes from "Yes," sometimes from "No," and sometimes from the "still point" in the center, Merton guides the reader through word and image into the pivotal realm of communion and presence. This chapter aims to ground the epistemological claim supporting the remainder of this study—namely, that Merton's theology makes old things new "not through the reason, but through the imagination, by means of direct impressions. . . . by description."[8]

The seeming contradiction between Merton's apophatic respect for the limits of language and his masterful exploration of its revelatory possibilities is softened if one views his theology not through the discursive gridiron of

---

4. Philip Endean, *Karl Rahner and Ignatian Spirituality* (New York: Oxford University Press, 2001), 140.

5. Cited in ibid., 141.

6. Ibid. In his lucid discussion of this issue in *Zen and the Birds of Appetite* (39–46), Merton rejects a "purely formalistic view of theological and philosophical doctrines, as if a fundamental belief were something that a mystic could throw off like a suit of clothes and as if his very experience itself were not in some sense modified by the fact that he held this belief" (ZBA, 43).

7. David Tracy, *The Analogical Imagination: Christian Theology and the Culture of Pluralism* (New York: Crossroad, 1981), 423.

8. Newman, GA, 89.

systematic theology but through the more fluid categories of a literary, sapiential, or poetic frame of reference. Keeping in mind his social context—not only was he a monk who prayed (and chanted) the Bible daily but he was also the lifelong student of Blake, Hopkins, Rilke, and countless other literary artists—what is needed with Merton is not the "reifying tendencies" of scholastic discourse but "the use of a linguistic-analytical approach, a method that attends to the dialectic structure of semantic strategies."[9]

Without attempting an exhaustive theory of language or knowledge, this chapter looks in turn to the religious epistemologies and semantic strategies of John Henry Newman and Abraham Joshua Heschel to examine the role of the imagination—"an *organon* more delicate, versatile, and elastic than verbal argumentation"[10]—in religious discourse as analogous to literary or poetic cognition. Newman's balanced appeal to the imagination as the dynamic faculty that aids and enlarges reason gives considerable sanction to the tradition of mystical theology in which Merton stands. It also ascribes a creative role to the imagination as the principle of vitality at the heart of ongoing doctrinal development, giving sanction to theology's task of making old things new for present and future generations. Heschel's Jewish philosophy of religion (or "depth theology") comprises one of the most profound defenses of revealed religion in the modern period, and his poetical method bears striking affinities with Merton's approach to language.[11]

With respect to how believers come to know Jesus Christ, questions of epistemology quickly implicate, as noted above, basic commitments in theological anthropology. Does the imagination or memory somehow have recourse to Christ already, so to speak, in "the grammar written on human hearts by the divine Creator,"[12] a grammar that "the great artistic, poetic, and theological

9. Mark S. Burrows, "Words That Reach into the Silence: Mystical Languages of Unsaying," in *Minding the Spirit: The Study of Christian Spirituality*, ed. Elizabeth A. Dreyer and Mark S. Burrows (Baltimore: Johns Hopkins, 2005), 207–14, at 210. By "dialectic structure" Burrows means the saying (cataphasis) and unsaying (apophasis) characteristic of mystical texts, a semantic strategy shared, as we shall see, by Merton, Newman, and Heschel.

10. Newman, GA, 217.

11. Following Edward Kaplan I use the terms "poetic," "poetics," and "poetical" somewhat interchangeably to refer not "to mere verse, prose sentences chopped into rhymes and rhythms" but more expansively to "an imaginative manner of experiencing language" that is "meant to disturb our habitual thought patterns and evoke our sense of the ineffable, the bud of spiritual awareness" (Edward K. Kaplan, "Language and Reality in Abraham J. Heschel's Philosophy of Religion," *Journal of the American Academy of Religion* 41, no. 1 [March 1973]: 94–113, at 95).

12. Pope Benedict XVI, "Message for World Day of Peace," cited in *America* 196, no. 2 (2007): 2.

exercises of the religious imagination throughout the Catholic tradition"[13] serve to remember, awaken, and cultivate anew in every new generation? Such questions will require us at times to distinguish between broadly Neoplatonic (or Augustinian) approaches to the imagination and more or less Aristotelian (or Thomistic), Kantian, or scientific frameworks.[14]

In sum, what this chapter seeks are basic insights about epistemology and method, markers for a way of doing theology that take account of the whole person. The heuristic we seek to establish, Merton's way through both "Yes" and "No," is the sacramental imagination, the pivot or center of which is the reconciliation of opposites (*coincidentia oppositorum*)[15]; more broadly, it is the way of wisdom, or *sapientia*, what Merton calls "a kind of knowledge by identification, an intersubjective knowledge, a communion in cosmic awareness and in nature. . . . a wisdom based on love."[16] Though it would be impossible here to adequately address all the issues at play, by chapter's end it should be clear that for the Catholic sacramental imagination, religious symbols are not merely aesthetic or literary tools but bear a deeply theological (i.e., revelatory) root in God's own freedom and self-communication in history. The chapter concludes with a meditation on how Merton employs images and symbols much in the way an iconographer applies colors to canvas, or a musician opens a revelatory space through the interplay of tone and silence.

Theology and the Sacramental Imagination: Lessons from Newman

Catholic theology should be wary of granting final epistemic authority to philosophical strictures that would have disallowed the great artistic, poetic, and theological exercises of the religious imagination throughout the Catholic tradition. The unity of that tradition suggests that the

13. John Thiel, "For What May We Hope? Thoughts on the Eschatological Imagination," *Theological Studies* 67 (2006): 517–41, at 529.

14. The problem of epistemology and method is an ancient one in the life of the church. Fifteen hundred years before moderns such as Gadamer, Ricoeur, and Wittgenstein, Augustine had already engaged many of the core issues; indeed, his theory of signs would become the foundation of medieval semiology and a precursor of postmodern epistemological debates (see R. A. Markus, *Signs and Meanings: World and Text in Ancient Christianity* [Liverpool University, 1996]). The modern form of the problem dates as far back as the rise of the medieval universities in Europe, where it marked the often contentious divide between monastic and scholastic approaches to theology.

15. "The essential note of catholicity, understood as a theological category, is, according to Avery Dulles, to reconcile opposites (*coincidentia oppositorum*) after the manner of our understanding of Christology itself." Lawrence S. Cunningham, "*Extra Arcam Noe*: Criteria for Christian Spirituality," in *Minding the Spirit*, 171–78, at 173.

16. Thomas Merton, *The Literary Essays of Thomas Merton*, ed. Patrick Hart (New York: New Directions, 1981), 108; hereafter LE.

scandal of an excluded past would make for an equally scandalous present or future.[17]

"The practice of theology," suggests Nicholas Madden, "can still arguably be thought to show an excessive respect for a scientific method that has its roots in the Enlightenment."[18] Madden finds evidence for this "excessive respect" in the dominance of the historical-critical method, still considered by many scholars of religion "to be the only valid way to truth."[19] Resisting what he judges to be the far-reaching implications for Christian theology and spirituality of a method that finds its principal analog in the empirical sciences, Madden looks to Gadamer's hermeneutical theory for a way of approaching theology more attuned to the way the humanities engage with truth. To truly get inside the meaning of a religious tradition, Gadamer suggests, one has to transcend the control of the scientific method and engage in something more like a conversation, albeit in this case, with interlocutors from the past. Just as in a conversation between living persons, where we "use words with our own private echoes, based on our own history," and what we say "is capable of several interpretations," so too with religious, literary, and mystical texts. Despite the difficulties of communicating meaningfully across boundaries of culture, distance, and time, "it is only as a result of engagement in conversation that we attain any mutual understanding."[20]

While the kind of responsive or imaginative listening advocated by Gadamer is laborious—and perhaps more to the point, *personally implicating*—the fruit of such an engagement, Madden suggests, is not so much rational, discursive knowledge, but something more akin to what Flannery O'Connor called "The Habit of Being": "an intuitive appropriation of reality grafted into one's life as a whole and which moves and determines the will."[21] Madden's model for a more holistic and personally engaged approach to religious truth is John Henry Newman, who stands out among modern Catholic thinkers, he suggests, not least for his ability to hold in fruitful tension seemingly

17. Thiel, "For What May We Hope?" 529.

18. Nicholas Madden, "Approaching Theology with Newman," *Irish Theological Quarterly* 69 (2004): 323–36, at 323.

19. Ibid.; cf. Thiel, who raises concerns about the degree to which modern theologians have embraced Kant's position on the limitations of human knowledge, a position that severely limits theological speech on matters outside the realm of sense experience. Thiel's primary concern is eschatology and the fact that when most theologians today address the "last things," "their work transpires as though Kant were looking over their shoulders" (Thiel, "For What May We Hope?," 519).

20. Madden, "Approaching Theology," 324, citing Andrew Louth, *Discerning the Mystery* (Oxford, Clarendon Press, 1983), 29.

21. Madden, "Approaching Theology," 324, citing Louth, *Discerning the Mystery*, 137.

opposite sensibilities in the tradition: the historical and the mystical, the dogmatic and the pastoral, the poetic and the scientific. Newman's capacity for reconciling opposites in a unified, though complex and mosaic view of things, shares not a little with Thomas Merton. Indeed, it is the mark of the Catholic theological imagination at its best.

Like many Christian thinkers of the nineteenth century, Newman struggled to reconcile the claims of Christianity with an increasingly scientific and pluralistic worldview. With his "theology of the religious imagination," he sought a middle way between the "mountain and the morass" of two opposing points of view. On one side was the prevailing rationalism of modernity represented by empiricists like John Locke, according to which scientific demonstration was seen as the only basis for verifying truth, and certitude in all matters was directly proportionate to the evidence available.[22] On the other side was Christianity's own form of "evidentialism," represented in Newman's day by William Paley. This was the traditional but increasingly reactionary view that defended revelation on the basis of external proofs, namely, the prophecies and miracles recounted in Scripture.

As a pastor, Newman held great respect for the piety of ordinary believers: "If children, if the poor, if the busy, can have true Faith, yet cannot weigh evidence, evidence is not the simple foundation on which Faith is built."[23] For him both the "liberal" left (Locke) and the "conservative" right (Paley) were guilty of a foreclosure of the mind, a kind of poverty (or captivity) of imagination. Neither did justice to the catholicity of the human mind, nor to the dynamic and holistic way in which most people come to certainty in matters of faith. When it came to faith in Jesus Christ, Newman privileged the "simple and distinct *facts* and *actions*" that meet us in Scripture, and not the "generalized laws or metaphysical conjectures"[24] of the dogmatic tradition. His epistemological starting point, in other words, was not linear, dogmatic rationality but "an *organon* more delicate, versatile, and elastic than verbal argumentation," that is, the religious imagination.[25]

The Dynamics of Revelation: "From Above" and "From Below"

For Newman, revelation takes root, or it does not, in the "concrete" and "living" soil of communal experience and, above all, the imagination. To say

22. For Newman's critique of Locke, see John Henry Newman, *An Essay on the Development of Christian Doctrine* (Notre Dame, IN: University of Notre Dame Press, 1989), 327–28; hereafter ED.

23. John Henry Newman, *Fifteen Sermons Preached Before the University of Oxford* (Notre Dame, IN: University of Notre Dame Press, 1997), 231; hereafter OUS.

24. Ibid., 27.

25. Newman, GA, 217.

it in contemporary terms, no matter how high our theology, or the degree to which it begins "from above," religious epistemology always begins "from below."[26] Not to pose the dialectic too sharply, however, Newman's epistemology in fact reflects a tensive or polar interplay of both subjective (low) and objective (high) elements. "Christianity is dogmatical, devotional, practical all at once."[27] While Newman expresses the subjective pole of religion in terms of the imagination, he refers to its objective aspect—that which exists (or rather *preexists*) outside and above the human mind—in terms of revelation, or what he calls the "original impression," "leading principle," or perhaps most tellingly, the "idea" of Christianity. For Newman this idea is the incarnation of the Son of God.[28]

Avery Dulles contends that Newman worked out his understanding of revelation within a Platonic framework of ideas.[29] For Newman the "idea" of Christianity is a living and comprehensive entity that "takes hold of a thousand minds by its living force," such that it "may rather be said to use the minds of Christians, than to be used by them"; "Wonderful, to see how heresy has but thrown that idea into fresh forms, and drawn out from it farther developments."[30] The Christian world of thought, Newman asserts, "is the expansion of a few words, uttered, as if casually, by the fishermen of Galilee."[31] In sum, concludes Dulles, "Christian revelation is a *real* idea. As a Christian Platonist in the Alexandrian tradition, Newman rebelled against the conception that ideas are simply products of the mind. For him, the idea pre-exists. 'The mind,' he writes, 'is below truth.'"[32]

Yet Newman also exhibits great respect for historical particularity, with personal and empirical sensibilities that Dulles sometimes understates. Thus while coming from outside human beings and indeed coming to completion

26. The imagination is also the means, Newman cautions, by which "sight" triumphs over "faith," and the world gradually beats down believers' attachment to the Gospel, that is, "It assails their *imagination*" (OUS, 132).

27. Newman, ED, 36. Scholars variously emphasize a range of influences on Newman's epistemology, including the Christian Platonism of the Alexandrian school, the Romanticism of Coleridge, and the British empiricism of Locke. All agree that Newman's epistemology, especially his defense of the "dogmatic principle," is an attack against "liberalism" in all its forms. See John Henry Newman, *Apologia Pro Vita Sua*, ed. Ian Ker (London: Penguin, 1994), 252–62; ED, 325, 357–59.

28. Newman, OUS, 35; ED, 324.

29. Avery Dulles, "From Images to Truth: Newman on Revelation and Faith," *Theological Studies* 51 (1990): 252–67, at 254. John Thiel subtly clarifies the sense in which Newman both is and is not a "Christian Platonist." See his *Senses of Tradition: Continuity and Development in Catholic Faith* (Oxford: Oxford University Press, 2000), 70–71.

30. Newman, OUS, 316–17.

31. Ibid., 317.

32. Dulles, "From Images to Truth," 254.

in apostolic times, revelation for Newman is far from an intellectual abstraction or disembodied concept, breaking in wholly extrinsically, as it were, from above. Faith for Newman always involves concrete historical engagement and participation, living assent; it must be kindled anew in communities, in children, from one generation to the next. But how? How does one rise, as Newman asks, to "what I have called an imaginative apprehension" of the mystery of God? How can I believe "as if I saw?"[33] The answer for Newman begins not strictly from above or from below but *from within* the ground of human experience, where the wordless presence of God comes to birth in conscience. Whether or not Newman is best described as "a Christian Platonist," the essential point is this: by affirming interiority as a first principle in his general theory of knowledge, Newman lays the ground for a sapiential (or contemplative) approach to epistemology and theological method.

Revelation "From Within": Conscience and Imagination

Few passages are more telling or moving than when Newman describes the dawning sense of religious imagination in childhood. In the first pages of the *Apologia*, he recalls his experience at age fifteen of resting "in the thought of two and two only absolute and luminously self-evident beings, myself and my Creator."[34] It is not hard to hear resonances of this early memory in the *Grammar of Assent*, where the elder Newman expands on the experience of conscience as the seedbed of religious imagination:

> Such is the apprehension which even a child may have of his Sovereign Lawgiver and Judge. . . . It is an image of the good God, good in Himself, good relatively to the child, with whatever incompleteness; an image, before it has been reflected on, and before it is recognized by him as a notion. Though he cannot explain or define the word "God," when told to use it, his acts show that to him it is far more than a word. He listens, indeed, with wonder and interest to fables or tales; he has a dim, shadowy sense of what he hears about persons and matters of this world; but he has that within him which actually vibrates, responds, and gives a deep meaning to the lessons of his first teachers about the will and the providence of God.[35]

33. Newman, GA, 96.
34. Newman, *Apologia*, 25.
35. Newman, GA, 104–5. It is illuminating to compare this passage with the much earlier second *University Sermon*, in which Newman, not yet thirty years old, lays down the bedrock principles of conscience and imagination that would ground his phenomenology of religions for the rest of his life.

Two points here need to be underscored. First, while conscience is an innate moral sense of right and wrong, it is more than this. The emotions aroused by the conscience further arouse the imagination, awakening the image "of some person, to whom our love and veneration look, in whose smile we find our happiness, for whom we yearn . . . in whose anger we are troubled and waste away"—in a word, "the image of the good God." Indeed, Newman often refers to conscience as an inner "voice": "Inanimate things cannot stir our affections; these are correlative with persons."[36] And second, the apprehension of this living object is *real*, a "fact of the imagination," and most important, it is so *before it has been reflected on, and before it is recognized*, named, categorized, or defined "as a notion."[37]

The significance of this point can hardly be overstated, for here we behold the seedbed of what Nicholas Lash calls Newman's imaginative, literary, or aesthetic mode of rationality, the first principles that separate him (quite self-consciously) both from classical rationalism and Lockean evidentialism.[38] The former reproduces the "mistake of the Aristotelians of the middle age, who, instead of what Bacon calls 'interrogating nature' for facts, reasoned out everything by syllogisms"[39]; the latter forgets how the great mass of human beings actually come to religious faith. With his discussion of conscience and imagination in the early pages of the *Grammar of Assent*, Newman counters the "scientistic" presumption of universal *doubt* as the only valid starting point for inquiry into truth with a presumption of universal *presence*, as it were, already built into the human person. "To gain religious starting points," Newman asserts, "we must . . . interrogate our hearts . . . interrogate our own consciences, interrogate, I will say, the God who dwells there."[40] This personal "interrogation" of the experiences, memories, and impressions that dwell in the heart is what grounds Newman's ascending theory of religious assent.

People come to faith, in other words, neither by rational arguments or irrefutable evidence, nor by a blind and sudden leap, but rather by the "slow-paced" convergence of impressions and "antecedent probabilities," all pointing in the same direction. Religious certitude is, for Newman, like a cable

---

36. Newman, GA, 101.

37. "When I make an act of certitude," proposes Newman, "I am contemplating a fact in itself, as presented to me by my imagination" (cited in Gerard Magill, "Moral Imagination in Theological Method and Church Tradition: John Henry Newman," *Theological Studies* 53 [1992]: 451–75, at 458). "Newman uses 'real' and 'imaginative' equivalently," Magill observes, "to indicate the importance of making knowledge personal in the imagination, the hallmark of real assent: 'Assent to a real proposition is assent to an imagination.'"

38. Nicholas Lash, "Introduction" to Newman, GA, 10.

39. *The Letters and Diaries of John Henry Newman*, cited in ibid., 9. Note here what seems to be an implicit criticism of Aquinas's Aristotelian methodology.

40. Newman, *Letters and Diaries*, cited in Lash, "Introduction," 9.

made up of many strands, "each feeble, yet together as sufficient as an iron rod."[41] Faith is a kind of reasoning that in fact enlarges or goes beyond reason, since it makes inferences based upon "holy, devout, and enlightened presumptions"[42] more than it rests on bluntly verifiable evidence. "The truth of our religion, like the truth of common matters, is to be judged by all the evidence taken together."[43] And one of the firm presumptions that the self-reflective person (i.e., one who "interrogates" his or her own heart) will bring into matters of discernment, "dim" and "shadowy" though it may be, is a personal interior sense of divine reality, the impression or memory of a living *Someone* to whom we owe our life and submission.

Wisdom: The Attunement of Conflicting Opposites

It is important to emphasize that when Newman describes the child's pre-rational, preverbal apprehension of God, that "dim, shadowy sense" within the child "*which actually vibrates*, responds, and gives a deep meaning" to the vast maze of reality, he is describing what he believes to be a universal human faculty.[44] This universalism proceeds, however, not from abstract or metaphysical principles (i.e., notions, doctrines), nor from a priori commitments to methods of observation only verifiable by others (as in science), but rather from a deeply personal and wordless (contemplative) experience of God, of God's very self, who has become a "fact of the imagination." Newman's universalism here, we may surmise, is rooted in his own experience of God, a realization so vivid and longstanding that he presumed its existence in human experience as such. The discussion of conscience in the *Grammar of Assent* peaks in Newman's account of the "theology of the religious imagination." It is a passage that resonates strongly with Merton's mystical or sapiential approach to reality; so too, the Russian theologians of Wisdom:

> To a mind thus carefully formed upon the basis of its natural conscience, the world, both of nature and of man, does but give back a reflection of those truths about the One Living God, which have been familiar to it from childhood. Good and evil meet us daily as we pass through

41. Cited in Avery Dulles, *Newman* (New York: Continuum, 2002), 41.
42. Newman, OUS, 239.
43. Cited in Dulles, *Newman*, 41.
44. "This vivid apprehension of religious objects, on which I have been enlarging, is independent of the written records of Revelation; it does not require any knowledge of Scripture, nor of the history or the teaching of the Catholic Church. It is independent of books" (GA, 107). For an expanded discussion, see Christopher Pramuk, "'They Know Him by His Voice': Newman on the Imagination, Christology, and the Theology of Religions," *Heythrop Journal* 48 (Jan 2007): 61–85.

life, and there are those who think it philosophical to act towards the manifestations of each with some sort of impartiality, as if evil had as much right to be there as good, or even a better, as having more striking triumphs and a broader jurisdiction. And because the course of things is determined by fixed laws, they consider that those laws preclude the present agency of the Creator in the carrying out of particular issues.

It is otherwise with the theology of a religious imagination. It has a living hold on truths which are really to be found in the world, though they are not upon the surface. It is able to pronounce by anticipation, what it takes a long argument to prove—that good is the rule, and evil the exception. It is able to assume that, uniform as are the laws of nature, they are consistent with a particular Providence. It interprets what it sees around it by this previous inward teaching, as the true key of that maze of vast complicated disorder; and thus it gains a more and more consistent and luminous vision of God from the most unpromising materials.[45]

For the religious or self-reflective person, regardless of religious tradition, an inner sense of God becomes the "true key" for understanding the way things "really" are in the world, for grasping the hidden harmony of "that maze of vast complicated disorder" coming to us through the senses.[46] Lacking this elemental sense of God's realness, a strictly empirical or picture-thinking mentality might lead people to reasonably conclude, as Newman suggests, that evil holds sway in the world, and has "as much right to be there" as the good. Furthermore, to the degree we have lost touch with an interior sense of God impressed upon the imagination, the doctrines and symbols of religion will likely appear as little more than a "heap of notions." For the person or community that cultivates within itself the remembrance of God, however, it is possible to see things differently:

When men begin all their works with the thought of God, acting for His sake, and to fulfill His will, when they ask His blessing on themselves and their life, pray to Him for the objects they desire, and see Him in the event, whether it be according to their prayers or not, they will find everything that happens tend to confirm them in the truths about Him which live in their imagination, varied and unearthly as those truths may be. Then they are brought into His presence as that of a Living Person,

45. Newman, GA, 106.

46. Following on Augustine's sign-theory, Markus conceives of a wider "interpretive community" (i.e., beyond the Jewish and Christian communities) formed by "those who are able to see the world of creatures as pointing beyond themselves to a Creator," those "who hear [creation's] outward voice and compare it with the truth within themselves" (Markus, *Signs and Meanings*, 34).

and are able to hold converse with Him, and that with a directness and simplicity, with a confidence and intimacy.[47]

What happens, then, for the scientist who begins all her work "with the thought of God"? The same thing, Newman implies, that happens for the teacher, the nurse, the cop, the monk, and the theologian. They will all find themselves doing their work in God's presence and with directness and simplicity "are able to hold converse with Him." This revelatory dimension of human life as such, when lived mindfully, is what finally separates Newman's account of the religious imagination from an Aristotelian, Kantian, or otherwise scientific lens on truth. While the latter framework ties all knowing to sensibility, which is said to provide the only trustworthy or "realistic" content to our mental operations, Newman insists that the religious imagination can grasp truths that are "really to be found in the world, though they are not upon the surface." Despite the complexity and seeming fragmentation of reality, there is a hidden wholeness to be found in the world, and the imagination—supported by right disposition, a holy heart, a willingness to believe—can hold this sense of unity-in-difference together. In short, the inner experience of God is real, and its transformative effect on the mind's grasp of reality is trustworthy.

As Gerard Magill has shown, Newman adopted Samuel Taylor Coleridge's view of the imagination as the dynamic mode of cognition that selects and organizes experience into a meaningful whole. For Coleridge, this productive or creative ability of the imagination was associated especially "with a mediating role to unify apparent dualisms, for example, head and heart."[48] This is what Merton calls "wisdom," as we shall see in chapter 3, a sapiential grasp of things he associates especially with Zen and other Eastern traditions. For both Merton and Newman, wisdom culminates not in "polymathy," the knowledge of many things, but more perfectly in *a sense of the whole of things* and "their mutual relations."[49] Wisdom is "the clear, calm, accurate vision, and comprehension of the whole course, the whole work of God"[50]; it "implies a connected view of the old with the new; an insight into the bearing and influence of each part upon every other; without which there is no whole, and could be no centre."[51]

47. Newman, GA, 106–7.
48. Magill, "Moral Imagination," 460.
49. Newman, OUS, 287.
50. Ibid., 293. Obviously, no person is able to view the whole work of God. The statement does not imply religious or rationalist hubris so much as the contemplative mode of seeing the forest for the trees.
51. Ibid., 287.

The heartbeat of wisdom for Merton is "the hidden attunement of opposite tensions,"[52] and the same dynamic saturates Newman's writings. In the passage cited above, for example, we find in Newman the attunement of complexity and unity, disorder and order, nature and Providence, vision and hiddenness, and so on. Of course this also calls to mind the coincidence of opposites at the heart of Christianity's leading idea, the incarnation. Real assent to such a mystery is possible, and not unreasonable, says Newman, provided reason is not uprooted from its imaginative mode, which can hold together seeming disparate truths (human/divine) in its grasp of Christ. Magill elaborates on this aspect of Coleridge's writings, which "had the greatest influence upon Newman":

> Coleridge understood the imagination as perceptive ("It dissolves, diffuses, dissipates, in order to recreate") and as crucial for religious belief ("a Symbol is characterized by the translucence of the Eternal through and in the Temporal"). On the one hand, for Coleridge the imagination was not separate from reason; rather it changed our mental focus and enabled us to reason differently by enlarging and reordering our powers of perception of reality, providing a new unity to our understanding and knowledge. That was the imagination's creative and mediating ability. On the other hand, Coleridge used images (which become meaningful symbols through the power of imagination) to structure religious discourse, based upon the analogous relation between poetry (as symbolic utterance) and religious faith. That was the imagination's interaction with religion.[53]

Two key points in this passage can help us link imagination as an epistemological category with its constructive role in theological method. First, imagination is not separate from reason, but rather enables us "*to reason differently* by enlarging and reordering our powers of perception." Second, there is an "analogous relation" between poetry and religious discourse, since the latter employs *images* that "become meaningful symbols through the power of imagination." Like poetry, theological language is "a type of rhetoric as creative persuasion about the truth of God."[54]

Magill notes that Newman, sensitive to the subjective and symbolic nature of theological language, extended this creative dimension of the imagination he found in Coleridge "to articulate a theological method for understanding

---

52. Thomas Merton, *The Behavior of Titans* (New York: New Directions, 1961), 76; hereafter BT.

53. Magill, "Moral Imagination," 460–61, citing Coleridge's *Biographia Literaria* (1817), *Lay Sermons*, and *Collected Works*, and several studies by Stephen Happel.

54. Magill, "Moral Imagination," 461, citing Happel.

the development of doctrine."[55] This dynamic, selective, and holistic manner of appropriating reality, this process of growing into the truth, we might say, Newman calls "the illative sense."[56] Where scientific rationality proceeds by linear, deductive, or syllogistic thinking, imaginative rationality (the illative sense) is closer to literary or poetic cognition, involving an intuitive process of discernment that Newman compares to the sensibilities of a climber on the face of the rock—we advance "not by rule, but by an inward faculty."[57] For most people, the illative sense is operative not in every sphere of knowledge but in one or two domains of expertise. But without this interior sense of discernment, Newman says, no matter our field or everyday concerns, we would forever be circling around the same questions and confined to the same sphere of knowledge. In short, we would be unable to really *live*, paralyzed by the assumption that incontrovertible demonstration or proof is required before commitment is possible.

We pause here to draw some parallels with Merton's turn to Wisdom imagery in the last decade of his life. Inspired by the book of Proverbs and the Russian theologians, Merton increasingly employed the evocative image of Sophia as a meaningful theological symbol "through the power of the imagination." As Coleridge says of symbols, Merton found in Sophia "the translucence of the Eternal through and in the Temporal," and he increasingly invoked her name for the purpose of "creative persuasion about the truth of God." In short, the appropriation of Sophia into Merton's corpus during the 1960s offers a lucid example of the illative sense at work in theological method. There seems to be no reason that the church and its theologians today, so long as we remain sensitive to the metaphorical nature of theological language, might not also invoke Sophia's memory and name in the task of theological development.

Returning to wisdom (or *sapientia*) as an epistemological category, we must not forget that the religious truths of which Newman and Merton speak are *not upon the surface* of things. If there is a "hidden ground of Love"[58] to be found in the world, despite the world's unspeakable violence and fragmentation, the term *hidden* must be accentuated. And nowhere perhaps is this more truly and mysteriously the case than in the imagination's encounter with God in the person of Jesus. Though it is a truth of faith hidden from ordinary sight, Newman does not hesitate to describe Jesus Christ as the source and center of all reality.

55. Ibid.
56. Newman, GA, 270–99.
57. Newman, OUS, 257.
58. HGL, 115.

Christ and the Sacramental Principle

> [No] religion yet has been a religion of physics or of philosophy. It has
> ever been synonymous with revelation. . . . Moses was instructed
> not to reason from the creation, but to work miracles. Christianity is
> a history supernatural, and almost scenic: it tells us what its Author is,
> by telling us what He has done.[59]

Throughout his writings Newman is clear in his belief that behind Christianity and the diverse religions—"wild plants indeed but living"[60]—there is a living *Someone*, not an impersonal or abstract "What" but an active and objective "Who," to whom human beings owe their submission. But this is where his personalism places so much weight on the life of Christ, for it is through Christ, the incarnation of God, that human history has beheld this living Object much more concretely, intimately, and perfectly than the hidden "Someone" of natural and universal conscience. For Newman, much as for Merton, the incarnation is the "result and completion" of "the natural course of things," and the life of Christ interprets for the believer "the faint or broken accents of nature."[61] Aligning himself with Clement of Alexandria and with St. Paul among the Athenians (Acts 17:22-23), Newman finds in the life of Christ the one great prism or lens by which all the disparate and fragmentary beams of *human being* converge in the center:

> The life of Christ brings together and concentrates truths concerning
> the chief good and the laws of our being, which wander idle and forlorn
> over the surface of the moral world, and often appear to diverge from
> each other. It collects the scattered rays of light, which, in the first days
> of creation, were poured over the whole face of nature, into certain intelligible centres, in the firmament of the heaven, to rule over the day and
> over the night, and to divide the light from the darkness.[62]

It is striking how much these lines anticipate Merton's own reflections on the incarnation in *New Seeds of Contemplation*: "As a magnifying glass concentrates the rays of the sun into a little burning knot of heat that can set fire to a dry leaf or a piece of paper, so the mystery of Christ in the Gospel concentrates the rays of God's light and fire to a point that sets fire to the spirit of man."[63] What must not be overlooked here is the concreteness and intensity with which both thinkers conceive of the life of Christ as it comes

59. Newman, GA, 91–92.
60. Newman, ED, 380.
61. Newman, OUS, 31.
62. Ibid., 26.
63. NSC, 150.

to meet us in the gospels, and which impresses itself upon the whole person. Newman calls this the *sacramental principle*: "The doctrine of the Incarnation is the announcement of a divine gift conveyed in a material and visible medium, it being thus that heaven and earth are in the Incarnation united. That is, it establishes in the very idea of Christianity the *sacramental* principle as its characteristic."[64]

It is difficult, if not impossible, Newman observes, "to create or to apprehend by description images of mental facts, of which we have no direct experience."[65] For this reason, he insists, "The Word was made flesh and dwelt among us." Newman repeatedly frames his glosses on the life of Christ with John's Prologue, and the words of 1 John: "That which we have seen with our eyes, which we have looked upon, and our hands have handled."[66] Revelation, in other words, meets us with a history "almost scenic," with "simple and distinct *facts* and *actions . . .* not with generalized laws or metaphysical conjectures, but with *Jesus and the Resurrection*."[67] In the life of Christ "we are allowed to discern the attributes of the Invisible God, drawn out into action in accommodation to our weakness."[68] It is important to note the thoroughly affective tenor of Newman's voice when it comes to the imagination's encounter with Christ. Those who believe do so "because they know Him to be the Good Shepherd; and they know Him by His voice; and they know His voice, because they are His sheep." Just as "they know and follow Christ, upon His loving them," so also "we *believe*, because we *love*."[69]

In short, there is nothing abstract about the revelation of God in Jesus Christ. The sacramental principle grasps the incarnation not as a doctrine or discursive notion so much as an *event* in the life of God—"the announcement of a divine gift conveyed in a material and visible medium."[70] It is for believers a "fact of the imagination" that marks Christian faith with an intensely personal and even visual character, proceeding from the vividness of the gospel itself. Yet Newman's phenomenology of faith embraces a paradox, or better, an attunement of opposites. For while Christian revelation meets us with a history "almost scenic," its salvific content is found in hiddenness and

64. Newman, ED, 325.

65. Newman, GA, 43.

66. John 1:14; 1 John 1:1; cited in Newman, ED, 324; OUS, 16, 26.

67. Newman, OUS, 27.

68. Ibid., 26.

69. Ibid., 236.

70. Newman, ED, 325. Rejecting both the Antiochene school of Christology (ED, 343, 358, 366) and Protestant devotion to Jesus as "an excellent human being" (ED, 428), Newman celebrates St. Ignatius's *Spiritual Exercises* (ED, 429)—the classic performance of a high Christology encountered from below, through imagination—and the *Theotokos*, which preserves "the faith of Catholics from a specious Humanitarianism" (ED, 426).

obscurity, namely, in the fact that God, the creator of the universe, comes to us in the life of Jesus through "an act of *self-denial.*" Like St. Paul, to the question of Christianity's distinctiveness amid the religions and philosophies of the world, Newman answers in boldest relief with the image of Christ crucified, rejected, and hidden in a life of humble servitude. The heart of Christian revelation, the pearl of great price, is the story of God's love "drawn out into action in accommodation to our weakness"—yet it is a truth to be found "not upon the surface" of things. This paradoxical attunement of both theophany and hiddenness resonates deeply, as we shall see later, with the kenotic Christology of Merton and the Russian theologians.[71]

Christ the Center: Anthropological Implications

For Newman, the believer's encounter with the love and mercy of Christ engages the whole person, transforming our way of seeing not only ourselves but all human beings, not least the stranger. As he put it with disarming beauty in a sermon preached on Christmas Day, 1837, "I say that Christ, the sinless Son of God, might be living now in the world as our next-door neighbor, and perhaps we not find it out. And this is a thought that should be dwelt on."[72] The encounter with God "in material and visible medium" through Jesus Christ becomes for the believer the "true key" for understanding the way things really are in the world, for grasping the hidden harmony within that "vast maze" of plurality and disorder coming to us through the senses. Here is the core of Newman's personalism that shares not a little with Merton's capacious imagination: "true religion is a hidden life in the heart; and though it cannot exist without deeds, yet these are for the most part secret deeds, secret charities, secret prayers, secret self-denials, secret struggles, secret victories."[73] God is mysteriously present in human beings always and everywhere, a "presence" that can be grasped, even if dimly and in shadows, before it has been reflected on, recognized, named, categorized, or defined (e.g., in explicitly christological terms) as a notion.

How can Christians reasonably claim this? Because our "collective memory and experience of Christ"[74] gives us both a norm and a living lens through which to make sense of the world and humanity's place in it. Like a lens

---

71. "Hiddenness" was a favorite theme of Soloviev in his reflections on Sophia (McCaslin, in MHPH, 241); Merton's *Hagia Sophia* closes with the image of a "homeless God, lost in the night, without papers, without identification, without even a number" (ESF, 69).

72. John Henry Newman, "Christ Hidden from the World," in *Parochial and Plain Sermons* (San Francisco: Ignatius, 1997), 886–94, at 888.

73. Ibid., 889.

74. ICM, 35–36.

that collects the "scattered rays of light," the Gospel of Jesus Christ helps us discern and communicate "the simple, deeply held convictions about the ultimate shape of the whole: God, who is personal, who creates, who is friendly, who loves creatures and enters into an interactive relationship with them."[75] Because the life of Christ exhibits continuity and not discontinuity with the shape of human life as a whole—its needs, desires, fears, joys—Jesus emerges for us as the Second Adam, the measure of divine-humanity in its very fullness, which is to say, as persons ever striving, in grace, toward communion in agapic love.

None of this is too far from Augustine, who grounds his epistemology not chiefly according to the model of philosophical ascent or in the study of the liberal arts but in "the participation of the believer in a sacred reality signified by religious symbols and rituals."[76] Augustine always has in mind (in Ricouerian terms) the person *in front of* the text, where signs are always bound to the *will*, the meaning of signs to *intention*, and intention to *community*. But the human community as such is imprisoned by a poverty or corruption of imagination rooted in the Fall: "Hence the radical ambivalence of signs, their ability to conceal no less than to reveal."[77] For Augustine, what allows us to permeate the opacity of signs—to "put them to the question"—is "right disposition," or "the right semiotic intention."[78] Right intention is the will of persons bound under the symbolic and ritual life that flows from *the confession of Christ*, who is finally, for Augustine, the only liberating and trustworthy hermeneutic. Confession is the condition for the possibility of right understanding of Scripture and the world, "so that the inner meaning of your words may be opened to me as I knock at their door."[79] This subjective aspect of Augustinian epistemology, not a little influenced by Christian Neoplatonism, is also quite marked in both Newman and Merton. It is what Newman calls "a holy heart," or "the willingness to believe."[80]

---

75. Roger Haight, *Jesus, Symbol of God* (Maryknoll, NY: Orbis, 1999), 408–9.

76. Sally Ann McReynolds, "Imagination," in *The New Dictionary of Catholic Spirituality*, ed. Michael Downey (Collegeville, MN: Liturgical Press, 1993), 531–35, at 532.

77. Markus, *Signs and Meanings*, 30.

78. Ibid., 27.

79. Conf. 11.2.4. "Only the Interior Teacher, which is the light of Christ dwelling in the mind, can teach by at once displaying to the mind the reality to be known and providing the language for its understanding. He is the source of both the objects encountered and the light which illuminates them for our understanding."

80. Yet, like Newman, Merton's appreciation for the concrete and particular of things brings him at times closer to the Romanticism of Hopkins, Blake, and Rilke—and the "conceptual realism" of Thomism—than the Neoplatonism of Augustine. See LE, 424–51, especially 443; NSC, 29–36; McReynolds, "Imagination," 533–34.

Many pluralist theologians today argue, not without merit, that no matter how well-intentioned or creative new articulations of christocentric inclusivism may be, to put Jesus Christ (or his body, the church) at the center of truth is to perpetuate a worldview that, at best, is no longer credible and, at worst, justifies a thousand forms of prejudice and imperialism. Yet for Christians who have been formed from birth by the Gospel, it is not ourselves whom we see at the center, but Christ. If all epistemology begins from below, Christians can hardly deny the fact that, for us, *Jesus holds the center*, such that when our eyes fall on him something deep inside "actually vibrates, responds, and gives a deep meaning" to what before was dim and shadowy, scattered and chaotic, unfamiliar and alien. To love one's neighbor as oneself is possible, as Newman suggests, only to the degree our spiritual senses have been *re*-centered or conformed in Christ, such that eventually something in us might actually "vibrate and respond" when we stand before the stranger, because in them we somehow recognize the visage of Christ, albeit the hidden Christ. Christ at the center does not necessarily lead to violence, conceptual or otherwise. Newman's corpus, about as well as any Christian thinker's I have seen (save Merton's), suggests to the contrary.[81]

To sum it all up, when Newman speaks of wisdom he means a holistic kind of knowing penetrated by love. If we really believe (not merely notionally) that Christ is somehow hidden in the world and in the mystery of the other, it is only *because we love*, and *have been loved by Christ* in the center of our being. It hardly matters whether we call the experience mystical, aesthetic, literary, sapiential, or sophianic—to move from faith to wisdom is to look upon the human mosaic with gratitude and wonder, always expecting to discover in ever new ways the presence of God, who is ultimately, as Merton insists, "beyond the reach of anything our eyes can see or our minds can understand."[82] One of the most beloved poets of this kind of wisdom—both christocentric and apophatic at once—is Gerard Manley Hopkins, converted to Catholicism by Newman in 1866, and one of Merton's favorite poets. When Hopkins wrote, "As kingfishers catch fire"—"for Christ plays in ten thousand places, / Lovely in limbs, and lovely in eyes not his"—he was surely attuned to that same spirit of Wisdom that saturated Newman's Catholic sensibilities, and that would find lyrical voice in Merton's writings a century later.

---

81. An inclusivism that identifies the other with Christ must be wary of turning them into a projection of ourselves or an idolatrous image of Christ. We must be satisfied with Christ's hiddenness, an apophatic respect for the other as irreducible other.

82. NSC, 131.

Theology and the Poetical Spirit: Making Old Things New

> Our theological philosophers are like the old nurses who wrap the un-
> happy infant in swaddling bands or boards, put a lot of blankets on him
> and shut the windows [so] that not a breath of fresh air may come to
> his skin—as if he were not healthy enough to bear wind and water in
> due measures. They move in a groove, and will not tolerate anyone who
> does not move in the same.[83]

In the last decades of his life, Newman was "increasingly dismayed," as
Terrence Merrigan notes, "by the prevailing theological conservatism [in
the Roman Catholic Church], especially in the face of the intellectual crisis
generated by 19th-century scientific advance."[84] It was in such a polarized
atmosphere, perhaps not too distant from our own, that Newman concluded
that theology needed a "Novum Organon": "A new question needs a new
answer," and new answers "can only be developed where there is a degree
of flexibility, a willingness to leave well-trodden paths however serviceable
they may have proved themselves to be."[85] The development of doctrine was
not for Newman "a chain of linked deductions and inferences in systematic
form—'a list of articles that can be numbered.'"[86] It is not a sudden leap over
conceptual chasms, nor does it follow from a sudden revelatory flash of insight. Newman saw the development of doctrine as "a never-ending series
of translations which must be adequate to the fact of Revelation and to the
situation in which we, the translators for the time being, find ourselves."[87]
In terms of his favored metaphor, it is like the polygon expanding into the
enclosing circle. Coulson elaborates: "The development of doctrine . . . is, in
fact, a prime example of imaginative responsiveness. It requires a determina-
tion to turn the mysteries of Revelation round until, suddenly, we discover
that they have 'clicked' into our present awareness, itself variable, relative
and changing—but this 'click' or 'focus' will not hold indefinitely, since 'here
below to live is to change, and to be perfect is to have changed often.'"[88]

In the year he was made a cardinal, Newman stated that "theology makes
progress by being always alive to its own fundamental uncertainties."[89] The

83. Newman, *Letters and Diaries*, cited in Terrence Merrigan, "Newman and Theological
Liberalism," *Theological Studies* 66 (2005): 605–21, at 614–15.

84. Ibid., 614.

85. Cited in ibid.

86. John Coulson, "Belief and Imagination," *The Downside Review* 90 (1972): 1–14, at 13.

87. Ibid.

88. Ibid., citing Newman's *Essay on Development*.

89. Cited in Coulson, "Belief and Imagination," 14. "This implies a claim about the nature
of theology," Coulson adds, "which brings [Newman] closer to Peguy and Hopkins, and of
course essentially to the Fathers, and separates him from the Neo-Scholastic tradition. No

statement captures well the tensive and discerning nature of the discipline today. The fact that we are always adjusting our focus does not imply doctrinal relativism, as Coulson asserts, since "to talk of approximation is to imply the existence, objectively, of what one is trying to approximate to."[90] The polygon of religious discourse, in other words, is always gesturing outward, asymptotically touching the enclosing revelatory circle. Or to recall the Tao, "Yes" becomes "No" and then "Yes" again, spiraling the imagination centripetally toward the center where speech turns to silence, only to be regenerated again from the event. In his preparatory papers to the *Grammar of Assent*, Newman describes this never-ending dance between "Yes" and "No" in theology, laying down what Merrigan calls a "charter" for the practice of theological science. "The essence of that charter is the willingness to live with the limitations that inevitably accompany the science of God, and even more, to see in them some clue to God's very being."[91] Newman writes:

> From the nature of the case, all our language about Almighty God, so far as it is affirmative, is analogical and figurative. We can only speak of Him, whom we reason about but have not seen, in terms of our experience. When we reflect on Him and put into words our thoughts about Him, we are forced to transfer to a new meaning ready made words, which primarily belong to objects of time and place. We are aware, while we do so, that they are inadequate, but we have the alternative of doing so, or doing nothing at all. We can only remedy their insufficiency by confessing it. We can do no more than put ourselves on the guard as to our own proceeding, and protest against it, while we do . . . it. We can only set right one error of expression by another. By this *method of antagonism* we steady our minds, not so as to reach their object, but to point them in the right direction; as in an algebraical process we might add and subtract in series, approximating little by little, *by saying and unsaying, to a positive result.*[92]

It should be clear at this point that theology in a Catholic mode, represented at its best in thinkers like Newman and Merton, is much more than

---

wonder that he found the scholastics 'cold'; but how right Manning was to see his preference for the Fathers as being a 'literary' one!"

90. Ibid.

91. Merrigan, "Newman and Theological Liberalism," 619.

92. Cited in ibid. Magill observes that Newman "was sensitive to the paradoxical character in the history of doctrine seeking verbal formulae that decisively avoid closures of meaning while creatively generating new metaphors. . . . He used the imagination, then, to maintain a paradoxical tension between disclosing the meaning of what is otherwise unavailable to us while veiling the transcendent mystery of religious truth" ("Moral Imagination," 471, citing Rowan Williams).

an aesthetic or literary operation, painting pictures, images, or narratives for reason's consideration. It speaks of God, rather, "whom we reason about but have not seen, in terms of our experience." For both Newman and Merton, the sacramental imagination spirals around two elemental experiences: first, the wordless but vivid sense of God's presence in the conscience, memory, "true self," or seat of the soul, an experience presumed available to all; and second, the experience of God's love and mercy poured out *in history* in the person of Jesus Christ. These two experiences, both personal and communal at once, spring forth in and from a polyphonic range of social forms, languages, and practices that make up Christian ecclesial life. "The Christian idea is . . . a complex, comprehensive fact of history."[93]

But what theological form best communicates the salvific content of revelation in the present historical and cultural moment? It is significant that "not long before his plea for the creative (theological) reappropriation of the Christian tradition," Newman "had pondered its essentially poetic, and hence, its essentially 'impenetrable, inscrutable, [and] mysterious' character."[94] Poetry, Newman observed, "does not address the reason, but the imagination and affections."[95] Poetry brings us to the boundaries of saying and unsaying, those "frontiers of consciousness," as T. S. Eliot puts it, "beyond which words fail, though meanings still exist."[96] It is the stuff of what the elder Newman would describe in the *Grammar of Assent* as real apprehension.

Newman did not suggest, nor will this study suggest, that poetics offers a conclusive "solution" to the myriad problems of theological method. And yet Newman's approach to theology does lend considerable support to the more modest view I take as my own here: namely, that "a poetic approach to epistemology—a poetic dimension of theological thinking or even a theological literature in search of a poetic form and voice—offers an insight into modern construals of reality that remain impoverished without it."[97] In other words, a theology proceeding solely or decisively from the historical-critical or scientific spirit is like Newman's "old nurse" who wraps the "unhappy infant in swaddling bands" and shuts the windows so that "not a breath of fresh air" may touch the pulsing body of faith. Mark Burrows gets to the

---

93. Merrigan, "Newman and Theological Liberalism," 616. Against "literary religion," i.e., religion conceived as solely a human projection of divine realities, Newman defends both the historical character of revelation ("the testimony of facts and events") and the dogmatic principle (the Spirit's guidance of the Church in doctrinal development). See GA, 89–92.

94. Merrigan, "Newman and Theological Liberalism," 617.

95. Cited in ibid.

96. T. S. Eliot, "The Music of Poetry," cited in Mark S. Burrows, "Raiding the Inarticulate: Mysticism, Poetics, and the Unlanguageable," in *Minding the Spirit* (n. 9 above), 341–61, at 349.

97. Burrows, "Raiding the Inarticulate," 348.

heart of the matter when he asks, "Can [theology] sustain itself in a form bereft of the musicality of language, a prosaic genre no longer edged with strong margins of the inarticulate, a limping literature that is incompatible with song?"[98]

We turn now to Abraham Joshua Heschel, whose depth theology achieved a remarkable marriage of form and content, that is, an extraordinary musicality, through the practice of poetics. Few accounts of the crisis of revealed religion in the modern period are more striking than that of Heschel's struggle to reconcile the piety of a Hasidic Jewish upbringing with the intellectual climate of Europe in the years surrounding the Second World War. And like his friend Thomas Merton, Heschel found "the seeds of transcendence within the practices of language itself."[99]

Holiness in Words: Lessons from Heschel

> Religion is what man does with the presence of God. And the spirit of God is present whenever we are willing to accept it. True, God is hiding His face in our time, but He is hiding because we are evading Him.[100]

Heschel arrived as a refugee in New York City on March 21, 1940, acutely aware "that his family and the thousand-year-old Jewish civilization of Europe were being annihilated."[101] Some twenty-five years later, in his inaugural lecture at the Union Theological Seminary in New York, he defined himself in terms of that unspeakable event: "I am a brand plucked from the fire, in which my people was burned to death. I am a brand plucked from the fire of an altar to Satan on which millions of human lives were exterminated to evil's greater glory."[102] Heschel's mother and two unmarried sisters had perished in the Warsaw Ghetto, while a third who lived in Vienna was sent to Treblinka with her husband and murdered in Auschwitz.

Much of Heschel's writing defies these personal and global human agonies. Over against the twentieth century's most devastating spiritual catastrophes, he set himself the task of preserving the essential principles of biblical re-

98. Ibid., 356.

99. Ibid., 350. I can fathom no better or more concise expression of a sapiential approach to religious epistemology and theological method than what Burrows offers as a general axiom in this phrase.

100. Abraham Joshua Heschel, *Man's Quest for God: Studies in Prayer and Symbolism* (New York: Scribner's, 1954), xiv.

101. Edward K. Kaplan, *Holiness in Words: Abraham Joshua Heschel's Poetics of Piety* (Albany: State University of New York Press, 1996), 10; hereafter HW.

102. Abraham Joshua Heschel, "No Religion Is an Island," *Union Seminary Quarterly Review* 21, no. 2 (January 1966): 117–34; also Kaplan, HW, 10.

ligion: the study of Scripture, commitment to a life of prayer and holiness, and the defense of "the divine image of so many human beings."[103] In addition to his magisterial studies in philosophy of religion—*Man is Not Alone* (1951) and *God in Search of Man* (1955), works that Thomas Merton knew well—no book illumines Heschel's epistemological concerns more lucidly than *Man's Quest for God: Studies in Prayer and Symbolism* (1954). In a rare autobiographical sketch titled, "From the Point of View of God," Heschel describes his arrival in 1927 at the University of Berlin, where he "came with great hunger" looking for "a system of thought, for the depth of the spirit, for the meaning of existence":

> Yet, in spite of the intellectual power and honesty which I was privileged to witness, I became increasingly aware of the gulf that separated my views from those held at the university. . . . To them, religion was a feeling. To me, religion included the insights of the Torah which is a vision of man from the point of view of God. They spoke of God from the point of view of man. To them, God was an idea, a postulate of reason. They granted Him the status of being a logical possibility. But to assume that He had existence would have been a crime against epistemology.
>
> The problem to my professors was how to be good. In my ears the question rang: how to be holy. . . . To have an idea of the good is not the same as living by the insight, *Blessed is the man who does not forget Thee.*
>
> I did not come to the university because I did not know the idea of the good, but to learn why the idea of the good is valid, why and whether values had meaning. Yet I discovered that values sweet to taste proved sour in analysis; the prototypes were firm, the models flabby. Must speculation and existence remain like two infinite parallel lines that never meet? Or perhaps this impossibility of juncture is the result that our speculation suffers from what is called in astronomy a parallax, from the apparent displacement of the object, caused by the actual change of our point of observation?[104]

In this remarkable passage, Heschel prefigures Merton's own response to the "death of God" theologians who would burst into popular consciousness during the 1960s. The implicit target of his critique is Kant, whose position on the limitations of human knowledge had become axiomatic in much religious discourse. The result, from Heschel's biblical perspective, was an intellectual and cultural climate in which the assumption that God is

103. Cited in Kaplan, HW, 10.
104. Heschel, *Man's Quest for God*, 94–95.

real, much less that human beings could experience ("taste") God's realness, and thus have a reasonable basis for *knowing* it, would have been "a crime against epistemology." Embraced theologically, Kantian epistemology traps its adherents, suggests Heschel, in a "parallax," a self-created exile in which "speculation and existence remain like two infinite lines that never meet." By a kind of "displacement of the object," God has become "*a name but no reality*"[105] for all who internalize this pattern of thinking, which is to say, for nearly everyone, including believers, living under the Cartesian climate of modernity.

Kaplan relates a poignant incident in which the young Heschel, having just arrived in Berlin to study at the university, was walking through its "magnificent streets" when he noticed that the sun had gone down, and suddenly realized that he had forgotten to pray. "I had forgotten God—I had forgotten Sinai—I had forgotten that sunset is my business—that my task is to 'restore the world to the kingship of the Lord.'"[106] Heschel challenges the theologian, the so-called specialist, to remember *God*, the God of Sinai and sunset, before settling too easily into well-worn "systems" and "frameworks" for speaking *about* God from a comfortable distance. Theology is a much more dangerous, intimate, and embarrassing business than its practitioners in the academy are generally wont to admit.

The Prophetic Perspective: "From the Point of View of God"

> Our problem . . . is how to share the certainty of Israel that the Bible contains that which God wants us to know and to hearken to; how to attain a collective sense for the presence of God in the biblical words. In this problem lies the dilemma of our fate, and in the answer lies the dawn or the doom.[107]

As with Merton, the beauty of Heschel's style is widely recognized, though often, as Kaplan observes, "to the detriment of serious consideration of the intellectual system implicit in his vision."[108] With his own masterful studies of what he calls Heschel's "poetics of piety," Kaplan has done much to correct this imbalance. Note how the term "poetics of piety" reinforces the central

---

105. Ibid., xii.

106. Heschel, "Toward an Understanding of *Halacha*," cited in Kaplan, HW, 16.

107. Abraham Joshua Heschel, *God in Search of Man* (New York: Farrar, Straus and Cudahy, 1955), 246.

108. Kaplan, "Language and Reality," 94. Kaplan has been at the forefront of scholarship exploring Merton's relationship with Judaism. See, e.g., his numerous contributions in *Merton and Judaism: Recognition, Repentance, and Renewal: Holiness in Words*, ed. Beatrice Bruteau (Louisville, KY: Fons Vitae, 2003).

theme of this chapter, namely, that every act of theology involves basic epistemological commitments with respect to revelation and a semantic strategy for joining epistemological commitments with method.

Heschel founds his philosophy of religion on the experience of the "ineffable," a sense of transcendence and mystery that "precedes conceptualization, on a level that is responsive, *immediate, preconceptual*, and *presymbolic*."[109] "Any genuine encounter with reality is an encounter with the unknown. . . . [We] sense more than we can say."[110] "Wonder" is the term Heschel gives to the sense of being caught up in transcendence, the experience of ourselves as the object of God's transitive questioning and concern. The term "experience" with reference to God, however, must be carefully qualified. The certainty of God's realness is given not from experience as such but "*from our inability to experience* what is given to our mind,"[111] our poverty before the mystery and meaning of life. It is precisely this gap between what we sense and what we can say (described negatively as the "ineffable") that discloses positive divine meaning. Heschel aims to move us beyond the beautiful and beyond even the good to the *holy*: "Wonder is not a state of esthetic enjoyment. Endless wonder is endless tension, a situation in which we are shocked at the inadequacy of our awe, at the weakness of our shock, as well as the state of being asked the ultimate question."[112]

Thus Heschel makes an elemental distinction (not separation) between the realm of objective divine reality and the human realm of conceptual and verbal cognition. The former is primary, and independent of the latter. "There is something which is far greater than my will to believe. Namely, God's will that I believe."[113] We do not grasp the transcendent, "we are present to it, we witness it."[114] In short, the existence of God does not depend on human consciousness of it. All human insight or intuition stands between these two realms. Concepts and symbols (as distinct from biblical revelation) are

109. Heschel, *God in Search of Man*, 115.

110. Ibid.

111. Ibid, 117.

112. Abraham Joshua Heschel, *Man Is Not Alone: A Philosophy of Religion* (New York: Farrar, Straus and Young, 1951), 68–69; also Kaplan, HW, 43. Kaplan argues that rather than rejecting Kantian categories outright, Heschel *extends* "Kant's notion of universal mental categories of space and time to *the ineffable*, which he considers to be an a priori category of consciousness, 'as if there were an *imperative*, a compulsion to pay attention to that which lies beyond our grasp'" (HW, 36–37).

113. Heschel, *Man's Quest for God*, 96.

114. Heschel, *God in Search of Man*, 116. This is not to say that there is no "connecting principle" between the transcendent and the human realms. Heschel roots human identity (and epistemology) in its exalted status as "image" of God: "The image is not in man; it *is* man" (*Moral Grandeur and Spiritual Audacity*, ed. Susannah Heschel [New York: Farrar, Straus and Giroux, 1996], 369).

second thoughts for Heschel; all conceptualization is symbolization. While religious symbols (doctrines, discursive theology) are necessary, Heschel rejects the assumption that they are the only access we have to God; he warns especially against the tendency to hypostatize dogmas as the object of worship. The task of depth theology, by contrast, is "to keep alive the meta-symbolic relevance of religious terms"; concepts "must not become screens; they must be regarded as windows."[115]

Once again, Heschel is reacting against broadly Kantian or scientific first principles that predicate God's "realness" on human consciousness, that is, as a postulate of reason. When truth is regarded as that which the mind creates, then "symbolism" becomes the sole technique of human understanding, casting about "for a goal that will forever remain unknown." "The premise of religious symbolism is the assumption that God lies beyond the ken of our minds and will. There is no God, but we go on worshiping his symbol."[116] A wholly subject-centered epistemology yields either the rationalist or aesthetic "trap": revelation becomes subordinate to the criteria of intelligibility or beauty. In neither case does the resultant "God" interrupt human hubris, or make moral demands.[117] Yet at the same time, and with equal rigor, Heschel also rejects dogmatic or biblical fundamentalism, in which, as Kaplan observes, "the literal minded are condemned to worshiping their own projective portraits of divinity."[118] While defending supernatural revelation, Heschel does not view the Bible as a flat description of historical events, nor does he advance a single interpretation of the Sinai revelation and its rabbinic codification.[119] "The surest way of misunderstanding revelation is to take it literally, to imagine that God spoke to the prophet on a long-distance telephone. Yet most of us succumb to such fancy, forgetting that the cardinal sin in thinking about ultimate issues is *literal mindedness*. The error of literal mindedness is in assuming that things and words have only one meaning."[120]

"Revelation is a cloudburst, a downpour, yet most of us are like moles, burrowing, and whatever stream we meet is underground."[121] Heschel fleshes out his view of biblical revelation and the polyvalent meanings of religious

115. Heschel, *God in Search of Man*, 116.
116. Heschel, *Man's Quest for God*, 130.
117. During an interview in 1973, Heschel challenged a too-facile conception of God as "Ground of Being": "Ground of being causes me no harm. . . . Isn't there a God who is above the ground? Maybe God is the source of qualms and of disturbing my conscience. Maybe God is a God of demands" (*Moral Grandeur and Spiritual Audacity*, 408); on the dangers of symbolism as rational or aesthetic "trap," see *Man's Quest for God*, 142–43.
118. Kaplan, HW, 59.
119. Ibid., 46.
120. Heschel, *God in Search of Man*, 178–79.
121. Ibid., 251.

language with a characteristic play on words. Biblical accounts are "not less but *more than literally true*: 'The prophets bear witness to an event. The event is divine, but the formulation is done by the individual prophet. According to this conception, the idea is revealed; the expression is coined by the prophet.'"[122] The words of Scripture are therefore not "coextensive and identical with the words of God."[123] To believe so is a kind of idolatry. Biblical words are "windows" or pregnant "meeting places"; they must not become screens, substitutes for direct verification of reality. As Kaplan notes, "Their words mix the divine and the human as does the meeting that produced them. . . . Analysis of biblical language trains us to read religiously, allowing us access to Holy Spirit, or God's continuing revelation."[124]

With his philosophy of religion Heschel thus seeks to give voice to "a different way of thinking"[125] that takes its cue from the Bible, especially those privileged moments in history when, like rain or lightning, God's word breaks into history through the prophets. Adapting Husserl's phenomenology, Heschel insists that for the pious person the awareness of the divine "intrudes" as a sense of wonder, a "pressure" that breaks in, weighs down, and makes demands. Where this kind of religious certainty is dead, insists Heschel, "the most powerful symbolism will be futile."[126] Moreover, for those who internalize the Scriptures, God is not the Unmoved Mover or "ground of being" so much as the "most moved Mover" whose pathos is rooted in freedom and loving will, not in necessity or human contingency. By taking as his starting point the category of the ineffable, Heschel's depth theology re-centers the locus of subjectivity from human consciousness to the divine perspective, stressing the God side, not the human side, of the revelatory event. "Its music remains."[127]

The "Fertile Paradox": Poetics and Presence

While Heschel appreciates the *via negativa*, the apophatic way of silence, he clearly acknowledges the formative power of religious tradition, including

122. Kaplan, HW, 46, citing *God in Search of Man*, 265.

123. Heschel, *God in Search of Man*, 258.

124. Kaplan, HW, 47. "The spirit of God is set in the language of man, and who shall judge what is content and what is frame?" (Heschel, *God in Search of Man*, 259).

125. Abraham Joshua Heschel, *The Prophets* (New York: Harper and Row, 1962), xxviii.

126. Heschel, *Man's Quest for God*, 142. "It is not right for us to be waiting for God, as if he had never entered history" (*God in Search of Man*, 164). The statement recalls Newman's emphasis on the experience of God in conscience and in the pluriform world, as well as his defense of revealed religion as rooted in historical events.

127. Kaplan, HW, 49, 56. Speculation, Heschel says, is a question *about* God. Religion is a question *from* God. "We find that it is we who are being questioned" (*God in Search of Man*, 110).

authoritative interpretations of biblical revelation and the communication of the ineffable through image and symbol. Yet ever determined to accentuate the divine perspective of theocentric thinking, Heschel's poetics "embraces a contradiction: he electrifies concepts frozen by ideologies, using them to surpass themselves."[128] This is what Kaplan calls the "fertile paradox" at the heart of Heschel's approach to language and metaphysical insight, a linguistic strategy joining epistemology with method that shares not a little with Merton: "'It is precisely the challenge involved in using inadequate words that drives the mind beyond all words.' . . . At the borders of speech we open ourselves to the positive value of silence. . . . Literary reading, through its complexity, its music, its suggestiveness, points to a fuller realm of being."[129]

Heschel is walking a fine line here. While acknowledging that the theologian must use conventional terms with all their dogmatic connotations, he laments the degree to which "Human weakness substitutes static images for intuitions of reality."[130] Thus the critique of imagery and symbolism does not imply an outright rejection of theology or traditional language, suggests Kaplan, nor an absolute refusal to communicate. What Heschel rejects is "a *literal* apprehension of such representations which replace experience of reality itself."[131] Poetics, says Kaplan, "is Heschel's solution to this logical bind, for it can preserve the social cohesion of a common tongue while exploiting the fluid relation of words to reality."[132] Committed to the struggle to communicate the ineffable "in linguistic terms shared by society," Heschel's writings "mix conceptual reflection with evocative prose, with the express purpose of surpassing creeds or systematic theology."[133] Indeed, Kaplan measures the success of Heschel's method by its capacity to arouse a sense of "presence" in believers and unbelievers alike, a gift also frequently ascribed to Merton. "It is at the gates of poetic participation in religious language that the believer and the faithless meet."[134]

Taking his cue from the Bible, or more precisely, from the experience of the prophets that produced biblical speech, Heschel offers a literary analysis of how religious words can function as "hyphens between heaven and earth,"[135] a claim that implies a formal connection between the two. To contrast a literal,

128. Kaplan, HW, 49.

129. Ibid., citing Heschel, *The Prophets*, 276.

130. Kaplan, "Language and Reality," 96. This is precisely the danger of systematic theology, dogma, or any other "systematized" view of reality, and a major theme for Merton, as we shall see in chap. 3.

131. Ibid.

132. Ibid.

133. Kaplan, HW, 49.

134. Kaplan, "Language and Reality," 95.

135. Heschel, *God in Search of Man*, 244; cf. Kaplan, HW, 55.

one-dimensional apprehension of words and a literary appreciation of their suggestibility, Heschel distinguishes between *descriptive* words, which "stand in a fixed relation to conventional and definite meanings," and *indicative* words, which "stand in a fluid relation to ineffable meanings."[136] The former includes concrete nouns such as "chair, table, or the terms of science"; the latter refers to "words such as God, time, beauty, eternity," which are not descriptive or denotative but allusive, evoking something that we intuit but cannot fully comprehend. They call forth "not so much a memory but a *response*, ideas unheard of, meanings not fully realized before."[137] In other words, "The real burden of understanding is upon the mind and soul of the reader."[138]

"How does one rise," asks Heschel, "from saying the word *God* to sensing His realness?"[139] As in poetry or any truly literary reading, when religious language is read *responsively*, the words can become a window or meeting point for meaning and presence. But how? The key to Heschel's "language of presence," Kaplan suggests, is the "semantic paradox." Religious declarations "possess both positive and negative valences," evoking simultaneously "two ontologically distinct dimensions: a reality surpassing human thought and an image of sublime value in a figure of speech."[140] Understanding the structure of metaphorical language prevents us from yielding to either fundamentalist literalism or rationalist disengagement from the text; most important, as Kaplan explains, it illumines "how language may link a person and God":

> The metaphor is a concrete image that alludes to another reality, based upon some analogy between the two terms. The "vehicle" of the metaphor is the term (or image) that appears in the text, alluding to the "tenor," the absent reality or concept. Metaphor may be used to express something less known, abstract, or even unknown, by something more familiar: for example, "A mighty fortress is our God." A fortress alludes to one particular aspect of the Deity, seen from a definitely human perspective. The common quality that enables the metaphorical equation or comparison is the "ground" of the metaphor, here God's strength and stability.
>
> Heschel depicts the "ground" of the biblical metaphor as a "hyphen between heaven and earth," since it hints to what is ultimately real. The vehicle and tenor themselves remain incomplete representations of their referents, for they must emphasize, in order to intensify them, only

---

136. Heschel, *God in Search of Man*, 181–82.
137. Ibid.
138. Ibid., 183. The word "revelation" itself is for Heschel an indicative word, invoking participatory meaning rather than a denotative one.
139. Heschel, *The Prophets*, 274.
140. Kaplan, HW, 53.

certain characteristics. In this sense as well, Heschel avers that religious assertion functions as *understatement*, for the vehicle of language can never completely express the divine tenor.[141]

Kaplan's analysis illustrates how the fertile paradox resolves the problem of biblical anthropomorphism, that is, "ascribing human characteristics to a Being whose essence transcends language and thought."[142] Words that appear to describe God are "but one pole of the dialectic," evoking by their very inadequacy "a sense of transcendence in relation to the known."[143] When taken "to be allusions rather than descriptions," says Heschel, "understatements rather than adequate accounts, they are aids in evoking our sense of His realness."[144] God is both "like" a fortress and "not-like" a fortress; "otherness and likeness" are inseparable. Yet the same words will undoubtedly comprise obstacles for the reader who takes them literally, descriptively, denotatively. As Kaplan comments, "the meaning of the assertion 'God's word came to me' depends upon the reader's intelligence, skill, and flexibility. Religious statements require us to recognize their literary range."[145]

What Kaplan underscores here is not only the paradoxical dynamic of mystical experience but also the degree to which Heschel's literary strategy stresses the divine tenor (God's "I") of religious speech, not the vehicle, as its metaphysically "pure" or "true" content. Thus God's "pathos," Heschel insists, grasped as a biblical and theological category, "is a genuine insight into God's relatedness to man, rather than a projection of human traits into divinity."[146] By characterizing prophetic assertions as understatements, and not hyperbole, Heschel presses us toward the divine tenor beyond words: "The speech of God is not less but more than literally real."[147] In this way he shows how the metaphorical character of biblical language in no way diminishes its ontological validity as a privileged "meeting place."[148] "On the contrary, linguistic awareness should bring us closer."[149] In like manner, a poetical method in theology does not deem to bring God down to the level of human words but involves the "accommodation of words to higher meanings."[150]

141. Ibid., 56.

142. Ibid.

143. Ibid., 53.

144. Heschel, *The Prophets*, 277.

145. Kaplan, HW, 52. "The use of anthropomorphic *expressions*," Kaplan writes, "does not itself prove belief in anthropomorphic *conceptions* of God" ("Language and Reality," 104).

146. Kaplan, HW, 57.

147. Heschel, *God in Search of Man*, 180.

148. Heschel, *Man's Quest for God*, 139.

149. Kaplan, HW, 57.

150. Heschel, *The Prophets*, 271.

The strength of Kaplan's analysis lay especially in his recognition of the "musicality of language"[151] and his insistence with Heschel that a theology bereft of this tensive and allusive quality lacks something essential—a point that recalls Tracy's insight (chap. 1) that theological form goes hand in hand with content. Yet Kaplan also recognizes that this implies a receptivity in the community that may or may not be present. To recall Newman, the spiritual senses of the community must be attuned to "hear" this music, to "realize" religious truths hidden in the world, just as we must be "linguistically prepared" to encounter the presence of God in the words of the Bible. What Kaplan affirms of Heschel on this point may also be said of Merton: his treatment of language seeks "to educate his reader's receptivity so that [the reader] might benefit from the spiritual treasures immanent to religious texts."[152] This educative or formative dimension of poetics is the methodological linchpin of what Kaplan calls Heschel's "apologetics": "not the justification of a fixed system but a program to convert our minds and hearts to God-centered consciousness."[153]

All of this comes to bear analogously in Merton's approach to theology, not least in his adoption of Sophia as a kind of sustained metaphor for the divine-humanity of God. To borrow Kaplan's formulation, it is possible for a linguistically prepared reader to experience the name Sophia "in its polar structure 'which of necessity combines otherness and likeness, uniqueness and comparability, in speaking about God.'" While Sophia as a metaphorical vehicle "can never render the tenor [God/Christ/Trinity] accurately and positively,"[154] nevertheless her name, precisely when voiced *as Name* (e.g., in prayer), can facilitate an experience of real presence, communion with the hidden God who is both beyond all words *and* ever waiting to break through from within them.

Prayer: Where Language Meets Reality

Thus far we have seen how Heschel counters the "displacement" or parallax of Kantian epistemology by ushering the reader into a poetic landscape that "rouses our audacity, requires intellectual flexibility and initiative,"[155] and makes theocentric thinking formally possible for human beings. Ultimately it is literary empathy that can enable both doubters and believers to apprehend a sense of transcendence in written prayers, in the Bible, or other kinds of

---

151. Burrows, "Raiding the Inarticulate," 356; see n. 96 above.
152. Kaplan, "Language and Reality," 103; cf. HW, 56.
153. Kaplan, HW, 19.
154. Ibid., 56.
155. Ibid., 50.

religious discourse. "By projecting our emotions into the words," Kaplan observes, "readers actualize the text's semantic richness and, reciprocally, their own inner life."[156] "A word is a focus," says Heschel, "a point at which meanings meet and from which meanings seem to proceed. In prayer, as in poetry, we turn to the words, not to use them as signs for things, but to see things in the light of the words."[157]

Most significant, with his phenomenology of prayer, Heschel draws very near to the monastic tradition of theology in which Merton stands, especially its practice of *lectio divina*. As in Christian monasticism, prayer for Heschel is the fullest realization of responsive reading, the window of presence: "It is the spiritual power of the praying person that makes manifest what is dormant in the text."[158] The aim of prayer "is not to find Him as an object in our minds but to find ourselves in Him."[159] "The task is not to know the unknown but be penetrated with it, to expose ourselves to him, not to judge and assert but to listen and be judged by him."[160] And ultimately it is not the words we say but the consciousness of our poverty, of "speaking under His eyes,"[161] that makes our prayers into hyphens between heaven and earth.

Thus the heart of prayer, once again, is the existential and semantic paradox. Heschel's extraordinary account of the praying person provides a fitting conclusion to our schematic overview of his depth theology. The account is, to my mind, one of the most penetrating descriptions of faith, understood as both a human act and as an event in the life of God, ever penned in the modern period:

> In no other act does man experience so often the disparity between the desire for expression and the means of expression as in prayer. The inadequacy of the means at our disposal appears so tangible, so tragic, that one feels it a grace to be able to give oneself up to music, to a tone, to a song, to a chant. The wave of a song carries the soul to heights which utterable meanings can never reach. Such abandonment is no escape, nor an act of being unfaithful to the mind. For the world of unutterable meanings is the nursery of the soul, the cradle of all our ideas. It is not an escape but a return to one's origins.
>
> What the word can no longer yield, man achieves through the fullness of his powerlessness. The deeper the need in which one is placed through this powerlessness, the more does man reveal himself in his essence,

156. Ibid., 52.
157. Heschel, *Man's Quest for God*, 26.
158. Ibid., 27.
159. Heschel, *Man Is Not Alone*, 127.
160. Ibid., 128.
161. Heschel, *Man's Quest for God*, 13.

and himself becomes expression. Prayer is more than communication, and man is more than the word. Should we feel ashamed by our inability to utter what we bear in our hearts? God loves what is left over at the bottom of the heart and cannot be expressed in words. . . . The unutterable surplus of what we feel, the sentiments that we are unable to put into words are our payment in kind to God.[162]

Three themes in this passage can serve here as heuristic markers for a theological method in which imagination and poetics play a significant role. First, "the fullness of [human] powerlessness" expresses in concise form the paradoxical and transformative experience at the heart of religious consciousness, mysticism, or piety.[163] Second, for all his emphasis on reaching beyond words, symbols, and images, we must not overlook the degree to which Heschel—much in the way of Merton—affirms here, and himself utilizes, the language of tradition ("a tone, a song, a chant") as an indispensable starting point or window through which we place ourselves under the eyes of God. On the lips of the praying person, sacred texts bear the potency to surpass mere communication and become vehicles of communion. Third, Heschel witnesses here to something of crucial importance in thinking about the task of theology in a mystical or sapiential mode. The "abandonment" of our selves to the ineffable in prayer, he says, "is no escape, nor an act of being unfaithful to the mind." It is, rather, "a return to one's origins," a remembrance of "the forgotten mother tongue."[164] Does this kind of remembrance, infused with prayerful receptivity, really have a place in the discipline of theology? A theocentric frame of reference answers "Yes," understanding the audacity and risks implied in such a first principle, the intellectual flexibility it presses upon theologians and believers alike. Indeed, if the discipline of theology (and with it the church) means to be attuned to the incomprehensibility of God, it will have to make itself more comfortable with the uncomfortable, with hints and gestures toward secret or forgotten meanings—all "to be gathered, deciphered and formed into evidence."[165]

In sum, Heschel's depth theology proffers much more than a semantic or rhetorical strategy. Like Newman, his manner of doing theology embraces foundational claims about God and the human person, claims rooted not only in Scripture but perhaps also in human experience as such. Without embar-

---

162. Ibid., 39–40.

163. Kaplan, "Language and Reality," 102.

164. Heschel, *Man Is Not Alone*, 75. The phrase could well stand as shorthand for Merton's own intuitive remembrance (i.e., *anamnesis*) of biblical Wisdom-Sophia.

165. Ibid.; compare with Newman's view of faith as a cumulative kind of reasoning that makes inferences based upon "enlightened presumptions" and "antecedent probabilities."

rassment or apology, Heschel evokes wellsprings of forgotten identity and memory, "our awareness of having been created in God's image, the Edenic rapport with the Creator."[166] From Heschel's theocentric perspective, the Bible reveals in inspired poetic form the divine source and center of human imagination, memory, will, and intellect: "For the world of unutterable meanings is the nursery of the soul, the cradle of all our ideas."[167]

Revelation as Breakthrough

The problem for theology after Nietzsche, after Kant, after Auschwitz, is not simply an epistemological crisis of images, symbols, or grand narratives that no longer find a foothold in the secular imagination. The problem is also ontological, that is, addressing the reigning intellectual conviction that "there is, not only no God, but no metaphysical order of any kind"[168] When the very possibility of speaking meaningfully of God is questioned by theology itself, it is no longer simply a question of which symbols from the tradition should be reclaimed or emphasized, but whether one can affirm at all (with biblical, mystical religion) any kind of real contact with God, "everywhere present but in an infinite variety of ways."[169] "As a tree torn from the soil," Heschel laments, "as a river separated from its source," we have lost the sense of God's reality. Again, *God is a name but no reality*."[170]

One of the first principles of epistemology that Heschel shares with Newman and Merton—and all three share with Augustine—is the conviction that in order to grasp things as they really are, deeply entrenched cultural patterns of seeing must be interrupted, critically questioned, and sometimes dismantled to make way for an integrally religious way of discerning the heart of reality.[171] Religion cultivates a "habit of being." Over against modern epistemologies that view reality in closed, Cartesian, or flatly anthropocentric terms, these thinkers

166. Kaplan, HW, 55.

167. Heschel's emphasis on the whole person "confirms our intellectual autonomy, our demand for verification through experience," even while broadening our concepts of experience and rationality to include interior realities—perhaps even archetypal "memories"—closed off to a Kantian or scientific epistemology (see Kaplan, HW, 85; also 34–37). This affirmation of communal or archetypal memory is also strong in Merton, as will be seen in chap. 3.

168. Michael Perry, "The Morality of Human Rights: A Problem for Nonbelievers?" *Commonweal* 133, no. 13 (July 14, 2006): 17. Perry notes (as Merton, Nietzsche, and many others have noted) the link between the undermining of metaphysics and the undermining of human dignity: i.e., the "death of God" corresponds closely with the "death of the subject."

169. Gerald O'Collins, *Christology: A Biblical, Historical, and Systematic Study of Jesus* (New York: Oxford University Press, 1995), 322.

170. Heschel, *Man's Quest for God*, xii.

171. As we shall see in chap. 3, Merton was attracted to Zen not least for its capacity to shatter illusory, idolatrous, or solipsistic notions of "self," "God," and "reality."

defend revelation as the breakthrough of the Word of God into human experi-ence, a breakthrough which, in the act of faith, has the capacity to liberate the modern person, as Merton insists, from "[his] inordinate self-consciousness, his monumental self-awareness, his obsession with self-affirmation."[172] Each protest the degree to which "totalitarian rationality and self-present subjec-tivity" empty the world and religious discourse of God, and their respective theologies were in no small part a response to that impoverishment.

In sharp contrast to a still pervasive theological method that exiles itself from the possibility of real engagement with the God of biblical revelation, Heschel's depth theology "seeks to meet the person in moments in which the whole person is involved, in moments that are affected by all a person feels, thinks, and acts."[173] Mining the very paradox that is the human person, Heschel's blending of ideational prose and indicative poetics trains the mind and spirit to open. By re-centering subjectivity from self to God, such a theol-ogy is able to "realize" or "actualize [the] nonsymbolic content" of religious discourse, electrifying "concepts frozen by ideologies, using them to surpass themselves."[174] Heschel thus models an experiential approach to theological method that shares much with Merton, and the mystical tradition of both East and West from which he drew inspiration.

Theology and Mysticism: Reclaiming a Divine Perspective

> The experience of a great mystic is always paradoxical, even disquieting, to any system. . . . Over the centuries the "friends" of Job have polished and honed their concepts until they possess an amazing perfection of logical clarity. "In this system . . . widespread everywhere today, God is not killed; He is assimilated." . . . In such "organized reality," the Gospel paradox, with its explosive truth, is conjured away.[175]

In his study subtitled "Mysticism, Poetics, and the Unlanguageable," Mark Burrows speaks of the "margins" where "language reaches for an utterance that finally eludes our voice."[176] Burrows suggests that poetics is a means of

---

172. ZBA, 31.

173. Abraham Joshua Heschel, *The Insecurity of Freedom* (Philadelphia: Jewish Publication Society of America, 1966), 119.

174. Kaplan, HW, 50, 49. In chap. 3 we shall consider how Merton "electrifies" and "actual-izes" the "nonsymbolic content" of Christian doctrines such as the incarnation.

175. Paul Evdokimov, *Woman and the Salvation of the World: A Christian Anthropology on the Charisms of Women*, trans. Anthony P. Gythiel (Crestwood, NY: St. Vladimir's Seminary Press, 1994), 206–7, citing Henri de Lubac, *Meditation sur l'Église* (1954).

176. Burrows, "Raiding the Inarticulate," in *Minding the Spirit* (see n. 9 above), 241–61, at 349.

reaching across "the necessary distances and absences" that these margins signify. Indeed, this very act of reaching "constitutes the erotic structure of metaphor, just as metaphor stands at the heart of poetics." "Can we find," Burrows asks, "a manner of *thinking* and *writing* theology that claims such an imagination as constitutive of its method?"[177] The question draws us back to Merton, the Russians, and Sophia, the feminine child who haunts the marginal spaces of Jewish and Christian memory:

> I love those who love me, and those who seek me diligently find me. (Prov 8:17)
>
> For she is a breath of the power of God, and a pure emanation of the glory of the Almighty. . . . For she is a reflection of eternal light . . . and an image of his goodness. (Wis 7:25-26)

In January of 1923, a few weeks after his expulsion from Russia, Sergius Bulgakov arrived in Istanbul, his first stop on the way to exile in Europe. There he visited the Cathedral of Hagia Sophia "to ponder the ironies of world history."[178] The great sixth-century church of Christian Byzantium was then still a Turkish mosque. The experience struck Bulgakov with the force of a revelation:

> Human tongue cannot express the lightness, the clarity, the simplicity, the wonderful harmony which completely dispels all sense of heaviness. . . . A sea of light pours from above and dominates all this space, enclosed and yet free. . . . It creates a sense of inner transparency; the weightiness and limitations of the small and suffering self disappear; the self is gone, the soul is healed of it, losing itself in these arches and merging into them. It becomes the world: I am in the world and the world is in me. . . .
>
> This is indeed Sophia, the real unity of the world in the Logos, the coinherence of all with all, the world of divine ideas. It is Plato baptized by the Hellenic genius of Byzantium. . . . How true was our ancestors' feeling in this temple, how right they were in saying that they did not know whether they were in heaven or on earth! Indeed, they were neither in heaven nor on earth, they were in St. Sophia—between the two: this is the *metaxu* of Plato's philosophical intuition. St. Sophia is the last silent testimony to the future ages of the Greek genius: a revelation in stone.[179]

177. Ibid., 350.

178. Paul Valliere, *Modern Russian Theology: Bukharev, Soloviev, Bulgakov: Orthodox Theology in a New Key* (Grand Rapids, MI: Eerdmans, 2000), 283; hereafter MRT.

179. From an autobiographical essay called "Hagia Sophia," cited in Andrew Louth, "Wisdom and the Russians: The Sophiology of Fr. Sergei Bulgakov," in *Where Shall Wisdom Be*

A great cathedral can be a "revelation in stone" in the same way sacred texts can function for the responsive reader as hyphens between heaven and earth. Both forms bear the capacity to engage the whole person in a revelatory space that is "enclosed and yet free," like the paradox of human embodiment itself. Great arches support the dome, just as bones frame the person, but the greater part of Hagia Sophia is light and shadow, color and mist. In like manner, a great musical work carries the attentive listener into the cathartic space between tone and silence. "In Mozart's *Mass*," Evdokimov wonders, "the solemnity of the music attains the liturgical value of a Presence. Mozart's *Mass* is an icon written in sound."[180]

Yet Bulgakov also understood the darker side of the imagination, how easily it can seize one side of the revelatory dynamic and reduce it to immobility. He understood, in other words, the thin boundary between the act of approaching some thing or place as an icon, a transparent sacrament or real symbol of divine Presence, and the act of approaching that very same thing as an idol.[181] The difference resides not in the thing itself but, to recall Augustine, in the disposition of the person or community standing before it. Bulgakov saw that the dome of St. Sophia, for example, which had once "been suspended as it were in midair," had in the context of the *imperium Romanum* come to rest on a hierarchical foundation. "The dome was no longer the symbol of eternity but of finite limitation. Everything was now defined, determined, coordinated, and correlated under the supreme authority of Christ's representative on earth."[182] Under the weight of political power and ossification, the dome was no longer a "window" for its pilgrims but an opaque "screen," mirroring back the hubris of ecclesial authority.

Still, for Bulgakov himself, the dome of Hagia Sophia served as a hyphen between heaven and earth, casting the world below and its diverse peoples in the unifying light of Wisdom's divine perspective. As Paul Valliere writes, "Bulgakov found himself admiring the discipline and sincerity of the Muslim worshipers. He rejoiced that the sanctuary had not been recovered for Orthodoxy by 'the bloody boots' of a Russian army. Ceasing to regard St. Sophia's as a monument to Orthodox tradition alone, he came to see it as a prophetic symbol of 'the Universal Church and universal humanity' to be

---

Found? Wisdom in the Bible, the Church, and the Contemporary World, ed. Stephen C. Barton (Edinburgh: T and T Clark, 1999), 169–81, at 178.

180. Evdokimov, *Woman and the Salvation of the World*, 132.

181. This is a persistent theme of Jean-Luc Marion in his *God Without Being*, trans. Thomas A. Carlson (Chicago: University of Chicago Press, 1991), 61–73; idem, *The Idol and the Distance: Five Studies*, trans. Thomas A. Carlson (New York: Fordham University Press, 2001).

182. Sergei Bulgakov, *Sophia: The Wisdom of God: An Outline of Sophiology* (Hudson, NY: Lindisfarne Press, 1993), 3.

realized at the end of history."[183] Trying to verbalize that experience, Bulgakov wrote, "The self is gone . . . I am in the world and the world is in me. And this sense of the weight on one's heart melting away, of liberation from the pull of gravity . . . is the bliss of some final knowledge of the all in all . . . of infinite fullness in multiplicity, and of the world in unity."[184]

It is striking how much Bulgakov anticipates here the catholicity of Thomas Merton. In his much-celebrated epilogue to *The Sign of Jonas*, "Fire Watch, July 4, 1952," Merton raises his own revelatory vault through the *metaxu* (the "inbetween") of language, bearing the reader from the bowels of Gethsemani, "the house that will one day perish," to the pinnacle of the abbey tower shrouded in night.

> And now my whole being breathes the wind which blows through the belfry, and my hand is on the door through which I see the heavens. The door swings out upon a vast sea of darkness and of prayer. Will it come like this, the moment of my death? Will You open a door upon the great forest and set my feet upon a ladder under the moon, and take me out among the stars? . . .
>
> Mists of damp heat rise up out of the fields around the sleeping abbey. The whole valley is flooded with moonlight and I can count the southern hills beyond the watertank, and almost number the trees of the forest to the north. Now the huge chorus of living beings rises up out of the world beneath my feet: life singing in the watercourses, throbbing in the creeks and the fields and the trees, choirs of millions and millions of jumping and flying and creeping things. And far above me the cool sky opens upon the frozen distance of the stars.[185]

Symphony soon passes into silence, just as life gives itself over to death: "The hand lies open. The heart is dumb. The soul that held my substance together, like a hard gem in the hollow of my own power, will one day totally give in." Saying passes into unsaying: "Although I see the stars, I no longer pretend to know them. Although I have walked in those woods, how can I claim to love them? One by one I shall forget the names of individual things." The divine perspective breaks through, as "the Voice of God is heard in Paradise: '*What was fragile has become powerful. I loved what was most frail. I looked upon what was nothing. I touched what was without substance, and*

183. Valliere, MRT, 283.

184. Cited in Louth, "Wisdom and the Russians," 178.

185. Thomas Merton, *The Sign of Jonas* (New York: Harcourt Brace, 1953; New York: Octagon, 1983), 360; hereafter SJ.

within what was not, I am.'" "Yes" becomes indistinguishable from "No," all speech yielding to *"Mercy within mercy within mercy."*[186]

Yet just as creation's breath finds its still point, "the great sun appears, and leaves stir behind the hushed flight of an escaping dove."[187] The day begins, and the circle of "Yes" and "No" begins again. The "most wonderful moment of the day," Merton writes some years later, in *Conjectures of a Guilty Bystander*, "is that when creation in its innocence asks permission to 'be' once again, as it did on the first morning that ever was. All wisdom seeks to collect and manifest itself at that blind sweet point."[188] This is what Merton calls *"le point vierge,"* when all creatures speak "not with fluent song, but with an awakening question that is their dawn state. . . . Their condition asks if it is time for them to 'be.' He answers 'yes.'"[189]

If it is true that "the artist is a sacrament maker, a creator of emphasized, clarified beauty designed to make us see,"[190] then Merton in such passages is the consummate artist. A theology shaped by a robust sacramental imagination sees, with Merton, that while the world is stricken deeply by sin, it is also limned in the light of resurrection. And in this "general dance"[191] between God and the world, the human person mysteriously holds a special place as image and icon of God. Here the Wisdom literature of the Bible boldly, almost recklessly, celebrates the connecting principle between cosmology and anthropology "from the beginning."

> When I look at your heavens, the work of your fingers
> the moon and stars that you have established;
> What are human beings that you are mindful of them,
> mortals that you care for them?
> Yet you have made them a little lower than God,
> and crowned them with glory and honor. (Ps 8:3-5)

For the Christian imagination, Sophia, "spread like a canopy over our sinful though still hallowed world,"[192] will find her deepest identity in Jesus Christ, the inbreaking Wisdom of God, who by his incarnation not only joins heaven with earth, but gives humanity a place in God, as it were, from the beginning: "When he established the heavens, I was there, when he drew

---

186. Ibid., 361–62.
187. Ibid., 362.
188. CGB, 131.
189. Ibid.
190. Andrew Greeley, "The Apologetics of Beauty," *America* 183, no. 7 (2000): 8–12.
191. The title of the final meditation in *New Seeds of Contemplation*, one of the most luminous of the many appearances of Wisdom-Sophia in Merton's corpus (see NSC, 290–97).
192. Bulgakov, *Sophia: The Wisdom of God*, 21.

a circle on the face of the deep . . . I was beside him" (Prov 8:27, 30). This reaching across the distances of eternity and history, heaven and earth, divinity and humanity, comprises the erotic structure of the whole Bible. Bulgakov thus envisions Sophia as the eros of God, the love between Father, Son, and Spirit that longs for incarnation from the beginning. We do not have to steal fire from heaven, as Merton says of Prometheus, for it has already been given in Christ. "*In a flash, at a trumpet crash/ I am all at once what Christ is . . . immortal diamond.*"[193] To do theology under the light of Wisdom is to do it in a mode of prayerful, sometimes painful, expectation. *Stay awake, the bridegroom is coming!*[194] This is, for Thomas Merton, "the heart of theology: not solving the contradiction, but remaining in the midst of it, in peace, knowing that it is fully solved, but that the solution is secret, and will never be guessed until it is revealed. . . . The wise heart lives in Christ."[195]

Concluding Remarks

> If imagination is the creative power that perceives the basic resemblances between things, then all sources, no matter how exotic, resonate in me as well. Imagination is fed by metaphor. Religion and the Scriptures, if perceived as such, are not a fundamentalist prison but an open field for visionary inspiration.[196]

If this chapter has demonstrated anything, it is the complex and laborious nature of epistemology. Yet as Newman understood a century and a half ago, in the modern context it has become an indispensable component of (and catalyst for) theological understanding, creativity, and development. Key epistemological markers examined here have been the "sacramental imagination," "wisdom," "the coincidence of opposites," and "the illative sense," while key methodological markers have been described in terms of "saying and unsaying," the "fertile paradox," and "poetics." It is important to reiterate that poetics is not being advanced here as a definitive solution to theology's task of negotiating between the claims of revelation and the value of critical thinking. The discussion of poetics is meant rather to illumine the fact that "as well as being a scientific or inferential discipline, theology

193. Gerard Manley Hopkins, "That Nature Is a Heraclitean Fire and of the Comfort of the Resurrection," in *Gerard Manley Hopkins: The Major Works*, ed. Catherine Phillips (New York: Oxford University Press, 1986), 181.

194. See Matt 25:1-13, "The Parable of the Ten Virgins," one of Merton's favorites.

195. CGB, 212, reflecting on the "eschatological secret" pervading the writings of Julian of Norwich, "a true theologian."

196. Claire Nicolas White, "And Then There Was Light: Five Generations of Stained-glass Makers," *Commonweal* 133, no. 22 (2006): 12–14, at 13.

is also a literary one. And it is to see to what extent belief begins, not in the notion or concept, but in the image and symbol."[197] It is further to insist that modern construals of reality will remain much impoverished without "a poetic dimension of theological thinking" or "a theological literature in search of a poetic form."[198]

Perhaps above all this chapter has sought to establish that there is such a thing as an imaginative mode of reasoning, and that this more capacious manner of knowing is fundamentally trustworthy with respect to the experience of God. As Newman's balanced approach demonstrates, granting a space in theological method for imaginative reasoning does not represent the abandonment of belief in the objective dynamic of revelation, nor does it represent, as Heschel insists, an "act of being unfaithful to the mind." A mystical or sapiential approach to theology engenders an open, we might even say electrified, posture of expectation, seeking after a goodness, a hidden wholeness in the world, that is still experienced by many as the deepest truth of reality. If that is putting it too strongly, then perhaps we can say that reading thinkers like Newman, Heschel, and Merton at least cultivates the desire and the willingness to believe, to pay attention to life's unfolding mystery and hidden glory. It is arguably Merton's luminous Imagination, after all, that continues to attract a remarkably diverse and frequently offbeat community of readers, many of whom would not otherwise be inclined toward traditional religiosity and doctrine.[199]

The point here is that something is profoundly at stake when by hints and degrees theology loses its depth dimension, its sense of confrontation with the irreducibly numinous, revelatory, and dramatic inscape of reality, indeed, of history. John Coulson's analysis is as cogent today as when it was published some forty years ago: "The danger point is reached when the language of theology ceases to nourish [the public language of a culture] and becomes even less sensitive than it to that sense of complexity, even paradox, which, in the public language of our poets, novelists, and dramatists, is, in origin, theological."[200] The fertile "complexity" and "paradox" of which Coulson speaks here apply not only to our confrontation with the unlanguageable mystery of God, but also to our encounter with the deepest mysteries of

197. Coulson, "Belief and Imagination," 14.

198. Burrows, "Raiding the Inarticulate," 348.

199. In a delightful aside during a lecture to the novices in 1962, Merton says: "One of the great graces of my life, as far as this question of being imaginative goes, is the fact of having more or less grown up among European cathedrals and monasteries and things like that. I mean to have all that around you when you are a kid is marvelous. And to grow up with that sort of stuff and with that kind of imagery, you see" (MHPH, 461).

200. Coulson, "Belief and Imagination," 14.

human being. All the more so in approaching the mystery of Jesus, where our manner of speech (i.e., our Christology) somehow has to be worthy of a memory and experience that enfolds both divine and human assertions, not in mutual antagonism or opposition but precisely in mutual reinforcement. The coincidence of opposites speaks to an intrinsic (i.e., historical and metaphysical) dynamic of relationality and mutuality, a "covenant" engendered not only *by* God but also, as Christianity dares to profess, *in* God, "in person," indeed, in our very human flesh. For "human nature, by the very fact that it was assumed, not absorbed, in him, has been raised in us also to a dignity beyond compare." In Jesus, we claim in wonder, God "has in a certain way united himself with each individual. He worked with human hands, he thought with a human mind. He acted with a human will and with a human heart he loved. Born of the Virgin Mary, he has truly been made one of us, like to us in all things except sin" (*Gaudium et spes* 22).[201] A Christology worthy of such a confession, of such disarming *good news*, will truly have to break itself open linguistically, metaphysically, kenotically, to the wisdom and presence of God in every natural and naturally human landscape, where Wisdom ever plays, beckons, provokes, and finds us.

For the Catholic sacramental imagination, the cultivation of a more holistic manner of apprehending truths "really to be found in the world, though they are not upon the surface" might even be capable of yielding an affirmative response to the modern anxiety about verification through experience. When Merton points to the "logos of a barn," the "real presence" of Christ in the psalms, or the "dance of Sophia" in the faces of children, we can begin to respond—whether to the modern skeptic, or that skeptic in ourselves—"Yes, it *is* true, though perhaps not precisely in the way that your question assumes." Or we might reply, as Merton did, with the Zen *mondo*: You are "trying to understand" when in fact you ought to try and *see*.

As we shall see in chapter 3, to the modern question, "Is it true?" Merton's writings have the effect of turning the question around, confronting the questioner's epistemological or solipsistic assumptions: "*Who is it* that asks?" Just as the Bible questions and transforms the life of the one who reads and prays it, Merton's theology provokes and trains the mind to open. To be "bitten by Merton" is to be initiated into a world of revelation, heightened expectation, and presence.

---

201. Citing the Council of Chalcedon (AD 451); Heb 4:15.

Drawing by Thomas Merton. Used with permission of the Merton Legacy Trust and the Thomas Merton Center, Bellarmine University.

3

In the Belly of a Paradox:
The Archaeology
of Merton's Sacramental Imagination

The sign Jesus promised to the generation that did not understand Him was the "sign of Jonas the prophet"—that is, the sign of His own resurrection. The life of every monk, of every priest, of every Christian is signed with the sign of Jonas, because we all live by the power of Christ's resurrection. But I feel that my own life is especially sealed with this great sign . . . because like Jonas himself I find myself traveling toward my destiny in the belly of a paradox.[1]

The years between 1958 and 1968 were years of extraordinary tension and creativity for Thomas Merton, a period that produced arguably his most stunning and enduring works. Consider just one of these, *Raids on the Unspeakable* (1966), a collection of thirteen pieces published in various venues between 1958 and 1965, the book that most unforgettably captures Merton's voice in the wilderness in an era spinning out of control. The title is presumably a variant on T. S. Eliot's description of poetry as "a raid on the inarticulate," with Merton substituting "the Unspeakable" to emphasize the vocation of the poet (the intellectual, the Christian) to resist the horrors of an age of apocalyptic violence.[2] Between the essays are placed fifteen of Merton's abstract drawings, described in a final note as "simple signs and ciphers of energy, acts or movements intended to be propitious" but "transcending all logical interpretation."[3] The book's message, a prefatory note hints, is to "be human in this most inhuman of ages, to guard the image of man for it is the image of God."[4] Note how this statement juxtaposes priestly annunciation with prophetic denunciation: Merton intends to reclaim the dignity of the

---

1. SJ, v.
2. Patrick F. O'Connell, "Raids on the Unspeakable," in TME, 379.
3. RU, 180, 182.
4. Ibid., 6, citing Berdyaev.

human person while launching "raids" on every dehumanizing force churning through the world in the twentieth century.

Poetics and Prophecy in Merton's Last Decade

One of the more autobiographically telling pieces in *Raids* is "Message to Poets," an essay Merton wrote for a gathering of Latin American poets in Mexico in 1964. Here Merton insists that poetry is not "word-magic," a claim he will stake, significantly, for theology in other contexts. In an age of mass society, observes Merton, it is not the poet or the theologian "who devoutly believes in the 'magic of words,'" it is rather "the businessman, the propagandist, the politician."[5] For the poet "there is precisely no magic" but "only life in all its unpredictability and all its freedom." The poet's task is not to manipulate the imagination or, like the advertising specialist, to "appeal mindlessly to the vulnerable will." The poet's task is "to seize upon reality in its moment of highest expectation and tension toward the new. This tension is discovered not in hypnotic elation but in the light of everyday existence." In this way, Merton says, poetry serves as a form of *prophecy*, by which he means, not prediction, but giving voice to "the flowering of ordinary possibilities" that are "hidden in everyday life," in order to harvest "fruits of hope that have never been seen before."[6]

A survey of other titles published in this period tells the story of a writer seized by both the poetic and prophetic spirits: *Disputed Questions, The Behavior of Titans, New Seeds of Contemplation, Emblems of a Season of Fury, Seeds of Destruction, Gandhi on Non-Violence, The Way of Chuang Tzu, Day of a Stranger, Seasons of Celebration, Conjectures of a Guilty Bystander, Mystics and Zen Masters, Cables to the Ace, Faith and Violence, Zen and the Birds of Appetite.* While Merton had strongly apophatic impulses, he chose the path of solidarity with a world in crisis, his prophecy taking the form of ruthlessly naming the present through the practice of language. Like Heschel, in whom mysticism, poetics, and prophecy were also one, Merton's mature voice is both "prophetic" *and* "apologetic," serving "not the justification of a fixed system" but the *interruption* of fixed systems—not least theological ones—in order "to convert our minds and hearts to God-centered consciousness."[7] Most striking is the way his writings continue to galvanize both believers and nonbelievers alike, a fact that should not be too quickly overlooked. Like Heschel, Merton's work still resonates deeply in people; it rings true

5. Ibid., 159.
6. Ibid., 159–60.
7. Edward K. Kaplan, HW, 19.

with basic human sensibilities. Heschel's biographer, Edward Kaplan, goes far in explaining this convergence: "It is at the gates of poetic participation . . . that the believer and the faithless meet."[8]

But poetic theology is not "word-magic," just as other theological forms, such as Scripture, liturgy, or iconography, hold no inherent power to magically transport the believer into communion with the hidden God. The point is, God is *already present*. Liturgy, iconography, and poetics function as vehicles of presence, even for the nonbeliever, to the degree they facilitate a re-centering of subjectivity from the self and community to God. This transformative dynamic unites the poet, prophet, priest, and mystic, and unites them with every human being who has experienced that paradoxical moment in which one "dies" or "loses oneself" in the immediacy of something (some One) infinitely greater. Indeed, this sense of "infinitely greater" is such that the thought of freezing it in any kind of a system, linguistic or otherwise, feels like a violation, an act of reclaiming the center for ourselves too quickly. Contemplatives become prophetic witnesses precisely when they interrupt this act, interjecting the divine perspective into an imaginative framework that has become opaque, forgetful, or contemptuous of God—that is, the nest of the Unspeakable.

It is no accident that in the last decade of his life, and corresponding with the church's turn to the modern world at Vatican II, Merton found in the Hebrew Bible lessons that would help to transform his understanding of the role of "contemplation in a world of action." Certainly his friendship with Heschel, corresponding with the council's radical reevaluation of Christianity's foundational relationship to the Jewish people, infused Merton's religious consciousness with a new, and unapologetically biblical, urgency. In 1967 he writes:

> Today a new and more Biblical understanding of the contemplative life is called for: we must see it as a response to the dynamic Word of God in history, we must see it in the light of Biblical eschatology. The contemplative finds God not only in the embrace of "pure love" alone but in the prophetic ardor of response to the "Word of the Lord": not in love considered as essential good but in love that breaks through into the world of sinful men in the fire of judgment and of mercy. The contemplative must see love not only as the highest and purest experience of the human heart transformed by grace, but as God's unfailing fidelity to unfaithful man.[9]

8. Edward K. Kaplan, "Language and Reality in Abraham J. Heschel's Philosophy of Religion," *Journal of the American Academy of Religion* 41, no. 1 (1973): 94–113, at 95.
9. CWA, 133.

To recall lessons from the previous chapter, revelation grasped from Wisdom's divine perspective—Bulgakov under the dome of Hagia Sophia, Merton's "Fire Watch"—is not the disclosure of some fixed truth so much as an invitation to participate in a "love that breaks through into the world"; it is an event in the life of God, "drawn out into action in accommodation to our weakness."[10] No less than Heschel, Merton believed responsive engagement in the Bible immerses us in the river of divine pathos. Kaplan describes the paradoxical inversion that follows: "Instead of remaining the object of human consciousness, God becomes experienced as the Subject of which the person is the object. *The Bible is God's anthropology, not human theology.*"[11]

This is an extraordinary statement, bound to irritate the sensibilities of many Jews and Christians today, to say nothing of the systematic or hermeneutical theologian. Yet it captures something essential if we mean to get inside Merton's religious imagination in the last decade of his life, especially his remembrance of Sophia. "The prophet," observes Kaplan, "lives at the crossroads of God, the individual, and the human community."[12] It was Proverb (Wisdom, Sophia) whom Merton invoked after his breakthrough at the crossroads of Fourth and Walnut in Louisville, by all accounts a significant turning point in his relationship to the world. From that moment forward, Merton would associate her name with "God's anthropology" in some of his most penetrating theological and social writings. Note how the metaphor itself—"God's anthropology"—underscores the disarming intimacy into which God invites humanity from the beginning; by an act of love-humility, God opens a space in Godself for the world, and consummately, for human freedom. It is the prophet who calls the human community back to itself in God, to its primordial task of incarnating God's love, mercy, and justice in the world.

This chapter explores both the priestly and prophetic contours of Merton's religious imagination. It builds on the previous chapter by examining Merton's epistemology and use of language, a semantic strategy shaped by the poetic symbols of the Bible and especially the monastic tradition in which he was steeped. Its aim is to show how theological symbols such as "Logos," "Christ," "Spirit," and "Sophia" are not "word-magic" for Merton, that is, aesthetic or literary fantasies, painting beautiful pictures for the mind's eye; nor are they merely signs, indicative pointers to a distant and abstractly conceived God-beyond-God, enshrouded in impenetrable darkness. Merton utilizes such

10. John Henry Newman, OUS, 26.

11. Edward K. Kaplan, "Contemplative Inwardness and Prophetic Action: Thomas Merton's Dialogue with Abraham Joshua Heschel," in *Merton and Judaism: Holiness in Words: Recognition, Repentance, and Renewal*, ed. Beatrice Bruteau (Louisville, KY: Fons Vitae, 2003), 253–68, at 259; emphasis added.

12. Ibid.

symbols, rather, in the manner they utilize him, which is to say, as *sacraments*, vessels of memory, presence, and hope that bring together realities, "the flowering of ordinary possibilities" ever present but hidden in the world.

Yet Merton also understood that the latent power of religious symbols will be lost on a community that has no awareness of its need for redemption.[13] His acute consciousness of the ills and idols of Western and American society comprises the tensive subtext, the sustained "negative contrast experience,"[14] of his entire corpus, from *The Seven Storey Mountain* to the posthumous *Peace in a Post-Christian Era*. This prophetic, ironic, and seemingly dialectical thrust of Merton's religious imagination came into devastating focus in the last decade of his life and will also be explored here.

In fact, two distinct epistemological trajectories within the Christian tradition will variously come into play in this chapter: one more or less biblical and sapiential, which embraces "the seeds of transcendence within the practices of language itself,"[15] the other broadly mystical and metaphysical, which moves more easily in the realm of unsaying and silence. It may be that Merton's extraordinary catholicity is most revealed in his wondrous capacity to bring together these distinct, but both thoroughly "Catholic," ways of wisdom.

The Archaeology of Catholicity

> Tao is obscured when men understand only one of a pair of opposites, or concentrate only on a part of being. Then clear expression also becomes muddled by mere wordplay, affirming this one aspect and denying all the rest.[16]

Christopher Nugent has written two penetrating studies on Merton's "way of seeing," or what he calls the "archaeology of catholicity."[17] It is, in a word,

---

13. "No need of feast days when everyone is just: no one needs to be saved. No one needs to think. No one needs to confess" (RU, 105).

14. The term refers to an experience of something that is so self-evidently wrong or evil as to elicit the more or less intuitive (transcendental) reaction that *this simply should not be*, and that further generates a positive impulse to action, the desire to right the wrong. See Edward Schillebeeckx, *Church: The Human Story of God* (New York: Crossroad, 1990), 5–6; idem, *God the Future of Man* (New York: Sheed and Ward, 1968), 153–54.

15. Mark S. Burrows, "Raiding the Inarticulate: Mysticism, Poetics, and the Unlanguageable," in *Minding the Spirit: The Study of Christian Spirituality*, ed. Elizabeth A. Dreyer and Mark S. Burrows (Baltimore: Johns Hopkins, 2005), 341–61, at 349.

16. WCT, 42.

17. Christopher Nugent, "Merton, the Coincidence of Opposites and the Archeology of Catholicity," *Cistercian Studies* 26 (1991): 257–70; idem, "*Pax Heraclitus*: A Perspective on Merton's Healing Wholeness" (unpublished manuscript, 2005).

the *coincidence of opposites,* "one of the oldest and . . . best kept secrets of human experience"[18]; indeed, the "best things in life are expressions of the coincidence of opposites: the rainbow, an admixture of rain in shine; great emotion, as with 'tears of joy'; the implosions of love; the 'travail' and 'joy' of birthing, as observed in the Gospel of John (16:21) . . . music with its alteration of sound and silence . . . the universe . . . with its simultaneity of expansion and contraction."[19] Of course for Christians, the coincidence of opposites is "enshrined at the center of the New Testament" itself in the person of Jesus, "Son of God" and "Son of Man," "the first and last," and consummately in "the paschal Mystery of life-through-death."[20] Thus Christian spirituality, our very way of being in the world, is patterned after our understanding of Christology itself: it "must do honor to the conjunction of the bodiliness (humanity) and the transcendence (divinity) of the human person without dissolving the coincidence into either one of its poles. In other words, the tradition is in a constant state of balancing the poles without letting go of the tension between them."[21] Nicholas of Cusa, the great Western exponent of the *coincidentia oppositorum*, considered it "the least imperfect definition of God."[22]

Nugent teases out how this fundamental memory and experience at the heart of Christianity is expressed in mystical theology: "It is related to the dialectical mode. . . . But the dialectical mode, rooted in classical traditions, is discursive, whereas the coincidence of opposites takes us beyond language and beyond logic. Or it would. As would poetry, or mysticism. It transcends rhetoric for what Newman called 'realization.' It is existentialist more than intellectualist. A composite, the 'opposites' of the construct implies its disposition for the apophatic, the *via negativa*; on the other hand, the 'coincidence' would relate it more to the cataphatic, the *via positiva*."[23]

Recall that Newman ascribed this capacity for the "realization" of apparent opposites to the imagination, which "dissolves, diffuses, dissipates, in order to recreate."[24] The imagination plays a further role in structuring religious discourse, where images become participatory symbols through the power of the imagination. The religious symbol bears the believing community

---

18. Nugent, "The Coincidence of Opposites," 260.

19. Nugent, "*Pax Heraclitus*," 5.

20. Ibid., 264.

21. Lawrence Cunningham, "*Extra Arcam Noe*: Criteria for Christian Spirituality," in *Minding the Spirit: The Study of Christian Spirituality*, ed. Elizabeth A. Dreyer and Mark S. Burrows (Baltimore: Johns Hopkins, 2005), 171–78, at 173.

22. Nugent, "The Coincidence of Opposites," 263.

23. Ibid., 260.

24. Gerard Magill, "Moral Imagination in Theological Method and Church Tradition: John Henry Newman," *Theological Studies* 53 (1992): 451–75, at 460.

"beyond language and beyond logic" into an experience of communion, a truth-in-wholeness that is obscured when the imagination fixes upon only one aspect or pole of manifold reality. Thus when theology fixes on the apophatic way, as Nugent notes, it "can issue in the esoteric"; when it fixes on the cataphatic way, it issues "in the mundane."[25] By contrast, the proper attunement of positive and negative theology, of saying and unsaying, is the mark of a symbolic, sacramental, and Catholic imagination. Catholicity is marked by "plentitude" of imagination, by contrast to "partiality" and "sectarianism"; it is "inclusive, paradoxical and ironic, and, when truest to itself, ascetic."[26] All of this will come to bear below in our consideration of the way Merton structures religious discourse through the biblical symbol—the Judeo-Christian *memoria*—of Sophia.

Breakthrough and Expectation

One of the few explicit references to the coincidence of opposites in Merton's work occurs in "Learning to Live" (1968), an essay honoring his alma mater, Columbia University. Here Merton likens the telos of the university to that of the monastery, suggesting that both should strive to cultivate a "consciousness that transcends all division, all separation."[27] Writing of the divine "spark" and its "realization," he writes: "This realization at the apex is a coincidence of all opposites (as Nicholas of Cusa might say), a fusion of freedom and unfreedom, being and unbeing, life and death, self and non-self, man and God. The 'spark' is not so much a stable entity which one finds but an event, an explosion which happens as all opposites clash within oneself."[28]

Clearly an "event" or "breakthrough" before it is an idea or "construct," the coincidence of opposites most often reverberates implicitly in Merton's writings on contemplation, or mystical experience: "For if God is immanently present, He is also transcendent," writes Merton. "The two ('absence') and ('presence') merge in loving knowledge that 'knows by unknowing' (a traditional term of mysticism). . . . [This] sense of absence is not a one-sided thing: it is dialectical, and it includes its opposite, namely presence."[29]

25. Nugent, "The Coincidence of Opposites," 260.
26. Ibid.
27. Thomas Merton, *Love and Living*, ed. Naomi Burton Stone and Patrick Hart (New York: Harcourt Brace Jovanovich, 1985), 9; hereafter LL.
28. Ibid., 10. It is illuminating to compare this passage to Merton's account of Zen realization, written around the same time: "Zen implies *a breakthrough*, an explosive liberation from one-dimensional conformism, a recovery of unity which is not the suppression of opposites but a simplicity beyond opposites. . . . This means a totally different perspective than that which dominates our society—and enables it to dominate us" (ZBA, 140).
29. CWA, 159.

As everywhere in Merton's writing, there are echoes here of his long love affair with John of the Cross: "Just as we can never separate asceticism from mysticism, so in St. John of the Cross we find darkness and light, suffering and joy, sacrifice and love united together so closely that they seem at times to be identified. It is not so much that we come through darkness to light, as that darkness itself is light."[30] In terms of everyday spirituality, the reconciliation of opposites "is the mark of true sanctity," giving "the soul of the saint a perfectly Christ-like character."[31]

The strange coincidence of presence and absence finds its liturgical and formative climax, Merton suggests, in the paschal Triduum, which draws the community body and soul into a wholesale confrontation with it[32]—the dreaded kiss of Jesus' bloodied feet, the watching in the night before the tomb, the Vigil fire suddenly breaking through in darkness—a mystagogical *anamnesis* and sensual feast that surely goes far in landscaping the Catholic imagination with its strong affinity for the ironic. Just as the incarnation and paschal mystery figure in many of Merton's late writings as God's exemplary irony, so he elegizes Flannery O'Conner's ability to exploit the "shocking" situation in which a Word "from above" breaks through "to bring man into confrontation with a whole new kind of destiny, a destiny to freedom in Christ."[33]

Nowhere does the coincidence of opposites manifest more vividly throughout Merton's corpus than in the realm of eschatology, that fertile paradox in Christian life between the joys of fellowship in Christ now, on this side of death, and our hopes for an all-embracing fulfillment yet to come. To be sure, Merton's imagination is as thickly eschatological as it is mystical and sacramental, and this has everything to do with his monastic vocation. Among his most celebrated passages, it would be hard to find a single one that did not reflect that tensive insertion of the monk "between present and future, moving back and forth between them, tasting here and now 'in this body . . . in this vessel' some piece of heaven"[34] *Will it come like this, the moment of my death? Will you open a door upon the great forest and set my feet upon a ladder under the moon, and take me out among the stars?*[35]

30. Thomas Merton, *Disputed Questions* (New York: Harcourt Brace, 1985), 212; hereafter DQ.

31. Ibid., 211.

32. See Thomas Merton, *The New Man* (New York: Farrar, Straus and Giroux, 1999; originally published 1961), 238–48; hereafter NM.

33. LE, 101; see also "Flannery O'Connor: A Prose Elegy," RU, 37–42.

34. William Harmless, *Desert Christians: An Introduction to the Literature of Early Monasticism* (New York: Oxford University Press, 2004), 392.

35. SJ, 360.

It is telling that near the end of his dialogue with Zen teacher D. T. Suzuki, Merton invokes the figure of John Cassian, the living bridge between East and West in ancient monasticism.[36] He calls to mind Cassian's teaching on purity of heart, a way of life involving unceasing meditation on the Scriptures, especially the psalms, which reassure the solitary, as Cassian puts it, "that help is always and everywhere present." Yet purity of heart is only a preparation, notes Merton, "for the real work of God which is revealed in the Bible: the work of the *new creation*, the resurrection from the dead, the restoration of all things in Christ. This is the real dimension of Christianity, the eschatological dimension which is peculiar to it, and which has no parallel in Buddhism."[37] No less than for Cassian, for Merton too the "living symbols" of the Bible— meditated, prayed, experienced integrally by the whole person—are crucial for interiorizing the "eschatological secret"[38] of Christian faith: the real (not merely notional) experience of Christ's living presence within us, the promise of resurrection, the "sign of Jonas." Merton closes the dialogue with Suzuki with one of his favorite gospel images, "the wise virgins who wait with lighted lamps,"[39] which captures for him the eschatological tension permeating the New Testament. *Keep awake therefore, for you know neither the day nor the hour.* As we shall see in chapter 4, he finds the same flash of vigilance in the pre-Christian fragments of Herakleitos the Obscure: *He that is awake lights up from sleeping.*

If Cassian and Herakleitos were Merton's ancient mentors in the coincidence of opposites, with many others in between, then William Blake was his modern guide. In "Blake and the New Theology" (1968), Merton defends Blake from the "death-of-God" theologian Thomas Altizer's attempt to draft him "into the militant ranks of the new antireligious Christians."[40] Merton takes pains to dissociate Blake's "reunion of contraries" from Altizer's Hegelian dialectic—"a purely intellectual operation [which] does not involve the whole man" and which results finally "in a return to the idol in a worse and more inexorable form."[41] What for Hegel "would be 'coincidence'—the shock of billiard balls against one another in an historical process . . . is for Blake something totally different," the restoration of a "higher unity" in "mercy, pity, peace. The work of this reversal is the epiphany of God in Man."[42] In lines that

36. ZBA, 130–32.

37. Ibid., 132.

38. CGB, 211–12; the term comes from Julian of Norwich, whose influence on Merton was considerable.

39. ZBA, 133; see also NM, 227–29.

40. LE, 4.

41. Ibid., 7.

42. Ibid., 6, 7.

could well apply to himself, his own theological mood in the 1960s, Merton describes Blake's vision as "a total integration of mysticism and prophecy, a return to apocalyptic faith which arises from an intuitive protest against Christianity's estrangement from its own eschatological ground. Blake saw official Christendom as a *narrowing* of vision, a foreclosure of experience and of future expansion, a locking up and securing of the doors of perception. . . . Blake, in other words, calls for 'a whole new form of theological understanding.'"[43]

Yet even Blake's "new form," Merton insists, maintains that God "is still the Creator and not the creation process—the ground of being, not the process of becoming."[44] While Merton affirms the kenosis of God in history—"The dynamism of eschatology is not a dynamism of the divine nature *ad intra* but a work of God in the world, 'in the Spirit' and 'in Christ'"—he rejects radical theology's Hegelian reduction of the "'Godhead' to a historical process." The Christian narrative is not the "fuzzy romanticism of a Godhead-process" but rather "an epiphany of God . . . *communicating and sharing himself.*" The "Kingdom of God" is God's free and unmerited "self-manifestation and self-expression in man."[45]

Eschatology and Peacemaking

The "realization" of eschatology itself becomes ever more the focus of Merton's writings during the chaos and fragmentation of the 1960s. In other words, in the midst of suffering, Christian hope does not seek fulfillment only in some distant day "over the river Jordan," but hope intensifies *in* and *for* the present moment. As with Blake and much in the pattern of the Russian theologians, Merton recognizes in human creativity and efforts for a peaceful and just society a divine source and empowerment in trinitarian life from the very beginning:

> I am coming to see clearly the great importance of the concept of "realized eschatology"—the transformation of life and of human relations by Christ *now* (rather than an eschatology focused on future cosmic events . . .). Realized eschatology is the heart of genuine Christian humanism and hence its tremendous importance for the Christian peace effort, for example. . . . The preaching of peace by a remnant in an age of war and violence is one of the eschatological characteristics of the life of the

43. Ibid., 6.
44. Ibid., 9.
45. Ibid., 9–10. While defending Blake here, at other times Merton critiques Blake's mysticism as "extremist" and corrects him by appealing to Aquinas and the Thomistic theology of Maritain and others (see, e.g., LE, 446).

Church. By this activity of the Church the work of God is mysteriously accomplished in the world.[46]

It is no accident that eschatology was foremost on Merton's mind in 1964 or that he inscribed these words just days after his grim reflection on "the stupor of the Church," including its "treatment of Negroes in the United States."[47] Merton's hope was both mystical and political, offering a rare model for reconciling two strands in the tradition that are "still commonly assumed [to be] inimical to one another and mutually exclusive."[48]

Clearly the "spark" in which the attunement of opposites is "realized" is not for Merton "a beautiful abstraction of a beautiful mind" or the height of Plotinian ascent toward "the alone with the Alone." To the contrary, as Nugent observes, the reconciliation of opposites is for Merton an "event" that is "intra-historical and open to engagement in human affairs. The Logos at its center is such that the 'opposites' can magnetize rather than repel—if we would let them." Its logic, in other words, "is centripetal, not centrifugal," seeking to reverse the centrifugal and egoic movement of the Fall.[49] Embracing unity-in-multiplicity, it seeks after the common good. War, of course, is its horrifying opposite, facilitating, as Merton writes, the mass "suspension of conscience" in a quasi-mystical "game" of life and death. "The satisfaction is all the greater when the suspension of conscience can be seen as a mystical summons: to destroy the devil by a delicious recourse to the devil's own methods."[50] And "the smoke of the victims is always justified by some clean sociological explanation."[51] St. Paul, as Nugent poignantly comments, "may have augured the death-knell of the demon [of war] in his marvelous annunciation of universality: 'There is neither Jew nor Greek, slave nor free, male nor female' (Gal. 3:28); but, alas, there *was*." The consequence of "failing to recognize common humanity," Nugent observes, is "millions of carcasses under a common headstone, inscribed, 'OTHER.'"[52] For Merton, only mercy—a free, unexpected, and illogical gift of grace—can liberate us from the self-perpetuating hatred that feeds the demon of violence.[53]

46. DWL, 87.

47. Ibid., 83–84; also Thomas Merton, *The Intimate Merton: His Life from His Journals*, ed. Patrick Hart and Jonathan Montaldo (New York: HarperCollins, 1999), 215–16.

48. A. M. Allchin, "Our Lives, a Powerful Pentecost," in MHPH, 138.

49. Nugent, "*Pax Heraclitus*," 6.

50. CGB, 228.

51. Thomas Merton, *Faith and Violence: Christian Teaching and Christian Practice* (Notre Dame, IN: University of Notre Dame Press, 1968), 153; hereafter FV.

52. Nugent, "*Pax Heraclitus*," 8.

53. Again, against a Hegelian kind of "vague optimism about an abstract reconciliation of ideological opposites," Merton describes eschatology as "the vision of a totally new and final

Against his own failures to recognize the common humanity and sanctity of the stranger, Merton narrates his awakening from a "dream of separateness" at the corner of Fourth and Walnut:

> I was suddenly overwhelmed with the realization that I loved all those people, that they were mine and I theirs, that we could not be alien to one another even though we were total strangers. . . . This sense of liberation from an illusory difference was such a relief and such a joy to me that I almost laughed out loud. . . . As if the sorrows and stupidities of the human condition could overwhelm me, now I realize what we all are. And if only everybody could realize this! But it cannot be explained. There is no way of telling people that they are walking around shining like the sun.[54]

Much overshadowed in *Conjectures of a Guilty Bystander* by the Fourth and Walnut passage, but no less wondrous, is the "Prayer to God the Father on the Vigil of Pentecost."[55] As in "Fire Watch" and innumerable other texts, here Merton celebrates the epiphany of wisdom in "the forms and individual characters of living and growing things, of inanimate beings, of animals and flowers and all nature,"[56] all holy in the sight of God. In short, Merton's peacemaking extends well beyond the human community to embrace the natural world:

> Today, Father, this blue sky lauds you. The delicate green and orange flowers of the tulip poplar tree praise you. The distant blue hills praise you, together with the sweet-smelling air that is full of brilliant light. The bickering flycatchers praise you with the lowing cattle and the quails that whistle over there. I too, Father, praise you, with all these my brothers, and they give voice to my own heart and to my own silence. We are all one silence, and a diversity of voices. . . . Here I am. In me the world is present, and you are present. I am a link in the chain of light and of presence.[57]

Rejecting an adversarial or instrumental view of nature, Merton narrates an ancient view of human being bound up with the well-being of all things.

---

reality, a cosmic reversal" that brings unity to "concrete and communal Mankind . . . not by politics but by mercy" (LE, 10). By "reversal" Merton does not mean a kind of deus ex machina that overpowers human subjectivity (his eschatology will be explored further in chap. 6).

54. CGB, 156–57.

55. Ibid., 177–79.

56. NSC, 30.

57. CGB, 177; cf. the superbly realized "Things in Their Identity," NSC, 29–36; also SFS, 214–15, where Merton invokes the biblical "I am" in describing the experience of communion with nature.

The restoration of sanity will require "a renewal of communion between the traditional, contemplative disciplines and those of science, between the poet and the physicist, the priest and the depth psychologist, the monk and the politician."[58]

Biography as Theology

Is it too much to suggest that the contours of a Catholic life may serve as a model for the contours of a vibrantly "catholic" theology?[59] If there are only a handful of instances in which Merton wrote explicitly about the reconciliation of opposites, it may be because, as Nugent suggests, "he was too close to it": "Merton *was* the seamless garment before it was articulated."[60] This striking insight, not merely hyperbole, calls to mind the pivotal journal of April 28, 1957, transposed into an even more universal key in *Conjectures of a Guilty Bystander*: "If I can unite in myself the thought and the devotion of Eastern and Western Christendom, the Greek and the Latin Fathers, the Russians with the Spanish mystics, I can prepare in myself the reunion of divided Christians. From that secret and unspoken unity in myself can eventually come a visible and manifest unity of all Christians. . . . We must contain all divided worlds and transcend them in Christ."[61]

Asked in 1961 to write a preface for *A Thomas Merton Reader*, Merton took the opportunity to assess the broad contours of his life:

> I have had to accept the fact that my life is almost totally paradoxical. . . . No matter. It is in the paradox itself, the paradox that was and still is a source of insecurity, that I have come to find the greatest security. I have become convinced that the very contradictions in my life are in some ways signs of God's mercy to me. . . . Paradoxically, I have found peace because I have always been dissatisfied. My moments of depression and despair turn out to be renewals, new beginnings. . . . All that matters is that the old be recovered on a new plane and be, itself, a new reality. . . . All life tends to grow like this, in mystery inscaped with paradox and contradiction, yet centered, in its very heart, on divine mercy. . . .

---

58. LL, 79.

59. Johann Baptist Metz laments the separation in Catholic theology between dogmatic theology and mystical biography, which he describes as "the articulation of one's life's story in God's presence." My method here generally accords with Metz's desire to view "dogmatic theology" and "mystical biography" as part of a single cloth. See Johann Baptist Metz, *Faith in History and Society: Toward a Practical Fundamental Theology*, trans. and ed. J. Matthew Ashley (New York: Crossroad, 2007), 198–207.

60. Nugent, "The Coincidence of Opposites," 261, 270.

61. CGB, 21.

> Without the grace of God there would be no unity, no complicity in our
> lives: only contradiction.[62]

Rendered theologically, the passage echoes Newman's wonderfully forthright axiom: "Theology makes progress by always being alive to its fundamental uncertainties."[63] *All that matters is that the old be recovered on a new plane and be, itself, a new reality.*

As Nugent puts it, "Merton's guiding instinct, conscious or not, is that when one has lost one's way, the way out is the way back. 'Archaeology,' freely, is the search for beginnings. And so Merton goes beyond the received scholastic theology (while by no means foreswearing it) to patristic and ancient traditions, whether East or West."[64] Much in the way of Newman, Merton's theology "excavates the past to move beyond it"[65]—an essential thrust of the Catholic imagination. In sum, from the earliest hymns of St. Paul to the African American spirituals rising up from the bloodied soil of slave religion, the mystical (i.e., real but hidden) encounter with Jesus Christ is a coincidence of opposites that finds expression in ten thousand Christian and Catholic forms. Merton is a mystical theologian because he moves beyond discursive theology to appeal directly to this "always already" experience, and to shape it, in the responsive imagination of his readers.

It remains to state the perhaps obvious but crucial fact that while the attunement of opposites is inclusive and seeks after a hidden wholeness, this does not mean that the way to its realization is free of friction, still less that mystical or speculative attainment is beyond good and evil. To the contrary, on this side of the reign of God, where at best the church and its theologians see "through a glass darkly," the way of catholicity will always be marked by sin and shortsightedness, struggle, and sometimes, as Merton avers, "depression and despair." The Catholic imagination makes no grand leaps from cognitive dissonance to unbending certitude. Arduously, the imagination has to "dissolve, diffuse, and dissipate" before it can begin to "recreate"—after which the process must begin again, like the climber discerning her way up the rock face. As Newman reminds us, Catholic theology is a "method of antagonism" by which "we steady our minds, not so as to reach their object,

---

62. Thomas Merton, *A Thomas Merton Reader: Revised Edition*, ed. Thomas P. McDonnell (Garden City, NY: Doubleday, 1974), 16–17.

63. Cited in John Coulson, "Belief and Imagination," *The Downside Review* 90 (1972): 1–14, at 14.

64. Nugent, "The Coincidence of Opposites," 265.

65. Ibid., 258.

but to point them in the right direction . . . approximating little by little, *by saying and unsaying, to a positive result.*"[66]

When realization dawns, and that which was dim and shadowy suddenly "clicks" into focus, it will not be our mental labor that sparks the event, but the silent gift of grace. Herein lay the ascetic dimension of theology, emphasized so lyrically in Merton's writings: Like the wise virgins of Jesus' vibrant imagination, the theologian must train the mind, heart, and body (i.e., the spiritual senses) to remain open and uncluttered, free to receive the gift of insight when it comes. No less than in poetry, the "tension toward the new" in theology has little to do with "word-magic," but it is instead a discovery to be made above all "in the light of everyday existence."

Modern Consciousness vs. Wisdom Awareness

> The new consciousness which isolates man in his own knowing mind and separates him from the world around him . . . makes wisdom impossible because it severs the communion between subject and object, man and nature, upon which wisdom depends. In the new consciousness man is . . . radically cut off from the ground of his own being, which is also the ground of all being.[67]

Like Newman a century earlier, Merton struggled to reconcile the terms of Christian faith with the secular, scientific, and global consciousness of modern Western society. Where Newman's "theology of the religious imagination" sought a middle way between rationalist empiricism and Christian "evidentialism," Merton's appeal to the mystical tradition and, above all, to the way of contemplation, sought a middle way between vague indifferentism and dogmatic triumphalism. The Catholic imagination at its very best, witnessed in these two figures, seems called on in the modern world to grapple its way toward truth and wisdom "in the belly of a paradox."

Two important essays of 1967 offer a lucid glimpse into Merton's mature effort to come to terms with modern epistemological assumptions and, further, his understanding of the role of the imagination in grasping the deepest truth of things. "The New Consciousness" is a crucial and somewhat understudied piece early in *Zen and the Birds of Appetite* that, though written chronologically later, sets the stage for Merton's dialogue with Suzuki presented in the latter part of the book. "'Baptism in the Forest': Wisdom and Initiation in William Faulkner" appears in *The Literary Essays of Thomas*

---

66. Cited in Terrence Merrigan, "Newman and Theological Liberalism," *Theological Studies* 66 (2005): 605–21, at 619.

67. LE, 108.

Merton and is representative of his remarkably fruitful forays into the world of literary criticism. The first essay, with one eye on Zen and the other on Cartesian rationalism, is decidedly metaphysical in its outlook; the second moves more freely and capaciously in what is undoubtedly Merton's greater comfort zone, that is, the realm of the imagination.

Subject/Object Dualism: "The New Consciousness" (1967)

As with the whole of *Zen and the Birds of Appetite*, "The New Consciousness" is vital because it gives us a glimpse of the mature Merton at his best, pressed to the limit of discursive communication on vexatious theological problems—and this after more than a decade of reflection and growth with respect to interfaith dialogue. The essay reveals him to be much more conservative than conservative caricatures make him out to be, and much more liberal by far than most progressives, insofar as he writes with the authority of a committed Christian who has actually immersed himself in serious dialogue, with all its challenges and risks, and not just as one who talks about it. Indeed, the essay strikes a polemical tone from the beginning, suggesting that "progressive Christians were never *less* disposed to this kind of openness," this despite the "somewhat disconcerting vogue for exploring Asian religious experience in the West."[68]

Yet Merton is less concerned with mounting a defense of Eastern religion (in which case "I should feel myself obliged to argue in favor of Buddhism") than with evaluating developments in Western Christian theology that render it profoundly suspicious of all mystical and metaphysical religion, not just outside Christianity but within it as well. The "new consciousness" Merton describes corresponds broadly with the shift from classical to historical consciousness in theology following the Enlightenment, the Protestant Reformation, and nineteenth- and twentieth-century attacks on Christian metaphysics. With the term "new," however, he refers more immediately to developments in mid-twentieth-century theology that yielded on the whole an "activistic, secular, and anti-mystical" conception of Christianity. These include the radical "Death-of-God" theologies; the influence of Barth and Bonhoeffer in Protestantism; and in Roman Catholicism, the anti-mystical bias implicit "in new studies of ecclesiology and of Christology, in the new liturgy"[69] after Vatican II, and in "the Biblical renewal everywhere."[70] What these widely divergent movements have in common is the tendency to

---

68. ZBA, 15, 17.
69. Ibid., 19–20.
70. Ibid., 17.

identify mysticism "with the 'Hellenic' and 'Medieval' Christian experience [which is] more and more rejected as non-Christian."[71]

What concerns Merton about this radical shift in consciousness is not primarily its undermining of the metaphysical stability of the classical view, which over the centuries "was comforting and secure,"[72] but the impact this shift will have on the Christian community's most basic identity and spirituality, that is, "the Christian's experience of himself in relation to Christ and to the Church."[73] According to the "new" and more "fluid" way of conceiving the life of faith, "the Christian is invited to repudiate all aspiration to personal contemplative union with God and to deep mystical experience, because this is an infidelity to the true Christian revelation, a human substitution for God's saving word, a pagan evasion, an individualistic escape from community." In place of everything "ancient," "medieval," "static," "metaphysical," "authoritarian," and "hierarchical," the new consciousness preaches the "return to a more dynamic and charismatic Christianity—claimed to be that of the first Christians."[74] It "naturally turns outward to history, to event, to movement, to progress, and seeks its own identity and fulfillment in action toward historic political or critical goods. In proportion as it is also Biblical and eschatological it approaches the primitive Christian consciousness. But we can see already that 'Biblical' and 'eschatological' thinking do not comfortably accord with this particular kind of consciousness, and there are already signs that it will soon have to declare itself completely post-Biblical, as well as post-Christian."[75]

The prescience of these lines hardly requires comment. What seems to irritate Merton most is the claim that the new wave of theological renewal marks a return to the "primitive Christian" experience: "Supposing that the only authentic Christian experience is that of the first Christians, can this be recovered and reconstructed in any way whatever? And if so, is it to be 'mystical' or 'prophetic'? And in any case, *what is it*?" In short, Merton is concerned that the mystagogical moorings of Christian faith and praxis down through the ages are being cut away, perhaps irretrievably. More than this, the new consciousness implies a certain basic attitude about the self, that is, it implies and engenders an overriding anthropology. It is here that Merton focuses the heart of his critique, first of all, by disavowing the notion that Christian consciousness today can "simply be the consciousness of a first-century inhabitant of the Roman empire." It is bound, rather, "to

71. Ibid., 20.
72. Ibid.
73. Ibid., 19.
74. Ibid., 20.
75. Ibid., 28.

be a modern consciousness," and the modern consciousness, he argues, is still overwhelmingly shaped by a Cartesian notion of the self as "thinking, observing, measuring and estimating 'self'":

> [This "self" is] the one indubitable "reality," and all truth starts here. The more he is able to develop his consciousness as a subject over against objects . . . the more he can manipulate these objects for his own interests, but also, at the same time, the more he tends to isolate himself in his own subjective prison, to become a detached observer cut off from everything else in a kind of . . . bubble which contains all reality in the form of purely subjective experience. Modern consciousness then tends to create this solipsistic bubble of awareness—an ego-self imprisoned in its own consciousness, isolated and out of touch with other such selves in so far as they are all "things" rather than persons.[76]

Because, as noted above, nothing is known "as it is in itself but only as it is in his mind," the person "is radically cut off from the ground of his own being, which is also the ground of all being."[77] Here Merton diagnoses the source of modern alienation amid the teeming crowds of mass society, the sense of being cut off not only from all the others, who are equally isolated, not only from the natural world, which is increasingly subjugated to utilitarian ends, but also the sense of alienation from God, who becomes a projection of the modern mind's own aloneness in an infinitely receding universe. Indeed, the modern God-as-object mirrors the Enlightenment "subject," the Cartesian "ego-self imprisoned in its own consciousness." And the "murder" of one, Merton suggests, corresponds closely with the desperation and despair of the other:

> Cartesian thought began with an attempt to reach God as object by starting from the thinking self. But when God becomes object, he sooner or later "dies," because God as object is ultimately unthinkable. God as object is not only a mere abstract concept, but one which contains so many internal contradictions that it becomes entirely nonnegotiable except when it is hardened into an idol that is maintained in existence by a sheer act of will. For a long time man continued to be capable of this willfulness: but now the effort has become exhausting and many Christians have realized it to be futile. Relaxing the effort, they have let go the "God-object" which their fathers and grandfathers still hoped to manipulate for their own ends. Their weariness has accounted for the element of resentment which made this a conscious "murder" of the deity. Liberated from the strain of willfully maintaining an object-God in

---

76. Ibid., 22.
77. LE, 108.

existence, the Cartesian consciousness remains nonetheless imprisoned in itself. Hence the need to break out of itself and to meet "the other" in "encounter," "openness," "fellowship," "communion."

Yet the great problem is that for the Cartesian consciousness the "other," too, is object. There is no need here to retail the all-important modern effort to restore man's awareness of his fellow man to an "I-Thou" status. Is a genuine I-Thou relationship possible at all to a purely Cartesian subject?[78]

The first thing to note in this dense passage is Merton's recognition of a positive impulse in the new consciousness, namely, its rejection of God-as-object, which marks a potentially fruitful liberation from a "God" who never existed, save in the Cartesian mind. Yet the individual or community freed from such an idol still remains "cut off from the ground of [its] own being." Seeking to fill the existential void, people everywhere, Merton observes, seem to be rushing headlong into the stranger's arms (the sexual revolution); the arms of the party, racial or ethnic identity group, or state (the Marxist revolution); the arms of their banker (the capitalist counterreaction); or the arms of Jesus (the ecclesial revolution, with its liturgical folksiness). Of course, another object of devotion had emerged in the 1960s: drugs, the new "*deus ex machina* to enable the self-aware Cartesian consciousness to extend its awareness of itself while seemingly getting out of itself." In other words, "drugs have provided the self-conscious self with a substitute for metaphysical and mystical self-transcendence. Perhaps also with a substitute for love? I don't know."[79]

"The Flight from God"

The time will come when they will sell you even your rain. At the moment it is still free, and I am in it. I celebrate its gratuity and its meaninglessness.[80]

One wonders what Merton would make of the reflexive consciousness pervasive in Western society at the dawn of the twenty-first century. If the revolutionary fervor of the 1960s has all but disappeared today from political and ecclesial life, what has not diminished since Merton wrote the above lines is the epidemic degree to which Americans (not least American Christians) still turn to drugs, alcohol, work, buying, consuming, nonstop news and entertainment, and a thousand other addictive means of escaping the "ego-self

78. ZBA, 23.
79. Ibid., 28.
80. RU, 9.

imprisoned in its own consciousness." Surely sex is perceived and utilized as much today, if not more (and more cynically) than in the era of "free love," as a "substitute for metaphysical and mystical self-transcendence," the best connection ("hook-up") that one can really hope for with other similarly isolated ego-selves.[81]

Even more, the omnipresence of the internet and other communication technologies casts Merton's diagnosis of the modern subject-object split in an especially foreboding light. For how much more do these proliferating technologies and gadgets serve to close off the symbiotic and fertile dance between human beings and the earth, not to mention between human bodies as such, face-to-face? How much more do they encourage a certain narcissism in the young, many of whom spend untold hours every day trying on various personae in virtual communities called "Facebook," "MySpace," and "YouTube"? How much more do they facilitate the culture's seamless (and profitable) efficiency for turning persons into things, whether masked behind the anonymity of a computer screen or exposed as objects for the arbitrary enjoyment of detached others, without cost or commitment, without real self-disclosure, without love? "The machines are meditating on the most arbitrary and rudimentary of essences, punched into IBM cards, defining you and me forever without appeal."[82] These words, penned in 1965, hardly seem like hyperbole today.

In *The Way of Chuang Tzu*, Merton chronicles the poignant words of Lao Tzu to a distraught disciple:

> "A moment ago
> I looked into your eyes.
> I saw you were hemmed in
> By contradictions. Your words
> Confirm this.
> You are scared to death,
> Like a child who has lost
> Father and mother.
> You are trying to sound
> The middle of the ocean
> With a six-foot pole.
> You have got lost, and are trying
> To find your way back
> To your own true self.

81. Merton cites the character Charlotte in D. H. Lawrence's *The Wild Palms*, who "for all her sexual freedom, is 'fallen' through willfulness and through the modern consciousness 'into herself alone . . . a god-lost creature turning upon herself'" (LE, 113).

82. DWL, 201; cf. ICM, 130, on the "demonic" aspects of technology.

You find nothing
But illegible signposts
Pointing in all directions.
I pity you."[83]

This is the tragedy that most concerns Merton in the last decade of his life: we run after "illegible signposts pointing in all directions," when that which we seek already rests deep within us, much nearer and deeper than we could ever fathom "with a six-foot pole." Against the radical commodification of nature, of sex, and of human beings everywhere, Merton will interject the gentle voice of Sophia, "at once my own being, my own nature, and the Gift of my Creator's Thought and Art within me."[84] And a lament: "We do not hear the soft voice, the gentle voice, the merciful and feminine. We do not see the Child who is prisoner in all the people."[85]

One of the recurrent themes of *Zen and the Birds of Appetite* is the irony of the Western spiritual predicament in which believers and unbelievers alike, while secretly congratulating themselves on their liberation from institutional religion and an alienating God-object, nevertheless find themselves seeking "a deeper dimension of consciousness than that of a horizontal movement across the surface of life—what Max Picard called 'the flight' (from God)."[86] Indeed, this yearning for the "deeper dimension," notes Merton, is what drives many Westerners to Eastern spirituality; surely it also goes far in explaining why so many people today describe themselves as "spiritual but not religious." Many of these are still deeply "attracted by the mystical consciousness," as Merton observes, "but repelled equally by the triumphalist institution of the Church and by the activist and aggressive noisiness of some progressives."[87] What reply can the long tradition of Christian mysticism give to them?

Of course nearly the whole of Merton's corpus may be seen as a polyphonic response to this question. In "The New Consciousness" Merton frames his reply in largely metaphysical terms that he believed had strong parallels in Zen practice, terms like "Being," "Ground of Openness," and "Presence." There is, however, an implicit tension in this approach for Merton, and throughout *Zen and the Birds of Appetite* one gathers that he is negotiating not just between Christianity and Zen but between two trajectories within the Christian tradition itself: on the one hand, the mystical and metaphysical, and on the other, the biblical and prophetic. How he navigates this tension

83. WCT, 130.
84. *Hagia Sophia*, ESF, 61.
85. Ibid., 63.
86. ZBA, 25.
87. Ibid.

while drawing from both trajectories will become clearer as this chapter progresses, but let us first consider his account of mystical intuition in "The New Consciousness."

God "Everywhere and Nowhere": The Intuition of Being

> Man's loneliness is, in fact, the loneliness of God. That is why it is such a great thing for a man to discover his solitude and learn to live in it. For there he finds that he and God are one: that God is alone as he himself is alone. That God wills to be alone with him.[88]

There is another kind of consciousness that is still available to the modern person, Merton insists, which "starts not from the thinking and self-aware subject but from Being, ontologically seen to be beyond and prior to the subject-object division."[89] This experience of Being is "totally different from an experience of self-consciousness. . . . It has in it none of the split and alienation that occurs when the subject becomes aware of itself as a quasi-object." The consciousness of Being, says Merton, "is an immediate experience that goes beyond reflexive awareness. It is not 'consciousness *of* but *pure consciousness*, in which the subject as such 'disappears.'" In fact the experience of our ego-selves as "self-aware" subjects, Merton says, is "posterior" to this immediate experience of Being. "[As] the Oriental religions and Christian mysticism have stressed, this self-aware subject is not final or absolute. . . . Its existence has meaning in so far as it does not become fixated or centered upon itself as ultimate, learns to function not as its own center but 'from God' and 'for others.'"[90] While Merton insists that this experience of "no-self" or "nondualism" is *real*—that is, it is "not an abstract objective idea but a fundamental concrete intuition directly apprehended in a personal experience that is incontrovertible and inexpressible"[91]—because it springs from "a totally different kind of self-awareness from that of the Cartesian thinking-self," he expects neither patience with nor understanding of it from modern "men of action."[92]

To be clear, Merton grants that dualistic conceptions of God (Christ, Spirit, self) are to some extent unavoidable, since the dynamics of Christian revelation come to bear, as it were, both "from above" and "from below."[93]

---

88. DQ, 190.
89. ZBA, 23.
90. Ibid., 24.
91. Ibid., 26.
92. Ibid., 24, 29.
93. "The self-centered awareness of the ego is of course a pragmatic psychological reality, but once there has been an inner illumination of pure reality, an awareness of the Divine,

He further acknowledges the dangers of "false mysticism" as narcissistic self-centeredness. Yet like Newman, Merton expresses a basic confidence that human beings always already have "real" access to the mystery of God in the "pivot" of being itself. Are the mystics down through the centuries simply wrong or deluded about the human capacity for a direct and immediate experience of God? Is mystical experience really reducible, as the modern consciousness assumes, to "a stubborn fixation on an imaginary object, on 'something out there,'" or alternately, a kind of "narcissistic repose of the consciousness in itself"?[94] To these questions Merton responds, if somewhat polemically, with his own: "To what extent does the theology of a theologian without experience claim to interpret correctly the 'experienced theology' of the mystic who is perhaps not able to articulate the meaning of his experience in a satisfactory way?"[95]

Contemplation cultivates a different way of experiencing (and thinking) reality, one that is closer to the deep truth, the unity-in-difference of God, self, and world. Like Newman and Heschel, who take their starting points in a phenomenology of religious piety, Merton describes mystical consciousness as the re-centering of subjectivity from the self to God: "Here the individual is aware of himself as a self-to-be-dissolved in self-giving, in love, in 'letting go,' in ecstasy, in God—there are many ways of phrasing it. The self is not its own center and does not orbit around itself: it is centered on God, the one center of all, which is 'everywhere and nowhere,' in whom all are encountered, from whom all proceed. Thus from the very start this consciousness is disposed to encounter 'the other' with whom it is already united anyway 'in God.'"[96]

The semantic inversion here is significant: God is not "in me" so much as "I" experience my "self" (the *death* of my ego-self) "in God." It is more or less the difference between pantheism (God-in-the-world-ism) and pan*en*theism (all-in-God-ism), the latter certainly coming closer to the Christian mystical tradition than the former. What these abstract spatial metaphors tend to obscure, however, is the ultimately personal character of any properly Christian metaphysics. Here again, the distinctively sacramental character of Christianity as a religion of the inbreaking Wisdom and Word of God comes into play—and perhaps where Christian metaphysics begins to part ways not only with Buddhism or nontheistic philosophies but also with Judaism and

---

the empirical self is seen by comparison to be 'nothing,' that is to say contingent, evanescent, relatively unreal, real only in relation to its source and end in God, considered not as object but as free ontological source of one's own existence and subjectivity" (ZBA, 26).

94. Ibid., 27.

95. ZBA, 45.

96. ZBA, 24; on the loss or "death" of the false self, see also DQ, 104; and NM, 18–19.

Islam. For the Catholic sacramental imagination, in other words, both the content of divine presence (as love, judgment, mercy) and the radical extent of union with God (adoption, theosis, deification), is shaped by the community's wholesale "memory and experience" of God's "incarnational" union with the world in the person of Jesus Christ. "This is more than a meeting," as Merton writes, "It is an identification,"[97] a union "not only of 'I and Thou,' but a transcendent union of consciousness in which man and God become, according to the expression of St. Paul, 'one spirit.'"[98] Russian sophiology, as we shall see, accentuates this divine reaching across the distances even further by envisioning a certain humanness or "anthropology" in God, as it were, from the very beginning.

While this intuition of radical love and giftedness is always "there" in the roots of our being, the gift has, at the same time, says Merton, "been lost and must be recovered." Even at his most philosophical, Merton here strikes existentialist and archetypal biblical themes: the coincidence of paradise and exile, light and darkness, fulfillment and loss, ecstasy and imprisonment, all themes that will play a central role in his dialogue with Suzuki. For both he and Suzuki agree that the "recovery of innocence" requires a way "back home," a spiritual discipline that will interrupt our illusory patterns of thinking and cultivate an awareness of who we already are, our original kinship in the "hidden ground of Love."[99] Again, what Zen realization shares with biblical-mystical faith is precisely the disarming experience of "*a breakthrough . . . a recovery of unity which is not the suppression of opposites but a simplicity beyond opposites. . . .* This means a totally different perspective than that which dominates our society—and enables it to dominate us."[100]

What must not be overlooked here is Merton's insistence on the close relationship between contemplative practice and receptivity toward the stranger. While Cartesian consciousness approaches the "other" dualistically like

97. Thomas Merton, *Bread in the Wilderness* (New York: New Directions, 1953), 122; hereafter BW.

98. FV, 222.

99. For the Suzuki-Merton dialogue, see "Wisdom in Emptiness," ZBA, 99–141.

100. ZBA, 140. Merton's best study of the similarities-in-difference between Zen realization and Christian mysticism is "The Zen Koan" (Thomas Merton, *Mystics and Zen Masters* [New York: Farrar, Straus and Giroux, 1967], 235–54; hereafter MZM), where he draws parallels "on the psychological level" between the "dark night" mysticism of John of the Cross and the "pure consciousness" of Zen—both involve a "death" of "a calculating and desiring ego"—even while drawing a crucial distinction between the two: "The difference is theological: the night of St. John opens into a divine and personal freedom and is a gift of 'grace.' The void of Zen is the natural ground of Being—for which no theological explanation is either offered or desired." The essay includes a fascinating riff on Paleolithic cave art as a celebration of "the *act of seeing* as a holy and transcendent discovery" (248), as well as a discussion of Rilke's poetic consciousness, or "in-seeing."

everything else, that is, as an "object" among an infinite world of objects that are "not-I," mystical consciousness is "from the very start" favorably disposed to encounter the other "with whom it is already united anyway 'in God.'" Like Newman and Heschel, Merton joins epistemology, anthropology, and theology into a vision of theandric unity—not from abstract notions or ideals about unity but from the living experience (and discipline) of letting go, of losing oneself in God, the hidden ground of Love.

Lest this all seem very abstract, we might call to mind the "mystical-prophetic" sensibilities of two contemporaries for whom Merton held the greatest admiration: Mahatma Gandhi and Martin Luther King, Jr. What Merton describes as the "Indian mind that was awakening in Gandhi" was not far, of course, from King's seminal belief in the "interrelated structure of all reality," a conviction rooted in his biblical faith that a divine, loving presence binds all life together in "an inescapable network of mutuality," a "single garment of destiny."[101] In his darkest moments of doubt, fear, and despair, King felt this presence reassuring and beckoning him forward, giving him new courage and strength to love. The vocation to unity is no mere slogan for Merton; it is the way of the cross, rooted in a daily giving over of oneself to the loving presence of God.[102]

Finally, insofar as we can discern Merton negotiating in "The New Consciousness" between two distinct trajectories in Christianity—that is, between Scripture (God as Freedom and Love) and metaphysics (God as Being and Openness)—the important thing, he insists, is not to oppose these two trajectories but to show where they "really seek to express the same kind of consciousness or at least to approach it in varying ways." The scholastic element was with Merton until the end, and here it serves him, and us, very well. Indeed, throughout *Zen and the Birds of Appetite* Merton shows himself to be the consummate practitioner of Maritain's *distinguer pour unir* ("to distinguish in order to unite"), giving us a model not only for a Catholic approach to interfaith dialogue but, no less important, for holding in fruitful tension distinct but mutually enriching (and mutually correcting) traditions within the Catholic tradition itself. Of course the impulse to distinguish in order to unite is not only scholastic; it is also monastic, literary, and sapiential. It is, in a word, the way of wisdom.

101. Martin Luther King, Jr., *Strength to Love* (Philadelphia: Fortress Press, 1963), 72.

102. Merton's reflections in *Faith and Violence* on the historical and paschal dimensions of Christian wisdom call to mind both King and Gandhi, not to mention Jesus: "The way of wisdom is no dream, no temptation and no evasion, for it is on the contrary a return to reality in its very root. . . . It does not withdraw from the fire. It is in the very heart of the fire, yet remains cool, because it has the gentleness and humility that come from self-abandonment, and hence does not seek to assert the illusion of the exterior self" (FV, 218).

Beyond Metaphysics to Sapientia: *"Baptism in the Forest" (1967)*

> Metaphysics can only show us God as an object of thought, vaguely
> foreshadowed in analogies: [it] can create in us the desire to love God
> but cannot satisfy that love.[103]

It is remarkable that even with his spirited defense of traditional mystical
and metaphysical language in "The New Consciousness," Merton concludes
the essay by acknowledging that "there must be a better reply" to the spiritual crisis of our times "than the mere reaffirmation of the ancient . . . and
classical positions": "It is quite possible that the language and metaphysical
assumptions of the classic view are out of reach of many modern men. It
is quite plausible to assert that the old Hellenic categories are indeed worn
out, and that Platonizing thought, even revivified with shots in the arm from
Yoga and Zen, will not quite serve in the modern world. What then? Is there
some new possibility, some other opening for the Christian consciousness
today?"[104]

In his introduction to *The Literary Essays of Thomas Merton*, Patrick Hart
notes that in the mid-sixties Merton had begun "to shift his attention from
formally religious writings to literary models."[105] That Merton was negotiating between philosophical, theological, and literary models in these years is
especially clear when one reads "The New Consciousness" alongside "'Baptism in the Forest': Wisdom and Initiation in William Faulkner." Indeed, the
latter seems to pick up almost precisely where the former ends, with Merton
asking whether there is "some other opening for the Christian consciousness
today" than traditional religious, philosophical, and scientific models:

> I would submit that the term "religious" no longer conveys the idea
> of an imaginative awareness of basic meaning. . . . And I would also
> say that the word "metaphysical" is not quite adequate to convey these
> values. There are other possibilities. One of them is *sapiential*.
>
> *Sapientia* is the Latin word for "wisdom." And wisdom in the clas-
> sic, as well as the Biblical, tradition is something quite definite. It is the
> highest level of cognition. It goes beyond *scientia*, which is systematic
> knowledge, beyond *intellectus*, which is intuitive understanding. It has
> deeper penetration and wider range than either of these. It embraces the
> entire scope of man's life and all its meaning. . . . Wisdom is not only
> speculative, but also practical: that is to say, it is "lived." And unless one

---

103. LE, 446.
104. ZBA, 29–30.
105. Patrick Hart, "Introduction," in LE, xv. To my mind the earliest seeds for Merton's
literary or sapiential shift were planted as early as 1958 with his study of Pasternak, an influence that will be considered in chap. 4.

"lives" it, one cannot "have" it. It is not only speculative but creative. It is expressed in living signs and symbols.[106]

This passage offers a concise summation both of Merton's mature epistemology (wisdom is "the highest level of cognition"; it is "not only speculative," but it is "lived") and his mature theological method (wisdom is "expressed in living signs and symbols"; it embraces the whole of life "and all its meaning"). Indeed, the powerful interplay of symbols, myths, and archetypes in Faulkner seems to spark the issue of method in Merton with a special urgency and perhaps even a new clarity. Much of what he says here of Faulkner could justly be said of his own mature work:

> Faulkner is typical of the creative genius who can associate his reader in the same experience of creation which brought forth his book. Such a book is filled with efficacious sign-situations, symbols, and myths which release in the reader the imaginative power to experience what the author really means to convey. And what he means to convey is not a system of truths which explain life but a certain depth of awareness in which life itself is lived more intensely and with a more meaningful direction. The "symbolic" in this sense is not a matter of contrived signification in which things point arbitrarily to something else. Symbols are signs which release the power of imaginative communion.[107]

Merton defines *sapientia* in terms that immediately call to mind Newman's account of wisdom and the "theology of the religious imagination": it is "a kind of knowledge by identification, an intersubjective knowledge, a communion in cosmic awareness and in nature. . . . a wisdom based on love."[108] Like Newman, whose epistemology favored the concrete over the abstract, Merton insists that sapiential (or "sophianic") awareness "deepens our communion with the concrete. It is not an initiation into a world of abstractions and ideals."[109] Its concern is not fixing upon "a system of truths which explain life" so much as cultivating "a certain depth of awareness in which life itself is lived more intensely and with a more meaningful direction." And like Newman, who affirmed the revelatory roots of "natural" or "pagan" religions, Merton here intuits that "there is a relation between all 'wisdoms,'" citing Clement of Alexandria as his authority.[110]

106. LE, 98–99.
107. Ibid., 98.
108. Ibid., 108.
109. Ibid., 100.
110. Ibid. In his journal of August 7, 1961, Merton comments on Newman's love of Clement of Alexandria: "To Newman he was 'like music.' This may look like a cliché but it is profound.

While Merton makes an important distinction between literary and theological symbols, what matters here is to reiterate that symbols are much more for Merton than mere "wordplay," more than conventional "signs," "contrived signification," or "mere artifacts of a few human minds." To the contrary, they bear archetypal meanings that are "anterior to any operation of the mind"; like theological symbols, literary symbols retain "their power and their seminal creativity in the unconscious even after conscious minds have agreed that 'God is dead.'"[111] This does not mean, however, that their apprehension is automatic. *Sapientia*, notes Merton, "is not inborn. True, the seeds of it are there, but they must be cultivated."[112] As in his essays on Zen and elsewhere on Christian education, Merton insists here that "wisdom develops not by itself but in a hard discipline of traditional training, under the expert guidance of one who . . . possesses it and who is therefore qualified to teach it." In short, "wisdom cannot be learned from a book. It is acquired only in a living formation; and it is tested by the master himself in certain critical situations."[113]

Notice once again how epistemological first principles implicate anthropological ones. Merton's affirmation of symbolism and archetype as a kind of corporate memory clearly implies a radically thick (i.e., universal) theological anthropology. As he notes in the dialogue with Suzuki: "The whole reality of the 'Fall' is inscribed in our nature in what Jung called symbolic archetypes, and the Fathers of the Church (as well as the Biblical writers no doubt) were much more concerned with the archetypal significance than with the Fall as an 'historical event'"—adding that Suzuki is "far more at home" with such traditional symbols "than many Western theologians."[114] The point to underline here is this: to the degree that we give our selves over to poetry, literature, and art—to the experiences of *strangers*—and find that something in these forms resonates within, their value is not "merely" aesthetic but potentially sacramental. Whereas "communication" takes place between a subject and object, *sapientia* opens onto a realm of "communion" beyond the division: "it is a sharing in basic unity," which "does not necessarily imply a 'pantheist metaphysic.'"[115] Nor does *sapientia* exclude truths gained through science.

For there are people one meets—in books and in life—with whom a deep resonance is at once established." Merton reflects on the meaning of "resonance"—*cor ad cor loquitur* ("heart speaks to heart")—and lists writers whose "music" has moved him. He closes with Clement's image of humanity as "a musical instrument for God" (TTW, 149).

111. LE, 98.
112. Ibid., 99.
113. Ibid.
114. ZBA, 64; cf. LE, 107, 115.
115. LL, 73.

To the contrary, it "gives a new dimension to science. What would our world of science be, if only we had wisdom?"[116]

Merton does not fail to draw critical distinctions between Christian wisdom and modern literature, or to confess his uneasiness with the latter. "What is the position of a believing Christian before the sick and bewildering gnosticism of modern literature?" On the one hand, the believing Christian must "accept the fact that we live in an age of doubt," in a world "where most people find Christian doctrine incomprehensible or irrelevant." In such an atmosphere, modern literature offers "authentic assurances of hope and understanding, provided that we are willing to tolerate theological discomfort."[117] Clearly Merton was willing, for his own part, to tolerate enough "theological discomfort" to recognize the "unimpeachable sincerity of modern sapiential literature." On the other hand, he observes that what we often find in literature "is not a coherent intellectual view of life but a creative effort to penetrate the meaning of man's suffering and aspirations in symbols that are imaginatively authentic. If God does appear in such symbols, we can expect to find Him expressed negatively and obscurely rather than with the positive and rewarding effulgence that we find in the poetry of other ages."[118] Many of the best modern writers, he concludes, are "writers 'of religious temperament nourished in a literary culture of doubt.'"[119] It is not so much their negative portrayals of God that trouble Merton but the inability of writers or artists "of religious temperament" to embrace faith precisely in and through the darkness of doubt: "They make no commitments and they contrive to affirm and to deny the spirit at the same time."[120]

While "Baptism in the Forest" is in no way an apology for Christianity, Merton does insists that there are Christian forms of *sapientia* available to the modern consciousness that can open doors to a living faith even in an age of radical doubt. "Christian wisdom is essentially theological, Christological, and mystical. It implies a deepening of Christian faith to the point where faith becomes an experiential awareness of the realities and values of man's life in Christ and 'in the Spirit' when he has been raised to divine sonship." He cites three examples of such a wisdom: first, Flannery O'Connor's ironic and "shocking" form of wisdom "based on a Word which is an offense"; second, the ancient wisdom "of the Eastern Church, which represents a much more peaceful approach [than that of O'Connor]" and "from which Hellenic elements have not been driven out"; and third, the story "of the Russian Pilgrim

116. Ibid., 68.
117. LE, 115.
118. Ibid.
119. Ibid., 116, citing Stanford's review essay on Dylan Thomas.
120. Ibid.

[*The Way of a Pilgrim*] that . . . informs us of a sapiential technique first devised by the monks of Sinai and transmitted from there to Mount Athos and then to Rumania and Russia."[121]

That Merton singles out these three examples of Christian wisdom in this late essay—Flannery O'Connor, Eastern Orthodox spirituality, and the "sapiential technique" of Russian hesychasm (the Jesus Prayer)—is not of passing significance. The latter two reflect the biblical and eschatological seedbed of Merton's religious imagination, and the first, his increasing affinity for the ironic. Indeed, the archaeology of Merton's religious imagination in the last decade of his life may be charted in three dimensions: it is biblical, eschatological, and ironic. At his poetic and prophetic best, as in *Raids on the Unspeakable*, his writing is all three at once.[122] What shapes these three aspects into a single Catholic vision, in existential terms, are the practices of contemplation, *lectio divina*, and liturgical *anamnesis*. In theological terms, what joins them together is not only Merton's remarkable fluency with the symbols of tradition but also the receptivity of his readers, that is, their attunement to the sacramental power of language.

Sacramentum Scripturarum: Words as Sacraments

> Any serious reading of the Bible means personal involvement in it, not simply mental agreement with abstract propositions. And involvement is dangerous, because it lays one open to unforeseen conclusions. That is why we prefer if possible to remain uninvolved.[123]

We have been circling around the same question from different angles, namely, the formal relation between language and reality, between biblical and doctrinal symbols and mystical experience.[124] It is important to recognize that Merton's confidence in (and facility with) the sacramental power of language is not merely an accident of circumstance, talent, or study, but reflects his wholesale immersion in the Catholic liturgical tradition and monastic theology. No less than Heschel's depth theology was shaped by Hasidic Jewish sensibilities, when it came to structuring theological discourse Merton did not think, pray, and write in isolation but intuitively retrieved a

---

121. Ibid., 101.

122. The fusion of irony and apocalypticism in Merton's late Christology will be explored in chap. 6.

123. Thomas Merton, *Opening the Bible* (Collegeville, MN: Liturgical Press, 1970), 43; hereafter OB.

124. This is arguably the central question with which Merton wrestles throughout *Zen and the Birds of Appetite*, at least in terms of the challenges raised for Christian theology and identity (*ad intra*) in the dialogue with Zen.

method with roots in ancient and medieval monasticism, from East to West. The remainder of this chapter aims to situate Merton's sapiential approach to theology within the monastic tradition, and then to indicate where he makes a rather extraordinary and radical departure.

Poetry and Symbolism in Monastic Theology

In his masterful study of monastic theology in the twelfth century, M.-D. Chenu cites the following lines of the Cistercian lay brother, theologian, poet, and preacher, Alan of Lille: "Poetry's lyre rings with vibrant falsehood on the outward literal shell of a poem, but interiorly it communicates a hidden and profound meaning to those who listen. The man who reads with penetration, having caste away the outer shell of falsehood, finds the savory kernel of truth wrapped within."[125] In these lines, says Chenu, Alan of Lille defines "the end and the means of the poetic art that dominated the great works of the century,"[126] in which poetry was employed in the service of philosophical and theological wisdom. For the monks of the twelfth century, symbolism, metaphor, and myth were employed "not as merely literary devices or tropes to give a poet's touch to some intellectual reality, but as consistent means for signifying the inner substance of things. They are not therefore part of a psychological game played by an esthete, even though literary elegance—*elegans pictura*—is also involved; at stake is the discernment of the profound truth that lies hidden within the dense substance of things and is revealed by these means." One could hardly find a better description of Merton's sapiential approach to theology and his capacity for bringing to the surface the inner "substance of things." No "word-magic" is implied here. To grasp "the kernel of truth" the reader must "listen," "discern," and read "with penetration."[127] This implies, of course, that the reader (i.e., the believing community) is trained to do so. *Sapientia*, we may recall, "is not inborn. True, the seeds of it are there, but they must be cultivated."[128]

"A symbol," said Hugh of St. Victor, "is a juxtaposition, that is, a coaptation of visible forms brought forth to demonstrate some invisible matter."[129] Yet, as Chenu adds, "the play of this sort of reasoning did not constitute proof. Hugh's 'demonstration' was hardly that of Aristotle," and to think otherwise "would be seriously to confuse two distinct modes of thought to the detriment of both."

125. Marie-Dominique Chenu, *Nature, Man, and Society in the Twelfth Century*, ed. Jerome Taylor and Lester Little (Chicago: University of Chicago Press, 1957), 99–145, at 99.

126. Ibid., 100.

127. Ibid., 99.

128. LE, 99.

129. Cited in Chenu, *Nature, Man, and Society*, 103.

Chenu alludes here to the widening split between monastic and scholastic theologies in the twelfth and thirteenth centuries. In an analysis that calls to mind our discussion of Coleridge and Newman in chapter 2, Chenu argues that for the monastic theologians to bring symbolism into play "was not to extend or supplement a previous act of the reason; it was to give primary expression to a reality which reason could not attain and which reason, even afterwards, could not conceptualize."[130] Imagination, in other words, the realm of the symbol, is not separate from reason but enables us "*to reason differently* by enlarging and reordering our powers of perception."[131]

Chenu's phenomenological analysis of symbolic participation calls to mind both the fertile paradox of biblical metaphors described by Heschel and Merton's description of wisdom as the attunement or realization of conflicting opposites within a single event:

> [Through symbols] it was not by total abstraction that one proceeded; the symbolized reality remained concretely present and visible, for every symbol in a certain way contained the reality it expressed. But the relationship between symbol and thing symbolized, between type and antitype, was qualitative. . . . Participation in the transcendent was not felt to be a matter of *identity* with it ("identity" was a term proper to conceptual logic); rather, such participation was sensed through a dialectic of the similar-dissimilar within a "figure," within the coexistence of the sensible and the spiritual. The same act both fixed and freed the understanding, because the material symbol was preserved in its concrete density.[132]

Note especially Chenu's claim that understanding is both "fixed and freed" through symbols, a tensive dynamic that allows us to taste the deepest truth of things in "the belly of a paradox."

Again, from the previous chapter, all so-called descriptions of God are necessarily metaphorical, for the human vehicle (even the inspired biblical symbol) can never render the tenor (the mystery of God) accurately and positively. Biblical, liturgical, and theological discourse always "combines otherness and likeness, uniqueness and comparability, in speaking about God."[133] Yet it is precisely by entering wholly into this tensive and paradoxical dimension of speech and sacrament making—"the similar-dissimilar within

130. Ibid. It is noteworthy that Chenu uses the metaphor of "play" in describing the "symbolist mentality," e.g., "the play of this sort of reasoning," "to bring symbolism into play," in distinction from linear or discursive mode of rationality and communication.

131. Magill, "Moral Imagination," 460–61.

132. Chenu, *Nature, Man, and Society*, 139–40.

133. Kaplan, HW, 56.

a 'figure,'" or to recall Heschel, "the fullness of human powerlessness"—that God's "more than literal" realness (i.e., the ineffable) is not merely affirmed, as in a proposition, but experientially "tasted." Whether through liturgy, iconography, sacred music, or *lectio divina*, the moment theological symbols evoke a sense of "communion" and "real presence" in the praying community, they are *not merely symbolic*, if by "symbolic" we mean "abstract, disconnected, fleshless."[134] Drawing the subject into the divine tenor of the event, like "Yes" and "No" turning toward the silent center of the circle, they are real, more than literally real, as Heschel suggests, "hyphens between heaven and earth."

Chenu cites the biblical names of God as a paradigmatic example of metaphorical speech in theology. For monastic theology, metaphors for God such as fire, light, lion, or king were not merely properties of the divine being expressed in more or less abstract or concrete terms; rather, "they concealed, in dialectical suspension between likeness and disparity, the intrinsic bond uniting the material and spiritual realms, here conjoined in a single stroke of thought." The poetic construction of the phrases "was not allowed to render suspect but rather made to display the innate power and energy of symbols, which abstract knowledge left behind."[135] In other words, the "innate power and energy" of such symbols to engage the whole person render them capable of facilitating qualitative participation in the divine. Just as the metaphor of "pathos" is for Heschel "a genuine insight into God's relatedness to man, rather than a projection of human traits into divinity,"[136] so too the names of God in the Bible offer real insight—not explanations or proofs, but *insight*—into the "anthropology" of God, the "life story" of God, the very "Being" of God.

What is true for Heschel and Jewish Hasidism is true for the tradition of monastic theology and *lectio divina* in which Merton stands: "the metaphorical character of biblical language in no way diminishes its ontological validity as a privileged 'meeting place.'"[137] Thus patterned after the poetic power of the Bible itself, literary elegance in monastic theology was not "part of a psychological game played by an esthete"; but instead it marked the discernment of truths really to be found in the world, though hidden. In sum, writes Chenu, monastic theology "was saturated with metaphor and symbol; and in these it found . . . the means of sustaining the vitality of the sacred texts and the freshness of its own faith, with no detriment to understanding."[138]

---

134. TTW, 18.

135. Chenu, *Nature, Man, and Society*, 114.

136. Kaplan, HW, 57.

137. Abraham Joshua Heschel, *Man's Quest for God: Studies in Prayer and Symbolism* (New York: Scribner's, 1954), 139.

138. Chenu, *Nature, Man, and Society*, 114. While "the symbolist mentality" has its roots in Christian Neoplatonism from East to West, Chenu draws a crucial distinction between "the

Chenu neither ignores nor downplays the excesses and abuses of allegorical exegesis of the Bible in medieval theology: "Scientific analysis by theologians would soon define the limitations inherent in the very nature of such metaphors."[139] Yet his appreciation of symbolic and poetic theology at its best goes far in explaining what continues to draw people to thinkers like Merton and Heschel today. As practiced by these two figures, a poetic method in theology does not deem to bring God down to the level of human words but involves the "accommodation of words to higher meanings."[140] By contrast to excessively discursive or scientific approaches to theology—which can range, no less than poetic theology, from the esoteric to the idolatrous—Merton presses the reader through symbol, image, and metaphor toward the divine tenor beyond the words. To the degree we give our selves over to that tenor, to its inner musicality, self-centeredness recedes and the divine perspective begins to break through; "old things" are made new again through the transforming power of imagination. Merton's poetic method gives us a model for "sustaining the vitality of sacred texts" and the "freshness" of Christian faith, "with no detriment to understanding."

Thus in "a single stroke of thought" the name "Sophia," no less than the name "Christ," can become—on the lips of the believing, praying, *and* thinking community—a privileged meeting place for the encounter with God. Her name tells us nothing new, communicates no "new information," but awakens what is and always has been, a union that "already exists but is not fully realized." And yet, in truth, her name does evoke something new, and something quite old, that has been forgotten.

Neoplatonism of Augustine and that of pseudo-Dionysius" (125) with respect to the weight each gives to *history*. On the one hand, "the cosmic symbolism of pseudo-Dionysius tended to relegate any reference to history to a place of secondary importance; this was no less true of sacred history, including the deeds of Christ which the sacraments represented" (127). On the other hand, Augustine supplied "materials and methods for a symbolism capable of laying hold upon time—Christian time: events, bound up with past and present and future as so many stages of the Old Testament, the New Testament, and the final kingdom, not only prepared for the future but prefigured it in the present" (128). While Merton draws deeply from the well of Dionysian mysticism, his sensibilities are more Augustinian with respect to time, i.e., the affirmation of history and corporeality as the playing field of the divine-human drama. If Merton is not by contemporary standards terribly interested in "the historical Jesus," there can be no question, as we shall see in the next chapter, that for him the "deeds of Christ" during his ministry *are* crucial, precisely as history, as Jesus' own exercise of freedom in grace.

139. Ibid., 114.

140. Abraham Joshua Heschel, *The Prophets* (New York: Harper and Row, 1962), 271.

Biblical Memory and Imagination

In his classic study of monastic culture, *The Love of Learning and the De-sire for God*, Benedictine scholar and close friend of Merton, Jean Leclercq, describes the effect that constant rumination on the Bible had on the medi-eval theologian. "The memory, fashioned wholly by the Bible and nurtured entirely by biblical words and the images they evoke, causes them to express themselves spontaneously in biblical vocabulary."[141] Such a vocabulary is "often poetic in essence," it "hints at much more than it says," and it proceeds from "the feeling of the presence of God."[142] Its whole orientation is toward love, "the basis for the whole program of monastic life."[143] In classic Cistercian formulation—*amor ipse intellectus est*—to experience love is already to know and remember oneself as caught up in the trinitarian life of God.

Because the monks were constantly praying or chanting its words, the Bible came to be learned "by heart." More than this, the wholesale effect of physically intoning the text, an effect amplified in choir, exceeds the merely visual memory that would result from silent reading; indeed it is more akin, notes Leclercq, to "taste" (*sapor, ruminatio*) or "resonance," as in the whole-body effect of music. "What results is a muscular memory of the words pro-nounced and an aural memory of the words heard," such that the sacred text is inscribed, so to speak, "in the body and soul."[144] Over time, "one becomes a sort of living concordance, a living library, in the sense that the latter term implies the Bible." Most important, the constant *meditatio* and *ruminatio* of biblical texts yielded a form of exegesis that was distinctively monastic, what Leclercq calls "exegesis by concordance": "it is largely an exegesis through reminiscence, and for this reason it approaches rabbinical exegesis. It consists in explaining one verse by another verse in which the same word occurs."[145] Of course one of the far-reaching fruits of this kind of exegesis, going as far back as Origen, is *typology*, that is, interpreting the Hebrew Scriptures in light of the New Testament, and thus finding in the former symbolic "types" and figures for Christ (the New Adam), the church (the New Creation), Mary (Eve), baptism (the flood), Eucharist (manna), and so on.

Without question Merton's memory and imagination were biblically satu-rated in every sense Leclercq here describes. We shall see later, for example, that typology holds a significant place in Merton's Christology; indeed, it would be extraordinary, given his monastic formation, if it did not. The

141. Jean Leclercq, *The Love of Learning and the Desire for God: A Study of Monastic Culture*, trans. Catharine Misrahi (New York: Fordham University Press, 1961), 75.

142. Ibid., 75–76.

143. Ibid., 85.

144. Ibid., 73.

145. Ibid., 77.

conviction underlying the ancient Christian practice of typology is that Jewish and Christian revelation are ultimately one, and thus (against Marcion) that the two Testaments form "an organic unity."[146] Yet there is also evidence, especially in the wake of his correspondence with Heschel during Vatican II, that Merton was rethinking the implications of this practice; he was certainly questioning the fulfillment theology beneath it, which understood Judaism solely in terms of its completion and perfection by Christianity. This is a point we shall have to return to later, for it comes to bear on the remembrance of Sophia in Christian theology.[147] What matters here is to underscore the degree to which Merton was plunged in the poetry of the Bible, thus patterning his theological imagination in this kind of exegesis by reminiscence. And to recognize, as Paul Evdokimov observes, that this kind of "remembrance"— what the mystagogical tradition calls *anamnesis*—"is more than just memory or even a memory. *It is an epiphanic calling forth*."[148]

Like "Fire from Heaven"

Nowhere is Merton's integral relation to the Bible more sublimely expressed than in his study of the psalms, *Bread in the Wilderness* (1953). Though a relatively early work, it opens an important window into Merton's thoroughly monastic approach to biblical and liturgical revelation, an approach that pulsed deeply in him to the end of his life. Of special significance is his discussion of "Poetry, Symbolism, and Typology," where Merton distinguishes between "cosmic" and "typological" symbolism in the Bible. The former he describes as the revelation of God in nature, consummately expressed in David's wonder before the grandeur of the natural world: *When I gaze at the heavens, the work of thy fingers, the moon and stars, which thou has made . . .*[149] The corruption of cosmic symbolism occurs, Merton suggests, when human beings no longer relate to the world as sacramental or iconic, as transparent to the God of creation, but view the world rather as a mirror, reflecting back their own glory and mastery over things. Here sacramentality morphs into idolatry; nature becomes opaque, utilitarian, self-referential. Rather than seeing through creation like a clear windowpane to the sun and stars, human beings "had begun to forget the sky, and to light lamps of their own, and presently

146. BW, 31.
147. For example, to what extent must Wisdom-Sophia language be linked explicitly with Christ (or the Second Person of the Trinity)? To what extent might her name evoke more theocentric valences (*Shekinah, ousia*, Spirit), not only a language but above all a "memory and experience" of God that Jews and Christians might more readily share?
148. Paul Evdokimov, *The Art of the Icon: A Theology of Beauty* (Redondo Beach, CA: Oakwood, 1990), 166.
149. Psalm 8, cited in BW, 61.

it seemed to them that the reflection of their own room in the window was the 'world beyond.' They began to worship what they themselves were doing. And what they were doing was too often an abomination."[150]

Throughout *Bread and the Wilderness* Merton places considerable import on cosmic symbolism (nature as sacrament) in the Bible, just as a decade later he will describe *theoria physike* ("natural contemplation") as a crucial preparation for supernatural (historical, categorical) revelation. Still, "the most important symbolism in the Bible is not cosmic symbolism," Merton suggests, "but typology," that is, symbols in the Hebrew Scriptures that foreshadow "the Incarnation of the Word of God, and . . . man's Redemption by the Sacrifice of Christ on Calvary, for this is the central Mystery of Christian faith."[151] Where cosmic symbolism easily lends itself to idolatrous worship of the world or humanity itself, typological symbols break through the tendency to perceive the world and its history in closed, Cartesian, or dangerously self-referential terms: "Cosmic symbols reflect the action of God like the light of the sun on the vast sea of creation. Typological symbols are meteors which divide the dark sky of history with a sudden, searing light, appearing and vanishing with a liberty that knows no law of man. Cosmic symbolism is like clouds and rain: but typology is like a storm of lightning wounding the earth unpredictably with fire from heaven."[152]

A close study of *Bread in the Wilderness*, no less than much later, more outward-looking texts, suggests that one should not underestimate the hold that biblical symbols have on Merton's religious imagination. Throughout his corpus certain biblical images flash in repeatedly like "fire from heaven," and where Merton employs such images, he does so with the conviction that their implicit power goes beyond the merely literary or psychological realm of consciousness. The symbols of Scripture "lead to contemplation precisely because their impact on us is *theological* rather than *psychological*."[153] Moreover, there are particular images and symbols of the Hebrew Scriptures that Merton "calls forth" to throw a brilliant and "unpredictable" light on the New Testament. One of these is the "Tree of Life," which he often links, not without haunting paradox and irony, to the cross of Jesus. Another is Sophia.

---

150. BW, 61; cf. TTW, 123, an arresting passage that begins quite simply, "The great work of sunrise again today."

151. BW, 62.

152. Ibid. 63; cf. Heschel: "Revelation is a cloudburst, a downpour, yet most of us are like moles, burrowing, and whatever stream we meet is underground" (*God in Search of Man* [New York: Farrar, Straus and Cudahy, 1955], 251).

153. BW, 14; cf. OB, 25: "[These passages] are somehow claiming that there has been a breakthrough of the ultimate word into the sphere of the human, and that what the Bible is about is this breakthrough, recorded in events, happenings, which are decisive not only for the Jewish people or for the disciples of Christ but for mankind as a whole."

Sophia: the feminine child of Proverbs 8, who delights before God at the dawn of creation, cannot help but reverberate (i.e., typologically) in the same sonorous landscape as St. Paul's hymn to Jesus in Colossians: *He is the image of the invisible God, the firstborn of all creation. For in him were created all things in heaven and on earth.* It is a connection Merton will make explicit in his most formal christological writings, as we shall see in chapter 4. And just as he finds her "unpredictable light" flashing in Russian icons of Christ, the *Pantokrator*, so too does she "appear and vanish" before him in the humblest of everyday guises—in the silent woods of Gethsemani, in the faces of passersby on a crowded street corner—breaking in "with a liberty that knows no law of man."

Theology as *Memoria*, Presence, and Hope

Merton is not a word magician but a sacrament maker, structuring religious discourse in such a way that the symbols and doctrines of tradition may be experienced not as mere words, explanations, or as a "heap of notions" (to recall Newman) but truly as vessels of memory and real presence, enablers of hope in the concrete circumstances of our lives. Indeed, with these three terms—memory, presence, and hope—we are prepared to distinguish (if not separate) Christian wisdom from artistic or literary forms of wisdom, and theological symbols from poetic ones.

First, the theological symbol is a privileged vessel of *memory*. Christianity is no gnostic evasion, nor merely a literary endeavor, but it flowers forth from the depths of human history and radically affirms it. Certain symbols ("Let there be light") awaken the *memoria* of God's loving intention for the world, dawning in the very act of creation and finding its fruition in human freedom ("God found it very good"). Other theological symbols (the exodus, the cross) insist that we remember (*never forget*) the radically threatened character of human existence, from which not even God chooses to remain apart. Note how Merton's remembrance of Christ dialectically embraces symbols of glory and abjection, victory and failure, eternity and history: "For though it is quite true that He is the King and Lord of all, the conqueror of death, the judge of the living and of the dead, the *Pantokrator*, yet He is also still the Son of Man, the hidden one, unknown, unremarkable, vulnerable. He can be killed."[154] Still other symbols (cloud of witnesses, communion of saints) invoke the living *memoria* of all who have gone before us in the journey of faith.

Second, following from the first, the theological symbol is a vessel of *real presence*. Catholic theology will embrace, or certainly will not rule out, the evidently

---

154. NSC, 293–94.

universal human intuition that there really are truths to be found in the world that are not upon the surface. This is to insist that contemplation (*theoria*) plays an indispensable role in the "science" of Catholic theology and, more broadly, that faith and reason are not incompatible gifts. Formed in a faith community in which the "Catholic" imagination is catholic enough to bring together seemingly disparate truths, the theologian will positively look for and expect to find God's light and presence hidden in all the world, not only in myriad cultures and religious traditions, but even in the most "God-forsaken" places, where sin and darkness seem to carry the day. Indeed, the passage through Holy Week, Merton suggests, teaches us the irony of presence in the midst of terrifying absence, and mercy as the doorway to rebirth and hope in God.[155] *Father, forgive them; for they do not know what they are doing* (Luke 23:34).

Third, the theological symbol is a locus of participatory *hope*. Without any palpable connection to meaning and hope in the mundane circumstances of human lives, Catholic theology loses not only its biblical and eschatological moorings but all contact with the person and message of Jesus. The hope Jesus embodied was not "pie in the sky," but neither was it a vision of fulfillment by human effort alone, that is, by human effort uncentered in God. The whole dynamic of the New Testament is that of the person, teaching, and resurrection of Jesus Christ breaking through all conceptions of reality (including religious ones) as a closed system and reorienting subjectivity from self-centeredness, complacency, or despair to trust in God. In the pattern of Jesus' own radical surrender to *Abba*, which did not deem to escape the terrifying passage through God-forsakenness, the symbols of Catholic theology should aim to cultivate, not suppress or explain away, the paradoxical tension "in the light of everyday existence" between presence and absence, fulfillment and longing, intimacy and expectation.

All three of these dimensions of Catholic theology—*memoria*, presence, and hope—imply a formal relationship between the mosaic symbols of tradition and the deep structure of reality, the "hidden ground of Love." In chapter 4, we shall see Merton further affirm the sacramentality of language in his analysis of *theoria physike* and its relationship to symbols such as "fire," "Christ," "Spirit," and "Sophia." In anticipation of that discussion, what must be emphasized here is that for Merton "symbolic" and "sacramental" theology are synonymous terms: both belong to that realm of *theoria physike*, which is "the reception of God's revelation . . . in creatures, in history, in Scripture."[156] No

---

155. See, e.g., "Called Out of Darkness" (NM, 225–48), one of Merton's most penetrating reflections on the formative power of liturgical *anamnesis*, in this case, the paschal Triduum.

156. ICM, 123. As Patrick O'Connell notes, it was Merton's conviction "that the tendency on the part of some spiritual theologians to deemphasize or skip over completely the intermediate levels of symbolic theology has been just as harmful to a full and adequate theology

matter whether we are immersed mindfully in nature, in the mundane tasks of everyday living, in liturgy, iconography, or in sacred texts, the experience of God's presence through *theoria* is real, and it is trustworthy. This is not, however, because the symbols of world, liturgy, and text simply stimulate, entertain, or overwhelm our aesthetic and imaginative faculties. It is because the presence of God—"the sign of Jonas"—is already written in our being.

There is no literary or aesthetic magic going on here, just a radical claim for the sanctity of the human person in God, God who already lives in the cradle of the soul. The religious symbol, in other words, tells nothing new, communicates no "new information." What is "new" in the symbol, Merton insists, is our "discovery of a new depth and a new actuality in what IS and always has been."[157] Its function is "to manifest a union that *already exists but is not fully realized*. The symbol awakens awareness, or restores it. Therefore, it aims not at communication but at communion."[158] Communion means "bringing together," which is the etymological sense of "symbol."[159] It is "the awareness of participation in an ontological or religious reality: in the mystery of being, of human love, of redemptive mystery, of contemplative truth."[160] Merton likens this ever-present but hidden mystery of being to the words of Jesus: "the Kingdom of God is within you." Again, it is important to try to get inside this experience not abstractly but rather in its immediacy as an "event" or "spark" of realization. As seen in chapter 1, Merton reflexively turns to biblical and patristic archetypes in describing this experience: Love is a *reunion*, a coming back "to somewhere I had been as a child."[161] While utterly gratuitous—"As if from her hand had come a new *life*"—love's embrace is also felt as a remembering, an awakening from sleep, "like waking from a dream of separateness."

---

of mystical experience as the unwillingness to move beyond the level of images and ideas into the darkness of unknowing" (ibid., xxix). Indeed, Merton locates the roots of the "disastrous" separation between spiritual and scholastic theology in the Middle Ages in the tendency of "professional mystical theologians" to artificially separate Dionysius's *Mystical Theology* from the *Hierarchies* and the *Divine Names* (xxviii), and thus to go directly from the ascetic life to contemplation without forms, that is, without passing through the necessary intermediate stages of *theoria physike* (ibid., xxix–xxxiv).

157. LL, 67. "The 'sacredness' of man consists . . . precisely in the fact that the truth for which and by which he lives is primarily within himself, and therefore prime importance belongs to the symbol which directs him to this truth, not as an external object, but as a spiritual and personal fulfillment" (ibid., 69).

158. Ibid., 68.

159. Ibid., 56.

160. Ibid., 68. Clearly by our "communion" in God Merton does not mean "sameness." In Merton's theological anthropology, the *coincidentia oppositorum* still applies: i.e., it is a unity-in-difference that celebrates the irreducible mystery of every human being, just as Blake glories in the distinctiveness of every "grain of sand."

161. DWL, 202.

For all of these reasons, and considering his work as a whole, it seems that the architectonic principle of Merton's religious epistemology is *memory*, understood in the Augustinian sense not merely in epistemological terms, as the storehouse of sense impressions and events that happened empirically and historically to individuals in the past, but rather in ontological, archetypal, and even cosmic terms. In its Augustinian sense, *memoria* refers to the presence of God "written into" the fabric of creation always and everywhere. It is the image and likeness of God in humankind, that elemental sense of spiritual freedom and responsibility, both wondrous and terrifying, as part of the created order. It is the sense of being itself as radical *gift*—"'The good is diffusive of itself,' or 'God is love.'"[162] Yet graced *memoria* also contains its opposite, a corporate sense of brokenness and radical failure, of human being as being haunted by sin and death from the beginning.[163]

The point is that for Merton, the symbols and doctrines of the tradition are living symbols not because like a catechetical fact sheet they communicate new information, still less because they merely resuscitate a deposit of old truths wrapped in Baroque packages. The symbols of tradition are living to the degree that, like the parables of Jesus, they break through solipsism and idolatry and wake us up to a Life and Love that is unimaginable by all lights of practical reason; they are alive and not dead to the degree they help us to remember who God is, and who we are in God. Because "there is something in the very nature of man that expects a Redeemer and resurrection from the dead,"[164] the paschal mystery of Jesus quickens in us "the sign of Jonas," the promise of new life flowering from death, even now, as a foretaste of the

162. ZBA, 25.

163. Augustine's conception of *memoria* is described by Étienne Gilson as follows: "Now at the summit [of the human faculty of knowing] God placed the memory, that is . . . the faculty of recognizing in itself at every moment the latent presence of God. . . . This memory . . . simply expresses the fact . . . that God is always with us even if we are not always with Him. At the summit of the mind . . . there is a secret point where resides the latent remembrance of His goodness and His power; and there also lies the most deeply graven trait of His image. . . [Thus man's 'natural' state is] that of a reason that knows naught but God, of a will that tends to naught but God, because the memory whence they proceed is filled with nothing but the remembrance of God. Such was also the divine image in man when it shone out in all its splendour, before it had been tarnished by sin; this is the likeness we have lost and which the apprenticeship of divine love should put us on the way to recover" (Étienne Gilson, *The Mystical Theology of St. Bernard*, trans. A. H. C. Downes [Kalamazoo, MI: Cistercian Publications, 1990], 203–5; cf. ICM, 124–25, including n. 348).

164. SJ, 341. The comment follows a story in which Merton describes a number of children's drawings sent to the monastery from "somewhere in Milwaukee," the "only real works of art I have seen in ten years, since entering Gethsemani. But it occurred to me that these wise children were drawing pictures of their own lives. They knew their own depths. They were putting it all down on paper before they had a chance to grow up and forget" (ibid.).

heavenly banquet. In like manner, note how a symbol like "the communion of saints" does not confine the *memoria* of the dead to the past, but attunes our spiritual senses to experience a deeper reality, no less real because hidden: the dead are not dead but are the *living dead*, the cloud of witnesses, guiding and interceding before God, preparing our place in the heavenly banquet yet to come.

Merton is by no means ignorant of the darker side of imagination and its capacity through symbolism (especially religious symbolism) to embrace and propagate the demonic. To the degree that the metaphorical character of biblical, theological, and liturgical speech is not preserved, and symbols are construed by the believing community as simply (undialectally) facts, as self-evident as a syllogism, we become more or less religious idolaters, worshipers of revelation as a closed system. Idolatry is the distorted face of a sacramental and liturgical imagination run wild.[165] This is not, however, the failure of symbolism as such, Merton insists, but rather of bad theology and bad education—that is, the failure to educate ourselves and our children to be "linguistically prepared" readers of the Bible, sensitive practitioners of religious discourse, and properly initiated participants in the mystagogical symbols of liturgy, iconography, prayer.[166]

The mystical tradition of the church is "a collective memory and experience of Christ living and present within her,"[167] a tradition that forms and affects the whole person. Merton's poetic theology cultivates this collective memory and experience in a way that cedes to neither triumphalism nor indifferentism. This is no small gift. Merton attunes our senses to the music of Catholicism in such a way that we can joyfully embrace ecclesial identity, even while mindfully (and joyfully!) seeking to encounter Christ outside the visible boundaries of the church.

The *Memoria* of Others: Against Revelation as a Closed System

The distinctiveness of Catholic theology has just been described in terms of its capacity for awakening *memoria*, presence, and hope through an integral engagement with the memories, narratives, and symbols of the Bible as well as the creeds and symbols of the Catholic dogmatic and liturgical tradition. Yet surely the most extraordinary thing about Merton's life and theology is his will-

---

165. John Thiel, "For What May We Hope? Thoughts on the Eschatological Imagination," *Theological Studies* 67 (2006): 517–41, at 525–26.

166. "[Living] and creative symbols elevate and direct [action] in a good sense, while pathogenic and depraved symbols divert man's energies to evil and destruction. The point is to educate men so that they can discern one from the other" (LL, 62–63).

167. ICM, 35.

ingness to give himself over to the *memoria* of strangers, the wisdom of other peoples and traditions well beyond his own existential, religious, and cultural horizon. For Merton, the "cloud of witnesses" would appear to exclude no one. In the following journal of September 8, 1960, note how Merton's conception of *memoria* reflects his dawning realization of being caught up in one human family, beyond boundaries of nation, race, religion, and even time:

> Importance of being able to rethink thoughts that were fundamental to men of other ages, or *are* fundamental to men in other countries. For me, especially—contemporary Latin America—Greek Patristic period—Mt. Athos—Confucian China—T'ang dynasty—Pre-Socratic Greece. Despair of ever beginning truly to know and understand, to communicate with these pasts and these distances, yet sense of obligation to do so, to live them and combine them in myself, to absorb, to digest, to "remember." *Memoria.* Have not yet begun.[168]

In this critical passage, we find Merton seeking in shadows after the boundless *memoria* of God. He is praying, in other words, for the divine perspective of humanity, with its manifold histories, religions, and cultures, to break through. If Merton, for his part, had "not yet begun" to "absorb, to digest, to 'remember'" across "these pasts and these distances," how far is Catholic theology today from beginning to do so? How far are we from even the desire, much less the sense of obligation, to remember the earth and its manifold peoples from the divine perspective?

"The experience of a great mystic," writes Paul Evdokimov, "is always paradoxical, even disquieting, to any system."[169] Merton is disquieting to the degree his theology and his very life pose an implicit challenge to any "Catholic" worldview that has become opaque, too sure of itself, too jealous of the Love and Mystery it claims to guard in fullness. Indeed, like Bulgakov under the dome of Hagia Sophia, who could rejoice in the piety of the Muslims worshiping there, Merton recoils against any view of revelation as a closed system, "a system of truths about God and an explanation of how the universe came into existence . . . what are its moral norms, what will be the rewards of the virtuous, and so on."[170] Such a view reduces Christianity to "a religious philosophy and little more, sustained by a more or less elaborate cult, by a moral discipline and a strict code of Law." Under the protective dome of such

168. TTW, 42.

169. Paul Evdokimov, *Woman and the Salvation of the World: A Christian Anthropology on the Charisms of Women*, trans. Anthony P. Gythiel (Crestwood, NY: St. Vladimir's Seminary Press, 1994), 206.

170. ZBA, 40.

a theological system, our experience of the inner meaning of revelation will not be a "living theological experience of the presence of God in the world and in mankind through the mystery of Christ, but rather a sense of security in one's own correctness: a feeling of confidence that one has been saved, a confidence which is based on the reflex awareness that one holds the correct view of the creation and purpose of the world and that one's behavior is of a kind to be rewarded in the next life."[171] Our experience of Christ under such a worldview is bound to tend toward idolatry, docetism, magic.

Like Heschel, Merton cautions that dogmatic formulas, even the most solemn definitions with respect to Jesus Christ, must not become screens but must serve instead as windows for ushering the community of faith into the transcendent presence of God: "The importance of the formulas is not that they are ends in themselves, but that they are means through which God communicates His truth to us. They must be kept clear. They must be clean windows so that they may not obscure and hinder the light that comes to us."[172] These lines underscore why tradition and mysticism have a reciprocal relationship in the history of the church. The insights of the prophet, theologian, and mystic are crucial for the church's vitality whenever Tradition (capital *T*) becomes opaque, triumphal, reactionary, listless, or stubbornly complacent. Merton's theology enfleshes a paradox. On the one hand, he is no theological renegade: "To experience the mystery of Christ mystically or otherwise is always to transcend the merely individual psychological level and to 'experience theologically with the Church.'"[173] On the other hand, in opening himself to the wisdom of other traditions (i.e., the boundless *memoria* of God) he takes upon himself considerable risk, both personally and theologically: "God speaks, and God is to be heard, not only on Sinai, not only in my own heart, but in the *voice of the stranger*. . . . We must, then, see the truth in the stranger, and the truth we see must be a newly living truth, not just a projection of a dead conventional idea of our own—a projection of our own self upon the stranger."[174]

The essential point is theological. To recall Clement of Alexandria, the seeds of the Word, and thus the seeds of theological renewal, are to be found

171. Ibid.; cf. NM, 35–36, where Merton describes "Promethean theology" as the obsession with what is "mine" and "thine": "So it is the drive which urged the prodigal son to bring about a clear separation between the heritage that was 'his' and the rest of his father's possessions. . . . The prodigal has not stolen anything, but he thinks that to 'find himself,' he must segregate whatever can be classified as 'his' and exploit it for his own self-affirmation."

172. NSC, 129–30.

173. ZBA, 46. Or, as Paul Valliere observes: "Tradition comprises mysticism and exceeds it" (MRT, 170).

174. Thomas Merton, *The Collected Poems of Thomas Merton* (New York: New Directions, 1977), 384–85.

not only in the Christian tradition itself—especially in those narratives and symbols that have been marginalized—but will also break in from beyond the Christian tradition "with a liberty that knows no law of man." Like Newman's polygon expanding into the enclosing revelatory circle, the movement is both expansive and centripetal. "The Logos at its center is such that the 'opposites' can magnetize rather than repel—if we would let them."[175] Indeed, to the degree that we "bring out clearly the mystical dimensions of our theology,"[176] we may discover with Merton that our lives in Christ share much more with non-Christians than we had once fearfully or complacently assumed.

Love and the Naming of God: Sophia

In this chapter we have seen how Merton's conviction that "there is a relation between all wisdoms" extends not only to non-Christian religions and non-Western cultures, not only to the literary and scientific realms, but also to distinct wisdom trajectories within Christianity itself. "Greek wisdom," he insists, "was not out of harmony with that of the Bible."[177] The Romantic epistemology of Blake, which celebrates the *claritas* in every "grain of sand" and in "the human form divine," shares not a little with the Thomistic notion of "connaturality," which can grasp "the perfection of an antelope or a flower" as much as "the perfection of a theorem or of a syllogism."[178] The point is that Merton does not stake his Christian hope wholly on one side of opposite ways, such that *sapientia* trumps *scientia*, East trumps West, or Greek wisdom trumps the Bible. To do so would be to perpetuate the violence in which "Yes" and "No" pursue each other around the circle, at great cost to human sanity and the restoration of wholeness. While there is no going back to premodern or prescientific consciousness, neither should biblical and eschatological sensibilities be set up in false contradiction to scientific and historical consciousness.

At the same time, Merton denounces in the starkest terms a global situation in which scientific, economic, and instrumental rationality, largely a product of Western industrial capitalism, threatens to wipe out the very memory of more ancient and holistic ways of wisdom, and increasingly dictates the shape of life everywhere on the planet. In such a world the presence of Christ will be ever more hidden, interruptive, and ironic, because personhood itself is becoming ever more hidden, interruptive, ironic:

175. Nugent, "*Pax Heraclitus*," 6.
176. ICM, 16.
177. LE, 100.
178. Ibid., 443, 445.

The primordial blessing, "increase and multiply," has suddenly become a hemorrhage of terror. We are numbered in billions, and massed together, marshalled, numbered, marched here and there, taxed, drilled, armed, worked to the point of insensibility, dazed by information, drugged by entertainment, surfeited with everything, nauseated with the human race and with ourselves, nauseated with life.

As the end approaches, there is no room for nature. The cities crowd it off the face of the earth. As the end approaches, there is no room for quiet. There is no room for solitude. There is no room for thought. There is no room for attention, for the awareness of our state. In the time of the ultimate end, there is no room for man.[179]

Merton makes clear his conviction that scientific rationality is not wholly to blame for the sweeping alienation and depersonalization of modern life. What passes for theological wisdom in modern Western Christianity has been of little help in cultivating a more holistic spirituality of sanity, harmony, and balance: "Those that lament the fact that there is no room for God must also be called to account for this. Have they perhaps added to the general crush by preaching a solid marble God that makes man alien to himself, a God that settles himself grimly like an implacable object in the inner heart of man and drives man out of himself in despair? The time of the end is the time of demons who occupy the heart (pretending to be gods) so that man himself finds no room for himself in himself."[180] There are clear echoes here of Merton's meditations on Prometheus, "the prophet and contemplative that is required by the atomic age,"[181] who has made for himself a pantheon of small and jealous gods. Imagining that he must fight the gods for his spiritual freedom, that he must "steal fire from heaven," Prometheus's life is a never-ending struggle between "heroism and despair." His gods, however, will "eventually devour him."[182]

It is precisely in this archetypal complex of bad science and bad theology—"the time of massed armies, 'wars and rumors of wars,' of huge crowds moving this way and that, of 'men withering away for fear,' of . . . technicians planning grandiose acts of destruction"[183]—that Merton seeks "some new possibility, some other opening for the Christian consciousness today."[184] What he discovered in the East was a way of knowing "which transcends and unites . . . which dwells in body and soul together and which, more by

179. RU, 70.
180. Ibid., 71.
181. NM, 27.
182. BT, 15.
183. RU, 67.
184. ZBA, 30.

means of myth, of ritual, of contemplation, than by scientific experiment, opens the door to a life in which the individual is not lost in the cosmos and in society but found in them."[185] It was a wisdom "which made all life sacred and meaningful—even that which later ages came to call secular and profane."[186] "The Indian mind that was awakening in Gandhi," for example, "was inclusive not exclusive. . . . It was a mind of love, of understanding, of infinite capaciousness. Where the extreme nationalisms of Western Fascism and of Japan were symptoms of paranoid fury, exploding into alienation, division, and destruction, the spirit which Gandhi discovered in himself was reaching out to unity, love, and peace. It was a spirit which was, he believed, strong enough to heal every division."[187]

Like Heschel, Merton believed that modern consciousness (and with it, much of modern theology) had lost touch with the depth dimension of human life: *You are trying to sound the middle of the ocean with a six-foot pole.*[188] He came to accept it as integral to his vocation as both monk and writer to help others learn how to "sound the ocean," that is, to make contact with the hidden ground of Love. Yet the great question remains: *How?* As ever, Merton was deeply attuned to a problem that dogs the church as much, if not more, today than it did four decades ago: "The great question then is how *do* we communicate with the modern world? If in fact communication has been reduced to pseudo-communication, to the celebration of pseudo-events and the irate clashing of incompatible myth-systems, how are we to avoid falling into this predicament? How are we to avoid the common obsession . . . to construct what seems to us to be a credible idol? It is a nasty question, but it needs to be considered, for in it is contained the mystery of the evil of our time."[189]

Certainly, as "the contemporary of Auschwitz, Hiroshima, Viet Nam and the Watts riots,"[190] Merton might have been excused had he chosen, like so many other Christian intellectuals, to curtail his biblical and eschatological imagination and adopt a rigorous apophaticism or agnosticism in word and speech. But he chose rather the opposite path. Texts such as *New Seeds of Contemplation*, *Conjectures of a Guilty Bystander*, *Raids on the Unspeakable*, and *Contemplation in a World of Action* were written, after all, during years of extraordinary tension and creativity for Merton, and written with special

185. Thomas Merton, *Gandhi on Non-Violence: A Selection from the Writings of Mahatma Gandhi* (New York: New Directions, 1965), 1; hereafter GNV.
186. Ibid.
187. Ibid., 5.
188. WCT, 130.
189. FV, 163.
190. CWA, 143.

concern for the "diaspora" church, that is, for fellow Christian pilgrims trying to find their way in a fractured and unspeakably violent modern world.[191] It is significant that Merton directs our gaze in these texts not to some nameless presence or hidden God-beyond-God, but to *Christ*, the Wisdom of God, whose light transfigures all creation with love and resurrection hope, and whose presence shines in the face of every human being.

It is also telling that when Merton is pressed to the limits of apophatic theology in his dialogue with Suzuki, he keeps returning to "the realm of concept and image,"[192] to the sacramental principle at the heart of Christian revelation. "[The] fact remains that Christianity is a religion of the Word," and thus "the understanding of the statements which embody God's revelation of Himself remains a primary concern. Christian experience is the fruit of this understanding, a development of it, a deepening of it."[193] Precisely because Christianity is a "religion of the Word," the intuition of the "ground of openness" in Christian mysticism still has "the character of a *free gift* of love, and perhaps it is this freedom, this *giving without reason, without limit, without return, without self-conscious afterthought,* that is the real secret of God who 'is love.'"[194] How apophatic can theology be and still justly communicate this experience? More pragmatically, can apophatic theology address the "great needs" of the human (and Christian) community in our time: the need for community, for meaning and purpose amid life's most mundane circumstances, the need to affirm and celebrate the dignity of human and planetary life on all its levels, "bodily as well as imaginative, emotional, intellectual, spiritual"?[195] Is apophatic theology capable of breaking through humanity's "elephantiasis of self-will"[196] and confronting it with its need for redemption?

Clearly Merton did not place his trust in any philosophical or even theological system, and he showed little interest in building a new one. Not unlike the Zen *roshi*—indeed, not unlike Jesus—his deepest impulse was to *tell a story*, or to interject observations and questions (as in the Zen *koan*) meant to interrupt the opaque, complacent, or despairing worldview of modern consciousness, and thus to help cultivate in his readers greater mindfulness, sanity, peace. But when it comes down to it, the story Merton most wanted

191. On Rahner's notion of the Christian "diaspora," see SD, 184–220; also FV, 237.
192. ZBA, 132.
193. Ibid., 40.
194. Ibid., 136.
195. Ibid., 30. At the end of "The New Consciousness" (ZBA, 30–31) Merton lays down a kind of charter for *any* approach—philosophical, literary, theological, scientific—that would seek to address the "great needs" of humanity today. This is a critical passage in Merton's late writings, reflecting his extraordinary attunement to the human situation, the wisdom of other traditions, and to the signs of the times.
196. Ibid., 31.

to tell is one without parallel in Zen or in any other philosophical, religious, or spiritual tradition. Thus while he certainly exercised his apophatic and "metaphysical affliction"[197] to the end, Merton was arguably much more attuned to his own Catholic sensibilities, and more successful, when he allowed himself to explore, in the pattern of monastic and patristic theology before him, the poetic symbols of the Bible, a text with no parallel in facilitating the encounter (and confrontation) with a God of judgment, mercy, and, to be sure, wordless Presence.[198]

In short, if the modern spiritual crisis is ontological at its root, Merton grasped that its solution, at least for the Catholic Christian imagination, will have to be both metaphysical and literary. And in this he shares much with Heschel, the philosopher-poet of Judaism. In contrast to religious discourse that stands apart from confessional language and the "dim and shadowy" realm of religious experience, Merton "seeks to meet the person in moments in which the whole person is involved, in moments that are affected by all a person feels, thinks, and acts."[199] Like Heschel, Merton mines the very paradox that is the human person, blending prose and poetics in a way that trains the mind, imagination, and spirit to open. By re-centering subjectivity from self to God—not God "out there," but God "called forth" from within—Merton's theology is able to "actualize" or "realize" *the nonsymbolic content of religious discourse* and thus to electrify "concepts frozen by ideologies, using them to surpass themselves."[200]

How, for example, does the word "incarnation" function in Merton's writings? Does it merely point to a beautiful and even morally compelling narrative about a God out there who comes down from Heaven and then goes back up to watch over and judge us? Or does the symbol become real, more than literally real, in the everyday movements that make up a human life? Consider how Merton structures religious discourse on the meaning of incarnation:

> The presence of God in His world as its Creator depends on no one but Him. His presence in the world as Man depends, in some measure, upon men. Not that we can do anything to change the mystery of the Incarnation in itself: but we are able to decide whether we ourselves, and that portion of the world which is ours, shall become *aware* of His presence, consecrated by it, and transfigured in its light.

197. See LE, 9.
198. "The Truth is a Way and a Person," Merton wrote in 1958, "and a Way and a Person have to be found and followed. Truth is to be lived" (SFS, 192); cf. TTW, 122–23, on Gandhi, Christ, and indifferentism.
199. Abraham Joshua Heschel, *The Insecurity of Freedom* (Philadelphia: Jewish Publication Society of America, 1966), 119.
200. Kaplan, HW, 49–50.

> We have the choice of two identities: the external mask which seems to be real and which lives by a shadowy autonomy for the brief moment of earthly existence, and the hidden, inner person who seems to us to be nothing, but who can give himself eternally to the truth in whom he subsists. It is this inner self that is taken up into the mystery of Christ, by His love, by the Holy Spirit, so that in secret we live "in Christ."[201]

In his account of prayer, Heschel says that the "inadequacy of the means at our disposal appears so tangible, so tragic, that one feels it a grace to be able to give oneself up to music, to a tone, to a song, to a chant."[202] Many readers today come to Merton's writings in much the same way. Just as the "wave of a song carries the soul to heights which utterable meanings can never reach,"[203] so too his writing bears us, body and soul, into the heart of the Christian Good News, such that one can begin not only to hear and see it, but believe it. Believe what? In a word, that one is loved, that one belongs in the world, that human life has meaning and purpose in the vast cosmos.[204] Such a love stirs and ignites the spiritual freedom that is already given to us, in God, from the beginning. "The root of Christian love is not the will to love, but *the faith that one is loved*. The faith that one is loved *by God*. . . . although unworthy—or rather, irrespective of one's worth!"[205] This is the nonsymbolic content of incarnation that Merton's writing electrifies, and makes us to believe, such that "one feels it a grace" to give oneself up to such a spiritual master. If nothing else, Merton's poetic theology cultivates the willingness to believe, the desire to fall on one's knees and beg to be loved in such a way, so that I might be freed from fear and loneliness, freed from compulsion and shame, in the knowledge that I am a beloved son, a beloved daughter, of God.

Is it beyond the pale of Catholic theology to suggest that this is the very same mind—let us for a moment call her "Sophia"—that we earlier said was awakening in Gandhi, "a mind of love, of understanding, of infinite capaciousness"? The same mind that "opens the door to a life in which the individual is not lost in the cosmos and in society but found in them"? The same mind which makes "all life sacred and meaningful—even that which later ages came to call secular and profane"? Whether or not such a suggestion is orthodox, perhaps we may still question whether it is reasonable or intelligible to the contemporary Christian. Yet what if, to the contrary, Heschel

201. NSC, 295.

202. Heschel, *Man's Quest for God*, 39.

203. Ibid.

204. Here we may recall the Cistercian emphasis on love as the highest form of knowledge—*amor ipse intellectus est*—drawing us into the immediacy of life in God.

205. NSC, 75.

is correct about our immersion in the revelatory landscape of the Bible: that such an abandonment "is no escape, nor an act of being unfaithful to the mind," that "this world of unutterable meanings is the nursery of the soul, the cradle of all our ideas"?[206] What if the remembrance of Sophia is no escape but rather a return to origins, a retrieval of the "forgotten mother tongue"?[207] What if we approach Sophia not as a mere symbol or figure pointing to a divine attribute, but rather as a divine *name*, bound up in faith and in mystery with the anthropology, the *memoria*, the life story of God?

If, when meditating on her voice and presence in the Scriptures, something within us "actually vibrates, responds, and gives a deep meaning to the lessons of [our] first teachers about the will and the providence of God,"[208] then our task is not only the task of hermeneutical scrutiny but also the task, and the grace, of slowing down, listening, praying, and perhaps allowing shadow-realms of *memoria* to rise to the surface:

> For in her is the spirit of understanding: holy, one,
>   manifold, subtile, eloquent, active, undefiled, sure,
>   sweet, loving that which is good. . . .
> For she is a vapour of the power of God, and a certain
>   pure emanation of the glory of the almighty God. . . .
> For she is the brightness of eternal light, and the unspotted
>   mirror of God's majesty, and the image of his goodness.[209]

The stars rejoice in their setting, and in the rising of the Sun. The heavenly lights rejoice in the going forth of one man to make a new world in the morning, because he has come out of the confused primordial dark night into consciousness. He has expressed the clear silence of Sophia in his own heart. He has become eternal.[210]

Concluding Remarks

For Catholics of a postconciliar generation, it is easy to overlook just how radical Merton's commitment to ecumenical and interfaith dialogue would have been in the years prior to Vatican II. In a journal entry dated June 8, 1959, Merton recognizes the precarious theological position he has gotten himself into with typical candor and self-deprecating humor: "You have put your nose in Dostoyevsky and Berdyaev and Zen Buddhism and now where are you? On the road to heresy. Well, what about St. Paul, and all the saints?

---

206. Heschel, *Man's Quest for God*, 39.
207. Heschel, *Man is Not Alone*, 75.
208. Newman, GA, 105.
209. Wis 7:22-26, cited in BT, 81.
210. *Hagia Sophia*, ESF, 64.

What about the gospel? Certainly, it is a dangerous problem, and I am in danger. Thank God for it. I beg Him to protect me and bring me through the danger. And I still do not know what to do."[211] That Merton would recognize his situation as "dangerous" in one breath and "thank God for it" in the next will surprise few readers familiar with his life and writings. But these lines reveal more than the musings of an insatiably curious monk in the late 1950s. Just as he captured the spirit of a war-ravaged generation in *The Seven Storey Mountain*, here again Merton had his finger on the pulse of the church he loved, a community standing on the brink of its new self-consciousness as a global church at Vatican II.[212]

We know, of course, that Merton would continue to cross boundaries, trusting in God's friendship and protection, right up to his Asian pilgrimage and sudden death in Bangkok in 1968. But what will be our part? Now over four decades removed from the council, it seems that most of us "still do not know what to do" with this new global consciousness. Driven by a creeping anxiety that too much dialogue with secular culture, much less with other religions, has put legions of believers "on the road to heresy," vague indifferentism, or moral relativism, and dogged by the fear that the "center cannot hold" in christological discourse, the church and not a few of its theologians seem to be expending a great deal of pastoral energy, and spilling a lot of ink, staking out old lines in the sand. Perhaps it should not surprise that Merton remains a polarizing figure in the Roman Catholic Church. It was in a similarly polarized atmosphere, we recall, that Newman concluded that theology needed a "Novum Organon": "A new question needs a new answer."[213]

Whether Merton's Christology and the Russian sophiological tradition gesture to anything like a new answer is the central question explored in the second half of this book. Yet even prior to an evaluation of the content of Merton's Christology, there is already a great deal to learn from, and celebrate, in his capacious method or way of doing theology. It is a way of both identity and catholicity, a way of poetics and peace, that does not fear to reach both deeply within and well beyond the boundaries of the Roman Catholic dogmatic tradition. As will become even clearer in the next chapter, Merton models a way of knowing, centered in Christ, that positively expects to find God's presence "at play" in every corner of reality to which we humbly give our selves over.

---

211. SFS, 288.

212. In a seminal article Karl Rahner describes the council as "the first act in a history in which the world-Church first began to act as such," and he forecasts the pastoral and theological significance of this self-realization. See "The Abiding Significance of Vatican II," in Karl Rahner, *Concern for the Church*, trans. Edward Quinn (New York: Crossroad, 1981), 90–102.

213. Cited in Merrigan, "Newman and Theological Liberalism," 614.

In his analysis of Newman's approach to theology, Terrence Merrigan concludes with an observation that expresses well the kind of Catholic theological sensibilities so many have celebrated in Thomas Merton, and that I have tried to convey in the first half of this study. What Merrigan says of Newman applies equally to Merton:

> One who would understand Newman must not . . . be dismayed at the superficial discord his writings often evidence. Instead, very much aware of this element, one must attend to the way in which Newman strives to fashion (or refashion) a unity out of the discord he has created (or is undergoing). When Thomas Huxley declared that he could compile a "primer of infidelity" on the basis of Newman's works, he was bearing unintended witness to this peculiar character of Newman's mind. Like many others, however, he was working with only half the picture. The key to Newman's complexity is his ability to hold in tensile unity apparently opposite tendencies and concerns. Indeed, it is in the attempt at synthesis that Newman is most truly revealed.[214]

Similarly, when Merton is accused of infidelity to the tradition, his accusers are often "working with only half the picture." It is certainly true, as noted at the beginning of this study, that the last decade of Merton's life was marked by an extraordinary explosion of activity in his heart and mind. Yet Allchin is right: it was "a *non-disintegrating explosion,*" the effects of which "were constructive and not destructive."[215] As with Newman, one has to attend to the way in which Merton "strives to fashion (or refashion) a unity out of the discord he has created" and is undergoing—both personally and theologically. Indeed, "it is in the attempt at synthesis" that Merton is most truly revealed. Nugent makes the same point, if whimsically, when he remarks that Merton could appear "a case study in 'chaos theory.' But chaos theory," he adds, "looks to the larger pattern, and so too did Merton."[216]

While the irruption of Sophia into Merton's consciousness in the late 1950s was just one thread woven into the "larger pattern" of his mystical biography, it was the *golden* thread that helped him to hold the fabric together, ever more centered in Christ. To borrow from one of his most important mentors in the way of wisdom, Boris Pasternak, it was the "inward music" of her voice that raised him up to a newfound love, the love of humanity, in whose spiritual freedom is written "the life story of God."[217]

---

214. Cited in ibid., 621.
215. A. M. Allchin, "The Worship of the Whole Creation," in MHPH, 103–20, at 113.
216. Nugent, "The Coincidence of Opposites," 259.
217. From Pasternak's *Dr. Zhivago,* cited in DQ, 67.

"Christ unveils the meaning of the Old Testament." Drawing by Thomas Merton. Used with permission of the Merton Legacy Trust and the Thomas Merton Center, Bellarmine University.

4

The Dawn of Wisdom:
Awakening to the World
and Self in Christ

> The Christian's vision of the world ought, by its very nature, to have in it
> something of poetic inspiration. Our faith ought to be capable of filling
> our hearts with a wonder and a wisdom which see beyond the surface
> of things and events, and grasp something of the inner and "sacred"
> meaning of the cosmos which, in all its movements and all its aspects,
> sings the praises of its Creator and Redeemer.[1]

Thomas Merton's religious imagination has been described in these pages as
sacramental, poetic, catholic, biblical, sapiential, and mystical, in the richest
possible sense of these terms; the term iconic would serve just as well, as
we shall see later. But no matter what term we use to describe his capacious
worldview, the point to underscore is this: in an era when Christian theology
had every reason to lose its nerve, to embrace an iconoclasm or asceticism
of speech that would more or less strip away the imaginative and symbolic
foundations of faith, foundations that are so evidently corruptible, Merton
called for the retrieval of an authentically Christian and poetic vision of the
world, for the cultivation of a faith that would fill our hearts "with a wonder and a wisdom which see beyond the surface of things and events, and
grasp something of the inner and 'sacred' meaning of the cosmos." Such a
renewal, he believed, would require a "new and more biblical understanding"
of the Christian life and especially of biblical eschatology, a conception of God
not only "as essential good" but as a Love "that breaks through into the world of
sinful men in the fire of judgment and of mercy."[2]

This chapter traces the emergence of Sophia in Merton's life and theology as a Love and a Presence that "breaks through into the world," a "living
symbol" and "Name" with which he increasingly chose to structure theological discourse. If the role of symbolism, as argued in chapter 3, is "to 'bring

1. LE, 345.
2. CWA, 133.

together' man, nature, and God in a living and sacred synthesis,"[3] if our capacity "to apprehend the visible and the invisible as a meaningful unity depends on the creative vitality of [our] symbols,"[4] if authentic Christian symbols are vessels of *memoria*, presence (*theoria*), and hope—then our task here is to illumine the emergence of Sophia as Merton's most vivid symbol for expressing "a living experience of unity in Christ which far transcends all conceptual formulations."[5]

Much of the chapter will bear something of a narrative or story-shaped structure, drawing freely from letters, journals, lectures, and other writings that open a window into Merton's study of Christian and non-Christian ways of wisdom, from East to West. A key question at play here is whether his dialogue with Zen and experiences in the Far East reflect an elemental continuity with his Christ-haunted past, or rather, as not a few have argued or assumed, its radical interruption and even reversal. Here I shall make the case for continuity and development: that in Russian sophiology Merton discovered a language, both ancient and new, for giving lyrical voice to the Christian answer to the question of reality's "suchness." Sophia is compassion (*karuna*) without reserve, poverty of spirit. She is, in a word, the loving kenosis of God, coming to birth in all things, and consummately in Jesus Christ and the inner movements of human freedom.

It is crucial to keep in mind that the breakthrough of Sophia was not something that simply happened to Merton but was instead the culmination of years of sustained study of patristic and Russian theology, Zen, meditation on Scripture and iconography, and surely more than we can know, untold hours of contemplation in the hills and woods of Gethsemani. Indeed, underlying and in many ways unifying the explicitly theological content of this chapter is the dynamic itself of breakthrough, discernment, struggle, and growth— or, to recall Newman's "illative sense," the process of growing into the truth about the mystery of God. In the pages that follow, I invite the reader to try to listen from the inside, as it were, so as to taste and even to savor something of the intuitive process itself through which Merton, by the turn of the 1960s, came to internalize the sophianic worldview fully as his own. All the influences and exploratory gestures examined here will come to sublime fruition in the prose poem *Hagia Sophia*, the focal point of the next chapter, and in many ways the theological convergence point of this book.

---

3. LL, 60.
4. Ibid., 56.
5. ZBA, 39.

Mentors in Wisdom

Whether inspired by his catholicity or scandalized by it, few serious students of Merton's life and writings would dispute that his conception of Christ changed as he allowed deeper encounters with Eastern traditions to interrogate his faith. What is less commonly understood, however, is how closely his engagement with Zen in the late 1950s corresponded with his internalization of a deep thread in the Christian East, namely, the Sophia tradition of Russian Orthodoxy. The striking coincidence of seeming opposites in Merton's life during the late 1950s was not merely a coincidence but hinges in part on epistemological difficulties he wrestled with in the midst of radically shifting cultural, ecclesial, and political horizons. Yet neither does this attunement of apparent opposites end simply with epistemology. What emerges in Merton's concurrent study of Russian sophiology and Zen is a kind of story-shaped Christology, a story told through the life of Merton, but haunted more and more by the mysterious figure of Sophia.

The task at hand is to test this hypothesis by looking in on four pivotal conversations (to recall Gadamer) in which Merton was engaged from about 1957 to 1961, the years of his turning to the world and also the height of his immersion in Russian theology. These conversations are pivotal because they involve key influences on Merton's thinking, mentors, if you will, in the way of wisdom: D. T. Suzuki, Herakleitos the Obscure, Maximus Confessor, and Boris Pasternak. We begin with these figures rather than the Russian theologians because their common thread is epistemology: each relates in some way to wisdom or *sapientia* as a way of seeing, and thus each plays a formative role in Merton's remarkable catholicity. Yet as emphasized in the previous chapters, epistemological commitments quickly implicate anthropological and theological ones. In each of these conversations Sophia emerges more or less as a lyric symbol of "God's anthropology"—a love in God, a certain humanness in God, that longs for incarnation from the beginning.

"Something Breaks through a Little": D. T. Suzuki

Nowhere is Merton's effort to bring together seemingly disparate truths of religious experience better illustrated than in his dialogue with Zen scholar D. T. Suzuki, a conversation that began in 1959 and continued until the year of Suzuki's death in 1965. Their dialogue was of such a depth and honesty that both men were changed for it; certainly on Merton's side the experience planted seeds that would bear fruit in his pilgrimage to Asia, in his conversations with the Dalai Lama, and perhaps symbolically, in his unexpected death in Bangkok in December of 1968, just a few days after his much-discussed "realization" at the Buddhist shrine of Pollanaruwa.

In a letter dated March 12, 1959, Merton introduced himself to Suzuki, then known worldwide for his gift for translating the precepts of Zen Buddhism to the West.[6] After receiving a warm reply and some poems from the Zen scholar, Merton wrote a second letter. His tone is warm and forthright, written as one might address a respected teacher or a longtime elder friend. What is most striking is the intimacy with which this Catholic monk from the West opens himself to a Japanese Buddhist he has never met reflecting on the mystery of Christ experienced in prayer:

> The Christ we seek is within us, in our inmost self, *is* our inmost self, and yet infinitely transcends ourselves. We have to be "found in Him" and yet be perfectly ourselves and free from the domination of any image of Him other than Himself. You see, that is the trouble with the Christian world. It is not dominated by Christ (which would be perfect freedom), it is enslaved by images and ideas of Christ that are creations and projections of men and stand in the way of God's freedom. But Christ Himself is in us as unknown and unseen. We follow Him, we find Him . . . and then He must vanish and we must go along without Him at our side. Why? Because He is even closer than that. *He is ourself.* Oh my dear Dr. Suzuki, I know you will understand this so well, and so many people do not, even though they are "doctors in Israel."[7]

The Christ of deep Christian experience is "unknown and unseen" because he "is even closer than that. He is *ourself.*" Why, we may ask, does Merton presume a Japanese Zen teacher will understand this paradoxical experience of Christ, even though many "doctors in Israel" (i.e., Christian theologians) do not? He continues, pointing to the problem of language and mystical experience: "As you know, the problem of writing down things about Christianity is fraught with ludicrous and overwhelming difficulties. No one cares for fresh, direct and sincere intuitions of the Living Truth. Everyone is preoccupied with formulas."[8] The dilemma is not merely dogmatic, suggests Merton, as in the inability to accept traditional formulas on the basis of authority or a flat appeal to tradition. In an age of scientific rationality and historical consciousness, the dilemma is also profoundly epistemological. How do we come to authentic Christian faith in such an age, if by "faith" we mean a real and not merely notional relationship with the living Christ?

In a letter of November 1959, Merton once again brings the epistemological dilemma before Dr. Suzuki, now in the guise of his struggle with the Buddhist notion of emptiness:

6. HGL, 561–62.
7. Ibid., 564.
8. Ibid.

I am much happier with "emptiness" when I don't have to talk about it. . . . As soon as I say something, then that is "not it" right away. Obviously the conclusion is to say nothing, and that for a great deal of the time is what I manage to do. Yet one must speak of it. Obviously one must speak and not speak. . . . But at any rate, I thought you would be happy to know that I struggle with . . . not [the] problem, but [the] *koan*. It is not really for me a serious intellectual problem at all, but a problem of "realization"—something that has to break through. Every once in a while it breaks through a little. One of these days it will burst out.[9]

By no means, as we have seen, does Merton set aside the importance of words, doctrine, or of theology: "Obviously one must speak and not speak." Still, what we call today the problem of Christian faith in a post-Christian world—including the problem of Christ among the religions—was not for Merton an intellectual or philosophical puzzle to be solved so much as a problem of realization: *something has to break through.* It is not a problem, as he wrote to Suzuki, but a *koan*.

While in these early letters Merton seems to be struggling for analogies between Christian mystical experience and Zen realization, some years later he revisits the issue more systematically and with greater confidence in the striking essay "The Zen Koan" (1965).[10] Here he observes that through the *koan* (a kind of nonsense question), the Zen master aims to awaken in the student a "way of seeing," a "pure seeing" of reality and a "pure subjectivity *that needs no object.*"[11] The struggle of the Zen student to "break" the *koan* leads to a gradual deepening of consciousness "in which one experiences reality not indirectly or mediately but directly, in which clinging to no experience and to no awareness as such, one is simply 'aware.'"[12] This kind of language, the language of immediacy, unity, or nondualism, inevitably confuses the Western mind, which tends to be Cartesian, dualistic, object oriented. "For the West consciousness is always 'consciousness of.' In the East, this is not necessarily so: it can be simply 'consciousness.'"[13] But most important, far from the Western caricature of Zen as cultivating a quietist or escapist tranquility, Zen demands and even forces an active response to life:

> What the *Roshi* [Zen master] wants is not a correct answer or a clever reaction but the *living and authentic* response of the student to the *koan*. If he finally responds directly and immediately to the *koan*, he shows

9. Ibid., 569.
10. MZM, 235–54.
11. Ibid., 238.
12. Ibid., 237.
13. Ibid., 238.

that he is now able to respond fully, directly, and immediately to life itself. . . . What is required is not the ability to repeat some esoteric formula learned from a book . . . but actually to *respond* in a full and living manner to any "thing," a tree, a flower, a bird, or even an inanimate object, perhaps a very lowly one. . . . When one attains to pure consciousness, everything has infinite value.[14]

If we substitute the word "Christ," "Spirit," or "Sophia" for the word *koan* in this passage, we will begin to hear the resonances Merton perceived between the Zen mind and Christian mystical experience, a mysticism which sees the whole cosmos transfigured in Christ, or as he writes in *New Seeds of Contemplation*, bursting forth in "the General Dance" of Sophia. Like Zen practice, Christian faith involves "a living and direct response" to life that is grounded in a posture of openness and expectation, of waiting to be grasped. Faith involves, as Jon Sobrino writes, "The willingness to be swept along by the 'more' of reality."[15] To the degree I attend directly to reality in its "suchness," no longer will I be conscious of my "self" as a separate thing in a world of parallel, competing objects. Liberation is the dawning awareness of our true selves already living in Christ, which is to say, resting in the womb of God, in creation, and in one another. It is, as Merton described his experience at Fourth and Walnut, "like waking from a dream of separateness."[16]

Thus what is required of us as students of the Gospel is not to construct new formulas or repeat old ones but to allow the living God (Christ/Wisdom/ Sophia) to break into our consciousness and restore the divine Image in us. Whether this liberation happens gradually through lifelong discipline or quite suddenly—think of Saul on the road to Damascus—the immediacy of divine presence liberates us from the exhausting effort to maintain the false, habitual, or socially constructed masks we wear. "It is no longer I who live, but it is Christ who lives in me" (Gal 2:20). The grace of discovering ourselves in Christ frees us to respond "in a full and living manner" to every human being, every tree, flower, and bird, even the lowliest objects, with the new eyes of faith. In Christ there is no Jew or Greek, male or female, slave or free (see Gal 3:28), clean or unclean, for everything has infinite value.

There is nothing novel, abstract, or esoteric, Merton insists, about this experience of creation transfigured in divine presence. It accords with an ancient conception of God as light, or, as Thomas Aquinas explained, not "that which" we see, but rather "that through which" we see. But more than this,

14. Ibid., 249–50.
15. Jon Sobrino, *Spirituality of Liberation*, trans. Robert Barr (Maryknoll, NY: Orbis, 1988), 19.
16. CGB, 156; cf. SFS, 182.

it is the intuition of creation's radical goodness and gratuity that turns into an accusation of every dehumanizing decision, every "Unspeakable" force or structure of evil churning through the world. For Merton, contemplation (*theoria*) is the living seedbed of a prophetic worldview that seeks always and everywhere to "guard the image of man for it is the image of God."[17]

What then is the *koan* that Zen offers to Christians? It goes something like this: How are we to speak not only *about* Christ—the Christ "out there" whom we tend to manipulate according to our personal needs or ecclesial agendas—but *in* Christ? What sort of language mediates the living Christ as experienced in prayer, liturgy, or contemplation, that is to say, "not as object of seeing or study, but Christ as center in whom and by whom one is illuminated"?[18] What kind of language allows Christ to walk along at our side, and then, if we will risk it, allows him to vanish, in a manner of speaking, trusting that he now lives in and through us, as in the disciples on the road to Emmaus? If our story-shaped Christology has a kind of metaphysical turning point, let it be Merton's words to Suzuki in 1959: "Something . . . has to break through. Every once in a while it breaks through a little. One of these days it will burst out."

The Divine Fire "One and Manifold": Herakleitos the Obscure

> The waking have one common world, but the sleeping turn aside each into a world of his own. It is not right to act and speak like men asleep. If you do not expect the unexpected, you will not find it.[19]

Published in 1961, the year he began the "Cold War Letters," *The Behavior of Titans* "marks a definite departure from the content and tone of Thomas Merton's earlier works."[20] Written at a time when the world, shadowed by the fresh memory of Hiroshima and Nagasaki, lived under the palpable threat of global nuclear war, the atmosphere of crisis drove Merton's thoughts back to the deepest roots of the human drama in history. Blending literary genres of different types—myth, parable, a broadside, reflective essay—Merton excavates the past to interrogate the present through ancient myth, symbol, and archetype. Indeed, the more cryptic and interruptive style of *The Behavior of Titans* probably accounts for its underappreciated status relative to more popular works of this period such as *New Seeds of Contemplation*. Yet a careful reading of the book's six enigmatic pieces reveals it to be a critical work, a

17. RU, 6, citing Berdyaev.
18. HGL, 643.
19. BT, 96.
20. William H. Shannon, "The Behavior of Titans," in TME, 25.

first eruption, in which Merton fully claims the prophetic voice as his own. It is here, for example, that Merton first indicts himself as a "guilty bystander," one of the intellectual class "paid to keep quiet," "nourished in order that we may continue to sleep."[21] The irony, of course, is that Merton would not at all keep quiet in the coming years but would do everything he could to awaken others from the slumber of groupthink, the blindness of "the many," that he saw poisoning the modern (Christian) consciousness.

The final piece in *The Behavior of Titans*, "Herakleitos the Obscure," has been rightly described as "one of Merton's most extraordinary but somehow unheralded essays."[22] When it was first published in 1960, Czeslaw Milosz wrote to Merton to express his "astonishment," describing the essay as "proof of our deep spiritual affinity."[23] Its subject was Herakleitos of Ephesus, the enigmatic pre-Socratic philosopher who lived at the turn of the fifth century BCE, who left no writings of his own, but is quoted by early Christian thinkers such as Clement of Alexandria and Origen. Justin Martyr, Merton notes, refers to Herakleitos "as a 'Saint' of pre-Christian paganism."[24] The Ionian world of Herakleitos was the world of Homer and of the Olympian gods, "a world that believed in static and changeless order, and in the laws of mechanical necessity—basically materialistic."[25] Herakleitos was "one of those rare spirits whose prophetic insight enabled them to see far beyond the limited horizons of their society." Against a society "that feared all that was not 'ordinary,'" he rose up to speak for "the mysterious, the unutterable, and the excellent."[26]

Above all Herakleitos spoke for the logos, "the true law of all being—not a static and rigid form, but a dynamic principle of harmony-in-conflict," which he represented in the symbolic form of fire, the "primary substance" of the cosmos. The logos and fire of Herakleitos, Merton suggests, has "much in common with the Tao of Lao-tse as well as with the Word of St. John." Herakleitos, we must remember, "comes *before* Aristotle's principle of identity and contradiction. He does not look at things with the eyes of Aristotelian logic, and consequently he can say that opposites can be, from a certain point of view, the same."[27] Merton expands further on the vision of Herakleitos:

> Our spiritual and mystical destiny is to "awaken" to the fire that is within us, and our happiness depends on the harmony-in-conflict that results

21. BT, 60.
22. Christopher Nugent, "*Pax Heraclitus*: A Perspective on Merton's Healing Wholeness" (unpublished manuscript, 2005), 1.
23. Cited in Shannon, TME, 27.
24. BT, 77.
25. Ibid., 75.
26. Ibid., 76.
27. Ibid., 78.

from this awakening. Our vocation is a call to spiritual oneness in and with the logos. But this interior fulfillment is not to be attained by a false peace resulting from artificial compulsion—a static and changeless "state" imposed by force of will upon the dynamic, conflicting forces within us. True peace is the "hidden attunement of opposite tensions"—a paradox and a mystery transcending both sense and will, like the ecstasy of the mystic.[28]

Clearly the heart of Merton's concern in this study is epistemology. Herakleitos "looks on the world not as an abstractionist," he says, "but from the viewpoint of experience." However, experience for Herakleitos "is not merely the uninterpreted datum of sense. His philosophical viewpoint is that of a mystic whose intuition cuts through apparent multiplicity to grasp underlying reality as *one*." Moreover, fire is not merely a symbol for him, nor only material: it is "a dynamic, spiritual principle. It is a divine energy, the manifestation of God, the power of God. God, indeed, is for Herakleitos 'all things.'" This is not to say, however, that God is identified strictly (i.e., monistically) with "fire" or "earth" or the other elements, "or all of them put together." Rather, "his energy works, shows itself and hides in nature. He Himself is the Logos, the Wisdom, not so much 'at work' in nature but rather 'at play' there."[29]

And here Merton interjects a striking typological link between the Wisdom-child of Proverbs 8:27-31, "playing in the world" at all times, and the "fragmentary" wisdom of Herakleitos: "Time is a child playing draughts. The kingly power is a child's." Indeed, in the play of the Wisdom-child Merton finds a metaphor for Herakleitos's dual intuition that not only are all cosmic things "in a state of becoming and change" but also that in this "dance" of elements there is a "hidden harmony" that "keeps everything in balance in the midst of conflict and movement." True wisdom is not "polymathy," Merton notes, "the scientific research which observes and tabulates an almost infinite number of phenomena"; nor does wisdom consist in seizing upon "one of many conflicting principles, in order to elevate it above its opposite."[30] True wisdom grasps "the very movement itself, and penetrates to the logos or thought within that dynamic harmony."[31] Thus, says Herakleitos, "Wisdom is one thing—it is to know the thought by which all things are steered through all things," a fragment Merton juxtaposes with Wisdom 7:21-26: *For she is a vapour of the power of God, and a certain pure emanation of the glory of the*

28. Ibid., 76.
29. Ibid, 79.
30. Ibid., 80.
31. Ibid., 80–81.

almighty God: and therefore no defiled thing cometh into her. For she is the brightness of eternal light, and the unspotted mirror of God's majesty, and the image of his goodness.[32]

Pressing this cross-cultural exegesis by reminiscence[33] still further, Merton suggests a continuity of experience beneath the biblical *memoria* of Proverbs, Wisdom, and the Gospel of John and the "fragmentary intuitions" of Herakleitos: "Here in the inspired language of the sacred writer we find the Scriptural development which perfects and completes the fragmentary intuitions of Herakleitos, elevating them to the sublime level of contemplative theology and inserting them in the economy of those great truths of which Herakleitos could not have dreamt: the Incarnation of the Logos and man's Redemption and Divinization as the supreme manifestation of wisdom and of the 'attunement of conflicting opposites.'"[34]

What these ancient mystical texts share, suggests Merton, is a revelatory power to break through solipsism and "awaken the mind of [the] disciple to a reality that is right before his eyes" but which human wisdom by itself, whether turned in upon itself or seizing upon only one aspect of manifold reality, is incapable of seeing. "The heart of Herakleitean epistemology is an implicit contrast between man's wisdom, which fails to grasp the concrete reality of unity-in-multiplicity and harmony-in-conflict, but which instead seizes upon one or other of the conflicting elements and tries to build on this static and one-sided truth which cannot help but be an artificial fiction. The wisdom of man cannot follow the divine wisdom 'one and manifold.' . . . In order to 'see' our minds seize upon the movement around them and within them, and reduce it to immobility."[35] And here, says Merton, is the tragedy that most concerns Herakleitos: "the fact that the majority of men think they see, and do not. They believe they listen, but they do not hear. They are 'absent when present' because . . . they substitute the clichés of familiar prejudice for the new and unexpected truth that is being offered to them."[36]

Thus "the life and thought of 'the many' is a conspiracy of sleep, a refusal to struggle for the excellence of wisdom which is hard to find." The many allow themselves "to be deluded by 'polymathy'. . . the constant succession of novel 'truths,' new opinions . . . fresh observations and tabulations of phenomena," a multiplicity that "beguiles the popular mind with a vain appearance of wisdom." Herakleitos, "wielding the sharp weapon of paradox

---

32. Ibid., 81.

33. The phrase hearkens to Jean Leclercq's description of monastic (and rabbinical) exegesis as "largely an exegesis through reminiscence"; see chap. 3, n. 145.

34. Ibid., BT, 81–82.

35. Ibid., 82.

36. Ibid., 85.

without mercy," seeks to awaken the mind of his disciples—whether from "the sleep of individualism" or the "willfulness, blindness, and caprice" of the many—by interjecting the divine perspective, the truth of unity-in-multiplicity, the One fire that is *common to all*: Logos (Spirit, Sophia). "But each individual loses contact with the One Fire and falls back into the 'coldness' and moisture and 'sleep' of his little subjective world."[37]

Passing from epistemology to theological anthropology, we can begin to see why this essay is, as Christopher Nugent suggests, pivotal to Merton's emerging "philosophy of peace."[38] In the lead essay on Prometheus in *The Behavior of Titans*, Merton had poignantly asked, "[Why] do we imagine that our desire for life is a Promethean desire, doomed to punishment? Why do we act as if our longing to 'see good days' were something God did not desire, when He Himself told us to seek them?"[39] Herakleitian epistemology counters with the liberating realization of our own identity in God, breaking through Promethean despair and Olympian formalism. We do not have to steal fire from heaven; the divine fire, nothing less than our spiritual freedom, is already ours "for the asking, a gift of the true God, the Living God."[40] War, of course, is the bitter harvest of Prometheanism on a global scale, a centrifugal struggle against life spinning tragically around the poles of "heroism and despair." Whereas war shatters the inclusive reconciliation of opposites— "Dogs bark at everyone they do not know,"[41] says Herakleitos—the intuition of the One fire flames out to an awareness of divine presence in all persons and things. Hearken "not to me but to my Logos," says Herakleitos, "and confess that all things are one."[42] (Or, as Hopkins would put it: "for Christ plays in ten thousand places, / Lovely in limbs, and lovely in eyes not his / To the Father through the features of men's faces."[43])

There is nothing facile or sanguine, insists Merton, in Herakleitos's vision of unity-in-multiplicity. It reflects "a desert spirituality, a place of wide-open spaces, exodus from our captivity to the ego, self-emptying. Its goal is harmony, its way is friction."[44] It "demands effort, integrity, struggle, sacrifice. It

---

37. Ibid., 83–84.
38. Nugent, "*Pax Heraclitus*," 11.
39. BT, 22.
40. Ibid., 18.
41. Ibid., 104.
42. Ibid., 95.
43. From "*As kingfishers catch fire*," in *Gerard Manley Hopkins: The Major Works* (Oxford: Oxford University Press, 1986), 129.
44. Nugent, "*Pax Heraclitus*," 11. Nugent acknowledges the darker legacy of Herakleitos, whose fire "would warm the hearts of philosophers of will such as Friedrich Nietzsche or philosophers of war such as Heinrich von Treitsche." Yet Merton "was undaunted" by the moral ambivalence of the *Fragments*, notes Nugent; following the tradition of "Catholic 'recapitulation

is incompatible with the complacent security" most of us mistake for "peace." Indeed, the disarming wisdom of Herakleitos is not far, suggests Merton, perhaps much closer than we are, from the "spiritual and intellectual climate of the New Testament," where "the Word that enlightens every man coming into the world is made flesh, enters the darkness which receives Him not: where one must be born again without re-entering the womb; where the Spirit is as the wind, blowing where it pleases." Christ too spoke in enigmatic parables: "He came to cast fire on the earth. Was He perhaps akin to the Fire of which Herakleitos spoke?"[45]

We have passed into Christology, spirituality, and the anthropology of God. The "supreme manifestation of wisdom and of the 'attunement of conflicting opposites'" is realized not only by the incarnation, says Merton, but ultimately by our participation in it. It comes as no surprise that Merton closes the essay invoking Hopkins, who links "Heraklitean fire" with "the comfort of the Resurrection." Hopkin's concept of "inscape," notes Merton, is both "Heraklitean and Scotistic": "an intuition of the patterns and harmonies . . . impressed by life itself revealing the wisdom of the Living God in the mystery of interplaying movements and changes. '*Million fueled, nature's bonfire burns on*.'" And the "'*clearest-selved*' spark of the divine fire is man himself."[46]

In these lines the Christian poet is not merely "playing with words," insists Merton, and neither is Herakleitos, whose fragmentary wisdom reverberates in the same eschatological force field as New Testament texts that beckon us to cast off fear and complacency and to *live* in the light of Christ's resurrection: "Man kindles for himself a light in the night time when he has died but is alive . . . he that is awake lights up from sleeping."[47] To recall a central theme of chapter 3, poetry here becomes one with prophecy, giving voice to "the flowering of ordinary possibilities" hidden in everyday life, and harvesting "fruits of hope that have never been seen before." With these fruits, says Merton, "we shall calm the resentments and the rage of man."[48]

Multiformis Sapientia: *Maximus Confessor*

> The love of Christ hides itself mysteriously in the inner logoi of created things.[49]

---

of the classics that goes back to Irenaeus," he "had to contain the fire, not douse it: to render it 'Brother Fire'" (ibid., 2–3).

45. Ibid., BT, 91.

46. Ibid., 92.

47. Ibid., 103, citing Herakleitos; cf. Eph 5:14: "Sleeper, awake! Rise from the dead, and Christ will shine on you."

48. RU, 160.

49. Maximus Confessor, cited in ICM, 124.

We turn now to what is clearly one of the most important conversations of Merton's last decade, his immersion in the mystical theology of Maximus Confessor (d. 662). In particular, Maximus's exposition of *theoria physike*, or "natural contemplation," would prove pivotal in centering Merton's theological imagination in this period of intense creativity and outreach at the turn of the 1960s. Our best evidence for the influence, despite their schematic form, are Merton's lecture notes for a course titled "An Introduction to Christian Mysticism," given in the spring of 1961 to young monks at Gethsemani. In the eighth of these lectures, "Contemplation of the Cosmos," Merton explores Maximus's doctrine of the divine *logoi* hidden in all things.[50] These are, as Patrick O'Connell observes, "among the most evocative and fully realized sections" of the conferences, and "not surprisingly the section that has attracted the most attention from scholars."[51] It is also important to keep in mind their chronological proximity to *The Behavior of Titans*, *The New Man*, *New Seeds of Contemplation*, and Merton's intensive study of the Russian theologians.

In the first lecture Merton had identified his principal sources, a "who's who" of theologians from East to West: Jean Danielou, Hans Urs von Balthasar, Vladimir Lossky, John Meyendorff, and Paul Evdokimov, adding that recent studies by the latter two promise "a very rich flowering" in the fields of Byzantine mysticism and the Greek fathers."[52] It was here that Merton offered his vital description of tradition as "a collective memory and experience of Christ" that "forms and affects the whole man."[53] In the eighth lecture, Merton draws from von Balthasar's seminal study, *The Cosmic Liturgy*, to introduce Maximus as "the Father of Byzantine mysticism" and "one of the greatest of the Greek Fathers"; Maximus both "corrected" and "went beyond" the "deviations of Origenism," especially "the Origenist idea that the world is in itself imperfect, being made up of fallen spiritual realities."[54] He did so above all through his teaching of *theoria physike*, the "mysterious, silent revelation of God in His cosmos and in the *oikonomia*, as well as in our own lives."[55]

More expansively, Merton defines *theoria physike* as the *multiformis sapientia* (multiform wisdom) that apprehends the wisdom and glory of God

---

50. ICM, 121–36.

51. Patrick O'Connell, "Introduction," in ICM, xxx; A. M. Allchin offers wonderful commentary on Merton's exposition of *theoria physike* in "'The Prayer of the Heart and Natural Contemplation," in MHPH, 419–29; and "The Worship of the Whole Creation," in MHPH, 103–20.

52. ICM, 34.

53. Ibid., 35–36.

54. Ibid., 123–24.

55. Ibid., 124.

1. in the spirit of Scripture and not in the letter;
2. in the *logoi* of created things, not in their materiality;
3. in our own inmost spirit and true self, rather than in our ego;
4. in the inner meaning of history and not in its externals (history of salvation, victory of Christ);
5. in the inner sense of the divine judgments and mercies (not in superstitious and pseudo-apocalyptic interpretations of events).[56]

That *theoria physike* includes an apprehension of the spiritual sense of Scripture is significant, as we saw in chapter 3. But Merton's focus here is above all on the natural world as an epiphany of divine presence. He cites Maximus: "We must not believe that sin caused this unique masterpiece which is this visible world in which God manifests Himself by a *silent revelation*."[57] There follows several extraordinary paragraphs in which Merton describes the crucial role played by human beings, through *theoria physike*, "in the spiritualization and restoration of the cosmos."[58] Just beneath the surface one can discern Bulgakov's theme of divine Wisdom, as well as Berdyaev's accent on grace working through human freedom and creativity in history. These several paragraphs take us to the very heart of Merton's mature religious imagination:

> The vision of *theoria physike* is essentially *sophianic*. Man by *theoria* is able to unite the hidden wisdom of God in things with the hidden light of wisdom in himself. The meeting and marriage of these two brings about a *resplendent clarity* within man himself, and this clarity is the Divine Wisdom fully recognized and active in him. Thus man becomes a mirror of the divine glory, and is resplendent with divine truth not only in his *mind* but in his *life*. He is filled with the light of wisdom which shines forth in him, and thus God is glorified in him.
>
> At the same time he exercises a spiritualizing influence in the world by the work of his hands which is in accord with *the creative wisdom of God* in things and in history. Hence we can see the great importance of a sophianic, contemplative orientation of man's life. No longer are we reduced to a *purely negative* attitude toward the world around us, toward history, toward the judgments of God. The world is no longer seen as merely material, hence as an obstacle that has to be grudgingly put up with. It is spiritual through and through. But grace has to work in and through us to enable us to carry out this real transformation. . . .

56. Ibid., 122.
57. Ibid., 123.
58. Ibid., 125.

The "will of God" is no longer a blind force plunging through our lives like a cosmic steamroller and demanding to be accepted willy-nilly. On the contrary, we are able to *understand* the hidden purposes of the creative wisdom and the divine mercy of God, and can cooperate with Him as sons with a loving Father. Not only that, but God Himself.[59]

In these lines we see, as O'Connell points out, why *theoria physike* is for Merton "the heart of a genuine theology of creativity,"[60] for God "hands over to man, when he is thus purified and enlightened, a certain creative initiative of his own, in political life, in art, in spiritual life, in worship: man is then endowed with a *causality* of his own"[61]; "*theoria physike* is actually a dynamic unity of contemplation and action, a loving knowledge that comes along with *use* and *work.*"[62] Merton offers examples of work attuned to the *logoi* of things, including Shaker furniture and handicrafts, even a fascinating riff on the logos of a Shaker barn, "which always fits right into its location," the logos "of the place where it is built, [which] grasps and expresses the hidden *logos* of the valley, or hillside, which forms its site."[63] The essential point here is that the apprehension of the *logoi* of things is never abstract but attends to the concrete nature (inscape) of things in relation to the whole.[64]

By constrast, the absence of this sophianic grasp of the material world tends toward a purely instrumental and exploitative relationship with nature, "a demonic cult of change and 'exchange'—consumption, production, destruction, for their own sakes."[65] This is why contemplation, as O'Connell observes, "is of tremendous practical importance in a world increasingly tempted by a 'demonic pseudo-contemplation, [a] mystique of technics and production'"[66]; indeed, it "is demanded by the cosmos itself and by history."[67] In honoring the *logoi* of all living and nonliving things, we become "conscious of their mute appeal to us to find and rescue the glory of God that has been

---

59. Ibid., 125–26. As Allchin notes of this material, Merton suddenly seems to be speaking quite personally, "partly out of his experience of prayer, partly out of his experience as a writer" (MHPH, 425).

60. ICM, xxxii.

61. Ibid., 126.

62. Ibid., 129.

63. Ibid., 133–34.

64. Thus Merton's judgment that Maximus, in his appreciation for the concrete and manifold diversity of things, "unites Plato and Aristotle, within the Christian framework," offering "the broadest and most balanced view of the Christian cosmos of all the Greek Fathers" (ibid., 124).

65. Ibid., 130.

66. Ibid., xxxii, citing Merton, ibid., 130.

67. Ibid., 125.

hidden in them and veiled by sin."[68] In lines reminiscent of Herakleitos, Merton goes on to explain how *theoria physike* grasps the logos or divine "fire" not only in nature but in human beings, and thus comprises a way of seeing central to any integral spirituality (and theology) of reconciliation and peace:

> The *logos* of a man is therefore something hidden in him, spiritual, simple, profound, unitive, loving, selfless, self-forgetting, oriented to love and to unity with God and other men in Christ. It is not an abstract essence, "rationality plus animality." [It is] the divine image in him. More deeply it is CHRIST in him, either actually or potentially. To love Christ in our brother we must be able to SEE Him in our brother, and this demands really the gift of *theoria physike*. Christ in us must be liberated, by purification, so that the "image" in us, clothed anew with light of the divine likeness, is able connaturally to recognize the same likeness in another, the same tendency to love, to simplicity, to unity. Without love this is completely impossible.[69]

Note how the apprehension of Christ in the other—never as "abstract essence," not merely symbolically but sacramentally, more than literally—depends first on the liberation of the image of Christ in ourselves. This is what Cassian, following the Beatitudes, calls "purity of heart" and "poverty of spirit": the clearing of mind and body of attachments and temptations through prayer, simplicity, solitude, asceticism. Purity of heart is none other than the cultivation of humility and love, crucial for the attunement of the spiritual senses.[70] "When a man has been purified and humbled," says Merton, "when his eye is single, and he is his own real self, then the *logoi* of things jump out at him spontaneously."[71] In this way *theoria physike* engenders "a sense of *community with things in the work of salvation*."[72] Again, there is no magic implied here: "Without love," Merton notes, "this is completely impossible."[73]

Summing up Maximus, Merton points to Scripture as the *fontal locus* and imaginative seedbed, as it were, of *theoria physike*: "it must be quite clear that the spiritual sense of Scripture . . . is something much more than mere allegory. . . . [It] is a direct contact with the Word hidden in the words of

68. Ibid., 130.
69. Ibid., 128.
70. "Mysticism and asceticism form an organic whole. . . . Asceticism leads normally to mystical life; at least it disposes for it, though of course the mystical life, its normal fulfillment, remains a pure gift of God" (ibid., 22).
71. Ibid., 132.
72. Ibid., 131.
73. Ibid., 128.

Scripture."[74] In contrast to a strictly scientific, technological, or materialist approach to nature, which excludes consideration of the *logoi* of things as an obstacle to their use and manipulation, the words of Scripture train our spiritual senses to "enter into the movement of all things from God back to God." Here Merton cites von Balthasar's vivid imagery: "The whole world is a GAME OF GOD. As one amuses children with flowers and bright colored clothes and then gets them later used to more serious games, literary studies, so God raises us up first of all by the great game of nature, then by the Scriptures [with their poetic symbols]. Beyond the symbols of Scripture is the Word."[75]

We are back, it would seem, to the divine Wisdom-child, Sophia, playing before the Lord at all times. Indeed, in these passages we are seeing much more than simply an excursus on the teaching of Maximus. Here we discover Merton discovering in Maximus the golden thread for bringing together many converging lines of thought into a single mosaic (or iconic) picture. Scripturally and metaphysically, existentially and theologically, something here is *breaking through*. Why is the vision of *theoria physike* "essentially *sophianic*"? Bound up closely with Hebrew creation texts, the Wisdom tradition running through both testaments (e.g., John 1:1-18; 1 Cor 1:24; Col 1:15-20) intimates that the living heart of the universe is not a "what," as in the impersonal fire, but rather a "Who," in whom all things are created, sustained, redeemed: YHWH, Wisdom, Word, Spirit, Christ, Sophia.

Whoever Sophia is at this point in Merton's theological imagination, there can be no doubt that her subsequent remembrance in his writings is bound to Christianity's communal memory and experience of Jesus Christ. But surely her dawning presence in his consciousness also reflects his desire to make old things new, to reinvigorate a biblical and poetic vision of life "in which the individual is not lost in the cosmos and in society but found in them."[76] Like Heschel, Merton sought to awaken the experience of God in a people for whom, like "a tree torn from the soil" or "a river separated from its source,"[77] the term "God," and perhaps even "Christ," had become a name, but no reality. For both men, the revelatory symbols of the Bible

74. Ibid., 130.

75. Ibid., 131–32. In a significant aside, Merton praises Teilhard de Chardin for his "noble striving to recover a view of the scientific world, the cosmos of the physicist, the geologist, the engineer, with interest centered on the *logos* of creation, and on value, spirit, an effort to reconvert the scientific view of the cosmos into a wisdom, without sacrificing anything of scientific objectivity or technological utility" (ibid., 130–31).

76. GNV, 1.

77. Abraham Joshua Heschel, *Man's Quest for God: Studies in Prayer and Symbolism* (New York: Scribner's, 1954), xii.

remain our "bread in the wilderness," a "forgotten mother tongue," calling us out of exile to remind us who God is, and who we are in God, from the very beginning.

Defending the Person in the "Reign of Numbers": Boris Pasternak

> [His] protest is . . . the protest of life itself, of humanity itself, of love, speaking not with theories and programs but simply affirming itself and asking to be judged on its own merits.[78]

We turn now to a conversation inaugurated by Merton in 1958 and which corresponds closely, both chronologically and in substance, with his study of the Russian theologians. Indeed, the private journals between 1957 and 1961 afford a fascinating glimpse into Merton's immersion in the world of Russian literature, history, and theology. In his exuberance for this new world of thought, Merton proclaims in his first letter to Boris Pasternak, rather typically, that he intends "to begin learning Russian"[79] so that he can read the author's work in the original. Simmering beneath their subsequent exchanges, of course, is the Cold War, rendering all the more remarkable this dialogue between a famous American monk and the Russian writer, who was by now an international symbol of artistic courage behind the Iron Curtain.

In May of 1958, Merton notes in his journal that he "thought several times of writing to Pasternak" but then dismissed the idea: "How absurd—as if I could contemplate the writing of such a letter."[80] Two weeks later, there is a statement flush with irony, given the years to come: "The more I read about Russia the more I think it is better to be silent about what goes on in the world and not mix oneself up in it."[81] In early August, when the abbot "announced with relish that the U.S. Army now has a sputnik flying over Russia," Merton notes that he "felt like vomiting."[82] And then, on August 14, 1958, the tenor suddenly changes: "There are things I will not know about my faith and about my vocation if I fail to understand Communism. This I have to do for myself and for others as well. It is part of my solitude which, as a matter of fact, is now very real."[83] Merton sent his first letter to Pasternak on August 22, 1958.

There comes a passage in late September that makes no direct mention of Pasternak but nonetheless speaks vividly to Merton's increasing bewilder-

---

78. Thomas Merton, "The Pasternak Affair," in DQ, 3–67, at 11.
79. CT, 88.
80. SFS, 204.
81. Ibid., 205.
82. Ibid., 211.
83. Ibid., 212.

ment with Cold War America, a society by no means innocent of its own pressures toward mass conformism, militarism, and increasing alienation from the natural world:

> Last time I was in town—we had to drop something at the G. E. plant— Appliance Park. We came at the enormous place from the wrong side and had to drive miles all around it. Surrounded by open fields with nothing whatever in them, not even thistles, marked "Property of General Electric. No Trespassing." The buildings are huge and go on forever and ever, out in the midst of their own wilderness. Stopped by guards, we signed in at the appropriate gate and promptly got lost in the maze of empty streets between the buildings, finally came out right. What struck me most was the immense seriousness of the place—as if at last I had found what America takes seriously. Not churches, not libraries. Not even movies, but THIS! This is it. The manufacture of refrigerators, of washing machines, of tape recorders, of light fixtures. This is the real thing. This is America. It is for this, then, that we are to fight Red China over Quemoy? I am afraid I lack faith. I don't like it. I do not find it in myself to lay down my life for General Electric or anything it represents.[84]

After receiving two warm letters of gratitude from Pasternak in response to the first letter, Merton writes again on October 23: "It has given me much food for thought, this bare fact of the communication between us: at a time when our two countries are unable to communicate with one another seriously and sincerely, but spend millions communicating with the moon . . . No, the great business of our time is this: for one man to find himself in another one who is on the other side of the world. Only by such contacts can there be peace, can the sacredness of life be preserved and developed and the image of God manifest itself in the world."[85] Merton had just finished *Dr. Zhivago*, the book for which Pasternak had been awarded the Nobel Prize, only to relinquish the honor under political pressure and the fear of exile. "The book is a world in itself," Merton professes to the author, "a sophiological world, a paradise and a hell, in which the great mystical figures of Yurii and Lara stand out as Adam and Eve and though they walk in darkness walk with their hand in the hand of God. The earth they walk is sacred because of them." Reflecting further, he asks, "Am I right in surmising that the ideas in this book run closely parallel to those in Soloviev's *Meaning of Love*? There is a great similarity."

---

84. Ibid., 218–19; cf. CGB, 195–96 on the "seriousness" of American society.
85. This and subsequent citations are from the letter in CT, 89–90.

And then he offers Pasternak a striking confession: "Shall I perhaps tell you how I know Lara, where I have met her?" Merton relates his dream in which

> a very young Jewish girl . . . embraced me so that I was moved to the depths of my soul. I learned that her name was "Proverb," which I thought very simple and beautiful. And also I thought: "She is of the race of Saint Anne." I spoke to her of her name, and she did not seem to be proud of it, because it seemed that the other young girls mocked her for it. But I told her that it was a very beautiful name, and there the dream ended. A few days later I happened to be in a nearby city, which is very rare for us. I was walking alone in the crowded street and suddenly saw that everybody was Proverb and that in all of them shone her extraordinary beauty and purity and shyness, even though they did not know who they were and were perhaps ashamed of their names—because they were mocked on account of them. And they did not know their real identity as the Child so dear to God who, from before the beginning, was playing in His sight all days, playing in the world.

What is behind these confessions? It seems Pasternak had released in Merton a new appreciation for the role that poetry and literature might play in advancing an integral Christian humanism: first, humanism as a celebration of life in its "barest and most elementary essentials"[86]; second, as an "intense awareness of all cosmic and human reality as 'life in Christ,' and the consequent plunge into love as the only dynamic and creative force which really honors this 'Life' by creating itself anew in [Christ's] image"[87]; and third, as a form of resistance and protest in an age of mass propaganda, depersonalization, and violence. It was a vision Pasternak shared, not incidentally, with his fellow countrymen Soloviev and Bulgakov, and which Merton himself would soon embrace, with extraordinary results.

In his important study of 1959, "The Pasternak Affair," Merton highlights a climactic passage from *Dr. Zhivago*: With the coming of Christ "the reign of numbers was at an end. . . . *Individual human life became the life story of God and its contents filled the vast expanses of the universe.*"[88] Because of the incarnation and resurrection, human beings no longer "die in a ditch like a dog" but are "at home in history, while the work toward the conquest of death is in full swing"; we live and die "sharing in this work."[89] Against the ascen-

---

86. DQ, 12.
87. Ibid.
88. Cited in ibid., 66–67. Pasternak's image of "the reign of numbers" stays with Merton, and is an implicit, sometimes explicit, subtext in his critique of mass society in many of his prophetic social essays.
89. Cited in ibid., 66.

dancy of grand abstractions, ideas, and systems, Merton praises Pasternak as a "prophet of the original, cosmic revelation: one who sees symbols and figures of the inward, spiritual world, working themselves out in the mystery of the universe around him and above all in the history of men. Not so much in the formal, and illusory, history of states and empires that is written down in books, but in the living, transcendental and mysterious history of individual human beings and in the indescribable interweaving of their destinies."[90]

The Fourth and Walnut experience was precisely this for Merton—an epiphany of human life as "the life story of God," ordinary persons going about their daily business in the crossroads of the secular city, each of them Christ, Sophia, "the Child so dear to God" from "before the beginning," each of their stories filling "the vast expanses of the universe." The key to this life story of God, reaching back to Soloviev, is love, "the highest expression of man's spirituality and freedom."[91] Love, Merton writes, echoing Russian literature from Pasternak to Dostoyevsky, "is the work not of states, not of organizations, not of institutions, but of persons."[92]

What must finally be emphasized here is Merton's attention to the way Pasternak uses language itself—its inner *musicality*, to recall Heschel—as a powerful force for raising human beings up to love and life in God. It is a dimension of speech by no means foreign to the Bible, least of all to Jesus, the prophet and storyteller from Nazareth, as Pasternak here confesses:

> What has for centuries raised man above the beast is not the cudgel but an inward music; the irresistible power of unarmed truth, the powerful attraction of its example. It has always been assumed that the most important things in the Gospels are the ethical maxims and commandments. But for me the most important thing is that Christ speaks in parables taken from life, that He explains the truth in terms of everyday reality. The idea that underlies this is that communion between mortals is immortal, and that the whole of life is symbolic because it is meaningful.[93]

Just as the "inward music" of the gospels can spark an immortal "communion between mortals," so does Pasternak awaken in Merton a new appreciation for the power of language to reclaim the sanctity of the human

---

90. Ibid., 18–19. "[W]hether he knows it or not, [Pasternak] is plunged fully into midstream of the lost tradition of 'natural contemplation' which flowed among the Greek Fathers after it had been set in motion by Origen. Of course the tradition has not been altogether lost, and Pasternak has come upon it in the Orthodox Church" (ibid., 17).

91. Ibid., 49.

92. Ibid., 65.

93. Cited in ibid., 16–17.

person. "Over against the technological jargon and the empty scientism of modern man, Pasternak sets creative symbolism, the power of imagination and of intuition, the glory of liturgy and the fire of contemplation. But he does so in new words, in a new way,"[94] a way that is "very simple, very rudimentary, deeply sincere, utterly personal,"[95] and humble. "In the face of our own almost hopeless alienation," Pasternak is proof that the poet can help us "get back to ourselves before it is too late."[96] In him, poetry becomes one with prophecy.

In contrast to the Soviet ideologist or the capitalist peddler of the American dream, for whom language "is simply a mine of terms and formulas which can be pragmatically exploited,"[97] Pasternak's poet Yurii "felt that the main part of the work was being done not by him but by a superior power that was above him and directed him. . . . And he felt himself to be only the occasion, the fulcrum, needed to make this movement possible."[98] This reverence for the practice of language as a "home and receptacle" for grace is "the very key to Pasternak's 'religious philosophy,'"[99] Merton writes, but surely, it is also the key to his own. Indeed, Merton here makes explicit his conviction that language, when writer and reader are so attuned, opens onto the deepest structure of reality, who is Love, Christ, Sophia. In praising Pasternak's ability to be a "fulcrum" between God and the world, Merton also celebrates, for us, his own:

> When in the moment of inspiration the poet's creative intelligence is married with the inborn wisdom of human language (the Word of God and Human Nature—Divinity and Sophia) then in the very flow of new and individual intuitions, the poet utters the voice of that wonderful and mysterious world of God-manhood—it is the transfigured, spiritualized and divinized cosmos that speaks through him, and through him utters its praise of the Creator.[100]

The Irruption of Sophia: 1957–61

By the late 1950s Merton's outlook had certainly come a long way from *The Seven Storey Mountain*, which was sharply dualist and triumphal in tone.

94. Ibid., 31.
95. Ibid., 30.
96. LE, 340.
97. DQ, 20.
98. Cited in ibid., 21.
99. Ibid., 21.
100. Ibid., 20–21; cf. CGB, 11, on wisdom as the attunement of "the divine and cosmic music" within us.

But something else was clearly breaking through into Merton's consciousness in these years and beginning to "burst out" in his theology. One has only to read the journals from 1957 through 1961 to be struck by the frequency and poignancy with which the Wisdom-figure of the Hebrew Scriptures began to haunt Merton's religious imagination, thanks largely to his close study of Russian Orthodox sophiology. Picking up on the brief overview in chapter 1, we turn now to a more detailed examination of the irruption of Sophia into Merton's theological consciousness.

We have already noted the earliest mention of the Russians in the journal of April 25, 1957, where Merton describes Bulgakov and Berdyaev as "writers of great, great attention" who have "dared to accept the challenge of the sapiential books, the challenge of the image of Proverbs where Wisdom is 'playing in the world' before the face of the creator."[101] Already Merton recognizes in sophiology not merely a speculative theology but a bold theological anthropology, a view of human life, history, and culture as bound together in the "life story of God":

> Most important of all—man's creative vocation to prepare, consciously, the ultimate triumph of Divine Wisdom. Man, the microcosm, the heart of the universe, is . . . called to bring about the fusion of cosmic and historic process in the final invocation of God's wisdom and love. In the name of Christ and by his power, man has a work to accomplish. . . . Our life is a powerful Pentecost in which the Holy Spirit, ever active in us, seeks to reach through our inspired hands and tongues into the very heart of the material world created to be spiritualized through the work of the Church, the mystical Body of the Incarnate Word of God.[102]

Three days later, Merton considers the more controversial aspects of Berdyaev's work, criticizing him for rejecting "the Gospel as incomplete and patristic theology as sterile. In wanting to free himself from limitations he fell into narrower limits."[103] Merton further rejects Berdyaev's implication that the Holy Spirit is given (in the present age) to "supplant" the Scriptures, and further, his language of a future "anthropological" revelation "which perfects the Gospel." What Berdyaev is "trying to say" with such ideas, Merton notes, "has been said better in the N. T. itself—by Colossians, Ephesians, etc." And then, rather suddenly, he interjects the important confession cited in chapter 1: "If I can unite in myself, in my own spiritual life, the thought of the East and the West of the Greek and Latin Fathers, I will create in myself a reunion of

---

101. SFS, 85–86.
102. Ibid., 86.
103. Ibid.

the divided Church. . . . We must contain both in ourselves and transcend both in Christ."[104] We should not overlook, however, what follows just after this passage, thoughts that also represent a kind of personal creed, but now with respect to the development of doctrine:

> Against those who rejoice in every dogmatic definition as a *new limita-*
> *tion* which *restricts* the meaning of such and such a dogma to *what is*
> *contained in this formula* [and] nothing more. Who desire to have more
> and more formulas, more and more limitations, so that in the end every-
> thing is narrowed down to a minimum of meaning which must be held.
> On the contrary, dogmatic definitions set limits beyond which error
> cannot pass, but does not set limits to truth, in the sense of forbidding
> a dogma to mean *more* than is envisioned in a given formula.[105]

Inspired by the creativity of the Russians, Merton here seeks after his own formulation of the correct balance between the conservative and creative dynamics of theology. On the one hand, he resists Berdyaev's "ethic of cre-ativity" as a "temptation" insofar as it seems to give the theologian license for overlooking the revolutionary message already present in the New Tes-tament and in patristic theology.[106] On the other hand, Merton rejects any view of revelation that would simply retrieve dogmatic definitions of the past as definitive and final statements. The mystery of God always exceeds what can be expressed in the Scriptures or in any particular formulation; the sources of the tradition, in other words, are not end points but medita-tive starting points for preaching and theological reflection in the present historical moment.[107]

Above all, what appeals to Merton in these early encounters with Berdyaev and Bulgakov is their celebration of human history as a "powerful Pentecost," an ever-possible marriage of human and Divine Wisdom: "In their pages . . . shines the light of the resurrection and theirs is a theology of triumph."[108] In this respect, Merton concludes that Berdyaev has "profound insights into the real meaning of Christianity—insights which we cannot simply ignore."[109] His is a bold theology of Christ and humanity, "the New Adam, the new

---

104. Ibid., 87.

105. Ibid.

106. See SFS, 288, a fascinating passage (June 8, 1959) where Merton wrestles with the implications of Berdyaev's distinction between "ethics of law" and "ethics of creativeness" not only for theology and spirituality but also in light of his personal struggle with community life at Gethsemani.

107. The general principle is taught by Vatican II's *Dei verbum* 5, 10; *Gaudium et spes* 44.

108. SFS, 86.

109. Ibid., 88.

creation," bound together in God. It is "good news" about human being, a revolutionary truth that hinges on the radical meaning of incarnation and its elemental empowerment of human freedom:

> By union with God in [Christ] God does not remain in heaven, a dictator and overseer. He becomes man in order that the creation should continue in God's manhood. . . . The creation in 7 days of the O. T. must come out into the 8th day of the New Adam, the new creation, in which God and man together continue the work done by the Father. . . . It is in the Holy Spirit that man lives up to his true vocation as a Son of God and creator (contrary to what [Berdyaev] says, this is the very heart of the New Testament if by creativity we mean the *power of charity* as a Source of life . . .). Reading such things one is struck with compunction. Look at us! What are we doing? What have I done?[110]

The power of charity as a Source of life—this is the "New Law" that reverberates from within "the very heart" of the New Testament, just as he finds it breaking through in the cosmic vision of Maximus Confessor. But it is also significant that Merton here begins to discern critical differences between Berdyaev and Bulgakov. Where Berdyaev errs in Merton's estimation by too quickly abandoning the foundational sources as incomplete, Bulgakov, by contrast, follows a surer path by taking the New Testament and patristic sources as incontrovertible starting points for his dogmatic theology. In other words, in Bulgakov's sophiology Merton discerns a trustworthy development of New Testament theology, patristic Christology, and especially of Maximus's mystical theology (recall: "The vision of *theoria physike* is essentially *sophianic*").

Even more, what Merton finds utterly new in Bulgakov is his willingness, following Soloviev, to reach deeply into the biblical (Jewish) sources of Christology to retrieve (excavate, remember) the feminine Wisdom-figure of Proverbs 8 and other Wisdom texts in his exposition of dogmatic theology. Bulgakov has dared to make explicit and expand on that which has remained largely implicit in the Wisdom Christology of the New Testament and the patristic period. How exactly Bulgakov renders this retrieval and development, and whether he does so in an orthodox way, will take Merton some time to consider, as the journals of late July and August 1957 bear out. In any case, after the initial passage on Berdyaev, it is Bulgakov's sophiology that captures Merton's attention.

Naturally enough, his early questions pertain to the identity of Sophia in relation to the one essence (*ousia*) of God and the three Persons (*prosopon*)

110. Ibid., 89.

of the Trinity: "Bulgakov's explanation of his sophianology seems to me clear and satisfactory. The divine nature is distinct from the 3 Divine Persons, but is not therefore a 4th principle superadded to make a 'quaternity.' No one imagines that it does. When the same nature is regarded as 'Sophia'—why should that constitute a 4th person?" Merton's comment that "no one imagines" Sophia to be a fourth hypostasis is curiously inaccurate, since this is precisely one of the key (mis)readings that led to the Orthodox accusation of heresy against Bulgakov. For his own part, Merton recognizes correctly that Sophia refers not to a Person so much as the divine nature, the Love between Persons, which in turn constitutes "the 'world' which they themselves are." Merton cites Bulgakov: "The divine nature is not only the dynamism of life but its content. . . . The life of God is this total positive unity and this total unity is the nature of God." And here, notably, he draws parallels with Western mysticism: "This would seem to throw light on Ruysbroeck, Tauler, etc. '*Grund*' [ground], '*Geburt*' [birth], '*Wesen*' [essence] names of God."[111] Near the end of this long and somewhat tortured passage, it is significant that Merton highlights the centrality of love in Bulgakov's sophiological vision.

In the following days Merton continues to cite from Bulgakov's *The Wisdom of God*, drawing nearer to its roots in Soloviev's doctrine of God-manhood, or the humanity of God. Two citations (July 31 and August 2, 1957) are of particular importance:

> Within ourselves humanity is so close that one can seek to discover and will discover that "God is all in all" . . . Divine Wisdom, the ground source of all ideas, is the eternal humanity in God—the divine prototype and foundation of the being of man. . . .
>
> Sophia is the Wisdom of God, the glory of God is humanity in God, the "theanthropy," body of God, the divine world which was in God at creation. It is there that one finds the sufficient reason of creation . . . the foundation of Wisdomness.[112]

In these lines we find a certain ambiguity—perhaps a fruitful ambiguity—with respect to the relation of Sophia to Christ, or Christology as such. On the one hand, Bulgakov identifies Sophia directly with the Logos, the Second Person of the Trinity: she is "the eternal humanity in God," the "divine prototype" of humanity. On the other hand, Bulgakov identifies Sophia with God's *ousia*, the divine nature: she is Love, the "ground source of all ideas," the "body of God"; still further, Sophia is the "divine world which was in God at creation."

111. Ibid., 101.
112. Ibid., 104–5.

Notwithstanding his difficulty in sorting out these metaphysical distinctions, Merton has no difficulty in grasping the exalted anthropology at play here, and its implications for a spirituality of divinization, or *theosis*. "Man's vocation is to *humanize* and *clarify* perfectly the potential 'human' Sophia of creation which is entrusted to him. To make God shine in its charity."[113] This cosmotheandric vision—that is, the marriage of cosmology and anthropology in a spirituality of divinization—seems to finally come together for Merton in a journal passage of August 7, 1957:

> I think this morning I found the key to Bulgakov's Sophianism. His idea is that the Divine Sophia, play, wisdom, is by no means a fourth person or hypostasis, yet in *creation* spiritualized by the church, it is, as it were, hypostasized, so that creation itself becomes the "Glory of God." Man has frustrated this to some extent—"created Sophia" is "fallen" with man. . . . Yet man remains the one who, in Christ, will raise up and spiritualize creation so that all will be "Sophia" and true glory of God. For this man must be himself perfectly united and subjected to the wisdom of God.[114]

To *"unite"* and *"subject"* ourselves to the wisdom of God—in these lines we discover the theological subtext beneath Merton's homage to Pasternak, just as they anticipate Sophia's irruption into his own consciousness in the years to follow.

First, there is his hauntingly intimate dream of "Proverb" (February 28, 1958), the young Jewish girl who "clings to me and will not let go." After waking from the dream, he comments, not a little sardonically, "I rationalize it complacently." Yet a week later, he addresses her a "love letter" of surprising intimacy and devotion:

> How grateful I am to you for loving in me something which I thought I had entirely lost, and someone who, I thought, I had long ago ceased to be. . . . I must be careful what I say, for words cannot explain my love for you, and I do not wish, by my words, to harm that which in you is more real and more pure than in anyone else in the world—your lovely spontaneity, your simplicity, the generosity of your love. . . . In your marvelous, innocent, love you are utterly alone: yet you have given your love to me, why I cannot imagine. . . . Dearest Proverb, I love your name, its mystery, its simplicity and its secret, which even you yourself seem not to appreciate.[115]

---

113. Ibid., 106.
114. Ibid., 107.
115. Ibid., 176.

To be loved in such a way by one, it would seem, had broken open Merton's capacity to love the many. Two weeks later (March 18, 1958), Proverb comes to him "in Louisville, at the corner of 4th and Walnut." It was "As if waking from a dream—the dream of my separateness, of the 'special' vocation to be different."[116] As he later recasts the account in *Conjectures of a Guilty Bystander*, Merton is "suddenly overwhelmed with the realization that I loved all those people, even though we were total strangers."[117] Proverb, it seems, had reclaimed in Merton an innocence that he thought he "had entirely lost," awakening in him a new capacity to "see" and embrace that which remains pure in every person: *le point vierge*, that "point or spark which belongs entirely to God," which shines "like a pure diamond, blazing with the invisible light of heaven." The divine perspective had broken through, and it seemed to him "like news that one holds the winning ticket in a cosmic sweepstake."[118]

In the original journal account Merton reflects on his feelings for the women he sees in light of his vow of chastity: "It is as though by chastity I had come to be married to what is most pure in all the women of the world . . . each one secret and good and lovely in the sight of God and to taste and sense the secret beauty of their girl's hearts as they walked in the sunlight." At the same time, Merton judges that "no special question arises" because of his vow. "I am keenly conscious, not of their beauty . . . but of their humanity, their woman-ness. . . . For the woman-ness that is in each of them is at once original and inexhaustibly fruitful bringing the image of God into the world. In this each one is Wisdom and Sophia and Our Lady—(my delights are to be with the children of men!)."[119]

Taking the two Fourth and Walnut passages as a whole—that is, the original journal entry and the substantially revised version in *Conjectures*—and especially in view of neighboring journal passages, the central theme of Merton's realization at Fourth and Walnut is the "secret beauty" and "innocence" not only of the women passing by but of *all persons*, of human beings as such. If any one moment can mark the birth of Merton's far-reaching Christian humanism, surely this is it: "Thank God! Thank God! I am only another member of the human race, like all the rest of them."[120] Indeed, this overwhelming

---

116. Ibid., 181–82.
117. CGB, 156.
118. Ibid., 158.
119. SFS, 182.
120. Ibid., 183. Jonathan Montaldo characterizes "Fourth and Walnut" as "a significant literary event in Merton's writing" but is "dissuaded from regarding it as an historical 'epiphany' or 'revelation.' It is a literary event with literary antecedents." This opinion, he is careful to add, "does not diminish 'Fourth & Walnut's' power or importance in the history of Merton's

sense of the epiphany of God in humanity is borne out further in the original passage, where Merton comments on a "marvelous book" he picked up "for a few pennies" in Louisville, a book called *The Family of Man*:

> All those fabulous pictures. And again, no refinements and no explana-
> tions are necessary! How scandalized some men would be if I said that
> the whole book is to me a picture of Christ and yet that is the Truth.
> There, there is Christ in my own Kind, my own Kind—"Kind" which
> means "likeness" and which means "love" and which means "child." . . .
> [There] is only the great secret between us that we are all one Kind and
> what matters is not what this or that one has committed in his heart,
> separate from the others, but the love that brings him back to all the
> others in one Christ. . . . It is the divine Power and the divine Joy—
> and God is seen and reveals himself as man . . . and there is no other
> hope of finding wisdom than in God-manhood: our own manhood
> transformed in God![121]

If the Proverb dream is the prelude to Fourth and Walnut, this passage is its critical coda, linking Sophia (Soloviev's "God-manhood," the feminine "child" of the Bible) explicitly to the "one Christ" who "sleeps" in the secret innocence of human beings always and everywhere. "If only they could all see themselves as they really *are*. If only we could see each other that way all the time."[122]

One month after the Louisville experience, Merton's poignant reaction to still another book, John Collier's *The Indians of the Americas*, sets the pro-phetic (and self-indicting) tone for the decade to follow: "Have we ever yet become Christians? The duty of the Christian [is] to see Christ being born into the whole world and to bring Him to life in all mankind. But we have sought to bring to birth in the world the image of ourselves and of our own society and we have killed the Innocents in doing so, and Christ flees from us into Egypt. Have we ever yet become Christians?"[123]

Finally, in September of 1959, Merton notes that he has been reading Paul Evdokimov, a student of Bulgakov's and member of the first graduating class of St. Serge Theological Institute in Paris: "Here is a real theologian," he

---

writing" (Jonathan Montaldo, "A Gallery of Women's Faces and Dreams of Women from the Drawings of Thomas Merton," *The Thomas Merton Annual* 14 [2001]: 155–72, at 157). While Montaldo's point is well taken, the detail and tenor of the original account justifies its descrip-tion as an event or awakening that happened to Merton much as he described it there, and as later recounted, for example, in the letter to Pasternak.

121. SFS, 182–83.
122. CGB, 158.
123. SFS, 197.

comments, "one of the few."[124] Evdokimov describes sophiology as "the glory of present-day Orthodox theology" because of its liturgical and iconic way of seeing, a worldview built on the twin doctrines of creation and incarnation. Merton had already seen the same birthing impulse in Bulgakov's sophiology: that God "created for the sake of the Incarnation"; that the incarnation is not "only the means of redemption but its supreme crown." Significantly, he adds, "It has always been difficult for me to see how a Christian would possibly think otherwise. . . . And of course, Proverbs 8 makes it seem obvious. But of course a theologian can always approach the mystery of Christ from some angle which leaves Wisdom out in the exterior darkness."[125]

It was Evdokimov's book *Woman and the Salvation of the World* that seems to have crystallized the many Wisdom strands converging in Merton's religious imagination.[126] At least three things struck him about Evdokimov's development of the sophiological tradition. First, like Bulgakov and Soloviev before him, Evdokimov emphasizes the sanctity of the natural world, *natura naturans*, the "living unity [of nature] which may be called the created Sophia," which is stamped "in the image" of the heavenly Sophia, the Wisdom of God.[127] Second, writing in Paris in the wake of World War II, Evdokimov confronts the problem of evil (theodicy) more adequately than his sophiological forebears. Drawing from the book of Job and Jungian archetypes, he expands on Soloviev's doctrine of the "night face" of Sophia, that is, the perversion of sophianic wisdom through human freedom gone awry.[128] Third, drawing from Maximus, the Song of Songs, and modern biological sciences, Evdokimov advances a positive vision of sexuality and sexual union as having a divine counterpart in Sophia, the divine Eros that "brings forth the cosmos from chaos."[129]

For Merton, Evdokimov's sophianic vision of the natural world, and especially his celebration of eros as rooted in the very life of God, cast a severe

---

124. Ibid., 330.

125. Ibid., 109.

126. Montaldo, "A Gallery of Women's Faces," 156.

127. Paul Evdokimov, *Woman and the Salvation of the World: A Christian Anthropology on the Charisms of Women*, trans. Anthony P. Gythiel (Crestwood, NY: St. Vladimir's Seminary Press, 1994), 65–66; originally *La femme et le salut du monde* (Paris: Casterman, 1958). If I understand him correctly, Evdokimov identifies Sophia not directly with God's *ousia* (as in Bulgakov) but with the divine "energies" of Gregory Palamas: "Only Palamism, with its doctrine on the divine energies, allows for a correct Sophiology" (203).

128. Indeed for Evdokimov, it is "the case of Job" (i.e., theodicy, the suffering of innocents) that "prompts the 'memory' (*anamnesis*) of Sophia" (ibid., 202–8). Merton is also struck by Evdokimov's "arresting" description of monasticism and of prayer as "apocalypse already realized," which "shows forth the Christian conscience burning with impatience" (SFS, 334). The apocalyptic tenor of Evdokimov's theology of history exerts considerable influence on Merton's prophetic social writings, as we shall see in chap. 6.

129. Evdokimov, *Woman and the Salvation of the World*, 67.

light on the instrumentalization of nature and of human bodies that he saw poisoning modern Western society; much more personally, it cast a harsh light on his own relationships with women in his younger years. On July 2, 1960, the feast of the Visitation, Merton records perhaps the most significant of all the Wisdom passages, that of his "awakening" by "the soft voice of the nurse" in a hospital. The experience seems to touch off in Merton not only a deep sense of gratitude and wonder—"as if the Blessed Virgin herself, as if Wisdom had awakened me"—but also a profound sorrow for the acute memory of sins past, sins that implicated him in the sufferings of the world:

> Who is more little than the helpless man, asleep in bed, having entrusted himself gladly to sleep and to night? Him the gentle voice will awake, all that is sweet in woman will awaken him. Not for conquest and pleasure, but for the far deeper wisdom of love and joy and communion.
>
> My heart is broken for all my sins and the sins of the whole world, for the rottenness of our spirit of gain that defiles wisdom in all beings—to rob and deflower wisdom as if there were only a little pleasure to be had, only a little joy, and it had to be stolen, violently taken and spoiled. When all the while her warmth, her exuberant silence, her acceptance, are infinite, infinite! Deep is the ocean, boundless sweetness, kindness, humility, silence of wisdom that is not abstract, disconnected, fleshless. Awakening us gently when we have exhausted ourselves to night and to sleep. O Dawn of Wisdom![130]

Merton has fully internalized one of the more striking insights at the heart of Russian sophiology, namely, that "continence toward woman and reverence for creation are intimately connected."[131] Or, negatively, as ecofeminist writers have long insisted, that society's wholesale commodification of women (and women's bodies) is bound up with the objectification and destruction of the natural world: Sophia, the Mother who bears and sustains life; Sophia, the Lover whose beauty and physical touch landscapes our basic sense of being at home in the cosmos. Of course the linking of the earth (Mother Earth) and the feminine (Mary, *Theotokos*) with divinity (Sophia) is a pervasive archetype in Russian literature, and where Merton cites Pasternak on this point, Evdokimov looks to Dostoyevsky: "The Mother of God is the Great Mother—the damp earth (Gen. 2:6)."[132]

---

130. TTW, 17–18. The passage is especially striking when juxtaposed with Merton's sketches of women's faces, as Montaldo's study (n. 120 above) beautifully demonstrates.

131. Rowan Williams, "Bread in the Wilderness: The Monastic Ideal in Thomas Merton and Paul Evdokimov," in MHPH, 175–98, at 180.

132. Evdokimov, *Woman and the Salvation of the World*, 221.

At the end of a retreat in January 1961, just a few months before composing *Hagia Sophia*, Merton wrote in his journal:

> Long quiet intervals in dark hours. Evdokimov on orthodoxy—once again, as I have so many times recently, I meet the concept of *natura naturans* [nature acting according to its nature]—the divine wisdom in ideal nature, the ikon of wisdom, the dancing ikon—the summit reached by so many non-Christian contemplatives (would that it were reached by a few Christians!) Summit of Vedanta?—
>
> Faith in Sophia, *natura naturans*, the great stabilizer today—for peace.
>
> The basic hope that people have that man will somehow not be completely destroyed is hope in *natura naturans*.
>
> —The dark face, the "night face" of Sophia—pain, trouble, pestilence.[133]

Three points stand out in this critical passage. First, Merton's reference to the "ikon of wisdom" evokes Evdokimov's reflections on iconography in *Woman and the Salvation of the World*: "An icon is a theology in lines and colors, a true *locus theologicus*, one of the most expressive elements of the Tradition. . . . It is a sacrament, not of divine action, but of a divine presence. . . . It makes the invisible visible to 'the eyes of the mind.'"[134] It is significant that *Hagia Sophia*, as we shall see in chapter 5, came to birth partly from Merton's meditation on a painting of Holy Wisdom by his friend, the artist Victor Hammer. In Orthodox spirituality, the act of praying before such an image or icon draws us into participation in the real presence of the saint, Christ, Mary, or in this case, God revealed as Sancta Sophia.[135] Second, Merton links this divine presence experienced in prayer before the icon with the "summit reached by so many non-Christian contemplatives," the "summit of Vedanta?" At the very least, in epistemological terms, the wordless experience shared by contemplatives across religious boundar-

133. TTW, 91.

134. Evdokimov, *Woman and the Salvation of the World*, 230; cf. SFS, 124, where Merton comments on a "deeply moving" article on icons by Evdokimov. "How rare it is to find such theology!" It is not incidental that late in his life Merton described his image of Christ as the "Christ of the icons," nor that the first stirrings of his faith came as a young man in Rome, where he found himself haunted by the mosaics of Christ in the city's ancient churches. See Thomas Merton, *The Seven Storey Mountain* (New York: Harcourt Brace, 1948; 1976), 108–10; hereafter SSM.

135. Prayer before an icon facilitates the re-centering of subjectivity from oneself to the divine, no longer related to as an object of self-fulfillment but as Person and Presence. By means of the icon something breaks through a little, such that, as Cassian describes mystical prayer, the one praying is no longer aware of who it is that is praying.

ies has to do with making "the invisible visible to 'the eyes of the mind.'"[136] Third, years of meditation on the Russian theologians had brought Merton here to the rather striking insight that faith in Sophia is "the great stabilizer today for peace"—an intuition that would find its most sublime expression in *Hagia Sophia*.

Communion in Wisdom/Growth in Love

By October of 1958, the dialogue with Pasternak had already convinced Merton that "simple and human dialogue" across religious, cultural, and political boundaries is the real basis for peace in the world, "worth thousands of sermons and radio speeches. It is to me the Kingdom of God, which is still so clearly, and evidently, 'in the midst of us.'"[137] Of course this conviction, rooted in the "whole Spirit of the New Testament,"[138] would grow in Merton to the end of his life. Nor would it die with him in Asia, but lives on today in Christians and non-Christians who dedicate themselves to the labor and grace of ecumenical and interfaith dialogue. The key theme here is *growth*, which implies risk, struggle, and discernment. While dialogue was always spiritually and intellectually invigorating for Merton, it was never easy or automatic, a fact that comes through clearly in the journals and letters of 1957 to 1961.

A few months after initiating the correspondence with Suzuki, for example, Merton interrogates himself about the meaning of his relationship with this Zen teacher, who makes "statements that would make theologians fall over into a dead faint, and yet behind them is a sharp intuition of a very great reality—our life in the Risen Christ." Merton recognizes it as "a basic fact of primary importance" that he and Suzuki "can speak the same language and indeed that we speak much more of a common language than I can, for instance, share with the average American business man, or indeed with some of the other monks." He reflects: "if I tried baldly and bluntly to 'convert' Suzuki, that is, make him 'accept' formulas regarding the faith that are accepted by the average American Catholic, I would, in fact, not 'convert' him at all, but simply confuse and (in a cultural sense) degrade him. Not that he does not need the Sacraments, etc. but that is an entirely different question."[139]

Clearly Merton was still struggling in 1959 with the theological predicament into which he had gotten himself. On the one hand, he thinks Suzuki

136. Evdokimov, *Woman and the Salvation of the World*, 230.
137. SFS, 225.
138. Ibid., 273.
139. Ibid.

"would be immeasurably more sincere and more saintly *per se*, if he came to the Sacraments and were a visible member of the Church"; on the other hand, "who says that Suzuki is not already a saint?" He further ponders that "*visibility . . .* is not the most important thing" and adds the humbling fact "that the visibility of the conversion we demand of others may, perhaps, be demanded not by our charity but by our weakness: as an exterior prop to our own lack of faith."[140] In a moment of evident lucidity, Merton fixes on what he judges to be "the most important thing," that is, fostering his "simple and human" relationship with Suzuki: "[If] I can meet him on a common ground of spiritual Truth, where we share a real and deep experience of God, and where we know in humility our own deepest selves—and if we can discuss and compare the formulas we use to describe this experience, then I certainly think Christ would be present and glorified in both of us and this would lead to *a conversion of us both*—an elevation, a development, a serious growth in Christ."[141]

Five years later, Merton would have the chance to meet his Buddhist friend on "common ground." On June 17, 1964, after traveling on an airplane for just the second time in his life, Merton met with Suzuki at New York's Columbia University. The two sat on a couch and "talked of all kinds of things to do with Zen and with life."[142] Assisted by Suzuki's secretary, they shared an informal tea ceremony. Merton describes the meeting in several warm, if strikingly spare, paragraphs. "These talks were very pleasant, and profoundly important to me—to see and experience . . . that there really is a deep understanding between myself and this extraordinary and simple man whom I have been reading for about ten years with great attention. A sense of being 'situated' in this world. . . . For once in a long time felt as if I had spent a moment in my own family."[143] Before departing the meeting, Suzuki had made a final comment: "The most important thing is Love!"—a statement that Merton later confesses left him deeply moved. "Truly *Prajna* and *Karuna* are one (as the Buddhist says), or *Caritas* (love) is indeed the highest knowledge."[144]

Did anything of significance happen on this occasion? In flatly empirical terms, two human beings sat together, talked about the concept of person, read poems, and drank tea. And yet, as Merton-Suzuki scholar Matthew Zyniewicz suggests, the situation contained something more "than what was

140. Ibid., 274.
141. Ibid., 273.
142. DWL, 116.
143. Ibid., 116–17.
144. ZBA, 62, referencing the traditional Cistercian emphasis on love as integral to knowledge and wisdom, or *amor ipse intellectus est* (William of St. Thierry).

immediately and expressly described in Merton's journal entries."[145] During their years of deepening exchange—in what Zyniewicz calls their developing "in-betweenness"—"Suzuki's silence became ever more relational," less and less a private or "exotic" activity hidden behind the caricatures of Western misunderstanding. After a struggle of many decades, the elderly Zen scholar had finally found "a capable, living, Western dialogue partner to whom and through whom he could communicate his enlightened wisdom to the West."[146] While Merton for his part had initially agonized over the question of Suzuki's conversion and need for the sacraments, by the time they met in New York he desired only to share with Suzuki his presence.

Why? What had changed? As Zyniewicz observes, Merton came to believe that in himself, "in his own person, [he] could unite Suzuki to God. For at the base of all reality was the wisdom of love (Sophia), a wisdom which deepened when a Christian loved a non-Christian."[147] In other words, Merton's evolving openness to Suzuki was neither the result of simply a psychological change nor merely a concession of religious diplomacy, a goodwill gesture of peacemaking. Rather, his growing willingness to accept and engage Suzuki on his own terms had both a contemplative and theological root in Christ/Sophia, the love and mercy of God, whose presence in all things and in all people had become ever more palpable in the eyes of his heart.

During an informal talk in Calcutta in October 1968, just over a month before his death, Merton described the character of such a communion across seeming impenetrable boundaries: "It is wordless. It is beyond words, and it is beyond speech, and it is beyond concept. Not that we discover a new unity. We discover an older unity. My dear brothers, we are already one. But we imagine that we are not. And what we have to recover is our original unity. What we have to be is what we are."[148] Fully a decade earlier, Merton had struggled to express the same paradoxical experience of unity he shared with Suzuki: "The fact that you are a Zen Buddhist and I am a Christian monk, far from separating us, makes us most like one another. How many centuries is it going to take for people to discover this fact?"[149]

It is fascinating that near the end of their dialogue, Suzuki's "Final Remarks" seem almost as if they could have been written by his friend, Thomas Merton: "Eschatology is something never realizable and yet realized at every moment of our life. We see it always ahead of us though we are in reality

---

145. Matthew C. Zyniewicz, "The Interreligious Dialogue Between Thomas Merton and D. T. Suzuki" (PhD dissertation, University of Notre Dame, 2000), 242.

146. Ibid., 240.

147. Ibid., 177.

148. AJ, 308.

149. HGL, 566.

always in it. . . . It is the Great Mystery, intellectually speaking. In Christian terms, it is Divine Wisdom. The strange thing, however, is: when we experience it we cease to ask questions about it, we accept it, we just live it. Theologians, dialecticians and existentialists may go on discussing the matter, but the ordinary people inclusive of all of us who are outsiders live 'the mystery.'"[150]

Discerning the Heart of Reality: God/Creation/Kenosis

As we have seen throughout this study, much of Merton's interest in Zen centered on what he believed to be a realm of shared wisdom (*sapientia*) with Christian contemplation that is more or less epistemological, centering on the pivotal experience of breakthrough and death of the false self. Yet Merton's dialogue with Suzuki pressed quickly beyond epistemological issues into the more difficult realm of metaphysics and theology, centering on the deepest ground and source of reality in all its "suchness." Indeed, the most compelling exchanges between Merton and Suzuki might be boiled down to one question: what is the *content* of reality's suchness, when laid bare of every false construction? It is precisely in this realm, specifically, in Suzuki's discussion of "Emptiness" (*Sunyata*) and Merton's conception of "God" (Christ/Sophia), that the lines of this chapter's underlying thesis might begin to emerge more clearly, namely, that in Russian sophiology Merton discovered a vital language, both ancient and new, for sacramentalizing the Christian answer to the question of reality's suchness. Let us return briefly to the Merton-Suzuki dialogue, now adopting Suzuki's point of view.

"The metaphysical concept of Emptiness," Suzuki writes in *Zen and the Birds of Appetite*, "is convertible in economic terms into poverty, being poor, having nothing: 'Blessed are those who are poor in spirit.'"[151] In one of the crucial threads in the dialogue, Suzuki compares Jesus' beatitude of poverty of spirit, so dear to ancient and Eastern Christian monasticism, to the Zen realization of Emptiness that breaks through when the mind or heart is emptied of "all things"—above all, of attachment to "self," since "all evils and defilements start from our attachment to it."[152] Thus the monk who "has anything to loan," says Suzuki, and remains "anxious to have it returned . . . is not yet poor, he is not yet perfectly empty."[153] Elaborating further on Zen poverty and Emptiness, Suzuki turns to Mahayana Buddhism's teaching of the Six Paramita, the "moral virtues of perfection" practiced in daily life.

150. ZBA, 134.
151. Ibid., 108–9.
152. Ibid., 109.
153. Ibid., 111.

The first of the Six Paramita is *Dana*, or "giving," and the last is *Prajna*, or "transcendental wisdom," "an intuition of the highest order" into "the truth of Emptiness." While the Buddhist life starts with *Dana* and ends in *Prajna*, Suzuki notes that "in reality, the ending is the beginning and the beginning is the ending; the Paramita moves in a circle with no beginning and no ending. The giving is possible only when there is Emptiness, and Emptiness is attainable only when the giving is unconditionally carried out."[154] This circular relationship in Zen between *Dana* (unconditional giving, emptying of self) and *Prajna* (the highest order of spiritual insight) is already deeply resonant with the Christian narrative of kenosis. Indeed, the classic New Testament formulas of preexistence (John 1:1-18; Col 1:15-20; Rev 1:8), kenosis (Phil 2:6-11; Jn 12:24), and awakening (Rom 8:14-17; 2 Cor 3:17-18; Eph 5:14)—texts saturated with a nonlinear or circular metaphysic—occupy the hub of Merton's christic imagination.[155] But let us linger for a moment longer with *Dana*.

In the path of "crossing over" to the shore of perfection, continues Suzuki, *Dana* "does not just mean giving in charity or otherwise something material"; more than this, it means "going out of oneself, disseminating knowledge, helping people in difficulties of all kinds, creating arts, promoting industry or social welfare, sacrificing one's life for a worthy cause and so on."[156] Yet even this "is not enough as long a man harbors the idea of giving in one sense or another." The way of perfect giving that ripens and flowers in *Prajna* "consists in not cherishing any thought of anything going out of one's hands and being received by anybody else; that is to say, in the giving there must not be any thought of a giver or a receiver, and of an object going through this transaction." This is poverty in its genuine sense, says Suzuki: "Nothing to gain, nothing to lose, nothing to give, nothing to take; to be just so, and yet to be rich in inexhaustible possibilities."[157]

How then, does this true poverty of spirit relate to the Absolute, to the Infinite, to God? "We are generally apt to imagine," Suzuki observes, "that when the mind or heart is emptied of 'self and all things' a room is left ready for God to enter and occupy it. This is a great error."[158] In contrast to this dualist or dialectical conception of God, Suzuki looks to Eckhart as the Christian mystic who draws nearest to Zen Emptiness and enlightenment (*Sambodhi*) when he describes union with God in nondualistic terms: "In

154. Ibid., 112.

155. Perhaps no single text offers a better window into the biblical roots of Merton's Christology (ecclesiology, sacramental theology) than *The New Man* (1961), explored in chap. 5.

156. ZBA, 112.

157. Ibid., 109.

158. Ibid.

my breaking-through . . . I transcend all creatures and am neither God nor creature: I am that I was and I shall remain now and forever. Then I receive an impulse which carries me above all angels. In this impulse I conceive such passing riches that I am not content with God as being God, as being all his godly works, for in this breaking-through I find that God and I are both the same."[159] As Suzuki interprets Eckhart here, "God is at once the place where He works and the work itself."[160] This circular intuition of oneness with God, the intuition in love that "God and I are both the same," accords closely, suggests Suzuki, with the realization of Emptiness, which is, paradoxically, a kind of fullness, ripening, and consummation:

> Zen emptiness is not the emptiness of nothingness, but the emptiness of fullness in which there is "no gain, no loss, no increase, no decrease," in which this equation takes place: zero = infinity. The Godhead is no other than this equation. In other words when God as Creator came out of the Godhead he did not leave the Godhead behind. He has the Godhead with him all along while engaging in the work of creation. Creation is continuous, going on till the end of time, which has really no ending and therefore no beginning. For creation is out of inexhaustible nothingness.[161]

Much more could be said about Suzuki's reading of Christian mysticism through the eye of Zen, but we have already struck upon the key metaphysical insight: "when God as Creator came out of the Godhead *he did not leave the Godhead behind.*" In an earlier exchange of letters, Suzuki had put the matter in similarly provocative terms: "God wanted to know Himself, hence the creation."[162] In his reply, Merton responded enthusiastically to Suzuki's insight by referencing Bulgakov: "The Russian view pushes very far the idea of God 'emptying Himself' (kenosis) to go over into His creation, while creation passes over into a divine world—precisely a new paradise."[163] A year later, in a

159. Ibid., 114.

160. Ibid., 110.

161. Ibid., 133–34. Borrowing again from biblical imagery, Suzuki writes: "Paradise has never been lost, [it] is right away with me, and the experience is the foundation on which the kingdom of heaven is built." In a string of typically paradoxical Zen formulations, he says Emptiness should be understood "not only statically but dynamically. It takes place between being and becoming. . . . It is and at the same time it is not." In any case, the "it" that begins in *Dana* and "breaks through" in *Prajna* is centered in the realization of "no self, no ego, no *Atman* that will pollute the mind" (107).

162. Cited by Merton in HGL, 563.

163. Ibid. On kenosis as a central category in Bulgakov's dogmatics, see Paul Valliere, MRT, 331–32, 337–44.

passage of March 25, 1960, Merton put kenosis at the very center of Christian mysticism, theology, and, to be sure, Christian anthropology:

> In emptying Himself to come into the world, God has not simply kept in reserve, in a safe place, His reality and manifested a kind of shadow or symbol of Himself. He has emptied Himself and is all in Christ. *Invisibilis in suis; visibilis in nostris.* [Invisible in his own; visible in ours.] Christ is not simply the tip of the little finger of the Godhead, moving in the world, easily withdrawn, never threatened, never really risking anything. God has acted and given Himself totally, without division, in the Incarnation. He has become not only one of us but even our very selves.[164]

Joining Zen insight, then, with kenotic Christology from the New Testament forward, Merton intimates (analogically) that the dance between *Dana* and *Prajna* comprises the very life, the very suchness of God.[165] While this revelation into the kenotic heart of the cosmos was already enshrined for Merton in the twin doctrines of creation and incarnation, in Russian sophiology he discovered a new (and also ancient) theological form, at once biblical, poetic, and metaphysical, for sacramentalizing this experience of divine Love without limit, of the free and unreserved self-donation of God. By "sacramentalizing" I mean that the speculative language of sophiology—and above all, the biblical *name* Sophia—is not mere wordplay for Merton but bears the analogical capacity to awaken in the responsive human community an authentic memory of God, a palpable hope for liberation, and a real Presence in whom we "live and move and have our being" (Acts 17:28). In other words, the breakthrough of Sophia marked not a radical break from Merton's Christ-haunted past but rather its lyrical consummation.

Dharmakaya–Sophia

Here we move decidedly from the realm of epistemology to Christology and the theology of God. Beneath their narrative, psychological, and metaphysical elements, what all the Wisdom texts of Merton's mature period share

---

164. SFS, 381. The full journal entry illustrates not only the influence of the Russian theologians; more broadly, it illumines Merton's dissatisfaction with the scholastic approach to theology in which he had been formed, and finds him pondering his own theological vocation.

165. "Pseudo-Dionysius says that the wisdom of the contemplative moves in a *motus orbicularis*—a circling and hovering motion like that of the eagle above some invisible quarry, or the turning of a planet around an invisible sun. The work of Dr. Suzuki bears witness of the silent orbiting of *Prajna* which is (in the language of the same Western tradition of the Pseudo-Areopagite and Erigena) a 'circle whose circumference is nowhere and whose center is everywhere'" (ZBA, 65).

is a contemplative vision of life in which terms such as "Creation," "Incarnation," and "Resurrection" leap off the page not as objective doctrines about God, or merely historical events that happened long ago, but as living and present realities—"facts of the imagination," as Newman would say—that break into consciousness from the ground of mystical experience. Bound up closely with Hebrew creation texts, the Wisdom literature of the Bible proclaims that the suchness of the universe is not a "what" but rather a "Who," a hidden Power and Presence (Hebrew: *Shekhinah*) in whom all things are created and sustained. A sophianic epistemology rules out a negative or gnostic view of the world and of history. The world "is no longer seen as merely material, hence as an obstacle that has to be grudgingly put up with. It is spiritual through and through."[166] By contemplation and grace we are able "to unite the hidden wisdom of God in things with the hidden light of wisdom" in ourselves, and so participate in the "communal eros" that gives birth, in every new moment, to the whole of creation.[167]

Following Western Catholic theology we may call this nondualist way of seeing and participating in divine life "sacramental," but in the pattern of Eastern Orthodox spirituality, we might just as well use the term "iconic." Merton's sophianic writings are iconic in the way that the theologies of Maximus Confessor, John Damascene, and the contemporary Orthodox theologian John Zizioulas are iconic. In contrast to a historicist imagination that takes as its starting point historical causality and continuity, here an appreciation of God's presence in the material world issues forth from a liturgical sensibility and a symbolic, meta-historical or eschatological approach to space and time.[168] To grasp the "real presence" of Sophia in an icon, mystical text,

166. ICM, 126.

167. Merton's "immanentism" carefully avoids a Hegelian or pantheistic view of creation by underscoring the utter freedom and gratuity of God's creative love at the ground of all being (ZBA, 136–37; CWA, 175). Nor can Russian sophiology be justly characterized (as we shall see in chap. 6) as a kind of pantheistic monism clothed in Hegelian (or "New Age") garb (see Valliere, MRT, 334–37). In any case it will surprise no one engaged in Buddhist-Christian dialogue that this is precisely where Merton and Suzuki agree to disagree, namely, on the question of whether the deep structure and dynamism of reality—*Sunyata*, God, true self—is experienced and so conceived in personal (biblical, theistic) terms as a gift of *grace*. Yet it is also clear that Suzuki shares with Merton the conviction that persons and cultures everywhere, especially in the West, need urgently to recover the contemplative way in the midst of, in Suzuki's words, the "industrialization and the universal propagandism of 'an easy life'" (ZBA, 115).

168. Noting the centrality of worship in Orthodox spirituality, Zizioulas describes his worldview as "theophanic" and "meta-historical," citing Yves Congar's description of Orthodox ecclesiology as embodying the idea of "a 'showing,' or a manifestation of invisible heavenly realities on earth" (John Zizioulas, *Being as Communion: Studies in Personhood and the Church* [Crestwood, NY: St. Vladimir's Seminary Press, 1985], 171); cf. Roger Haight, *Christian Community in History*, vol. 2, *Comparative Ecclesiology* (New York: Continuum, 2005), 441–42.

or in the "text" of the world implies no magic, literary or otherwise. It does imply that the person or community situated before the text has to listen, discern, and read the signs "with penetration."[169]

It is crucial to reiterate that there was nothing abstract or esoteric for Merton about the experience of Christ as Sophia, the Wisdom of God. "It is simply opening yourself to receive. The presence of God is like walking out of a door into the fresh air. You don't concentrate on the fresh air, you breathe it. And you don't concentrate on the sunlight, you just enjoy it. It is all around."[170] Note how much Merton sounds here like his friend Suzuki, when he insists that theologians "may go on discussing the matter," but ordinary people, including religious outsiders, simply "live the mystery."[171] To say it another way, the marriage of Sophia and Zen shines forth most vividly not in Merton's Christology or theology so much as in his *life*.

Consider Merton's much-discussed "illumination" at the Buddhist shrine of Pollanaruwa, just days before his death:

> Looking at these figures I was suddenly, almost forcibly, jerked clean out of the habitual, half-tied vision of things, and an inner clearness, clarity, as if exploding from the rocks themselves, became evident and obvious. . . . The thing about this is that there is no puzzle, no problem, and really no "mystery." All problems are resolved and everything is clear, simply because what matters is clear. The rock, all matter, all life, is charged with dharma-kaya . . . everything is emptiness and everything is compassion.[172]

At the risk of over-reading a multivalent account that Merton himself never had the chance to revisit, there is more than an echo here of Russian theology's bold accent on sacred corporeality, *natura naturans*—as if "the rocks themselves" profess the incarnation! There are echoes too of Hopkins— "There lives the dearest freshness deep down things"[173]—and Maximus on *theoria physike*, about which Merton had noted: "When a man has been

---

I am grateful to Roger Haight for suggesting to me the resonances between Merton's iconic imagination and that of contemporary thinkers like Zizioulas.

169. Marie-Dominique Chenu, *Nature, Man, and Society in the Twelfth Century*, ed. Jerome Taylor and Lester Little (Chicago: University of Chicago Press, 1957), 99; here, as detailed in chap. 3 above, Chenu describes monastic theology's appeal, through biblical memory and imagination, to the whole person, inclusive of the senses.

170. Cited in MHPH, 454.

171. ZBA, 134. Or as Suzuki writes elsewhere, with characteristic directness, when realization comes it comes to "the ordinary Toms, Dicks, and Harrys we had been all along" (ZBA, 114).

172. AJ, 233, 235.

173. From "God's Grandeur," in *Gerard Manley Hopkins: The Major Works* (Oxford: Oxford University Press, 1986), 128.

purified and humbled, when his eye is single, and he is his own real self, then the *logoi* of things jump out at him spontaneously."[174] One might even recall Jesus' playful (i.e., sophianic) response to the Pharisees during his final entry into Jerusalem. The "whole multitude of the disciples began to praise God joyfully . . . for all the deeds of power that they had seen." When the Pharisees ask Jesus to silence the crowd, he proclaims: "I tell you, if these were silent, the stones would shout out!" (Luke 19:28-40). In short, Pollanaruwa need not be interpreted as a complete break from Merton's Christ-haunted view of reality. To the contrary, Pollanaruwa sums up what is for him the whole climate of the New Testament: "all matter, all life, is charged with dharmakaya,"[175] the self-emptying love and mercy of God.

Finally, much overshadowed in *The Asian Journal* but no less wondrous or significant than Pollanaruwa, there is the record of Merton's meeting some weeks earlier (November 16, 1968) with the Nepalese Buddhist hermit Chatral Rimpoche, "the greatest rimpoche I have met so far and a very impressive person." The passage is just as significant as Pollanaruwa, if not considerably more, because it reveals Merton at what may be his Christ-saturated best: not the solitary living in the woods or standing silently before the great figures of the Buddha but the man who simply loved to be with people, all kinds of people, and whose capacious spirit continues to draw people everywhere to himself and his extraordinary writings:

> Chatral looked like a vigorous old peasant in a Bhutanese jacket tied at the neck with thongs and a red woolen cap on his head. He had a week's growth of beard, bright eyes, a strong voice, and was very articulate, much more communicative than I expected. We had a fine talk and all through it Jimpa, the interpreter, laughed and said several times, "These are hermit questions . . . this is another hermit question." . . . We must have talked for two hours or more, covering all sorts of ground . . . but also taking in some points of Christian doctrine compared with Buddhist: dharmakaya . . . the risen Christ, suffering, compassion for all creatures. . . . He said he had meditated in solitude for thirty years or more and had not attained to perfect emptiness and I said I hadn't either.
>
> The unspoken or half-spoken message of the talk was our complete understanding of each other as people who were somehow *on the edge* of great realization and knew it and were trying, somehow or other, to go out and get lost in it—and that it was a grace for us to meet one another. I wish I could see more of Chatral. He burst out and called me a rangjung Sangay (which apparently means a "natural Buddha"). . . .

174. ICM, 110.
175. The term is Sanskrit for the most sublime or essential reality in the universe, "the cosmical body of the Buddha, the essence of all beings" (AJ, 372, citing Murti).

> I was profoundly moved, because he is so obviously a great man . . .
> marked by simplicity and freedom. He was surprised at getting on so
> well with a Christian and at one point laughed and said, "There must
> be something wrong here!"[176]

An entire theology lies hidden in Merton's desire to "see more of Chatral,"
and in his understated, almost plaintive observation that "it was a grace for
us to meet one another." Indeed, one might say that the two strangers, in
the simple warmth and hospitality of their presence to each other, were no
longer "on the edge" of realization but were fully immersed in it, "lost in
it"—irrespective of the need to name "it" with an explicit theology. Grace, it
seems, is surprising like that, breaking through with "simplicity and freedom,"
and surely provoking in us a little less seriousness, and a great deal more joy,
desire, spontaneity, creativity, and laughter.

I was there, rejoicing before him always, and delighting in the human race.

Concluding Remarks

When one first approaches Merton's mature Christology against the horizon
of religious pluralism, it appears to risk little by way of traditional dogmatic
and trinitarian formulations. Yet when his Christology is approached holisti-
cally as a piece with his life, a very different picture emerges. In particular,
Merton's sophiological turn during the late 1950s and early 1960s emerges as
the theological subtext that would both center and catalyze an uncommonly
radical openness to others during the 1960s. Russian sophiology seems to have
carved out something rather new and unexpected in Merton, a space and a
language in which there was enough room, both conceptually and imaginatively, to envision God's unbounded freedom, love, and presence to peoples and
cultures everywhere. In a period of tremendous social, political, and religious
fragmentation, what breaks through in Merton's last decade is not only a daring
affirmation of Christ's presence in all things but perhaps even a new kind of
theology, rooted in forgotten realms of *memoria*, presence, and hope. Faith in
Sophia had become for Merton "the great stabilizer today for peace."

Merton's great sophiological shift began on the corner of Fourth and Walnut,
where God's incarnation in Christ became real for him not only in the "hushed
flight of the escaping dove,"[177] as he had written in "Fire Watch," but in the
stranger, who once seemed alien and even threatening to his monastic vocation. This experience of holding "the winning ticket in a cosmic sweepstake,"[178]

176. AJ, 143–44.
177. SJ, 362.
178. CGB, 157.

this epiphany of God with a human face, is surely not far from the music of the Sermon on the Mount; nor is it alien to the world's poets, as Gustavo Gutierrez notes, citing César Vallejo: "The lottery vendor who hawks tickets 'for the big one'. . . somehow deep down represents God. But every person is a lottery vendor who offers us 'the big one': our encounter with that God who is deep down in the heart of each person."[179] The sophiological perspective is alive to God's presence in the world never as "abstract essence" but concretely, sacramentally, more than literally. "As if the sorrows and stupidities of the human condition could overwhelm me, now I realize what we all are."[180]

One of the great challenges facing Catholic theology today is finding the right balance between historical and iconic sensibilities, and probably nowhere is this challenge more acutely felt than in the realm of Christology. Given this situation, one of the most attractive things about Merton's mature theology is precisely its successful attunement of historical and iconic, prophetic and mystical, intellectual and poetic sensibilities. One measure of that success, as I have noted often, is that his writing continues to resonate with ordinary seekers everywhere, young and old, Christian and non-Christian. Merton's writing rings true for people from a remarkable range of backgrounds. Yet what accounts for this resonance is more than literary elegance, and it goes deeper than epistemology. Classic works such as *New Seeds of Contemplation* and *Hagia Sophia* do not just paint pretty pictures. What is at stake is "the discernment of the profound truth that lies hidden within the dense substance of things."[181]

The poet Susan McCaslin puts a fine point on the argument in the final lines of her exegesis of *Hagia Sophia*: "While Merton recognizes the limitations of language, he assumes a metaphysical and ontological ground of being beyond language; that is, the 'real presence' of Wisdom behind and within the signs."[182] To grasp the "real presence" of Sophia in an icon, mystical text, or in the text of the world and human history implies no magic, literary or otherwise. It does imply that the person or community situated before the icon, text, or particular historical reality has to listen, discern, and read the signs "with penetration." That is our task in the remaining pages of this study: to read and try to understand "with penetration" the implications of the sophiological tradition from East to West and, above all, its classic poetic formulation in *Hagia Sophia*.

179. Gustavo Gutierrez, *A Theology of Liberation: History, Politics, and Salvation*, trans. Caridad Inda and John Eagleson (Maryknoll, NY: Orbis, 1973), 202, where he also cites Yves Congar's notion of the neighbor as "sacrament."

180. CGB, 157.

181. Chenu, *Nature, Man, and Society*, 99.

182. MHPH, 253.

Drawing by Thomas Merton. Used with permission of the Merton Legacy Trust and the Thomas Merton Center, Bellarmine University.

5

Hagia Sophia:
The Marriage of East and West

[His] rebellion is the rebellion of life against inertia, of mercy and love against tyranny, of humanity against cruelty and arbitrary violence. And he calls upon the feminine, the wordless, the timelessly moving elements to witness his sufferings. Earth hears him.[1]

By the early 1960s Thomas Merton had embraced the sophiological world-view fully as his own, and had begun to translate it with intellectual and poetic vitality into the West. In his narration of "the great Joy," the great "secret," in which God "has acted and given Himself totally" and "has become not only one of us but even our very selves,"[2] Merton would by no means leave Wisdom "out in the exterior darkness"[3]; to the contrary, he would weave her name quietly into a burgeoning theology of engagement with the world. As detailed in the previous chapter, the opening salvo came in texts like "The Pasternak Affair," in his lecture notes on mystical theology ("An Introduction to Christian Mysticism"), and especially in *The Behavior of Titans*, a stunning marriage of mysticism and prophecy that opens and closes with two sophianic essays: the first on Prometheus, the last on Herakleitos. Yet the full flowering of Merton's sophiological voice was still to come. This chapter brings us to the theological heart of things, exploring the fruition of Merton's mature Christology in his view of Christ as the Wisdom of God, Sophia, in whom the cosmos is created and sustained.

We begin by exploring the more traditional features of Merton's mature Christology in two key texts of this period: *The New Man* (1961) and, perhaps his most beloved book, *New Seeds of Contemplation* (1962). Simmering beneath both, and occasionally bursting out, one finds the converging influences of both Russian sophiology and Zen. While both works brilliantly develop his theology

---

1. BT, 13–14, on Prometheus, as portrayed in Aeschylus's *Prometheus Bound*, "one of the most heart-rending, pure and sacred of tragedies." The lines could just as well be taken as autobiographical, capturing in miniature the sophiological tenor of Merton's last decade.

2. SFS, 381.

3. Ibid., 109.

of contemplation, in neither case does Merton's Christology as such stray from a more or less traditional framework. The second half of the chapter, and in many ways the theological focal point of this book, takes up a close reading of the prose poem *Hagia Sophia* (1962). Here, Merton allows himself greater freeplay with biblical, archetypal, and paradoxical images of the divine. Like the Russians before him, we might say, Merton dares "to make mistakes . . . in order to say something great and worthy of God."[4] The chapter concludes by asking whether indeed Merton "makes mistakes" in the poem or, rather, whether the poem gives voice to something deep and essential, though forgotten, in the Christian (and human) experience of God. Moving from textual study to systematic reflection, we shall have to ask not only *Who* is Sophia? but *Why* Sophia? And what significance might her remembrance have for the way we conceive of, and above all experience, the living God?

It is important to bear in mind that while Merton did not write as a systematic theologian, neither did he write merely as a storyteller, cultural critic, or poet. Immersed body and soul in the tradition, he wrote as a mystical theologian, a poet of the presence of God, "intuitively receiving and shaping images and symbols for the divine."[5] As Susan McCaslin observes, he was aware that the sophiological tradition "had been marginalized within Western Christianity," and with *Hagia Sophia* and other writings he "attempts to restore it."[6] In short, while Merton would never develop a formal sophiology as such, many of his most enduring writings come to us in an unmistakably sophiological key. In these he "calls upon the feminine, the timelessly moving elements" to witness not only his own sufferings but indeed the sufferings of all the world. And Sophia, it would seem, hears him.

Christ the Divine Image and Human Prototype:
The New Man (1961)/*New Seeds of Contemplation* (1962)

> [The Church must] break out continually into . . . lyrical notes to make up for the shortcomings of theological prose. . . . A toned down Christology is absurd. It must be all or nothing—all or nothing on both the divine and the human side. That is the very extreme of paradox . . . the derivative paradox which is the distinctive secret of the Christian life.[7]

Donald Baillie's description of the paradoxical secret of Christian life serves well to introduce Merton's more traditional and formally crafted reflec-

---

4. Ibid., 86.
5. Susan McCaslin, "Merton and 'Hagia Sophia,'" in MHPH, 235–54, at 253.
6. Ibid., 252.
7. Donald M. Baillie, *God Was in Christ* (New York: Scribner's, 1948), 132.

tions on the mystery of Jesus Christ. For Merton, the dogmatic and mystical teachings of the church may be summed up in "the twin doctrines of incarnation and deification, which are in fact two sides of the same mystery."[8] Thus one could say that his Christology begins quite lyrically from above, but only if one adds that this descending movement is mirrored by an equally lyrical ascent to God from below. These spatial metaphors do not really serve, however, because they foster a dualism that Merton ultimately rejects. That is, they cannot convey what is the heart of Christian spirituality for him: the discovery of our true selves already resting *in* Christ, not Christ "out there" as a separate Object, but "as the Reality within our own reality, the Being within our being, the life of our life."[9]

In other words, the paradox of incarnation faith is not dialectical for Merton so much as analogical. To borrow Baillie's language, it is not only a "toned down Christology" that is absurd, but also a toned down anthropology. "If we believe in the Incarnation of the Son of God," Merton writes in *New Seeds of Contemplation*, "there should be no one on earth in whom we are not prepared to see, in mystery, the presence of Christ."[10] Or again, in lines that presage almost verbatim the Christ-centered humanism of Vatican II's *Gaudium et spes*: "In Christ, God became not only 'this' man, but also, in a broader and more mystical sense, yet no less truly, 'every man.'"[11] *This* is precisely the paradox that becomes "an accusation" of every dehumanizing ideology and Unspeakable force churning through the world, the heart of a theology that seeks above all to "guard the image of man for it is the image of God."[12]

There are few places where Merton aims systematically to work out such a Christology. For this reason, the texts in which he did do so are crucial for grasping his Christian theological vision. *The New Man* is certainly one such text. Originally written in 1954 under the title *Existential Communion*, revised in 1959, and published in 1961, *The New Man* reflects Merton's masterful ability to weave together a theological vision from a dizzying range of sources: John's gospel, the Pauline epistles, Irenaeus, Augustine, Gregory of Nyssa, Bernard of Clairvaux, Duns Scotus, John of the Cross, John Ruysbroeck, contemporaries such as Henri de Lubac, and just beneath the surface, Russian Orthodox theology. In short, "Merton makes absolutely no break

---

8. A. M. Allchin, "The Worship of the Whole Creation," in MHPH, 103–20, at 107.

9. NM, 19.

10. NSC, 296. Here, and throughout NSC, Merton's theological anthropology resonates with that of Karl Rahner.

11. Ibid., 294–95; cf. *Gaudium et spes* 22, promulgated December 7, 1965, three years after the publication of NSC.

12. RU, 6, citing Berdyaev.

between the New Testament writers and the post-apostolic writers. Scripture and tradition form one whole."[13] Of the book's nine chapters, we focus here mainly on the sixth, "The Second Adam," because it gets to the heart of our topic: both the source and re-creation of all humanity in Christ.

Creation/Incarnation/Deification

In "The Second Adam," Merton is bent on illuminating Christ not only as the fulfillment of creation but also as its source and beginning. "The far ends of time meet in His hands."[14] Merton begins with the Pauline parallel of Christ and Adam, but he makes the case that the New Testament writers clearly subordinated Adam to Christ. The incarnation, in other words, was not an afterthought following a failed creation. Christ is the Word, the uncreated Image of God, who has already decided "from the beginning" to enter fully into humankind. "The whole character of the creation was determined by the fact that God was to become man and dwell in the midst of His own creation."[15] Merton then turns, as he so often does, to Saint Paul's "Captivity Epistles," drawing from a text that resonates strongly with the Wisdom-figure of the Hebrew Scriptures:

> The cosmic mediation of Christ is brought out clearly in St. Paul's Captivity Epistles, especially in the one to the Colossians. Here he says: "(Christ) is the image of the invisible God, the firstborn of every creature. For in Him were created all things in the heavens and on the earth. . . . All things have been created through and unto Him, and in Him all things hold together." [Colossians 1:15-17]. In reading words like these, one is astounded that they receive so little attention from Christians today. It is the Man-God, the Redeemer, Who is the "firstborn of every creature" and who is consequently "born" before Adam. . . . [In] Him Adam is created, like everything else in Heaven and on earth. . . . In Him they "hold together." Without Him they would fall apart.[16]

13. Allchin, "Worship of the Whole Creation," in MHPH, 108.

14. NM, 132.

15. Ibid., 137. George Kilcourse charts a range of early influences on Merton's Christology, including Bernard, Bonaventure, Duns Scotus, Gregory the Great, and Hopkins, and further distinguishes Merton's Cistercian and Franciscan sensibilities from those of Aquinas and scholastic theology: "Put somewhat baldly, for Thomas and the dominant theology the Incarnation of the Son of God was *necessary* because of sin; for Scotus and the Franciscan school of theology, the Incarnation of the Son of God was *inevitable* because of God's love!" (George Kilcourse, *Ace of Freedoms: Thomas Merton's Christ* [Notre Dame, IN: University of Notre Dame Press, 1993], 32; cf. pp. 9, 30–40).

16. NM, 136.

In these lines Merton begins to raise a latticework for the twin doctrines of incarnation and deification, for both a cosmic Christology and the most exalted anthropology. On the one side, Merton makes his own the patristic emphasis on Christ as the "*Alpha and the Omega, the beginning and the end*" (Rev 21:6) who is eternally before humanity, before Adam. "He is the uncreated Image of which we are created images." On the other side, it is the free choice, the "delight" of the Image, to become one with humanity. And here Merton gestures explicitly toward an ontological kinship between Sophia and humankind: "Thus even our natural life is rooted in the divine life of our Creator. It flows directly from the Image 'Who is the Wisdom of God, in Whom God knows His power, His wisdom and His goodness.'"[17] Our vocation as images of the Image, living reflections (icons) of Sophia, is already written, so to speak, in the eternal dance of trinitarian life. Human life always and everywhere "is ontologically suspended from the life of God."[18]

What, then, does the incarnation add to humanity that it did not already have? For Merton the hypostatic union is both the sign and ontological instrument of our own "spiritual perfection," the font of grace that makes deification possible: "And we shall see that the soul of Christ, united to the Word in a union closer than any other union of two natures that ever has existed or ever will exist, is not only the model of our existential communion with God, but is the *source of grace by which that union is effected in our souls.*"[19] While the incarnation is inseparable from the redemptive work of Christ's life, death, and resurrection, it is clear that Merton is not concerned here with the history as such of Jesus of Nazareth. Again, in Merton's view, we know Jesus because he is risen, because the light of his victory over sin and death is real, though hidden, in history; we know him because he is the Christ.[20] The problem of our failure to know him as such, as coming to birth in ourselves and in all the world, is for Merton a problem of awareness, or better, of realization.

We pause here to recall the broad theological context with which this study began, namely, the struggle to (re)formulate Christian self-identity before the horizon of religious pluralism and interfaith dialogue. Note that for Merton, the paradoxical mystery at the heart of a robustly analogical and incarnational faith—that "He is the uncreated Image of which we are created images," that "even our natural life is rooted in the divine life of our Creator"—is the positive foundation for the ontological and spiritual unity of all human beings in Christ. "If Adam, in whom we are all 'one image of

17. Ibid., 142.
18. Ibid., 143.
19. Ibid., 139. Note the phrase "existential communion," the original title of *The New Man*.
20. See the discussion "Historical Jesus/Mystical Christ" in chap. 1.

God' is created in Christ, then we are all one image of God, by creation, in Christ."[21] To say it in the terms of the contemporary theology of religions, our status as "images of the divine Image" is Merton's basis for an all-encompassing Christian inclusivism, the ground for an openness and dialogue that positively expects to encounter Christ, the light and Wisdom of God, hidden in the stranger. "It is to be noticed that this uncreated Image of God is one and the same in all the souls that receive their life from Him. *At the center of our souls we meet together*, spiritually, in the infinite source of all our different created lives."[22]

Recapitulation and Creative Freedom in the Body of Christ

In the midst of his robust apologia for the mystical and cosmic Christ, Merton interjects this rather bald understatement: "To us, no doubt, this all seems very strange."[23] The reasons he gives, however, for its strangeness—that is, our incapacity to comprehend the "mysterious com-penetration" of Christ with the whole cosmos—have little to do with the usual epistemological objections of post-Enlightenment theology. The presence of Christ remains hidden for two reasons: first, because of sin, which radically obscures our capacity to perceive the divine image and light in the world, in ourselves, and in others; and second, because Christ is so near to us that *he is ourselves*.[24] In both cases Merton points to contemplation as "a most important part of man's cooperation in the spiritualization and restoration of the cosmos."[25] To appreciate the significance of contemplation in Merton's posture toward both the Christian life (*ad intra*) and other religious paths (*ad extra*), it is necessary to dwell a little more on the soteriology presented in "The Second Adam," that is, its doctrine of sin, redemption, and recapitulation in the Body of Christ, the New Adam.

The central myth from which Merton operates is that of Genesis: humanity's loss of an original paradisal unity.[26] "Humanity, which was one image of God in Adam, or, if you prefer, one single 'mirror' of the divine nature, was shattered into millions of fragments by that original sin which alienated each

---

21. NM, 138.

22. Ibid., 142–43; emphasis added. Bulgakov's conception of Wisdom as the "theanthropy," or the "eternal humanity in God," is clearly at play here (cf. SFS, 104–7, 381).

23. NM, 137.

24. See NM, 138, 160; cf. SFS, 381; and the letter of April 1959 to Suzuki: "We follow Him, we find Him . . . and then He must vanish and we must go along without Him at our side. Why? Because He is even closer than that. *He is ourself*" (HGL, 564).

25. ICM, 125.

26. McCaslin, in MHPH, 246; McCaslin associates Merton on this point with William Blake.

man from God, from other men and from himself. But the broken mirror becomes once again a perfectly united image of God in the union of those who are one in Christ."[27] How is the "broken mirror" made whole again? Significantly, Merton places freedom—first the freedom of Jesus, then our own—at the center of his soteriology of recapitulation. "The second Adam, by the perfect use of His freedom in obedience to the Truth, reintegrated man into the reality of the spiritual order. He restored man to his original existential communion with God, the source of life, and thus opened again to him the closed gates of Paradise."[28] Freedom is not only the means by which the divine image is shattered—through pride, illusion, self-assertion, and inordinate desire—it is also the means by which all creation is recapitulated in Christ. The labor of the second Adam comes to its completion and cosmic fulfillment in the resurrection.

While it is true, then, as William Shannon notes, that it is "the risen Christ (especially the Christ of the Pauline epistles), rather than the Jesus of the Gospels, who is most prominent in Merton's writings,"[29] we must not overlook the central importance Merton gives to Jesus' freedom as the means of our redemption, even if his poetic manner of expressing it may seem to distance his "Christ" from "Jesus of Nazareth," or for that matter, from the rest of us. Merton's high Christology, in other words, must never be separated from his high anthropology, his robust doctrine of the "true self." The true self, enlightened by the divine "fire" or spiritual freedom given to us as adopted sons and daughters of God, and which does not need to be "stolen," represents the deepest principle of continuity with Christ, and not separation. Thus his meditation on the "mystery of Christ" in *New Seeds of Contemplation*, a text considered in relation to Newman's sacramental principle in chapter 2:

> As a magnifying glass concentrates the rays of the sun into a little burning knot of heat that can set fire to a dry leaf or a piece of paper, so the mystery of Christ in the Gospel concentrates the rays of God's light and fire to a point that sets fire to the spirit of man. . . . Through the glass of His Incarnation He concentrates the rays of His Divine Truth and Love upon us so that we feel the burn, and all mystical experience is communicated to men through the Man Christ.
>
> For in Christ God is made Man. In Him God and man are no longer separate, remote from one another, but inseparably one, unconfused and yet indivisible. Hence in Christ everything that is divine and supernatural becomes accessible on the human level to every man born of woman,

27. NM, 148–49.
28. Ibid., 151.
29. William Shannon, "Christology," in TME, 51–54, at 53.

to every son of Adam. What is divine has now become connatural to us in Christ's love so that if we receive Him and are united with Him in friendship, He Who is at the same time God and our brother, grants us the divine life that is now able to be ours on our human level. We become sons of God by adoption in so far as we are like Christ and His brothers.[30]

Note how the text moves "from the mystery of Christ that meets us in the Gospel to the action of the risen Christ who comes to us through the Spirit."[31] As Merton notes a few pages later, "We read the Gospels not merely to get a picture or an idea of Christ but to enter in and pass through the words of revelation to establish, by faith, a vital contact with the Christ Who dwells in our souls as God."[32] Yet this passing through must not be misunderstood as an ascent from the humanity of Christ to his divinity, falsely posited as the goal of the spiritual life.[33] To the contrary—and this is a critical point that keeps Merton's Christology from drifting into gnosticism or Nestorianism—faith in Jesus Christ is radically personalistic. "Our love and knowledge of Christ do not terminate in His human *nature* or in His divine *nature* but in His *Person*. . . . We do not love Christ for what He has but for *Who He is*."[34] In Christ, God comes to us not as a "what" but as a "Who," and herein, notes Merton, lay the real mystery and latent power of Christian agape:

> The power of a direct and simple contact with Him, not as with an *object* only, a "thing" seen or imagined, but in the transsubjective union of love which does not unite an object with a subject but *two subjects in one affective union*. Hence, in love we can, so to speak, experience in our own hearts the intimate personal secret of the Beloved. . . . Thus He Who is, is present in the depths of our own being as our Friend,

---

30. NSC, 150. Merton's soteriology reflects Orthodoxy's emphasis on divinization, recapitulation, and *apokatastasis*. In "the most typically Eastern lines of thought," writes Paul Evdokimov, "the Atonement is better expressed in physical-ontological terms rather than ethical-legal. The aim here is not 'redemption' (from the Latin *redimo*, 'to buy back, to ransom'), nor even 'salvation' (in the individualistic sense of 'Salvationism')—but *apocatastasis*, universal healing and restoration" (Paul Evdokimov, *Woman and the Salvation of the World: A Christian Anthropology on the Charisms of Women*, trans. Anthony P. Gythiel (Crestwood, NY: St. Vladimir's Seminary Press, 1994), 68.

31. Shannon, "Christology," in TME, 53.

32. NSC, 156.

33. The crucial distinction in patristic Christology, suggests Merton, is not between "the two abstract natures in Christ, still less between the Person of Christ and the divine essence" but "between the state of the God-Man before His passion and resurrection, and after His triumph over death" (Thomas Merton, "The Humanity of Christ in Monastic Prayer," in *The Monastic Journey*, ed. Patrick Hart [Kalamazoo, MI: Cistercian, 1992], 87–106, at 96).

34. NSC, 153; cf. *Monastic Journey*, 104–6.

and as our other self. Such is the mystery of the Word dwelling in us by virtue of His Incarnation and our incorporation in His Mystical Body, the Church.[35]

It is important to dwell a little longer on the centrality of freedom in what may now be called Merton's *person*-centered Christology. The issue at stake is whether Merton's lyrical and cosmic approach to Christology distances Jesus (and the preexistent Logos-Christ) irreconcilably from the rest of us. In a letter of June 1967 to June Yungblut, Merton acknowledges that he is "still hung up" on the traditional Christology of Nicaea and Chalcedon, not the Jesus of historical criticism but, as he clarifies in a later letter, "the Christ born in us in poverty, as [in] Eckhart; the Christ of Julian of Norwich; the Christ of immediate experience all down through the mystical tradition."[36] While, on the one hand, Merton would not hesitate to identify Jesus with God, on the other hand, when pressed into the discussion, he much favors the term "God-Man" to emphasize the unity of the one Person, Jesus Christ.[37] The point is, in emphasizing the Person and not the two Natures in the abstract, it is clear that Merton interprets Chalcedonian Christology as an expression not of discontinuity but of Christ's elemental continuity with human beings, with concrete *persons*, a continuity that corresponds with our spiritual freedom as adopted sons and daughters of God. For Merton, the paradoxical formula at the heart of Christology (truly human/truly divine) expresses a mystery that applies not only to Jesus Christ but analogically to all human beings, to every person, by virtue of the incarnation, and the potency for *theosis* that the incarnation inscribes into human being.[38]

In his lecture notes of 1961 on Christian mysticism, Merton cites the classic formulation of Athanasius on this point: "He became man in order that we

35. NSC, 153–54.

36. HGL, 637, 643; the clarification comes in the important follow-up letter (March 29, 1968), detailed in chap. 1, in which he describes his Christ as the "Christ of the ikons."

37. On this point Kilcourse underscores Merton's affinity with Gerard Manley Hopkins, who in a letter to Robert Bridges, distinguishes between his own Catholic sensibilities and Bridges' non-Catholic sense of Christ: "To you [says Hopkins to Bridges] it comes to: Christ is in some sense God and in some sense he is not God—and your interest is in the uncertainty; to the Catholic it is: Christ is in every sense God and in every sense man, and the interest is in the locked and inseparable combination, or rather it is in the Person in whom the combination has its place" (Kilcourse, 35).

38. In Orthodox doctrine there is a sense in which the gift of deification "has already been planted in human soil" through the incarnation: "A certain ontological reformation or regeneration of human nature was *already* accomplished in Christ, since human nature was given back its essential character of being in the image of God, i.e., of being in communion with God" (J. D. Kornblatt and R. F. Gustafson, "Introduction," in *Russian Religious Thought*, ed. by idem [Madison, WI: University of Wisconsin Press, 1996], 12, citing Beatrice de Bary).

might become God. He made himself visible in his body in order that we might have an idea of the invisible Father. He underwent outrages from men in order that we might have part in immortality."[39] Divinization is not only "the result of the Incarnation" but also "the very *purpose* of the Incarnation."[40] In other words, for Athanasius, "divinization and salvation are regarded as one and the same thing. . . . We are called to 'be sons of God in Christ.'"[41] And while Athanasius "is not explicitly concerned with what we would call mystical experience," his doctrine "is the theological foundation for all such experience."[42]

In short, in a manner that is real, though hidden, individual human life (to recall Pasternak) has become "the life story of God," and henceforth the contents of history "fill the vast expanses of the universe."[43] With the incarnation "the reign of numbers was at an end." Human beings are not meant to "die in a ditch like a dog" but to be "at home in history," to celebrate life in its "barest and most elementary essentials."[44] Above all, we are destined and empowered to love, which is to share in no less than Jesus' manner of life and victory over death.[45] It is precisely in this shared personhood, this shared freedom and potency for love and for life—but also, therefore, for terrible suffering, for failure unto death—that Merton can say that God "is *all* in Christ," that God "has become not only one of us but even our very selves."[46]

Once again, there is nothing passive or static about Merton's conception of salvation in Christ. Returning to *The New Man*, Merton writes that Christ's victory over death is the source of the grace that empowers *our* free and creative participation in the dawning of a "new creation":

> We shall see that in order to enter fully into communion with the life brought to us by Christ we must in some sense—sacramentally, asceti-

---

39. ICM, 62.

40. Ibid., 60.

41. Ibid., 61.

42. Ibid., 62. Merton notes that Athanasius's emphasis on divinization "is so strong that it almost constitutes an exaggeration . . . [What] he says about the Incarnation must not make us forget the prime importance of the Cross and the Redemption of man" (60); cf. pp. 51–52, where he responds to Harnack's criticisms of patristic theology.

43. DQ, 66–67.

44. Ibid., 12.

45. Thus the climactic pages on freedom concluding "The Pasternak Affair": "Will we never grow up, and get down to the business of living productively on this earth, in unity and peace? . . . Christ has planted in the world the seeds of something altogether new, but they do not grow by themselves" (DQ, 65).

46. SFS, 381. Compare with Merton's devastating critique of the "satanic theology," which convinces us that Christ "was *not like you*": "He knew He was God. He knew He was *not like you*. He thought of this and was secretly pleased all the time. He thought: I am God, I am *not like them*" (CGB, 141–42).

cally, mystically—die with Christ and rise with Him from the dead. . . . The New Adam creates himself, not only by the work and suffering and triumph of the Head, Jesus Christ, but also by the labors and sufferings and cooperation of each one of the members. . . . We must never forget this active and dynamic view of the Kingdom of Christ. For if we are all "one man in Him" that does not mean that we float into heaven on the tide of His merits, without any efforts or merits of our own.[47]

Taking his lead from Pius XII's *Mystici Corporis Christi* ("On the Mystical Body of Christ"), Merton calls our participation in redemption the birth of the "New Adam," or the "New Man." A history played out in Christ is a history in which human freedom and creativity matters. The life of discipleship is both a task—"an ascetic struggle, in which our spirit, united with the Spirit of God, resists the flesh, its desires and illusions"[48]—and a profound, unmerited grace, crowned by the resurrection. Joining himself to the cosmotheandric worldview of Orthodoxy, Merton proclaims that a toned-down view of the human person will not do for those who believe in, and experience in mystery, the incarnation of the Son of God.

It is significant that throughout *The New Man* both sides of the dialectic we are discussing here (incarnation/deification) reverberate together "in a typically Orthodox understanding of realized eschatology."[49] "For with the death and resurrection of Christ we are in a new world, a new age. The fullness of time has come."[50] Merton's conception of time, no less than space, is profoundly nondualistic; history, for the pilgrim Christian community, is more than "a horizontal movement across the surface of life."[51] In the age of resurrection, the present is seeded with eternal life; the cosmic victory that was before and remains yet to come is available to experience, not only epistemologically, through memory of the past or hope for the future, but ontologically, through the divine agency of light, Spirit, and presence. Realization dawns above all, for Christians, through participation in the Scriptures and liturgical life of the church.[52]

---

47. NM, 154–55.
48. Ibid., 157.
49. A. M. Allchin, "Our Lives a Powerful Pentecost," in MHPH, 121–40, at 129.
50. NM, 148.
51. ZBA, 25.
52. Allchin underscores the impact of the eschatology of Vladimir Lossky (d. 1958), and through him Gregory Palamas, on Merton's thinking in the early 1960s (MHPH, 135–38); cf. Merton's "Orthodoxy and the World," MHPH, 481–84; DWL, 181–82. Merton's emphasis on the redeemed present resonates deeply, of course, with Zen.

The Natural and Supernatural Orders

But where, we may ask again, does this leave all those who are outside the visible structures of Christianity? Merton's focus in the latter part of "The Second Adam" shifts from the "natural unity of man in the divine Image" to the "supernatural union with God in the Spirit and in Christ," that is, to the church, our existential communion with God in the Mystical Body of Christ, fired by our participation in sacramental life. Indeed, the ecclesiology throughout *The New Man* truly soars. The issue I wish to raise here is Merton's use of the natural/supernatural distinction of neoscholasticism, which at times conveys, if not the triumphalism of pre-1950s Catholicism, then still a vapor of that condescension with which Catholic theology prior to Vatican II looked upon the non-Christian world. In other words, if Merton's Christology is leaning here in the direction of a broadly christocentric inclusivism, his ecclesiology, it would seem, had not quite caught up. The following passage provides an important bridge back into the topic of contemplation:

> The natural unity of man in the divine Image is therefore far different from their supernatural unity in Christ. First of all, the natural unity does, perhaps in rare cases become an object of consciousness, but ordinarily it is never thought of by men. Secondly, the natural union with the divine Image as source of our physical life does nothing, of itself, to sanctify us or to make us virtuous except in a very imperfect way which contributes nothing to our true happiness. Thirdly, although by nature we are united to God, we cannot be said to possess Him or to know Him as He really is and this natural union does nothing to reduce the distance of our exile from Him and from His Paradise. Finally, the fact that we are all united to God in one natural image and in one human nature has never contributed much to a true union among men. It cannot keep them from fighting and hating one another, from enslaving and exploiting one another and from destroying in one another the very image of Him they ought to love above all things.[53]

We have to be careful—as no doubt Merton was being careful when he drafted *The New Man* in the mid-1950s—not to read too much (or too little) into such passages where he tries to distinguish, perhaps not altogether successfully, between the life of grace inside the visible body of the church and outside; between humanity's natural unity "in Adam" and the supernatural unity of the "New Adam," which is "heavenly" and "totally spiritual." Nevertheless, it is hard to overlook the largely negative tenor of this account of the non-Christian, secular, or natural world, especially in light of the transfor-

53. NM, 146–47.

mation he was undergoing when the book was finally published in 1961. It is hard to imagine Merton writing such a passage in 1961, or even in 1959, with its suggestion that only in "rare cases" do people outside the church become explicitly conscious of their existential communion with God, that a purely natural union with God "as the source of our physical life" by itself "does nothing" to lead us to holiness or "true happiness."

On the other hand, Merton does not entirely subjugate "natural" union with God to the "supernatural"; still less does he advance a vague or condescending theory of "natural religion." In the first place, while every person is naturally joined to God, this does not imply that all persons (including Christians) are conscious of it in a meaningful way, that is, in a way that yields a life of holiness or "true happiness." To become fully aware of oneself in God requires a community, a tradition that immerses one in a sacred ("supernatural") history, a living praxis in relationship to God, the world, and others. Even more, what stands out most in this passage is Merton's lament for the historical enmity between different peoples and (implicitly) the religions of the world. The fact that most of us rarely ponder, much less see, our kinship with one another in God, he suggests, is the chief reason we fight, hate, enslave, and exploit one another, "destroying in one another the very image" of God that we "ought to love above all things."

It follows that liberation and peace for the human race will require the grace of correct thinking and correct seeing. What exactly do we fail to see? Just this: that the image of God "is one and the same in all the souls that receive their life from Him. At the center of our souls we meet together, spiritually, in the infinite source of all our different created lives." Again, "God speaks, and God is to be heard, not only on Sinai, not only in my own heart, but in the *voice of the stranger*."[54] It is more than possible, of course, that talk of "seeing Christ in the other" has become so reflexive or platitudinous in the Christian mind that the radical transformation implied by Merton's conception of contemplation—"a kind of knowledge by identification, an intersubjective knowledge, a communion in cosmic awareness and in nature . . . a wisdom based on love"[55]—will completely escape us. Yet the crucial point to take from this text is this: Because of humanity's essential kinship in the creative life of the Trinity from the beginning, Christians share at least potentially with non-Christians an intuitive, existential illumination that is neither merely epistemological nor stuck on this side of an impenetrable dualism, whether Kantian, historicist, empiricist, agnostic, or otherwise.

54. Thomas Merton, *The Collected Poems of Thomas Merton* (New York: New Directions, 1977), 384–85.
55. LE, 108.

We share, rather, an existential communion that is "naturally" theological, "ontologically suspended from the life of God."[56]

We must say that this friendship in wisdom is potential, of course, because not all Christians or non-Christians are engaged in this sort of contemplation. Of those who are, too few are talking with one other. Merton grows to lament this fact deeply, suggesting that if religion is going to save and not destroy us, it will do so only to the degree it engenders a more contemplative approach to reality, to all our relationships in the social, political, and environmental spheres. To be clear, Merton harbored no illusions about the manifold differences across religious and cultural boundaries, or the difficulty of dialogue across deep and often painful historical and conceptual divides. Nevertheless, he came to believe that dialogue across religious boundaries involves the human community not only in an existential "exchange of gifts,"[57] as Pope John Paul II has written; when engaged in humility and love, dialogue reverberates inside the very life of God. It is not merely communication but communion in the "hidden ground" of Love.

Contemplation and Nondualism: "Waking from a Dream of Separateness"

> Now the Lord is the Spirit, and where the Spirit of the Lord is, there is freedom. And all of us, with unveiled faces, seeing the glory of the Lord as though reflected in a mirror, are being transformed into the same image from one degree of glory to another; for this comes from the Lord, the Spirit. (2 Cor 3:17-18)

It was said above that the presence of Christ remains hidden from the world for two reasons—because of sin, which obscures the divine image, and because of his nearness: "he is closer to us than we are to ourselves and that is why we do not notice Him. It is harder for us to see Him than for us to see our own eyes."[58] In the climactic final pages of "The Second Adam," Merton reflects on Second Corinthians, adding his own dynamic terms of "transformation," "realization," "awakening," and "awareness" to St. Paul's vivid visual metaphors of "unveiling," "image," and "glory." What Merton

---

56. "The capacity for contemplative experience and the fact of its realization . . . are therefore implicit in all the great religious traditions, whether Asian or European, whether Hindu, Buddhist, Moslem, or Christian" (MZM, 209).

57. See *Ut unum sint* 28: "[All] dialogue involves a global, existential dimension. . . . [It] is not simply an exchange of ideas. In some way it is also an 'exchange of gifts'"; cf. *Gaudium et spes* 91–93.

58. NM, 138.

signals with such terms is an understanding of salvation that is bound up inextricably with transformation through contemplation.[59]

In the opening pages of *The New Man* Merton describes contemplation as the means of liberation from the Cartesian prison of the false self and, not least, from the dangerous tendency to own and domesticate the mystery of God: "[The] experience of contemplation is the experience of God's life and presence within ourselves not as object but as the transcendent source of our own subjectivity. Contemplation is a mystery in which God reveals Himself to us as the very center of our own most intimate self—*intimior intimo meo* as St. Augustine said. When the realization of His presence bursts upon us, our own self disappears in Him and we pass mystically through the Red Sea of separation to lose ourselves (and thus find our true selves) in Him."[60] Thus we come to the extreme paradox of nondualism, which expresses, as Baillie puts it, both the "distinctive secret of the Christian life" and "the shortcomings of theological prose" in expressing it.

On the one hand, Merton grants that dualistic conceptions of God and Christ are unavoidable in the Christian imagination: "we see Him as an object separate from ourselves, as a being from whom we are alienated, even though we believe that He loves us and that we love Him."[61] Not only in existential terms does God seem to dwell "out there," so also theological language cannot help yielding to a certain dualism: "in respecting the metaphysical distinction between the Creator and creature we have to emphasize the I-Thou relationship between the soul and God."[62] On the other hand, "in contemplation this division disappears, for contemplation goes beyond concepts and apprehends God . . . as the Reality within our own reality, the Being within our being, the life of our life."[63] It is only by passing through "the Red Sea of separation" that we wake up as our true selves, "with faces unveiled," reflecting as in a mirror the glory of the Lord. "And when a mirror is full of light, you do not see the glass—you are blinded by the light."[64]

As with Newman's work, the poetic exuberance of such passages should not obscure the concreteness with which Merton conceives of the face-to-face encounter with the other. In other words, it is not only the Christian whose

59. Merton's focus on transformation through contemplative practice suggests that interfaith dialogue center not on the language of "salvation" so much as conversion and holiness. See Anne Carr, "Merton's East-West Reflections," *Horizons* 21 (1994): 243–45; William H. Shannon, "Thomas Merton in Dialogue with Eastern Religions," in *The Vision of Thomas Merton*, ed. Patrick O'Connell (Notre Dame, IN: Ave Maria Press, 2003), 219–20.

60. NM, 19.

61. Ibid., 18.

62. Ibid.

63. Ibid., 19.

64. Ibid., 159.

unveiled face "shines like the sun," but every human person, in all their luminous distinctness. It is this paradoxical experience of light, presence, and
unity—somehow both christocentric and apophatic at once—that Merton has
in mind in his letter to Suzuki in 1959, when he describes Christ as "unknown
and unseen": "We follow Him, we find Him . . . and then He must vanish and
we must go along without Him at our side."[65] Why must we "go along without
Him at our side"? Because "we ourselves are Adam, we ourselves are Christ"
and because "we are all dwelling in one another."[66] Liberation is the dawning
realization of who we already are "in one another and in him."

Finally, for Merton, the way of contemplation and *theosis* always implies
an ascetic struggle, self-purification, and love, which is to say, an integral
way of life.[67] It is not surprising that of all the religious traditions he studied, it was above all in Zen discipline and practice that Merton perceived
"a very real quality of existential likeness"[68] with Christian contemplation.
Nor is it insignificant, as we saw in chapter 4, that he would describe Zen in
terms of wisdom: "the true purpose of Zen [is] awakening a deep ontological
awareness, a wisdom-intuition (*Prajna*) in the ground of the being of the one
awakened."[69] Such awareness, resting its gaze with love on the concrete and
particular, on the intrinsic goodness of things, has little to do with a gnostic or
world-denying spiritualism. To the contrary, by contemplation "in Christ" we
awaken in mystery to our essential kinship and unity with the whole cosmos—
or better, every rock, every creature, every blade of grass within it.

Like waters through a dam, this gathering sophianic vision bursts forth in
the final pages of *New Seeds of Contemplation*, where we meet the Wisdom-
child of Proverbs 8, "playing in the world, playing before Him at all times."[70]
"We do not have to go very far," Merton writes, "to catch echoes of that game,
and of that dancing. When we are alone on a starlit night; when by chance we

65. HGL, 564.

66. NM, 161.

67. This is not an incidental point. For Merton "mysticism and asceticism form an organic
whole," and he laments their separation in Christian spirituality as "an unfortunate modern development" (ICM, 21–22). His approach is balanced, describing asceticism both in the familiar
negative terms ("renunciation," "taking up one's cross") and in positive terms ("development
of the *life of grace* in us, cooperation with the Holy Spirit more than conformity with a moral
or ascetic system") (19). On the one hand, "asceticism must be *real*. [We] must not cherish
illusions. [There is] no spiritual life when we are merely attached to ease, comfort, human
consolations" (20). On the other hand, its goal is wholly positive, namely, to engender "trust
in God" and "generosity with no second thought." It is "the liberation of charity in oneself" on
the way to "a more complete conformation to Christ" (21, citing de Guibert); see O'Connell's
discussion, ICM, xxiv–xxv; xxxii–xxxiii.

68. AJ, 312.

69. ZBA, 48.

70. NSC, 290.

see the migrating birds in autumn descending on a grove of junipers to rest and eat; when we see children in a moment when they are really children; when we know love in our own hearts." All of these, "if we could let go of our own obsession with what we think is the meaning of it all," would no longer appear trivial, but would strike us as invitations to "forget ourselves on purpose, cast our awful solemnity to the winds," and join in "the general dance" of Sophia, at play in the garden of the Lord.[71]

The Marriage of East and West: *Hagia Sophia* (1962)

Hagia Sophia is a prose poem that celebrates divine Wisdom as the feminine manifestation of God. Structured in four parts based on the canonical hours of prayer, it is Merton's most lyrical expression of "Christ being born into the whole world," especially in that which is most "poor" and "hidden." It is a hymn of peace. Yet as this study has intimated from the beginning, *Hagia Sophia* is more than a powerful locus of personal and even communal transformation, or *lectio divina*. It also merits sustained study as a classic of modern Christian mysticism, not only for its bold rendering of the Catholic sacramental imagination, but also for its rare and wondrously realized marriage of Eastern and Western spirituality. While many of the personal, theological, and literary antecedents of the poem have already been traced, a brief description of events surrounding its composition and publication will set the stage for a close theological reading of the text.[72]

Art, Insight, and Conversation: The Birth of Hagia Sophia

One day in early 1959, Merton was visiting his friends Victor Hammer, the Vienna-born artist and printmaker, and his wife Carolyn, at their home in Lexington, Kentucky. As they sat together at lunch Merton noticed a triptych that Victor had painted, its central panel depicting the boy Christ being crowned by a dark-haired woman.[73] As the artist later recalled, Merton ("Father Louis" to the Hammers), while looking at the triptych, "asked quite abruptly, 'And who is the woman behind Christ?' I said, 'I do not know yet.' Without further question he gave his own answer. 'She is Hagia Sophia, Holy

---

71. Ibid., 296–97.

72. By no means have we considered all the relevant sources for *Hagia Sophia*. Most notably missing is Julian of Norwich, whose influence during this period, by Merton's own account, rivaled that of St. John of the Cross earlier in his life (see SD, 275). Jonathan Montaldo also suggests the influence of the psychologist Karl Stern and his book *The Flight from Woman* (Jonathan Montaldo, "A Gallery of Women's Faces and Dreams of Women from the Drawings of Thomas Merton," *The Thomas Merton Annual* 14 [2001]: 155–72, at 156).

73. See page 300.

Wisdom, who crowns Christ.' And this she was—and is."[74] Some days later Hammer wrote to Merton, asking him to expand on what he had said about Holy Wisdom. Merton obliges in a letter of May 14, 1959: "The first thing to be said, of course, is that Hagia Sophia is God Himself. God is not only a Father but a Mother. He is both at the same time. . . . [T]o ignore this distinction is to lose touch with the fullness of God. This is a very ancient intuition of reality which goes back to the oldest Oriental thought. . . . For the 'masculine-feminine' relationship is basic in all reality—simply because all reality mirrors the reality of God."[75]

As the letter continues, Merton's thoughts seem to spill onto the page as if by stream of consciousness. His friend's inquiry seems to have opened a kind of conceptual and imaginative floodgate in Merton. Over the next five or six paragraphs, he identifies Sophia as "the dark, nameless *Ousia* [Being]" of God, not one of the Three Divine Persons, but each "at the same time, are Sophia and manifest her." She is "the Tao, the nameless pivot of all being and nature. . . that which is the smallest and poorest and most humble in all." She is "the 'feminine child' playing before Him at all times, playing in the world' (Proverbs 8)." Above all Sophia is unfathomable *mercy*, made manifest in the world by means of the incarnation, death, and resurrection of Jesus Christ.

"Pushing it further," Merton identifies Sophia as God's love and mercy coming to birth in us. "In the sense that God is Love, is Mercy, is Humility, is Hiddenness, He shows Himself to us within ourselves as our own poverty, our own nothingness (which Christ took upon Himself, ordained for this by the Incarnation in the womb of the Virgin) (the crowning in your picture), and if we receive the humility of God into our hearts, we become able to accept and embrace and love this very poverty, which is Himself and His Sophia." Mercy is the key to our participation in the life of God, notes Merton, because it expresses "the infinitely mysterious power of pardon" revealed in the life of Jesus; mercy "cuts across the divisions and passes beyond every philosophical and religious ideal."[76] Indeed, as Sophia, mercy "is not an ideal, not an abstraction, but the highest reality . . . [which] must manifest herself to us not only in power but also in poverty." As he had written in *The Sign of Jonas*, "*What was poor has become infinite. . . . I loved what was most frail. . . . I touched what was without substance, and within what was not, I am.*"[77] It is

---

74. Cited in MHPH, 234. Prov 4:8-9 reads: "[Wisdom] will honor you if you embrace her. / She will place on your head a fair garland; / she will bestow on you a beautiful crown."

75. Thomas Merton, *Witness to Freedom: The Letters of Thomas Merton in Times of Crisis*, ed. William H. Shannon (New York: Harcourt Brace, 1995), 4; hereafter WF. All citations from the letter in the following paragraph are from WF, 4–5.

76. Ibid., 5.

77. SJ, 362.

as if Merton is again hearing the Voice of God in Paradise—*"Mercy within mercy within mercy"*—but now in an unmistakably feminine key: Sophia.

By the time he concludes the letter, Merton seems to realize that their conversation has given birth to something significant, and he asks Hammer: "Maybe we could make a little broadsheet on Sophia, with the material begun here???"[78] Of course this is precisely what would happen. Drawing material from the letter and his journal entries, especially the "awakening" passage of July 2, 1960, Merton completed *Hagia Sophia* during Pentecost in the spring of 1961. Note that this is the very same Pentecost in which the sublime "A Prayer to God My Father on the Vigil of Pentecost" came to birth, and also the same Pentecost that marked the conclusion of the course on mystical theology. In short, the spring of 1961 was a time of endings but also of extraordinary beginnings for Merton, the discovery and dedication of himself as an intimate son and friend of God: "[Here] You see me. Here You love me. Here You ask the response of my own love, and of my confidence. Here You ask me to be nothing else than Your friend."[79] It is also significant that the original Vigil of Pentecost prayer (May 20, 1961) concludes with Merton asking for the courage to "be a man of peace and to help bring peace to the world," to learn the way "of truth and nonviolence," and for the grace to accept whatever difficult consequences might follow.[80]

The journals of 1961, just as the Pentecost prayer, reflect Merton's struggle to come to terms with the fact that his increasingly public stance on issues of peace and social justice would put him at odds with many Catholics (including the leadership of his own order) who preferred the pious persona of *The Seven Storey Mountain*. "What hurts me most is to have been inexorably trapped by my own folly. Wanting to prove myself a Catholic—and of course not perfectly succeeding. They all admit and commend my good will, but frankly, I am not one of the bunch, am I?"[81] Finally, on July 23, 1961, in what seems to be a spiritual turning point, he writes: "I will stop making any kind

---

78. WF, 6. It was Merton's habit to keep a record of his correspondence by typing letters with carbon paper. Halfway through the letter to Hammer, he pauses to express his anxiety about losing the insights now finding their way to the page: "I wrote that first page without keeping a carbon, but I am getting someone to copy it because I am going to want to know what I said. I say these things and forget them" (WF, 5).

79. TTW, 120; cf. CGB, 177–79.

80. TTW, 121. On this point it is striking to compare the Vigil of Pentecost prayer with Sergius Bulgakov's commentary on John the Baptist's friendship with Christ, and the self-sacrifice that it involves: "Every soul that comes to Christ must become not only a bride but also a friend of the Bridegroom, i.e., has to pass through the self-immolation of human self-will, human self-assertion . . . to reject self-deification and the divinity of humanity, to taste the voluntary death of self-sacrifice" (cited in Paul Valliere, MRT, 317).

81. TTW, 125.

of effort to justify myself to anybody. To prepare a place for myself anywhere, among any group. . . . Peace is impossible until I fully and totally realize, and embrace the realization, that I am already forgotten. . . . Render unto God the things that are God's."[82]

In January of 1962, *Hagia Sophia* came to print in a stunning limited edition on Hammer's handpress.[83] It was reprinted in a second edition with the artist's icon illustrating the text, and finally became the centerpiece of Merton's book of poems, *Emblems of a Season of Fury*. The prominent placement of *Hagia Sophia* in this collection, which includes devastating poems on racism ("And the Children of Birmingham"), genocide ("Chant to Be Used in Processions around a Site with Furnaces"), and political oppression ("A Picture of Lee Ying"), calls to mind the journal of January 26, 1961: "Faith in Sophia, *natura naturans*, the great stabilizer today—for peace." It seems that God had responded generously to Merton's prayer for courage, and would do so to the end of his life.

An Exegesis of Hagia Sophia

The best grasp of mystical texts, as Mark Burrows reminds us, comes "not in criticism of the text, but in the 'performance' of reading, that moment when the mystical text becomes the occasion for a 'merging of the way of knowledge and the way of love.'"[84] If *Hagia Sophia* is anything, it is just such a mystical text, a realization of knowledge and love that came to slow birth in Merton, but that now awaits gestation in readers willing to give themselves over to its play of images and silences, its haunting evocation of divine-human *memoria*. Notwithstanding its status as one of Merton's most secret and daring works—and its title, which may sound exotic to Western Christian ears—there is nothing intrinsic in the poem itself that should give the uninitiated reader pause in entering into its revelatory landscape; for those familiar with it already, the poem bears many repeated readings. For all of these reasons I encourage the reader to linger reflectively in the text of *Hagia Sophia* before reading further.[85]

---

82. Ibid., 143–44. One can almost hear echoes of Herakleitos: "The wise man must make tremendous efforts to . . . keep himself alert, he must constantly 'seek for himself' and he must not fear to strive for the excellence that will make him an object of hatred and mistrust in the eyes of the conventional majority" (BT, 84).

83. Thomas Merton, *Hagia Sophia* (Lexington, KY: Stamperia del Santuccio, 1962).

84. Mark S. Burrows, "Words That Reach into the Silence: Mystical Languages of Unsaying," in *Minding the Spirit*, ed. Elizabeth A. Dreyer and Mark S. Burrows (Baltimore: Johns Hopkins, 2005), 213, citing Michael Sells.

85. All citations from the poem below are taken from *Emblems of a Season of Fury*, 61–69, repeated in its entirety in the final section of this book. The poem is also found in *A Thomas*

"Dawn. The Hour of Lauds."

The poem opens in a hospital room at dawn. The speaker is awakened "out of languor and darkness" by the soft voice of a nurse. The experience is all gift, belying its setting in a place of disease and subjugation to machines: for in "the cool hand of the nurse there is the touch of all life, the touch of Spirit," which "flows out to me . . . welcoming me tenderly, saluting me with indescribable humility." There are no sterile hospital walls and invasive florescent lamps here, only "a dimmed light," rising up "in wordless gentleness . . . from the unseen roots of all created being." It is "as if Nature made wise by God's Art and Incarnation were to stand over him and invite him with unutterable sweetness to be awake and to live." This "hidden wholeness" brought on by the nurse's touch is "Wisdom, the Mother of all, *Natura naturans*," who "is at once my own being, my own nature . . . speaking as Hagia Sophia, speaking as my sister, Wisdom."

The setting—"July the second, the Feast of Our Lady's Visitation. A Feast of Wisdom"—suggests that Mary, whose womb bears Christ into the created world, is a manifestation of Sophia, a theme taken up in the fourth part of the poem. The speaker's awakening by Wisdom, by the Blessed Virgin, by Eve, is a telescoping of biblical *memoria*: it is like suddenly "standing in clarity, in Paradise." Here Christ is before Adam, or perhaps *is* Adam, before Adam drifts into languor, forgetfulness, sleep. The touch of Eve's hand is restorative: it is like "the One Christ awakening in all the separate selves" and "coming back together into awareness . . . into unity of love." Sophia is an eschatological presence, an *Alpha* and *Omega*: she is present on "the first morning of the world" and "the Last Morning of the world when all the fragments of Adam will return from death at the voice of Hagia Sophia, and will know where they stand." As Susan McCaslin notes, her power "to quicken through her voice echoes the divine 'Fiat' of God at creation, the calling forth of new life through the Word."[86] As dawn's light breaks, she beckons "to all who will hear (*Sapientia clamitat in plateis*) and she cries out particularly to the little, to the ignorant and the helpless."[87]

From Proverbs 8 the text moves seamlessly, if implicitly, into the Beatitudes, invoking one of most ancient themes in Christian life: *poverty of spirit*. "Who is more little, who is more poor than the helpless man who lies asleep in his bed without awareness and without defense?" The poverty of the

Merton Reader, 506–11; MHPH, 255–60; *The Collected Poems of Thomas Merton*, 363–71; and *Thomas Merton: Spiritual Master: The Essential Writings*, ed. Lawrence Cunningham (New York: Paulist, 1992), 257–64.

86. Susan McCaslin, "Merton and 'Hagia Sophia,'" in MHPH, 235–54, at 245.

87. ESF, 62.

one who entrusts himself to the care of the nurse is contrasted sharply with the one "who has defended himself, fought for himself in sickness, planned for himself, guarded himself, loved himself alone and watched over his own life all night." The first one awakens "refreshed, beginning to be made whole"; the second "is killed at last by exhaustion. For him there is no newness. Everything is stale and old."

Thus the poem's intimations of paradise on earth—of being "born again . . . from the depths of divine fecundity," of "inexhaustible sweetness and purity," of "a silence that is a fount of action and joy"—are shadowed by suggestions of a world exiled from Sophia, a region of unlikeness, of noise, languor, war, and death. While the "helpless one," the one who admits his need and vulnerability, will awaken "strong at the voice of mercy," the restless and grasping one, the one "who fought for himself in sickness," will be "killed at last by exhaustion." Whereas war, and endless preparation for it, is predicated on the Promethean obsession with what is mine, and which must therefore be captured and defended without rest, peace begins with the awareness of what is already freely given, a deep sense of who I am, who we are: beloved daughters and sons of God. Peace, then, and healing, begins with poverty of spirit. *For theirs is the kingdom of heaven.*

In his conferences on prayer, John Cassian counsels the Christian to constantly recite the words of Psalm 69: "O God, come to my help, Lord, hurry to my rescue."[88] Why? When this verse is on our lips at all times, says Cassian, accompanying us in all our works and deeds, it "keeps us from despairing of our salvation." It not only reminds us of our frailty but also gives us the "assurance of being heard," that "help is always and everywhere present."[89] "What greater poverty," Cassian asks, "than the one who recognizes that he has no defense and no strength and begs each day for the largess of another?"[90] This is the "littleness" and "poverty" of the one who entrusts himself in all things to divine mercy, to the "cool hand" of Hagia Sophia. "What is the reward of his trust?" the poem asks. "Love takes him by the hand, and opens to him the doors of another life, another day."[91]

"Wisdom is one thing," says Herakleitos, "to know the thought by which all things are steered through all things."[92] The opening of *Hagia Sophia*, as Christopher Nugent suggests, in many ways represents "the re-birthing" of Herakleitos: "But if so, Merton is returning the favor, as it were, softening the severely bred Heraclitus with the feminine. He is 'confronting reality' . . . and

---

88. John Cassian, *Conferences*, trans. Colm Luibheid (New York: Paulist, 1985), 132.
89. Ibid., 133.
90. Ibid., 136.
91. ESF, 63.
92. Cited in BT, 98.

finding it to be gentleness."[93] Yet this gift of "inexhaustible sweetness"—"my Creator's Thought and Art within me"—is predicated on a difficult uncentering and asceticism of the self, a humility and self-emptying that begins with the recognition of one's own limitations, one's need for God, and one's undeniable need for the other. Such is the kenotic "beginning" that marks *Lauds*, the paradoxical "death" of ego that allows us to be born into life again without reentering the womb (John 3:4), and that frees us "to be made whole" again, with the dawn of each new day.

"Early Morning. The Hour of Prime."

In the opening section, "*The Hour of Lauds*," Merton evokes *le point vierge* described in *Conjectures of a Guilty Bystander*, that "blind sweet point" of dawn awakening, "when all creation in its innocence asks permission to 'be' once again, as it did on the first morning that ever was."[94] But by "*The Hour of Prime*," Wisdom's invitation has already been roundly spurned: "We do not hear the soft voice, the gentle voice, the merciful and feminine."[95] Indeed, morning is the hour of prime efficiency for modern "men of action," as Merton writes in *Conjectures*: "We face our mornings as men of undaunted purpose. We know the time and we dictate terms. We are in a position to dictate terms, we suppose. . . . We are in touch with the hidden inner laws."[96] Whether ensconced in cars on deadlocked freeways, hidden behind computer, TV, or cell-phone screens, we do not hear the "blessed, silent one, who speaks everywhere!"[97] Again, from *Conjectures*: "Lights on. Clocks ticking. Thermostats working. Electric shavers filling radios with static. 'Wisdom,' cries the dawn deacon, but we do not attend."[98]

The poem implicitly questions its audience: Can anyone still hear the song of "Nature made wise by God's Art and Incarnation"? Who sees "the uncomplaining pardon that bows down the . . . flowers to the dewy earth"? Yet Sophia remains "the candor of God's light, the expression of His simplicity,"[99] re-creating herself in generous splendor—*natura naturans*—moment to moment, year after year, despite human disregard and exploitation.

If nations worldwide are now waking up, in fits and starts, from a "conspiracy of sleep"[100] with regard to the destruction of the natural world, global

93. Christopher Nugent, "*Pax Heraclitus*" (unpublished, 2005), 4.
94. CGB, 131.
95. ESF, 63.
96. CGB, 131.
97. ESF, 63
98. CGB, 132.
99. ESF, 63.
100. From "Herakleitos the Obscure," BT, 83; see chap. 4.

society shows few signs of awakening from its nightmarish commitment to militarism and violence as the primary means of communication with all strange and sinister others. Indeed, our evident need for violence carries all the hallmarks of a religious and liturgical feast, as Merton saw four decades ago: "Instead of taking care to examine the realities of our political or social problems, we simply bring out the idols in solemn procession. 'We are the ones who are right, *they* are the ones who are wrong. We are the good guys, *they* are the bad guys.'"[101] "Dogs bark at everyone they do not know," says Herakleitos—a ritual played out with liturgical precision over the airwaves every morning, filling not only radios, but hearts and minds, "with static." Why the rhetoric, machinery, and obscene liturgy of war—with its collateral damage of rape, torture, imprisonment without trial, destruction of cultures, infrastructures, and hopes for future generations—ad nauseum? Because "we do not hear mercy, or yielding love, or non-resistance, or non-reprisal. . . . We do not see the Child who is prisoner in all the people, and who says nothing."[102]

While "*The Hour of Prime*" is the shortest of the four sections, its invocation of "the Child" yields the poem's most poignant image of innocence and hope, an image that Merton returns to repeatedly in his late writings. In his encounter with Proverb at Fourth and Walnut, the Child is the "secret beauty" within every person's heart, "the core of their reality, the person that each one is in God's eyes."[103] As he later describes the experience to Pasternak: "And they did not know their real identity as the Child so dear to God who, from before the beginning, was playing in His sight all days, playing in the world."[104] In "The Time of the End is the Time of No Room," she is the ironic Christ-child of the Nativity, who still comes into a world in which there is "no room," and whose place is therefore "with those who do not belong, who are rejected by power because they are regarded as weak, those who are discredited, who are denied the status of persons, tortured, exterminated."[105] Of course, when set in the context of other poems in *Emblems of a Season of Fury*—"And the Children of Birmingham," "Chant to Be Used in Processions around a Site with Furnaces," "A Picture of Lee Ying"—the description of the Child as a bound prisoner "who says nothing" becomes almost unbearably poignant. That is to say, it becomes an accusation.[106]

---

101. FV, 154.

102. ESF, 63.

103. CGB, 158.

104. CT, 90.

105. RU, 72–73.

106. Recall the journal of April 25, 1958: "we have killed the Innocents . . . and Christ flees from us into Egypt" (SFS, 197). Merton's eschatological identification of Christ with the innocent victims of history—whether the child of the nativity or the crucified Jesus—suggests

Nevertheless, the Child herself does not yield to despair. In the stroke of a single image, the poem resounds with disarming hope: "She smiles, for though they have bound her, she cannot be a prisoner."[107] The line evokes Pasternak's celebration (and protest) of individual human life and of love in the "reign of numbers." No matter how badly the divine image in humanity has been mocked and desecrated, there remains an elemental goodness and divine light rising up in the hidden fabric of countless lives that can never be extinguished. Often, in conditions that would merit hatred and despair, love abounds and overflows in human hearts, resisting "the Unspeakable." As Merton professes in an impromptu prayer offered in Calcutta, shortly before his death: "Love has overcome. Love is victorious. Amen."[108]

And not only love as *agape*, but love as *eros*, initiating the playful dance of new life in sexual union, an implicit act of hope; love as *filios*, nurturing friendships across racial, economic, religious, and cultural boundaries, and laboring for healing and justice against resentment, cynicism, violence; and love as *creativity*, building up and inspiring the community in the labor of artists, teachers, scientists, civil servants, and so on. In these manifold expressions of social love and creativity, or what Paul Tillich calls a "communal eros,"[109] the hidden Christ finds a home in human history. It is not that the Child "is strong, or clever, but simply that she does not understand imprisonment."[110]

The symbol of the Child figures prominently in the striking opening of *Conjectures of a Guilty Bystander*, which recounts the story of a dream that Karl Barth, the great Protestant theologian of the early twentieth century, has about Mozart, in which "he was appointed to examine Mozart in theology." What moves Merton most of all in the story is Barth's suggestion that "it is a child, even a 'divine' child, who speaks in Mozart's music to us." "Each day, for years," Merton writes, "Barth played Mozart every morning before going to work on his dogma: unconsciously seeking to awaken, perhaps, the hidden sophianic Mozart in himself, the central wisdom that comes in tune with the divine and cosmic music and is saved by love, yes, even by *eros*. While the other, theological self, seemingly more concerned with love, grasps at a

---

that just behind the veil of the visible world, countless lives and bodies cut down, tortured, raped, dismembered, and turned to ash by war shall be (are *already*) rekindled and made whole again by "God's Art and Incarnation." See, e.g., Merton's striking letter to Suzuki (April 11, 1959) in which he apologizes for "the huge burden of the sins of the Western World": "The victims of Hiroshima and Nagasaki are before me and beside me every day when I say Mass. I pray for them and I feel they intercede for me before God" (HGL, 566).

107. ESF, 63–64.
108. AJ, 319.
109. Cited in LL, 64.
110. ESF, 64.

more stern, more cerebral *agape*: a love that, after all, is not in our own heart but *only in God* and revealed only to our head."[111]

Barth's dream, Merton suggests, has to do with his salvation: perhaps he "is striving to admit that he will be saved more by the Mozart in himself than by his theology." The passage calls to mind Pasternak's comment on the "inner music" of the gospels, with Merton here contrasting the *eros* and playfulness of Mozart (and Mozart's Catholicism!) with the "more cerebral *agape*" of Barth's theology. Thus the hidden Child (the "hidden sophianic Mozart") in Barth—in the teachings of Jesus, in all of us—is "the central wisdom that comes in tune with the divine and cosmic music and is saved by love, yes, even by *eros*." He closes the passage with a proclamation directed no less at himself than at Barth: "Fear not, Karl Barth! Trust in the divine mercy. Though you have grown up to become a theologian, Christ remains a child in you. Your books (and mine) matter less than we might think! There is in us a Mozart who will be our salvation."[112]

The final two stanzas of *"The Hour of Prime"* are the most lyrical of the poem, invoking the Spirit of gentleness and creativity, truth and nonviolence that lives hidden in all things. This "fount of action and joy"—"one Wisdom, one Child, one Meaning, one Sister"—flows out "from the roots of all created being" and awaits our yielding consent. When we say yes, our lives become "the life story of God," and our simple acts of love fill "the vast expanses of the universe."[113]

> The stars rejoice in their setting, and in the rising of the Sun. The heavenly lights rejoice in the going forth of one man to make a new world in the morning, because he has come out of the confused primordial dark night into consciousness. He has expressed the clear silence of Sophia in his heart. He has become eternal.[114]

---

111. CGB, 11.

112. Ibid., 12. There are several memorable passages in which Merton associates Sophia or "Proverb" directly with children (e.g., SFS, 270; NSC, 296; DWL, 259), and many more where he simply celebrates their spontaneity and joy. Still, the "innocence" of the Child who blazes "with the invisible light of heaven" (CGB, 158) in everyone should not be mistaken for a vaguely New Age, naive, or narcissistic "regression to the freshness of childhood." It is, rather, "a new birth, the divine birth in us" that empowers our freedom and creativity in history as cocreators with God. "To love you have to climb out of the cradle, where everything is 'getting,' and grow up to the maturity of giving, without concern for getting anything special in return" (LL, 34).

113. DQ, 67.

114. ESF, 64.

"High Morning. The Hour of Tierce."

At High Morning, the Sun as the "Face of God" is "diffused" mercifully into the softer light of Hagia Sophia, which shines not on all things so much as from within them, speaking "to us gently in ten thousand things." The phrase certainly recalls Hopkins, but also Merton's notes on *theoria physike*: "When a man has been purified and humbled, when his eye is single, and he is his own real self, then the *logoi* of things jump out at him spontaneously"[115]; *theoria* "implies a sense of community with things in the work of salvation."[116]

> All the perfections of created things are also in God; and therefore He is at once Father and Mother. As Father He stands in solitary might sur-rounded by darkness. As Mother His shining is diffused, embracing all His creatures with merciful tenderness and light. The Diffuse Shining of God is Hagia Sophia. . . . In Sophia His power is experienced only as mercy and as love.[117]

Lyrical passages of naming and unnaming follow, marking the hour of High Morning with palpable wonder and mystery, as if the speaker has ex-perienced something extraordinary and cannot be silent, yet struggles to say exactly what or who Sophia is. "Perhaps in a certain very primitive aspect Sophia is the unknown, the dark, the nameless Ousia. Perhaps she is even the Divine Nature, One in Father, Son and Holy Ghost. . . . This I do not know. Out of the silence Light is spoken." Biblical *memoria* rises to the surface, as diffuse light is sought out in primordial darkness, "in the Nameless Begin-ning, without Beginning." Most striking here, as McCaslin observes, is the oxymoronic coincidence of male and female metaphors, light and darkness, theophany and hiddenness: "The efforts to name Sophia, to catch her in the net of language defer to the apophatic tradition of 'unnaming.' Every naming becomes an unnaming, a backing off from language, and an insistence that words and names are inadequate before mystery. Sophia herself becomes 'the unknown, the dark, the nameless,'" reminding us that "God is not an object of knowledge. The God who is male and female, father and mother, is simultane-ously neither male nor female, transcending gender categories."[118]

But then there is a sudden shift in tone, a new confidence and seeming clarity: "Now the Wisdom of God, Sophia, comes forth, reaching from 'end to end mightily.'" She wills to be "the unseen pivot of all nature . . . that which is poorest and humblest, that which is most hidden in all things," yet

115. ICM, 132.
116. Ibid., 131.
117. ESF, 65.
118. McCaslin, in MHPH, 248–49.

also that which is "quite manifest, for it is their own self that stands before us, naked and without care." She is the feminine Child "playing in the world, obvious and unseen, playing at all times before the Creator," who "wills to be with the children of men. She is their sister. . . . She is God-given and God Himself as Gift."[119]

While, as McCaslin points out, a feminist reading of the text could find "the identification of the feminine with mercy and tenderness" problematic, in fact there is no hierarchical "subordination of Sophia to a masculine God."[120] Qualities of tenderness and mercy are also attributed to God the Father, just as Sophia exercises power and authority throughout the poem, as when she crowns the Logos and sends him forth into the world in section 4. In short, gender metaphors are "interconnected and interchangeable" in the poem, "an expression of two aspects of a single dynamic at play, like Wisdom at the foundation of the world."[121] Merton's metaphors remain fluid; Sophia "is not just the feminine face of a masculine God, or a masculine God with feminine attributes (God in a skirt), but an active power permeating all things."[122]

And yet what makes this section of *Hagia Sophia* so striking is not only its apophatic dance of saying and unsaying—that is, the traditional tension between X and *not-X* often found in mystical texts—but even more its cumulative layering of positive images for the divine in the pattern of X and Y and Z. By juxtaposing images that have long been separated in the Christian imagination, only rarely emerging in conjunction—"Jesus our mother" (from Julian of Norwich), "He is Father and Mother," "We call her His 'glory,'" "She is the Bride and the Feast and the Wedding"—Merton carries us beyond the dialectic of positive/negative theology into a kind of mystical third moment, where idols are shattered not in the silence of negation but in the plenitude of affirmation, unity-in-difference, and ecstatic praise. In short, Merton ushers us into a mosaic experience of God brimming with positive content, spilling over its linguistic containers.[123]

The last part of section 3 considers the wonder of Sophia's reception in the world of creatures. Though the fallen world prefers darkness to light, she is nevertheless received by many, and is the secret wellspring of beauty, creativity, and tenderness: "In her they rejoice to reflect Him. In her they are united with him. She is the union between them. She is the Love that unites them. . . . All

---

119. ESF, 65–66.

120. McCaslin, in MHPH, 248.

121. Ibid.

122. Ibid., 253.

123. See ICM, 142–43: "Mystical theology is not just [the] *via negationis*, apophatic theology, dialectical. It is beyond both forms of discursive theology, cataphatic and apophatic. It is the FULFILLMENT OF BOTH."

things praise her by being themselves and by sharing in the Wedding Feast."[124] The notion of all things giving glory to God simply "by being themselves" echoes a classic theme of transcendental Thomism, and calls to mind one of Merton's most celebrated texts, "Things in Their Identity," which opens simply, and unforgettably: "A tree gives glory to God by being a tree."[125]

Yet the softer light of Hagia Sophia casts the veil joining heaven and earth in a particular kind of radiance, which "would almost seem to be, in herself, all mercy."[126] Reprising themes from the letter to Hammer, Merton describes Sophia consummately as "the mercy of God in us," the "mysterious power of pardon [that] turns the darkness of our sins into the light of grace." Indeed, as mercy "she does in us a greater work than that of Creation: the work of new being in grace, the work of pardon, the work of transformation." Echoing the Wisdom literature of the Bible and St. Paul's theology of adoption in Christ, the poem here ascribes to human beings the highest place of honor and responsibility in creation, an honor that bears with it, however, a painfully kenotic sting.

To recall Merton's prayer on the Vigil of Pentecost: As daughters, sons, and friends of God, each of us is called by name "to help bring peace to the world," to learn the way "of truth and nonviolence," and to bear the consequences that follow. The third part of the poem thus leads to the need for the incarnation, the focus of the final section.[127]

"Sunset. The Hour of Compline. Salve Regina."

"The Hour of Compline" invokes Hammer's image of the woman crowning the boy Christ. "It is she, it is Mary, Sophia, who in sadness and joy, with the full awareness of what she is doing, sets upon the Second Person, the Logos, a crown which is His Human Nature. Thus her consent opens the door of created nature, of time, of history, to the Word of God." As Michael Mott observes, "Where Merton expects us to see the image from the painting" in these lines, "he also expects us to hear music."[128] When the *Salve Regina* is sung by the monks at the Abbey of Gethsemani, all lights in the abbey church are extinguished except for one, directed at the image of Mary in a window over the altar.[129]

---

124. ESF, 66–67.
125. See NSC, 29–36.
126. ESF, 67.
127. Patrick O'Connell, "Hagia Sophia," in TME, 191–93, at 192.
128. Michael Mott, *The Seven Mountains of Thomas Merton* (Boston: Houghton Mifflin, 1984), 362.
129. McCaslin, in MHPH, 249.

Yet Mary crowns her son "not with what is glorious, but with what is greater than glory: the one thing greater than glory is weakness, nothingness, poverty."[130] It is thus through Mary's wisdom and "sweet yielding consent" that "God enters without publicity into the city of rapacious men." Indeed, her "sadness" and "full awareness of what she is doing" reflect a wisdom well beyond her years, a wisdom deeply attuned to the "wisdom and foolishness" that will one day cause a sword to pierce her own heart. "She sends the infinitely Rich and Powerful One forth as poor and helpless, in His mission of inexpressible mercy, to die for us on the Cross."

It is significant that Mary is depicted in Hammer's picture neither as the mother of an infant nor as a royal Queen of Heaven. Her crowning of the boy Christ, notes McCaslin, is "an act of feminine power," subverting traditional depictions of "the Coronation of the Virgin" in which Mary is crowned by Christ, rather than she actively empowering him. In crowning the Child with his "human nature," the poem reminds us "that all men and women come from a common womb (the earth, the Feminine) and are alike vulnerable, frail, and utterly dependent on the earth and the feminine matrix."[131] Moreover, by depicting the Child not as an infant but on the brink of adulthood, both the picture and the poem underscore our common humanity with Jesus—not only "as ones who have undergone birth,"[132] as McCaslin suggests, but also as a people called to serve in a world riven by sin and contradiction. As the incarnation of divine Wisdom, "the Child goes forth to . . . crucifixion and resurrection. As humanity the child goes forth, an Everyman or Everywoman, into exile from paradise."[133]

Mary, in her "wise answer," accepts the contradiction. Through her understanding, God enters "without publicity" into human history. The final scene of the poem, as Michael Mott notes, is a scene of haunting "solemnity, great beauty, and a piercing loneliness"[134]:

> The shadows fall. The stars appear. The birds begin to sleep. Night embraces the silent half of the earth.
>
> A vagrant, a destitute wanderer with dusty feet, finds his way down a new road. A homeless God, lost in the night, without papers, without identification, without even a number, a frail expendable exile lies down in desolation under the sweet stars of the world and entrusts Himself to sleep.[135]

130. ESF, 68.
131. McCaslin, in MHPH, 250.
132. Ibid., 249.
133. Ibid.
134. Mott, *The Seven Mountains of Thomas Merton*, 363.
135. ESF, 69.

McCaslin sees in these lines "a strangely modern figure of the exile or God as exile in us"[136]—suggesting that human destiny in a world exiled from Sophia is not altogether different from that of Jesus, the Son of Man who "has nowhere to lay his head." O'Connell makes a similar point, citing Philippians 2:6-11, Paul's striking hymn of kenosis, God's self-emptying in Jesus: "In identifying fully with the human condition, Christ is the perfect epiphany of Sophia, embodying and extending to all the redemptive mercy of God."[137]

The final scene of *Hagia Sophia* unforgettably reprises Merton's celebration of Pasternak, whose protest is "the protest of life itself, of humanity itself, of love" against the "reign of numbers,"[138] against the alienation and anonymity of mass society. What meaning can our lives have, after all, in "the vast expanses" of an evolutionary universe? Like the hospital patient in the opening section of the poem; like Mary, receiving with astonishment the message of the Angel Gabriel; like Joseph, who struggles in faith to make sense of it all; like Mary Magdelene, Peter, Nicodemus, John, all the hidden but crucial players in the narrative subtext of the gospels—when "night embraces the silent half of the earth," everything depends on our laying ourselves down "under the sweet stars of the world" and giving ourselves over to the hidden Wisdom of God. Though our heads may pound with the clamor of many doubts and fears, and though it is more difficult than ever to see the stars, or even to remember to look for them through the glow of towering, sleepless cities, there is an inner music of Love, Mercy, and Understanding that rises up from the earth itself, *Natura naturans*, and from the still point of the human heart, asking to be set free in the world. She is Wisdom, our Sister: "God-given and God Himself as Gift." When we attend to her tender voice and give our quiet consent, she effects in us a work greater than that of Creation: the work of new being in grace, the work of mercy and peace, justice and love.

Who, then, is Hagia Sophia? She is the Spirit of Christ but more than Christ. She is the Love joining the Father, Son, and Spirit that longs for incarnation from before the very beginning. She is Jesus our mother, and Mary, the *Theotokos*. She is the "pivot" (*le point vierge*) of nature, *Natura naturans*, and all creation in God from the beginning. Perhaps most of all, Merton's Sophia is our "true self," when we (like Mary, seat of Wisdom) allow Christ to be birthed in us, and so realize the hidden ground of mercy, creativity, and presence in our very selves, the mystical Body of Christ. The moment her name awakens in us a sense of mercy, communion, and presence, Sophia— "one Wisdom, one Child, one Meaning, one Sister"—is not symbolic, but real,

---

136. McCaslin, in MHPH, 250.
137. O'Connell, "Hagia Sophia," in TME, 193.
138. DQ, 11, 66.

more than literally real. The remembrance of Sophia opens onto a mystical-political spirituality of engagement in the world.

Theological Significance of *Hagia Sophia*

As has been emphasized throughout this study, Merton's remembrance of Sophia was not something that simply happened to him but was the fruit of sustained study of Russian and patristic theology, Zen, biblical *lectio divina*, and, much more than we can know, untold hours of contemplation and prayer in his life as a monk at Gethsemani. While the Wisdom passages in Merton's corpus bear the tenor of historical events, inbreakings, irruptions, they are also, as Montaldo notes, literary events, with clear antecedents in Pasternak, Bulgakov, and Evdokimov, to name a few. This does not imply, however, that they are merely literary, just as the myriad genres of the Bible are not merely literary. Again, while Merton is not writing as a systematic theologian in *Hagia Sophia*, neither is he writing merely as a storyteller, songwriter, or poet. He is writing as a mystical theologian, excavating the past, and through both past and present, making old things new through the power of *memoria* and imagination.

As noted at the outset of this chapter, Merton is certainly aware that the sophiological tradition "had been marginalized within Western Christianity," and with *Hagia Sophia* he "attempts to restore it."[139] The intentionality and depth of realization in *Hagia Sophia* are undeniable—yet there is no artifice, no hidden agenda anywhere in its lines. Like the poet in Pasternak's *Dr. Zhivago*, Merton had become a "fulcrum" between God and the world; in *Hagia Sophia*, it "is the transfigured, spiritualized and divinized cosmos that speaks through him, and through him utters its praise of the Creator."[140]

Of course, such a judgment raises a compelling thought experiment for Christian theology, one that has long been raised by feminist and biblical theologians, and with much greater scriptural acuity than is possible here. What would be the effect on the Christian (and human) community of re-membering God not only as a "Person" (as in Jesus Christ) but as a Woman, calling out tenderly from the crossroads, urging the peoples of the world to come together and to recognize one another as members of one diverse, but radically interdependent, family? As a Mother, bent over her children in fierce protection, or crowning them with purpose and strength for the difficult journey ahead? As a Child, playing joyfully in the mountains, deserts, and watercourses of creation?[141] As a Lover, not abstract and fleshless, but

---

139. McCaslin, in MHPH, 252.

140. DQ, 20–21.

141. O'Connell surveys the significance of Merton's turn to wisdom not only in the social and interfaith realm but also "in light of the present critical state of human development"—

as one who loves us precisely in and through our bodies, and who despite our many failings, still recognizes and calls forth something strong and beautiful in us, something that (as Merton wrote to Proverb) we have "long ago ceased to be"?

Without question, all "gender-bound metaphors for ultimate reality are inadequate," as McCaslin notes, "since God is not an object of knowledge."[142] It is also significant that Merton uses gendered metaphors interchangeably in *Hagia Sophia* "to suggest a presence and a power beyond" traditional gender binaries. Yet we should not be too quick to move "beyond" female images (and names) of God prior to having lingered with them for a very long while, allowing depths of memory, thought, and feeling to rise to the surface. By "we" I mean first of all the Roman Catholic community, and from there, Christians (and Christian theologians) from East to West who share the same Scriptures. But surely the point radiates outward, at least as a kind of thought experiment, to include Jews and Muslims, other "Peoples of the Book" whose religious imaginations (and therefore families, communities, societies) also call for the healing of patriarchal deformations.

It is a delicate thought experiment, to be sure, but not a gratuitous one. For if Christian theology seeks to discern "the profound truth that lies hidden"[143] within all things, its scope cannot be merely parochial or contextual but must reach toward the universal—both in its literary and metaphysical dimensions, as indeed the Bible and traditional Christology do. To be very clear, the theological naming of God is not about identifying and circumscribing God with this or that political badge or theological button, and then trying to get as many people as you can, by hook or by crook, by threat of religious authority, or even by violence, to pin your God-badge on their chest. If Merton would be our guide, the naming of God is not about identification, but *identity*. It involves the slow and sensitive discernment of who God is, and who we are, through long meditation on the images and poetical symbols that shine through quietly, like forgotten stars, or break through dangerously, like flashes of lightning, from the revelatory firmament of the Bible.

Thus the essential argument of these five chapters: in "a single stroke of thought,"[144] the name Sophia can become a privileged meeting place for the encounter with God, the one God of all peoples. Her name tells us nothing

---

and highlights wisdom's association with the feminine, with spontaneity, play, joy, freedom, and delight, as a counter to the modern hegemony of scientific and instrumental rationality ("Wisdom," in TME, 535).

142. McCaslin, in MHPH, 249.

143. Marie-Dominique Chenu, *Nature, Man, and Society in the Twelfth Century*, ed. Jerome Taylor and Lester Little (Chicago: University of Chicago Press, 1957), 99; see chap. 3 above.

144. Ibid., 114.

essentially new, communicates no new information, but awakens what is and always has been, a union that already exists but is far, tragically far, from being realized. And that is why her name is disruptive, uncomfortable, dangerous—awakening timeless *memoria*, disturbing conscience, inviting and provoking response. *Hagia Sophia* is an implicit rebellion "of life against inertia, of mercy and love against tyranny, of humanity against cruelty and arbitrary violence."[145] The poem disrupts all self-enclosed worldviews, every arrogance, idolatry, patriarchy, or religious fundamentalism that would justify the erasure or diminishment of persons, any person, in the name of God.

And yet, like Pasternak, Merton renders his protest not by shouting louder than everyone else but with words that are "very simple, very rudimentary, deeply sincere, utterly personal"[146] and humble, that is, in a way that requires our consent, our participation. By stirring biblical imagination and memory—and by narrating his own awakening to Sophia's gentle voice—Merton interrupts our own ideologies and "dreams of separateness" to draw us back into the realization of radical kinship and social interdependence. "It is like all minds coming back together into awareness from all distractions, cross-purposes and confusions, into unity of love."[147] In *Hagia Sophia*, Merton not only anticipates the concerns of feminist and environmentalist theologies, he gives us "an elemental model on the birthing of peace."[148]

Concluding Remarks

After receiving a finished copy of the poem from Victor Hammer, Merton, somewhat typically, was unsure of what to make of it: "It is pretty, but my theology is strange in it. It needs revision and reformulation."[149] While in one sense *Hagia Sophia* is the fruition of a long discernment process in Merton, in another sense the text now belongs to the church and is a starting point for the kind of theological reflection undertaken in this book. If he judged the theology of the poem in need of "revision and reformulation," it is fair to conclude that he left it for others in the West, those more systematically inclined, to carry the reception of sophiology forward. As we turn toward our final chapter, we begin to take up questions of a more broadly historical and systematic nature, questions that Merton himself never addressed in any sustained way.

---

145. BT, 13–14; see n. 1 above.
146. DQ, 30.
147. ESF, 61–62.
148. Nugent, "*Pax Heraclitus*," 4.
149. TTW, 230.

The first of these relates to Sophia's place in traditional Christology or trinitarian theology. As we have seen, in works such as *The New Man* and *New Seeds of Contemplation* Merton's Christology generally conforms with the traditional pattern of identifying Wisdom with the Second Person of the Trinity, the Logos/Word/Wisdom of God. In *Hagia Sophia*, however, Merton allows himself greater freeplay with traditional conceptions and experiences of the divine. In doing so, he challenges complacent images of God that most Christians (and Christian theologians) will bring to the text. Like the Russians, Merton dares "to make mistakes . . . in order to say something great and worthy of God"[150]; but not only of God, for the text also makes claims for the natural world and the human community. But does Merton make mistakes in *Hagia Sophia*? Does he err in speaking of the feminine in God, of "Jesus our mother," of God as the "pivot" of nature? Does he violate God's transcendence by thinking too highly of human beings, too analogically, associating our personhood too closely with the very "Person" or anthropology of God? Does he blaspheme the divine Name by directing our gaze to the "homeless God," the God "without papers, without identification, without even a number"? Or rather, do we exempt Merton from such scrutiny by characterizing (and so dismissing) the text as poetry, not "real theology," thus exempting ourselves from the disarming memories and presences of God surfacing in authentic mystical insight?

A second question, proceeding from the first: is it possible or even desirable to translate mystical texts such as *Hagia Sophia* into the terms of systematic theology, as in, for example, a Wisdom-centered "Christology of presence"?[151] Or rather, to the contrary, are such texts, along with Russian sophiology, better left at the margins, like Sophia herself, with those narratives that form a kind of "penumbra around the canon"[152]? On the

---

150. SFS, 86.

151. Gerald O'Collins, e.g., gestures toward a "Christology of presence" proceeding from the image of Lady Wisdom. See his *Christology: A Biblical, Historical, and Systematic Study of Jesus* (New York: Oxford University Press, 1995), 304–23.

152. Wayne Meeks uses this phrase to describe the noncanonical gospels and their influence in the community long after the canon of the New Testament had been fixed (cited in Lawrence Cunningham, "*Extra Arcam Noe*: Criteria for Christian Spirituality," in *Minding the Spirit: The Study of Christian Spirituality*, ed. Elizabeth A. Dreyer and Mark S. Burrows [Baltimore: Johns Hopkins, 2005], 171–78, at 177n5). Arguing against any "systematization" of sophiology that would turn it into an abstract ideal, Paul Valliere describes Sophia in similarly evocative terms: "Sophia is the Lilac Fairy, not Sleeping Beauty. Sophiology works on dogmas in all sorts of wonderful ways . . . but it does not discard dogmas or invent new ones. It catalyzes new relationships within dogma and between dogma and culture" (Paul Valliere, "Sophiology as the Dialogue of Orthodoxy with Modern Civilization," in *Russian Religious Thought*, ed. Judith Kornblatt and Richard Gustafson [Madison, WI: University of Wisconsin Press, 1996], 176–92, at 190).

other hand, if "it is the imagination which governs our experience of God," as Sandra Schneiders writes, and further, that our imagination needs to be healed of patriarchal deformations, is not the remembrance of Sophia the most promising resource in the tradition for doing so?[153] One may wonder with Merton if our theological cautiousness with respect to celebrating the feminine as *imago Dei*, as *imago Christi*, is not after all "the sign of a fatal coldness of heart, an awful sterility born of fear, or of despair."[154]

Third, and perhaps the most compelling question: why did Sophia capture the imaginations of this small (and subsequently marginalized) group of thinkers living in the ashes of World War I, the Bolshevik Revolution, Auschwitz, Hiroshima, urban race riots, and the Vietnam War—a century in which Christian theology had every reason to lose its nerve? Might Sophia be grasped against this fractured horizon as a kind of apocalyptic figure? The potential rendering of Sophia in terms of the apocalyptic genre—no stretch in view of Merton's affinity with William Blake and Paul Evdokimov—is certainly intensified when one considers the terrifying contents of reality for so many women in the world today, not to mention the looming global environmental crisis.

All of these questions may be boiled down to one: *why Sophia*—and not simply a renewal of the more familiar terms of christological or trinitarian discourse?[155] Our final chapter seeks to illumine Merton's life and theology still further in view of the Russian theologians from whom he drew his inspiration—and in doing so, to appreciate how the remembrance of Sophia in Christian theology, worship, and spiritual practice might infuse our lives with a more palpable sense of the whole of things, the "all in all."

153. Sandra Schneiders, *Women and the Word: The Gender of God in the New Testament and the Spirituality of Women* (New York: Paulist, 1986), 70. Just as images of self and world can be healed, Schneiders argues, "so can the God-image. It cannot be healed, however, by rational intervention alone" (19).

154. SFS, 86.

155. As Valliere frames the question: "Would anything essential be lost if the sophiological aspect [of Bulgakov's dogmatics] were discarded?" ("Sophiology as the Dialogue," 188). Many Orthodox commentators have critiqued sophiology for being superfluous; i.e., it is not clear why "in treating of the spiritualization of humanity the theologian cannot get on well enough with the doctrines of the Incarnation and the indwelling of the Holy Spirit" (ibid.).

Drawing by Thomas Merton. Used with permission of the Merton Legacy Trust and the Thomas Merton Center, Bellarmine University.

6

Wisdom, Our Sister:
Human Beings in the Life Story of God

At the moment when the world comes undone, disintegrates—is not
Christianity overcome by a heavy, tragic sleep? . . . The absolutely new
derives from the eschatological return to the sources that *lie ahead*. This
is the art of apocalyptic times: "We remember what is to come."[1]

Writing in Paris in 1949, Russian Orthodox theologian Paul Evdokimov
described the atmosphere of post-war Europe as a "time of the catacombs,"
when the "horsemen of the Apocalypse cover the entire world."[2] In such a
world, he suggested, "The artist will recover his priesthood only by perform-
ing a theophanic sacrament: drawing, sculpting or singing the Name of God,
in which God dwells."[3] The task seemed painfully urgent for many amid the
wreckage of Western Christian civilization, but pointless and even revolting
to others: to draw, sculpt or sing the Name of God. Where was God, after
all, when the cattle cars rolled with their terrible rational efficiency into
Auschwitz? Where was Christ when the United States, the world's preeminent "Christian" nation, dropped its "original child bomb"[4] on Hiroshima,
immediately incinerating some 80,000 human beings, and three days later,
when a second was dropped on Nagasaki, turning another 40,000 souls to
dust? Has not Christianity, with its *Christus Victor* narrative, been exposed
irreparably for its "heavy, tragic sleep"? Is Christ the Lord of *this* history?

Yes, offers Evdokimov, but with a piercing qualification that the church
has too often forgotten through the centuries, or refused to see: Christ is
Lord of history in the manner "of His entry into Jerusalem: in a concealed,

---

1. Paul Evdokimov, *Woman and the Salvation of the World: A Christian Anthropology on
the Charisms of Women*, trans. Anthony P. Gythiel (Crestwood, NY: St. Vladimir's Seminary
Press, 1994 [first published in 1949]), 128, 130.

2. Ibid., 128.

3. Ibid., 130.

4. The title of Thomas Merton's unforgettable prose poem on the dropping of the first atomic
bomb (*Original Child Bomb* [New York: New Directions, 1962]). The bomb was affectionately
named "Little Boy" by its makers; the second they called "Fat Man."

kenotic matter (behind a veil of humility), which is imperceptible to the senses, but more than visible, and absolutely evident to faith."[5] As Thomas Merton would drive home the point less than a decade later, the Christ of our times is "the Christ of the bombed city and of the concentration camp. We have seen Him and we know Him well."[6]

"The Kingdom of God," Evdokimov writes, "is accessible only through the chaos of this world. It is not an alien transplant, but rather the revelation of the hidden depth of this very world."[7] In a world that despairs of God, the artist's task, says Evdokimov, is both priestly and prophetic: she "creates the transcendental and attests to its presence": "A little dust of this world, a board, a few colors, a few lines—and there is beauty. . . . *a vision of things which cannot be seen.*"[8] Sacred music stirs in our hearts again "the voice of Christ,"[9] the imprisoned and everywhere muted (bombed, starved, forgotten) sophianic child. The poet, "attuned to the beginning of things," helps us remember that "beauty is the fulfillment of truth, and that moment when 'all is fulfilled' is always marked by glory."[10] Or much more soberly, as Edward Kaplan describes the young Heschel, "The poet must speak for a silent God."[11] Is not the same terrible paradox also true today for the theologian?

Our final chapter proceeds from the intuition that theology today is and must be to some extent "the art of apocalyptic times." Yet the kind of apocalyptic we shall have in view here centers the imagination not so much on "the End" as the locus of God's decisive in-breaking or unveiling (Gk: *apokalypsis*), but rather "the Now," the critical present moment of tension, pregnancy, and possibility upon which the story of divine-human freedom ever hinges. "Christ has planted in the world the seeds of something altogether new," as Merton writes, "but they do not grow by themselves. . . . For the world to be changed, man himself must begin to change it, he must take the initiative, he must step forth and make a new kind of history."[12] Christ/Sophia is the presence of God breaking into history now, calling human persons to a decisive

---

5. Evdokimov, *Woman and the Salvation of the World*, 120.

6. BW, 1.

7. Evdokimov, *Woman and the Salvation of the World*, 128. During the German occupation of Paris, Evdokimov's family hid people who were targeted for arrest; after the war they ran a hostel for displaced persons and political refugees.

8. Ibid., 130.

9. Ibid., 132. "In Mozart's Mass, one hears the voice of Christ; the solemnity of the music attains the liturgical value of a Presence." The line recalls the "child" of "Barth's Dream": "Fear not, Karl Barth! . . . There is in us a Mozart who will be our salvation" (CGB, 12).

10. Evdokimov, *Woman and the Salvation of the World*, 129.

11. Edward Kaplan, "Introduction," in Abraham Joshua Heschel, *The Ineffable Name of God: Man* (New York: Continuum, 2005), 7–18, at 15.

12. DQ, 65.

break from the past, and renewing in the world, through human hearts and hands, a "sense of community with things in the work of salvation."[13]

The Eschatological Climate of the Gospels

Jesus of Nazareth narrated his apocalyptic "vision of things which cannot be seen" in part by invoking the Jewish memory of Sophia: "Come to me, all you that are weary and carrying heavy burdens, and I will give you rest" (Matt 11:28; cf. Sir 24:19, 51:23-26).[14] Surrounded by crowds of the burdened in an oppressive reign of numbers—"sheep without a shepherd" (Mark 6:34)—Jesus announced in word and deed a different kind of existence for human beings: the reign of God, a reign of compassion, forgiveness, and sacrificial love, where all are welcome and cared for as children of one Father. There was music in his words, to be sure, but there was also discord, urgency, and danger. "For as the lightning comes from the east and flashes as far as the west, so will be the coming of the Son of Man" (Matt 24:27); "As he came near and saw the city, he wept over it, saying, 'If you, even you, had only recognized on this day the things that make for peace! But now they are hidden from your eyes'" (Luke 19:41-42). In enigmatic parables he warned that the wise ones are those who stay awake, for no one knows "neither the day nor the hour" (Matt 25:13). So it was, we recall, in the obscure fragments of Herakleitos: "It is not right to act and speak like men asleep. . . . He that is awake lights up from sleeping."[15]

And so it is today, Merton suggests, for the church gathered around the world on Easter Vigil, when the new fire of the paschal candle is lit, and when, through the medium of the liturgy, "the Word Himself, uncreated Truth, enters into our spirits and becomes our theology."[16] In this "feast of light," hope flames out "like shook foil" from the roots of the earth itself, *natura naturans*, not as a last desperate cry before a violent end but as the silent herald of new birth and new creation, a hush-filled remembrance of what was, is, and will

---

13. ICM, 131.

14. Biblical scholars have long recognized the Hebrew Wisdom foundations of New Testament Christology, the texts of greatest interest being John's Prologue (John 1:1-18); Matthew's naming of Jesus as Emmanuel (Matt 1:23); certain redactions of Q (Matt 11:19, 29; 23:34); and Paul's cosmic hymnology (1 Cor 8:6; Col 1:15-17; Heb 1:1-3), texts that resonate with Prov 8:22-31. The literature examining the influence of Hebrew Wisdom on Jesus' self-identity and New Testament Christology is enormous. James D. G. Dunn provides a clear and balanced summary of the issues and texts at play in his *Christology in the Making: A New Testament Inquiry into the Origins of the Doctrine of the Incarnation* (Grand Rapids, MI: Eerdmans, 1996), 163–212; idem, "Jesus: Teacher of Wisdom or Wisdom Incarnate?" in *Where Shall Wisdom Be Found?* ed. Stephen C. Barton (Edinburgh: T and T Clark, 1999), 75–92.

15. BT, 96, 103; see chap. 4.

16. NM, 241.

be: *Resurrection!* Merton narrates the birth of Wisdom in the community that gathers before the tomb of Jesus, "watching in the night":

> The first voice that speaks in the silent night is the cold flint. Out of the flint springs fire. The fire, making no sound, is the most eloquent preacher on this night that calls for no other sermon than liturgical action and mystery. That spark from cold rock, reminds us that the strength, the life of God, is always deeply buried in the substance of all things. It reminds me that He has power to raise up children of Abraham even from the stones. . . .
>
> The fire that springs from the stone speaks, then, of his reality springing from the alienated coldness of our dead hearts, of our souls that have forgotten themselves, that have been exiled from themselves and from their God—and have lost their way in death. But there is nothing lost that God cannot find again. Nothing dead that cannot live again in the presence of His Spirit. No heart so dark, so hopeless, that it cannot be enlightened and brought back to itself, warmed back to the life of charity.[17]

There is "nothing lost that God cannot find again," no heart so cold that it cannot be "warmed back to the life of charity"—these words sum up well the climate of mercy, hope, and imminent expectation that Merton finds springing forth vividly and unpredictably, from the most unpromising materials, in the pages of the New Testament.

This is the "art of apocalyptic times." Theology must find new ways—or rediscover old ways—"of singing the Name of God in which God dwells." Against every temptation to theological despair or complacency, the church must keep alive the paradoxical good news at the heart of New Testament faith: Christ, the wisdom and power of God, enters history *still* "behind a veil of humility," judging every Promethean vision of reality in light of a deeper mystery, no less real because hidden. Hope springs forth again, like a mustard seed, from the most unpromising materials: acts of mercy, self-sacrifice, kindness, creativity; the beauty of nature, the wonder of children—these are the unlikely sacraments of God's own glory, presence, and hope breaking into history. This is the wonder, and the risk, of God's incarnation in creatures who are free.

---

17. Ibid., 241–42. Merton describes "Our life of 'watching in the night,' of sharing in the resurrection of Christ," as "the very essence of Christianity" (238).

Wisdom and the Russians: Foundations[18]

> I saw all, and all was but one—but one image of feminine beauty . . .
> The boundless entered into its measure—Before me, within me, are
> you alone.[19]

For both Vladimir Soloviev, the philosopher-poet and father of the Russian Sophia tradition, and Sergius Bulgakov, who developed Soloviev's ideas into a comprehensive dogmatic theology, Sophia was much more than an idea. She was, in the first place, a central figure of mystical experience, and within that experience, she represented the divine-human feminine. Yet Sophia was not less than an idea either, and she would come to play a central role in their respective theological metaphysics.[20] For Soloviev and his heirs, theological discourse about God's relationship to the world leads to the dogmatics of the humanity of God, or sophiology: "Christ as Sophia is the humanity which God sees and loves from all eternity."[21]

The word "love" here must not be taken for granted. Notwithstanding its highly philosophical and distinctive cultural content, Russian sophiology begins and ends in the ecstasy of love, of being loved gratuitously by God, spilling over into a profound sense of unity with all things, of being at home in the universe, even amid profound disruption, sin, and sorrow. Over against a century of unspeakable violence and fragmentation, sophiology seeks not just the retrieval of traditional Christology but also its transformation into

18. The best introduction to sophiology in the English language is Bulgakov's *Sophia: The Wisdom of God* (Hudson, NY: Lindisfarne, 1993), a mature work (orig. 1937) written with Western readers in mind, and the book that introduced Merton to Bulgakov. Bulgakov's magnum opus, *The Bride of the Lamb*, has recently been published in an acclaimed English translation (trans. Boris Jakim [Grand Rapids, MI: Eerdmans, 2002]). The following overview is much indebted to several excellent English studies that have appeared in recent years: Paul Valliere, *Modern Russian Theology: Bukharev, Soloviev, Bulgakov: Orthodox Theology in a New Key* (Grand Rapids, MI: Eerdmans, 2000); Catherine Evtuhov, *The Cross and the Sickle: Sergei Bulgakov and the Fate of Russian Religious Philosophy* (Ithaca, NY: Cornell University Press, 1997); Rowan Williams, ed., *Sergeii Bulgakov: Towards a Russian Political Theology* (Edinburgh: T and T Clark, 1999); Judith Kornblatt and Richard Gustafson, eds., *Russian Religious Thought* (Madison, WI: University of Wisconsin Press, 1996); Andrew Louth, "Wisdom and the Russians: The Sophiology of Fr. Sergei Bulgakov," in *Where Shall Wisdom Be Found?* 169–81; also *St. Vladimir's Theological Quarterly* 49, nos. 1–2 (2005), dedicated entirely to the question of Bulgakov's legacy. In what follows, I rely heavily (and gratefully) on Valliere's work, for not only does it go far in making sense of sophiology as a theological response to catastrophic shifts in Russian social and ecclesial life, it will also help us (by analogy, as it were) to make sense of Merton's own "turn" to Sophia as he turned to a world that seemed to be fragmenting out of control.

19. From Soloviev's third vision of Sophia, cited in Louth, "Wisdom and the Russians," 172.

20. Louth, ibid., 172–73.

21. Valliere, MRT, 159.

a positive theology of God's integral relationship to the world, nature, and human life and culture from the beginning.

It would be impossible here to do justice to the breadth and complexity of Russian sophiology, still less to the distinctive contributions of its proponents over the course of more than a century. Our task here is more modest, namely, to try and understand in broadest contours the thought of its two seminal figures, Soloviev and Bulgakov, and thus to grasp Merton's contribution as part of a much larger historical and theological fabric. As with Merton's theology, Russian sophiology cannot be understood apart from the mystical biography of its proponents. For this reason we begin with a narrative overview of key events in the lives of Soloviev and Bulgakov, a story-shaped approach that will help us to keep in view the existential and soteriological roots of sophiology. It will also illumine the strong, sometimes uncanny, resonances between their experiences of God as Sophia and those of Merton. The chapter then details how the sophiological perspective breaks open and potentially revitalizes the theology of God in four major areas: (1) Christology (or theological anthropology), (2) Trinity (or cosmic theology), (3) Earth (or environmental theology), and (4) eros and the feminine in God (sexuality, feminist theology). The chapter concludes by exploring what amounts to a fifth area: apocalyptic (or the sanctification of time), with special attention to Merton's prophetic writings and theology of the cross.

Two themes unify the material that follows: first, the "humanity of God," sophiology's core doctrine that takes as its starting point the divine-humanity of Christ as defined at Chalcedon, as well as the dance of divine-humanity at play everywhere in the gospel narratives; and second, the experience of God as "Presence," the heart of a Wisdom-centered Christology that seeks to affirm that Christ is "everywhere present but in an infinite variety of ways."[22]

Christ/Sophia in the Lives of Soloviev and Bulgakov

Vladimir Soloviev was a remarkable figure in the spiritual and cultural renaissance of late nineteenth-century Russia, the so-called Silver Age that preceded the cataclysmic events of the Russian Revolution.[23] Born in Moscow in 1853, his father was a professor of history but came from a long line of Orthodox priests; Soloviev himself would never be ordained or marry. As a young man at the University of Moscow, he studied physics and mathemat-

---

22. Gerald O'Collins, *Christology: A Biblical, Historical, and Systematic Study of Jesus* (New York: Oxford, 1995), 322.

23. See Evtuhov, *The Cross and the Sickle*, 1–17. Georges Florovsky writes of the Russian Silver Age that "in those years it was suddenly revealed to many that man is a metaphysical being" (cited in ibid., 50).

ics, but soon changed to history and philosophy, devouring the works of Schelling, Plato, the church fathers, and mystics like Jakob Boehme. Like many intellectuals of the period, he was a "Slavophile," that is, "one who opposed Westernizing tendencies in Russian society, and sought out what he believed to be a peculiarly Russian (and Orthodox) tradition." At the same time Soloviev "believed deeply in the unity of the Church, and saw Rome as a necessary safeguard of that unity."[24]

Soloviev was a friend of Dostoyevsky, and indeed, his life, as Andrew Louth notes, "is quite as bizarre as any of the characters of his novels."[25] At the age of twelve, standing in church, Soloviev had a vision of a young girl, surrounded by azure light, holding a flower and smiling. Ten years later, he was in London conducting research on the gnostic and mystical notion of Sophia, the Wisdom of God. While sitting under the dome of the reading room in the British Museum, the Lady again appeared before him. He later wrote of the vision: "I said to her, 'O bloom of divinity! You are here, I feel it; why have you not shown Yourself to me since my childhood years?'"[26] Looking into her face, he heard a voice say, "To Egypt!" Obediently he packed his bags, set off, and before long was in the Egyptian desert, "wandering around in his black overcoat and top-hat."[27] After nearly losing his life at the hands of hostile Bedouins, Soloviev found himself alone, at night, in the desert. Here he had his third and final vision of Sophia:

> Somnolent, in fear, I lay there.
> But then a breeze whispered, "Sleep, poor friend!"
> And I slept. When I woke up
> The earth and heavenly vault breathed roses.
> And in the violet splendor of the heavens,
> With eyes of azure flame
> You gazed at me, like the first rays
> Of the universal day of creation.[28]

The similarities to Merton's *Hagia Sophia* are striking: the "poverty" and "helplessness" of the one "who must entrust himself" to sleep; the awakening "out of languor and darkness" at the "sweet voice of Wisdom," as on "the first morning of the world," inviting him "with unutterable sweetness to be awake and to live. This is what it means to recognize Hagia Sophia."[29]

24. Louth, "Wisdom and the Russians," 171.
25. Ibid.
26. Cited in Valliere, MRT, 112.
27. Louth, "Wisdom and the Russians," 172.
28. Cited in Valliere, MRT, 113.
29. *Hagia Sophia*, ESF, 62–63.

After four months in Egypt, Soloviev returned to Russia by way of Italy and France. While in Italy he had a brief but intense affair with a married woman, and shortly after his arrival in Russia he fell in love with another married woman, Sofia Petrovna Khitrovo, for whom he would compose love poetry to the end of his life. As Valliere wryly characterizes these relationships, "Soloviev's mystical preoccupations had not eradicated his susceptibility to earthly love."[30] Though he never would marry, these intense, if passing, relationships with women undoubtedly shaped his poetic and religious imagination. Soloviev died on August 13, 1900, having influenced a generation of philosophers, poets, and theologians, some of whom would make their mark on Russian intellectual and cultural life as exiles in Europe after the revolution of 1917.

Principal among these was Sergius Bulgakov, born in 1871 in the province of Orel in central Russia. Like Soloviev, Bulgakov came from a long line of Russian Orthodox priests, though as a young man he abandoned his priestly roots in favor of a secular education. "The problem," as Valliere writes, "was spiritual: Sergei had lost his faith in God and decided to commit himself instead to the struggle for social and economic justice."[31] For a young radical of the day, that meant embracing Marxism, "the rising star in the Russian ideological firmament."[32] Sometime in 1895, in the midst of his busy student days, Bulgakov was on a train in the hills of the Caucasus, when the beauty of the mountains at sunset confronted him with questions that, as a committed Marxist and atheist, he thought he had left behind:

> It was dusk. We were riding through the southern steppe, basking in the honeyed odors of grass and hay, golden in the rays of the serene sunset. In the distance we could see the blue hills of the Caucasus. This was the first time I had seen them. And as I gazed greedily into the unfolding hills, breathing in air and light, I received nature's revelation. My soul had, although with a dull, aching pain, become accustomed to seeing nature as nothing more than a dead, arid desert wearing a mask of beauty; my soul could not reconcile itself to a nature without God. And then, at that moment, my soul began to tremble in unease and happiness: what if there is? . . . [what] if it is not a desert, not lies, not a mask, not death, but if He is there, the divine and loving Father with His forgiveness and His love . . . ? My heart pounded to the rhythm

---

30. Valliere, MRT, 113.

31. Ibid., 228.

32. Ibid. Valliere notes that "Vladimir Ulianov (Lenin) made the same choice at about the same time, as did many . . . who went on to play leading roles in the Russian revolutions of 1905 and 1917."

of the moving train as we rushed toward this fading gold and these graying mountains.[33]

The vision was fleeting and largely forgotten as Bulgakov plunged himself into academic and political work. Yet it "remained with him," as Catherine Evtuhov notes, "surfacing at unexpected moments and in new ways."[34]

Three years later Bulgakov was preparing himself for study abroad in Germany, full of enthusiasm for the place "that had long been his ideal—'culture,' comfort, Social Democracy!"[35] Just prior to leaving, in January of 1898, he married Elena Tokmakova. Usually reticent about writing of his personal life, he later described the spiritual significance of his marriage in terms of the revelatory experience in the hills of the Caucasus: "But I soon recognized the same thing the hills had told me in their triumphant glow, in the shy and quiet glance of a maiden, by other shores, under other hills. That same light glowed in the trusting, frightened and humble, half-childish eyes, full of the holiness of suffering. The revelation of love spoke of another world that had been lost to me."[36] The poignant association of nature's "glow" with the "shy and quiet" humility of his bride; the identification of her "half-childish eyes" with "the holiness of suffering," the "revelation" of conjugal love as "another world that had been lost to me"—such lines anticipate the sophianic worldview that would become the matrix of Bulgakov's theology. They also foreshadow the same themes, six decades later and a vast culture apart, in Merton, namely, Merton's association of the Wisdom-child not only with the beauty and "wordless gentleness"[37] of nature but also with "the true (quiet) inner woman I never really came to terms with in the world," the "part of the garden I never went to."[38] "How grateful I am to you for loving in me something that I thought I had lost entirely."[39]

In the spring of 1898, Bulgakov visited the Zwinger gallery in Dresden; knowing nothing about art at the time, he thought of the gallery "as merely an obligatory tourist stop."[40] Yet as he stood before the canvas of Raphael's Sistine Madonna, Bulgakov found himself overcome by joy. The "purity and conscious sacrifice" of the Madonna's eyes rendered him dizzy: "ice melted on

33. Cited in Evtuhov, *The Cross and the Sickle*, 39.
34. Ibid.
35. Ibid., 40.
36. Cited in ibid., 41.
37. *Hagia Sophia*, ESF, 61.
38. From the journal of June 26, 1965, in which Merton remembers "Ann Winser," the sister of a childhood friend he used to visit "on the Isle of Wight, in that quiet rectory at Brooke": "She was the quietest thing in it, a dark and secret child" (DWL, 259).
39. From the journal of March 4, 1958, following his dream of Proverb (SFS, 176).
40. Evtuhov, *The Cross and the Sickle*, 44.

my heart, and some kind of knot in my life was resolved."[41] "One wonders," Bernice Rosenthal remarks, "why a Western, Catholic holy picture had such an impact on Bulgakov, who must have been well acquainted with the icons of the Mother of God."[42] Though still an atheist, he visited the gallery every day and "prayed and wept before the image of the Mother of God."[43]

Like many others before and since, Bulgakov's encounter with a culture other than his own was a transforming, revelatory experience. It is not hard to think here of the young Merton in Rome, haunted by the city's Byzantine mosaics and finding himself, "without knowing anything about it," becoming "a pilgrim": "And now for the first time in my life I began to find out something of Who this Person was that men called Christ. It was obscure, but it was a true knowledge of Him, in some sense, truer than I knew and truer than I would admit."[44] Bulgakov would write much later, "Religion is born in the experience of God . . . and however proud the wisdom of this age may be, incapable of apprehending religion for lack of the necessary experience, still, behind its numbness and lack of religious talent, those who once have seen God in their hearts possess an absolutely certain knowledge of Him."[45] While neither Bulgakov nor Merton had been brought to "certain knowledge" of God in these early revelations, the dormant seeds of faith had been stirred, and done so, significantly, through an immersion in cultures quite different from their own.

Nevertheless, after two years in Germany Bulgakov came home disillusioned, "having lost firm soil under my feet, my faith in my ideals broken." His meetings with European revolutionary leaders he had so admired left him, after all, less than inspired, as he later recalled: "The earth was moving unrestrainably under me. I worked stubbornly with my head, posing 'problem' after 'problem,' but internally, I no longer had any means to believe, to live, to love."[46] As Evtuhov notes: "The foundations of his Marxist worldview were cracking, yet his occasional moments of revelation had provided him with no positive alternative."[47] We must pass over here the tumultuous intellectual and political currents of these years to now consider an event that Evtuhov

41. Cited in ibid.

42. Bernice Rosenthal, "The Nature and Function of Sophia in Sergei Bulgakov's Prerevolutionary Thought," in *Russian Religious Thought*, 154–75, at 169.

43. Evtuhov, *The Cross and the Sickle*, 44. It is worth noting that the Sistine Madonna survived the fire-bombing of Dresden in February of 1945 and was brought to Russia at the end of the war. It was later returned to Dresden, where it presently resides.

44. SSM, 109; cf. Evtuhov, *The Cross and the Sickle*: "To meet Christ is to meet one's own; that which is familiar if long forgotten" (54).

45. Cited in Evtuhov, *The Cross and the Sickle*, 45.

46. Cited in ibid., 40.

47. Evtuhov, *The Cross and the Sickle*, 45.

calls "one of the crucial moments of [Bulgakov's] spiritual evolution," more than "any purely intellectual discovery or political experience"[48]: the death of his four-year-old son in the summer of 1909. The boy's funeral brought "yet a third revelation of the existence of God":

> Oh, my lovely, my pure boy! As we carried you up the steep hill, and then followed the hot and dusty road, we suddenly turned off into a shady park, as if we had entered into the Garden of Eden; suddenly, after the unexpected turn, the church, as lovely as you, looked at us with its colored windows as it waited for you. I had not known it before and, like a miraculous vision, the church stood before us, sunk in the garden below the shadow of the old castle. Your mother fell, crying, "The sky has opened!" She thought she was dying and saw heaven. . . . And the sky had opened, it had witnessed our apocalypse. I felt, almost saw, our rise to heaven. Pink and white oleanders surrounded you like the flowers of paradise, waiting to bend over you, to guard your coffin. . . . So this was it! Everything became clear, all of the suffering and the heat dissipated and disappeared in the heavenly azure of this church. We thought that events took place only below, in the heat, and didn't know that these heights existed and were, it turns out, waiting for us.[49]

The raw humanity and poignancy of the passage requires no comment, but note also its apocalyptic tenor and invocation of "heavenly azure," which recalls Soloviev's visions of Sophia. The image of "flowers of paradise, waiting to bend over you, to guard your coffin" resonates not too distantly in at least two of Merton's poems: first, from *Hagia Sophia*—"We do not hear the uncomplaining pardon that bows down the innocent visages of flowers to the dewy earth"[50]; and second, the elegy to his younger brother, John Paul, killed in a bomber crash in the English Channel on April 17, 1943—"*Sweet brother, if I do not sleep / My eyes are flowers for your tomb*."[51] For both Bulgakov and Merton, it would seem, the "flowers of paradise" were indelibly scented with the "holiness of suffering."

In a letter to a friend shortly after his son's death, Bulgakov identifies the boy unambiguously with the Christ Child: "This boy of ours was entirely extraordinary, not of this world, 'not an inhabitant,' as was said about him.

---

48. Ibid., 133.

49. Cited in ibid., 134. Evtuhov cites Rilke in relation to this event: "But when you went, a flash of reality broke upon this stage through the chink you went through: the green of real green, real sunshine, real forest" (127). From the sophiological perspective, apocalyptic may be defined precisely as "a flash of reality," an awakening to the "real."

50. ESF, 63.

51. SSM, 404.

(In fact he was born on Christmas Eve and this was always very important for me.) Kind, gifted, advanced beyond his years, with big wonderful eyes. One could always look at him and love him only with a piercing pain and anxiety in one's heart."[52] A month later, he goes further: "The messenger of heaven has risen to heaven."[53] His son's death, as Evtuhov notes, "became a direct and personal experience of Christ's Resurrection."[54]

It was in the years following the death of his son that Bulgakov began to reread the philosophy of Vladimir Soloviev, where he found everywhere the figure of "the Eternal Feminine, the Divine Sophia, the Soul of the world." Wholly immersed, Bulgakov began to internalize Soloviev's thought as a kind of scaffolding for his own. The encounter came none too soon, for like every other Russian in this period, Bulgakov's life was about to be turned upside down. As Evtuhov notes, "The Bolshevik regime was born in the explosion of terror, blood, and chaos that was the Russian Civil War." Moments of inspiration "dissolved in the unmitigated horror of civil war . . . like a series of successively closing doors, shutting out one possibility after another, eventually obliterating even the memory of the intense religious and cultural renewal of the turn of the century." It was an ominous portent of what would become the twentieth century's darkest legacy: "The essence of total war is that it is inescapable."[55]

After being removed from his position at Moscow University in 1918, Bulgakov managed to teach for two more years in the Crimea but lost the position when the Bolshevik troops took the city in 1920. In October of 1922, he was arrested as one of many thousands of "unreformable" intellectuals; two months later he was deported, with his wife and all but one of their children. Thus in January of 1923, while Russia was being consumed by the flames of civil war, he came as a refugee to the mosque of Hagia Sophia in Constantinople, an episode considered in chapter 2. No less than Prince Vladimir's envoys had been awestruck by this jewel of Byzantium a thousand years earlier, Bulgakov too did not know whether he was in heaven or on earth. "My soul became the world: I am in the world and the world is in me." He felt his freedom in Sophia "as a release from the endless slavery, the 'slavery to slaves and to hunger, the emptiest and most deadening elements in the world.'"[56] Evtuhov's penetrating reading turns our narrative toward a conclusion:

---

52. Cited in Evtuhov, *The Cross and the Sickle*, 134. Cf. Merton's journal of March 19, 1958: "there is Christ in my own Kind, my own Kind—'Kind' which means 'likeness' and which means 'love' and which means 'child'" (SFS, 183).

53. Cited in Evtuhov, *The Cross and the Sickle*, 135.

54. Evtuhov, *The Cross and the Sickle*, 135.

55. Ibid., 230.

56. Ibid., 232, citing Bulgakov.

In the midst of these sensations, Bulgakov experienced a new apocalyptic vision. As he stood at the very source of Orthodox Christianity, Bulgakov was struck by the dignity and grace of the Muslims who now prayed to Allah in Justinian's church; and he felt the misguidedness of wartime Slavophile dreams of restoring a cross to Hagia Sophia, their misunderstanding of Sophia's true ecumenical mission. And if the world crisis had at once destroyed the first and second Romes, there would be a new, true third Rome, in which, before the end, the church must appear in its fullness and entirety. St. Sophia would fulfill its designated role of universal, ecumenical church—a role it had lost in history. It would become again the meeting place of heaven and earth experienced by Vladimir's emissaries almost a thousand years earlier.

Bulgakov chided himself immediately: The time for such visions was over, for "launching new schemes" and building "houses of cards." Was this not mere "dreaminess," and had he not just seen where projects of that kind might lead? Was he merely dizzy, having been released from a "stone bag" into the world of freedom? But in the end he could not resist. The powerful vision won him over, and he concluded that in this vision lay the voice of the church. Bulgakov had come full circle: in this moment inside Hagia Sophia, his return to the church was complete. The last twenty years of Bulgakov's life were a playing out of the vision in the mosque as . . . he launched an extraordinarily ambitious, messianistic effort to reinterpret Christian doctrine for the modern age.[57]

At the end of chapter 2, I suggested a kinship between Bulgakov's experience under the dome of Hagia Sophia and Merton's account of the "Fire Watch" at Gethsemani, noting that both accounts cast the world under the unifying light of Wisdom's divine perspective. The comparison is enough to remind us that well before his epiphany at Fourth and Walnut in the spring of 1958, the mystical seeds of Merton's universal vision were already firmly rooted. As he wrote in *The Sign of Jonas*, "It is a strange awakening to find the sky inside you and beneath you and above you and all around you so that your spirit is one with the sky, and all is positive night."[58] Would it be stretching the data too far to discern a kind of parabolic line joining these apocalyptic revelations across space, culture, and time—Caucasus and Hagia Sophia, Fire Watch and Fourth and Walnut—and forging in Bulgakov and Merton a mystical kinship between East and West, a reunion wherein "lay the voice of the church" and its "true ecumenical mission" in our times? In chapter 4, we considered another apocalyptic convergence point: Merton's illumination at the Buddhist shrine of Pollanaruwa. "Surely, with . . .

57. Ibid., 232–33.
58. SJ, 340.

Pollanaruwa my Asian pilgrimage has come clear and purified itself. I mean, I know and have seen what I was obscurely looking for. I don't know what else remains but I have now seen and have pierced through the surface and have got beyond the shadow and the disguise."[59]

In 1925, as dean of the newly established Russian Orthodox seminary in Paris, the St. Sergius Theological Institute, Bulgakov began to work out his dogmatics of the humanity of God. Twenty years later, with two magisterial trilogies and not a little controversy behind him, Bulgakov died in Paris on July 12, 1944. Thirteen years later, in the spring of 1957, Merton would record his first ecstatic notes on Bulgakov's "daring" efforts "to say something great and worthy of God."[60]

Epistemological Foundations: Soloviev's "Free Theosophy"

Soloviev's early thought took shape amid the tumultuous backdrop of Turkish violence against Orthodox Christians in the Balkans, and Russia's subsequent declaration of war against the Ottoman Empire in early 1877. "Hitching religious philosophy to Russian messianism,"[61] Soloviev delivered a rousing lecture in April of that year titled "Three Forces." His thesis, as Valliere explains, "was as simple as it was bold":

> The world is dominated by two opposed, but equally flawed, religious principles: the Islamic or oriental principle of "the inhuman God," a formula justifying universal servitude, and the modern European principle of "the godless human individual," a formula validating "universal egoism and anarchy." The conflict between these principles can only end in a vicious circle. Fortunately for humanity there is a country, Russia, where East and West meet and transcend their spiritual division in a higher religious principle: *bogochelovechestvo*, the humanity of God. As history's "third force," Russia is destined to blaze the path not just to Constantinople but to the universal, divine-human cultural synthesis of the future.[62]

Soloviev would develop the visionary schema of "Three Forces" in a series of public lectures in St. Petersburg in 1878–81, published as *Lectures on the Humanity of God*.[63] While, as Valliere notes, the Russian *intelligentsia* who

---

59. AJ, 236.

60. SFS, 86.

61. Valliere, MRT, 114.

62. Ibid.

63. Often translated as "Lectures on Godmanhood," the Russian term *bogochelovechestvo* is rendered by Valliere rather as "the humanity of God," both for semantic and theological reasons. The latter makes it clear that sophiology does not imply a kind of "synthesis of commensurate or complementary entities," that "God and humanity are, so to speak, two halves of a whole,"

attended may not have grasped much of their speculative content, they would have had no trouble understanding Soloviev's dedication: "for the Red Cross, but also in part for the restoration of St. Sophia's in Constantinople."[64] Now in his late twenties, Soloviev was also busy writing his doctoral dissertation, *The Critique of Abstract Principles.* The "critique" of the title is two pronged. On one side, Soloviev critiques the reigning epistemologies of modernity for lacking an integral connection with "positive religion"; on the other side, he critiques traditional theology for exiling itself from empirical and rational modes of inquiry. A brief overview of these twin criticisms will set the stage for his "theosophical" turn to Sophia in the *Lectures on the Humanity of God.*

Soloviev construes human knowledge as a synthesis of three elements: the natural (or empirical), the mystical, and the rational. Modern thought neglects the mystical, producing the extremes of abstract rationalism (e.g., Hegelianism, "a system of concepts without any reality") and abstract empiricism (e.g., positivism: "a system of facts without any inner connection").[65] Many moderns, confronted by the failures of these positions, resign themselves to "the emptiness and nullity of a fruitless skepticism." Meanwhile, conservative religious thinkers call for the reassertion of traditional systems of thought. Thus as Valliere notes, Pope Leo XIII "would have the modern world return to Thomas Aquinas," and certain Russian thinkers "would have it return to the fathers of the eastern church."[66] While Soloviev appreciates these conservative proposals—believing patristic theology comes "closer to the truth than any of the abstract philosophical systems"—"nevertheless, *always alert to the positive side of every philosophical position,* Soloviev sees good spiritual and intellectual reasons for the modern bias against traditional theology."[67]

Theology as it is traditionally practiced, Soloviev argues, tends to exclude "the free relationship of reason to the content of religion, the free appropriation

---

which is "a theological absurdity" ("Sophiology as the Dialogue of Orthodoxy with Modern Civilization," in *Russian Religious Thought,* 176–92, at 191). Sophiology "assumes that humanity can never reach God . . . [or] be joined to the divine on the basis of equality; but that God condescends to the human condition, 'taking the form of a slave' (Phil. 2:7). . . . The human may be engulfed in the divine, but not the divine in the human. One may therefore speak of the humanity of God . . . but not of the divinity of man. Indeed, the latter was regarded by Russian religious thinkers as the demonic perversion of the humanity of God" (ibid.; see also MRT, 11–15, where he draws parallels between the Russian use of the term and Karl Barth's late essay *The Humanity of God* [1956]).

64. Cited in Valliere, MRT, 115. The statement renders Bulgakov's later experience in the mosque of Hagia Sophia all the more remarkable. It would be some years, Valliere notes, before Soloviev's humanitarianism and "pan-humanism" would displace the Slavophile imperialism so evident in his early work.

65. Valliere, MRT, 138.

66. Ibid.

67. Ibid.; emphasis added.

and development of this content by reason; second, it does not implement the content [of religion] on the empirical plane." These exclusions undermine not just theology's credibility before its "cultured despisers" but its actual truth, "for if reason and experience without mystical knowledge lack truth, truth without reason and experience lacks fullness and reality."[68] Again, as Valliere sums up, "Only a synthesis of empirical, rational and mystical elements is finally 'true'. . . . For all its magnificent architecture, traditional theology is one-sided and exclusive, and thereby falls short of the truth about the whole of things. Reason and science are right to turn away from it."[69]

Theology that attempts to validate its claims based on mystical or traditional grounds alone, Soloviev argues, cannot help but yield an "abstract dogmatism," which is insufficient not only on rational and empirical grounds but on religious grounds as well. "In the field of theology, we know the truth as absolute or divine, but absolute or divine truth by definition cannot be one-sided, exclusive; it must be the whole truth, it must be all in all." How, then, must theology proceed in the age of critical reason and empirical science? The task, argues Soloviev, is "not to restore traditional theology in its exclusivity but, on the contrary, to free it from abstract dogmatism, to put religious truth into the form of free-rational thought and implement it with the data of experimental science, to link theology internally to philosophy and science and so to organize the whole field of true knowledge into a full system of free and scientific theosophy."[70] In a word, theology must dare to continually break itself open in dialogue with the social and natural sciences, seeking after the whole of things, the "all in all."

Valliere takes pains to distinguish (if not separate) Soloviev's "free theosophy" from "the modern theosophists"—the precursors, as Louth suggests, of contemporary New Age spirituality[71]—and from positivists such as Comte. Like the positivists, Soloviev saw modernity "as a positive age in which truth claims have to be validated in the material world."[72] But unlike the positivists, "he believed religion could pass this test," as Valliere explains: "The positivists saw humankind as advancing through a series of negations: theology is negated by metaphysics, which is in turn negated by modern science. For Soloviev knowledge advances through ever more inclusive forms of insight. Thus the critique of traditional theology ('abstract dogmatism') does not lead to the negation of theology but to its assimilation in a richer synthesis

68. Cited in ibid., 138–39.
69. Valliere, MRT, 139.
70. Cited in ibid.
71. See Louth, "Wisdom and the Russians," 169–70, 180.
72. Valliere, MRT, 140.

of divine truth, or free theosophy."[73] The point is crucial to bear in mind as we consider the theological content of sophiology. In turning to Sophia, what Soloviev and Bulgakov sought after is *a positive religious synthesis* in which "the religious or mystical element is not reducible to the empirical and rational elements."[74] Why? Because the fullness of truth, as near as we can hope to discern it on this side of the divine-human tapestry, requires all three: "The *theos* of free theosophy is not an abstract principle but God, the living divine reality."[75]

A final point is necessary here relative to apophatic (negative) theology, the dominant mode in Orthodox theology in the twentieth century, and certainly a strong current throughout Merton's corpus. As Valliere describes it, "Apophatic theology honors the transcendence of God by avoiding positive propositions, stating the truths of revelation by means of negation instead: God is not a creature, not remote from his creation, the Persons of the Trinity are not reducible to each other, the two natures in Christ are neither divided nor confused, and so on."[76] While the concern to safeguard divine transcendence through apophasis is praiseworthy, Soloviev believed that as a general program it fails because it leaves us, as Valliere explains, "with a God who, though acknowledged as real, is less interesting than the living, pulsating, endlessly productive world which we actually experience." Abstract theology is "the first step in the direction of atheism, for people will naturally pay more attention to living nature than to abstract deity. Moreover, as they enjoy and study nature, they will not look for God in it because they have been taught by abstract theology not to do so. . . . Eventually the God-abstraction is discarded altogether."[77]

Beginning in the 1930s, neopatristic scholars privileged apophasis both in their interpretation of the church fathers and in their own constructive work, establishing what Valliere calls an "apophatic bias" in Orthodox theology from East to West.[78] For Bulgakov, however, the "negative formula of the Council of Chalcedon cannot . . . be understood as a *ban* on positive

---

73. Ibid.

74. Ibid., 141.

75. Ibid. Soloviev's vision parallels that of Teilhard de Chardin in the West, perhaps especially his notions of "convergence" and "centration" (see *Pierre Teilhard de Chardin: Writings Selected*, ed. Ursula King [Maryknoll, NY: Orbis, 1999]); cf. Newman's description of wisdom (chap. 2, p. 43) as "a connected view of the old with the new; an insight into the bearing and influence of each part upon every other; without which there is no whole, and could be no centre."

76. Valliere, MRT, 299.

77. Ibid., 158; cf. 269, for Bulgakov's perspective on apophasis.

78. Vladimir Lossky, one of Eastern Orthodoxy's preeminent twentieth-century theologians and a rigorous apophaticist, was also one of sophiology's more severe critics. Rowan Williams

definitions, but only as a *preliminary* definition, not complete, not exhaustive, but awaiting continuation."[79] Carrying the point fully into dogmatics, Bulgakov described the Chalcedonian dogma as "the supreme and final problem for theological and philosophical comprehension" and called his Orthodox colleagues "to a new religious and theological discovery and appropriation of this gift of the church."[80] Bulgakov's dogmatics of the humanity of God—a vision of the world built on the incarnation as a positive religious ideal (i.e., both already and not yet fully realized)—is thus his enduring contribution to the continuation of Chalcedon.

Significantly, Valliere does not downplay the apophatic tenor of mystical experience, which mystical theology communicates through paradox and unsaying. He sees the Russian theologians, rather, as placing apophasis in its prior context of "saying": namely, the seedbed of positive religion, living traditions "brimming with content." "On the level of pure theory," Valliere argues, " mysticism may appear to contain and exceed tradition, as the whole exceeds the part. In actual religious life the opposite is the case. Tradition comprises mysticism and exceeds it. Without a traditional framework mystics cannot talk to anybody, not even to each other, indeed not even to themselves. As soon as communication begins, however, so does engagement with the mediating structures of tradition."[81]

We have made the same case for Merton throughout this study: namely, that Wisdom dawned in his consciousness and served in his writings ("as soon as communication begins") as a kind of "mediating structure," his most vivid means for attuning modern readers to Christ's real presence behind and within the signs of nature, in the sacramental life of the church, and in the dignity of persons everywhere. He did so classically insofar as his theology holds in fruitful tension the dynamic of saying and unsaying, fullness and emptiness, light and darkness, a dialectic at the heart of the Christian memory and experience of God in Jesus Christ from the beginning.[82] Yet

---

offers a brief but lucid discussion of the Sophia controversy of 1935–36. See Williams, *Sergeii Bulgakov*, 172–81; cf. Valliere, MRT, 287–89, 300n22.

79. Cited in Valliere, MRT, 300. On this point Bulgakov critiques patristic theology for failing to develop the humanistic implications of Chalcedon: "[In] stressing divine omnipotence to the exclusion of the human element the fathers risked reducing the incarnation to a *deus ex machina*. They affirmed the human truth of the incarnation theoretically but ignored it in practice" (Valliere, MRT, 297).

80. Cited in ibid., 298.

81. Ibid., 170. Mark S. Burrows advances a strikingly similar argument in "Words That Reach into the Silence: Mystical Languages of Unsaying," in *Minding the Spirit: The Study of Christian Spirituality* (Baltimore: Johns Hopkins, 2005), 207–14.

82. Whether Merton's theology strikes sufficient balance between cataphasis and apophasis depends much on the text in question, and, significantly, its intended audience. What bridges

given Merton's oft-stated predilection for apophasis, perhaps it is no surprise that scholars have sometimes understated the degree to which his work in fact advances a positive theology of divine-human presence, a vision of the world redeemed in Christ, not in spite of, but precisely *in* and *through*, its inescapable strickenness. It is toward this conclusion that the remainder of this chapter is bent.

Sophiology: Major Contributions to Positive Theology

The transcendent God has united himself with the world, has become God and the world, and this *And* is the union of the two natures in one divine hypostasis, divine and human, without division and without confusion, in a single life. The Chalcedonian dogma retains its significance even in heaven.[83]

I. Christology/Theological Anthropology

We have already identified the intuition at the heart of Soloviev's sophiology: that "Christ/Sophia is the 'world' which God experiences from all eternity, the world which he begets for himself."[84] From the beginning Soloviev treated sophiology as a branch of Christology, with Sophia strongly linked to the human nature of Christ. "Christ as Logos is the self-manifestation of God; but '[this] manifestation presupposes another . . . in relation to which God manifests himself, i.e., it presupposes a human being'"; "Sophia is the ideal and perfect humanity,"[85] the humanity that God sees and loves in Christ from all eternity. This should not be misconstrued as "a statement about Divine foreknowledge"; rather, it speaks of God's life "as Love from all eternity—Love which is always going beyond itself and creating that which has no source other than Divine Love. . . . The Chalcedonian dogma carries within itself not simply a Christological assertion, but also necessarily cosmological, soteriological and anthropological assertions."[86]

Once again, Soloviev's guiding impulse is not esoteric speculation on the inner life of God but the experience of *love*, of being drawn into participation in God's ongoing kenosis for all the world. As a branch of Christology, sophiology's concern is pragmatic: the salvation of actual human beings in

---

the tension, without resolving it, is his theology of contemplation, which always seeks to relate the positive formulas of faith to (wordless) experience.

83. From Bulgakov's *The Lamb of God*, cited in Valliere, MRT, 343n112.

84. Valliere, MRT, 159.

85. Cited in ibid.

86. Myroslaw Tataryn, "History Matters: Bulgakov's Sophianic Key," *St. Vladimir's Theological Quarterly* 49 (2005): 203–18, at 207–8.

history. The divine-human being, writes Soloviev, "in order to be real, must be one and many. . . . Every one of us, every human being, is essentially and actually rooted in the universal or absolute human being and participates in it."[87] In other words, Christ is not just an individual human being, but the "pan-human organism": "As members of this organism human beings have a share in divine freedom and immortality. In a word, they are divinizable."[88]

The theme of divinization brings us to the crucial question of Soloviev's motive in introducing the name Sophia. As Valliere asks, "If his point was to articulate the traditional Orthodox doctrine of theosis (deification), why was 'Sophia' necessary? 'God-human' and 'second Adam' would have sufficed." Indeed, the name Sophia itself would become (and remains) a "major stumbling block" for many Orthodox in understanding, much less embracing, sophiology. What does the name suggest that traditional christological terms do not? The answer, as intimated throughout this study, hinges on the notion of divinization *as participation*, and the degree to which the Wisdom literature of the Bible accentuates this extraordinarily high, even cosmic, calling of humanity.

> Before the mountains had been shaped,
>   before the hills, I was brought forth—
> when he had not yet made earth and fields,
>   or the world's first bits of soil.
> When he established the heavens, I was there,
>   when he drew a circle on the face of the deep. . . .
>   then I was beside him, like a master worker;
> and I was daily his delight,
>   rejoicing before him always,
> rejoicing in his inhabited world
>   and delighting in the human race. (Prov 8:25-31)

To repeat a point laid out in the introduction, Soloviev, the philosopher-poet, hears in these lines the music of an expansive divine-human mystery, a dual hymn evoking not only the presence of Christ, the uncreated Word-Wisdom of God, but also, through Christ's humanity, as it were, the primordial presence and participation of the human race, created Sophia, in life story of God. Soloviev, the metaphysician, translates this imagery into a portrait of Wisdom in two distinct but eternally related aspects, as Andrew Louth explains: "Within God, wisdom is God's essence, that in virtue of which the three divine persons are consubstantial. In the created order, wisdom is that which from chaos makes cosmos, that is, order. These two aspects of

---

87. Cited in Valliere, MRT, 160.
88. Valliere, MRT, 160.

wisdom—uncreated and created—are complementary, so that God and the created order intrinsically belong together, rather than being conceived as fundamental opposites, something that the Christian doctrine of creation *ex nihilo* . . . tends to suggest."[89]

Here is the key metaphysical affirmation: "God and the created order intrinsically belong together." What sophiology adds is a bold attempt to spell out just *how, where, and to what degree*. Valliere sees in Soloviev's doctrine of divine-human Sophia a dramatic broadening of the traditional concept of theosis from the individual (e.g., monk, artist, prophet) to "all human beings living in the world community."[90] Sophiology, as Valliere argues, reflects the broader project of Orthodox engagement with modern civilization: "Christ as the humanity of God has the power to divinize human 'wisdom,' i.e., culture, and in this capacity is appropriately called Sophia. The name fits the function. The function supports the project of Orthodox engagement with modern civilization."[91] In short, human beings are divinizable as beings "full of content," which is to say, "as creative agents engaged in the pursuits that fulfill humanity in the flesh, such as politics, science, education, the arts, technology, and so on."[92]

This is precisely what Merton saw in the Russians: the doctrine of the humanity of God as a basis for Christian humanism, ecumenism, interfaith dialogue, and the church's engagement in the modern world. Much of Merton's later theology, including his embrace of *Gaudium et spes*, can be discerned in Valliere's thesis: "Sophiology is not a gnostic quest for truths beyond the world but reflection on creative processes taking place within the world. It does not warrant an ethic of detachment or stillness (*hesychia*) but 'an ethic of joyful and creative labor.'"[93]

Most striking, Soloviev radicalizes the doctrine of theosis by positing not just the spiritualization of human beings "but also a kind of humanness in God,"[94] to which he gives the name Sophia. While "'God as absolute is transcendental to the world, is NO-thing,' i.e., not a 'thing,'" as Creator God brings to light the creature, "giving it a place [within] Himself by an act of love-humility."[95] As Bulgakov will develop the idea, God's world (Sophia)

89. Louth, "Wisdom and the Russians," 173.

90. Valliere, MRT, 161n40; here citing from Richard Gustafson, "Soloviev's Doctrine of Salvation," in *Russian Religious Thought*, pp. 31–48, at 40.

91. Valliere, MRT, 161. Valliere later cites N. N. Afanasiev on this point: "'The face of the Church is turned not to the desert but to the world, in relation to which she has creative and constructive work to do'" (cited in ibid., 386).

92. Valliere, MRT, 161.

93. Ibid., 261, citing Catherine Evtuhov.

94. Valliere, MRT, 335.

95. Rosenthal, "The Nature and Function of Sophia," 165.

is a *humanized world*: "Sophia is the Wisdom of God, the Glory of God, Humanity in God, the Humanity of God, the Body of God . . . the Divine World existing in God 'before' the creation."[96]

To the extent that traditional christological symbols such as Logos, God-Man, or Second Person risk detaching Christ in the imagination from nature and human history by accenting his absolute uniqueness, the remembrance of Sophia reclaims an elemental (or analogical) *continuity* between Christ and humanity, every human being, in the life story of God, a trinitarian communion that is "eternal"[97] (not just a divine forethought), "real," and in some measure already "realized"[98] through the incarnation; nor is matter merely a dead mechanism of atoms, but instead it is part of living nature, a universal organism, "the World Soul, *natura naturans . . . the anima mundi*."[99] The central place in this heavenly and earthly hierarchy belongs to humanity both as a collective universal and an individual organism, and to this "positive all-unity" Soloviev gives the biblical name Sophia.

In sum, by a kind of reaching behind the economy of the Second Person to Sophia—the Love or *eros* in God that longs for (makes room for) the world from the beginning—sophiology explodes the narrative of incarnation in a way that boldly reclaims God's love of all things in Christ. While not diminishing Christ's utter uniqueness as God-Man, sophiology presses the analogical implications of Chalcedon even further in Athanasius's direction, boldly amplifying the Eastern doctrine of theosis: like Jesus and because of him, every person has "a share in divine freedom and immortality."[100]

Of course there are dangers in pressing Chalcedon too far in this direction. As Merton cautions in his lectures on mystical theology, Athanasius's emphasis on incarnation and divinization "is so strong that it almost constitutes an exaggeration," and it "must not make us forget the prime importance of the Cross and the Redemption of man."[101] It is one thing to affirm that the world,

---

96. Cited in Valliere, MRT, 336.

97. Rowan Williams notes that the "uncreated" or "eternal" dimension ascribed to humanity should not be understood in a gnostic sense, but rather "that the spirit in us is not a thing that is brought into being like material objects; it is a *relation*, to God and others and the natural, given environment, that can as such have no beginning in time, since God's side of the relation is eternal" (Williams, *Sergeii Bulgakov*, 169–70). Still, the issue of a certain "preexistence" of humanity and/or the cosmos remains murky, at least in Bulgakov's early work.

98. See chap. 5, notes 30 and 38 on the Orthodox doctrine of deification.

99. Rosenthal, "The Nature and Function of Sophia," 165.

100. Valliere, MRT, 160. Bulgakov "is open at all times," writes Valliere, "to new discoveries—not of a new Christ, to be sure, but of a grander Christ than the one known to traditional exegesis, grander not just in divinity, but in humanity as well" (MRT, 338). The analysis has striking implications, not least for ecumenical and interfaith dialogue.

101. ICM, 47.

in Christ, has "a share in divine freedom and immortality"; it is another to foreclose the (painful/joyful) historical path by which we must live and grow into this mystery. To say it another way, the doctrine of theosis constitutes for the Russians a positive religious ideal; as such, it is both a given (now) and a mandate (not yet realized). The eschatological tension, the *human* tension, remains and must not be collapsed into a wholly realized vision of things.

Where Soloviev's theosophy tends to drift dangerously above the historical tenor of the gospels, Bulgakov's dogmatics of the humanity of God makes it patently clear that sophiology "is oriented to the actual world [which] is always under construction."[102] Indeed, proceeding on the axiom that "uninterrupted humanity in the God-human is the basic fact and basic premise of the gospel narrative,"[103] Bulgakov's portrait of Jesus in *The Lamb of God* aims explicitly to *correct* the docetic and monophysitic tendencies of neo-patristic exegesis. The significance of this point can hardly be overstated. As exotic as sophiology might appear to Western readers, Bulgakov takes the soteriological content of his dogmatics from the inner dynamism of the gospels, that is, the divine-human drama ("synergy") played out not only in the life of Jesus but in all the founders of the church.[104] Here, as was evident in Merton's Christology (chap. 5), the integral human freedom and receptivity of Jesus—and of all persons, by extension—takes center stage.

For Bulgakov to affirm the "uninterrupted humanity" of Jesus is to insist that Jesus "prayed for the same reason other human beings pray: to draw closer to God."[105] Likewise Jesus' freedom involved the capacity to err, marking his victory in the desert over Satan, at Gethsemane, and on the cross, as *both* a human victory (Russian: *podvig*) and the fulfillment of a divine plan. The gospels portray Jesus' manner of being not as if divinity were "operating in him mechanically" but as a "synergy of the divine and the human in which the contribution of human effort—spiritual toil, asceticism, prayer—must not be minimized. Human freedom in Jesus 'was not paralyzed or eliminated by His Divinity, but only inspired by it.'"[106] In a similar way, both John the Baptist

---

102. Valliere, MRT, 336. "In the Schellingian tradition, to be sure, there is a danger dogmatic religion will be dissolved into philosophical mysticism, an outcome that tempted Soloviev from time to time. The antidote lies in recognizing 'positive' realities are by definition concrete, particular, historical things" (296). For Bulgakov's critique of Soloviev on this point, see ibid., 292n4.

103. Cited in ibid., 338.

104. As we shall see below, Merton's metaphysics of "presence" likewise takes its cues from biblical revelation, climactically, from the "Word of the Cross."

105. Valliere, MRT, 338.

106. Ibid., 339, citing Bulgakov's *The Lamb of God*. For Bulgakov, Jesus' fully human freedom corresponds with the unreserved kenosis of the Son. Even the resurrection, Valliere explains, "should not be viewed through the prism of conventional triumphalism [i.e., as a sheer *deus*

and Mary emerge in Bulgakov's dogmatics as first among "the children of Wisdom" (see Luke 7:35). What can this mean?

Above all, it underscores the centrality of *human receptivity* in the gospels, the attunement of divine-human Wisdom on the fulcrum of freedom. Bulgakov goes to great lengths to show that John and Mary were "creative receivers, not passive recipients, of the Word made flesh," that they were *agents*, and not merely instruments, of divine power: "While the annunciation was surely a divine miracle, a human grandeur also was involved."[107] It is on this point that Bulgakov objects to the Roman Catholic dogma of the immaculate conception, arguing that the teaching, by removing Mary from original sin, removes her from humanity, and makes "it impossible to regard Mary's life as a *podvig*, a winning-through to purity by means of asceticism, virtue and piety." By a kind of "dogmatic *deus ex machina*," the teaching "makes it impossible to construe history as 'the *common task* of humanity, a single and connected action having the incarnation as its center.'"[108] Even more striking, Bulgakov objects that the dogma alienates Mary from "the whole human side of the preparation for the Incarnation."[109] Mary's moral horizon, in other words, her *Fiat*, never exists in a social vacuum; as a daughter of Israel her personal sinlessness is "not just Her personal accomplishment [*podvig*] but the accomplishment of the whole Old Testament church of all [her] forefathers and fathers in faith as well."[110] Here Bulgakov shows not only a deep respect for historic Israel and the integral Jewishness of Mary and Jesus; in doing so he affirms the social and historical matrix of all spirituality.

---

ex machina] but as 'a kenotic glorification, a glorification in humiliation'" (ibid., 341, citing *The Lamb of God*).

107. Valliere, MRT, 321.

108. Ibid., 322, citing Bulgakov. "If Bulgakov is right to believe that one of the faults of traditional dogmatics is insufficient appreciation for the human side of the incarnation, then the dogma of the immaculate conception clearly represents a step backwards." Valliere is careful to note that Bulgakov affirms the "personal sinlessness" of Mary. "The issue is how this purity came about. Was it the result of a divine miracle, or was it in some measure also Mary's personal accomplishment?" (ibid.).

109. Ibid., 322.

110. Cited in ibid., 322–23. Note that Bulgakov's objection is not the Protestant objection, which hinges on the lack of scriptural basis for Marian dogma, nor does he reject the dogma "because it is a modern innovation," as Valliere notes. Unlike conservative Orthodox theologians, for whom "the most important dogmatic issues were settled by the fathers of the seven ecumenical councils" (AD 325–787), Bulgakov "is much more heavily invested in the idea of tradition as an ongoing, organic process"; new Marian dogmas therefore "lie within the realm of possibility." Indeed, as Bulgakov saw it, "no preordained forms are prescribed for church tradition—the Holy Spirit, living in the Church, blows where it wills" (Valliere, MRT, 321). None of this diminishes the exalted tenor of Bulgakov's mariology (see ibid., 325–28).

In like manner, Bulgakov interprets Jesus' teachings in continuity with the Jewish prophets. The teachings of Christ "should not be handled as an oracle or manifesto of the Absolute Word . . . 'loaded with impossible demands, oriented to utopian maximalism and lacking a religious connection.'"[111] In the mouths of the prophets, "the *Divine Word* [is] a *human word*. . . . The prophet [is] a living mediator between God and human beings, not an oracle, which would be nothing but a mechanical tool for delivering messages unintelligible even to the prophet himself."[112] Thus Bulgakov sees the Sermon on the Mount as "a prophecy of the incarnate Word inviting a human response"; as such, "one has to figure 'earthly, relative, transitory values' into the equation. The difficulty of the task cannot be eased."[113] Again, the central dynamic of the gospels Bulgakov aims to preserve is that of revelation as *an invitation to participation in the life story of God*; the eschatological tension, the decisive Yes or No required of Jesus' audience, remains.[114]

Most striking and significant for our purposes is the way Bulgakov humanizes Jesus' apocalyptic sayings, emphasizing their hopeful but contingent thrust toward the kingdom of God. "We must not forget the *humanity*," he writes, "hence also the relativity of the prophetic visions if we are to have a correct view of them, free from exaggerations."[115] Thus where Jesus' limited knowledge of the future posed a stumbling block to patristic commentators— "But about that day or hour no one knows" (Mark 13:32)—Bulgakov, by contrast, "takes it as stunning evidence of the kenosis of the Son and as a vindication of the centrality of human reception in the gospel."[116]

> One of the meanings of Jesus' testimony about not knowing the time of the end of the world may be that this time is determined not just by the will of God but by human response. The latter has yet to be completed and represents a variable, undetermined quantity, the sphere of free, human creativity. The Son of Man takes the side of humanity here and, on its behalf, faced with an unconsummated and as yet unknown future with respect to which prophecy is *conditional*, speaks about His ignorance [of the end of the age].[117]

---

111. Ibid., 339, citing *The Lamb of God*.
112. Cited in ibid., 339.
113. Valliere, MRT, 339, citing *The Lamb of God*.
114. "Over against the unitary moralism of Tolstoyanism and other forms of utopianism, [Bulgakov] looks to an ongoing, ever-dynamic relationship between Son, Sermon and humanity. Over against the authoritarian Teacher of patristic exegesis, he sees a kenotic Son granting human beings the space and time they need to respond creatively to the Word" (ibid., 340).
115. Cited in ibid., 340.
116. Valliere, MRT, 340.
117. Cited in ibid.

In sum, the prophetic word of God, even that which comes from the lips of Jesus, is *conditional*, inviting and awaiting the "human response" which "has yet to be completed." With the incarnation, Bulgakov writes, "God reigns over the world *in a new way*, in human beings and through human beings in the God-human."[118] Henceforth history, indeed the life story of God, hinges on the fulcrum of the present human moment, where God speaks in the silence of the human heart: *Sophia*. The whole climate of the New Testament witnesses to "the flowering of ordinary possibilities" that are "hidden in everyday life." It remains for human beings, in every new generation, to harvest the "fruits of hope that have never been seen before."[119]

II. Trinity/Cosmodicy

If Soloviev set his early philosophy against the "inhuman God" of Islam and the "godless individualism" of Western culture, Bulgakov framed his early thinking in *The Unfading Light* (1911–16) in terms of the intellectual and spiritual collision of "Germanism" with the Orthodox world. In opposing Germanism Bulgakov countered not only the abstract philosophy of Kant but also German mysticism, which he criticized as pantheism or "immanentism," a "fatal turn to this world" which led to "man-deification of various types."[120] Equating German thought with the Protestant Pietism of its leading philosophers, he criticized the "gnostic rationalism" of Jacob Boehme and later that of Hegel; he objected in particular to Boehme's vision of "*Jungfrau* Sophia," whose perpetual virginity "reveals the negative attitude to femininity, and to the flesh in general," that Bulgakov considered juridical, monophysite, and 'typically Protestant.'"[121]

The tension between immanentism and transcendentalism haunts modern theology, and Bulgakov's sophiology is no exception. The vocation of modern religious thought, he asserts, is "to unite the truth of both, to discover not 'a synthesis' but the living unity [between them], to know God in the world and the world in God."[122] In his early analysis of the problem in *The Unfading Light*, Bulgakov introduces an imaginative neologism in his discussion of Plato's theory of forms: *cosmodicy*. The discovery of the sophianic nature of

---

118. Cited in ibid., 343–44. Bulgakov's emphasis on the integral freedom of the "hearers of the word" seems to presage the same theme in Karl Rahner.

119. RU, 160. The "pan-dogmatic scope" of Bulgakov's concern is clear: "the humanity of God entails not just the humanity of the gospel but the humanity of all scripture, the humanity of all Israel, the humanity of all revelation" (Valliere, MRT, 324).

120. Rosenthal, "The Nature and Function of Sophia," 164.

121. Ibid.

122. Cited in Valliere, MRT, 272.

the world, he writes, is "the essence of the cosmodicy of Platonism."[123] With the term "cosmodicy" Bulgakov announces the central concern of sophiology, as Valliere explains: "not theodicy, the justification of the ways of God to human beings" but "the justification of the world to the guardians of divine truth. Adumbrated by Plato and the biblical Wisdom tradition, cosmodicy comes into its own in modern times when the creaturely world, with modern secularism as its tribune, steps forward to claim its rights."[124]

The *justification of the world to the guardians of divine truth*—this is the fundamental (liberal) thrust of Bulgakov's philosophical thought. Yet it would take some time before he would bring this project into dogmatic theology or theology of revelation. While Sophia in *The Unfading Light* still "hangs in metaphysical limbo between God and the world," in his magisterial trilogy, *On the Humanity of God* (1933–45), Bulgakov finally brings the conversation with secular thought and the sciences "into dogmatics itself, the inner sanctum of theology." And when dogmatic theology dares to enter into this conversation in earnest, "it enters the force-field of modern 'creativity,'" making unprecedented demands on every discipline willing to engage. "Theology is challenged to orient itself not just to divine things, not just to God as it were, but to the humanity of God. The other side is challenged to deal not just with human things, but with God-filled humanity."[125]

While Bulgakov's mature trinitarian theology more or less follows the traditional lines of Greek patristics, his account of God's kenosis in the act of creation yields a somewhat more complex picture of *creatio ex nihilo*. As Valliere explains: "The act of creation is not just a manifestation of divine might, but 'a voluntary self-diminishment, a metaphysical kenosis,' whereby the divine Absolute admits the existence of beings outside itself. Moreover, the creatures of the world are not passive material in the hands of the creator but are endowed with a life of their own, a creaturely divinity so to speak, precisely because they bear the image of their divine creator."[126] There are hints here, as everywhere in Bulgakov's dogmatics, of Jewish kabbalism's notion of *zimzum*, a mystical narrative with strong maternal (sophianic) overtones. That is, by contrast to a sheer act of omnipotent power, God freely and lovingly wills to "open a space" in Godself for the world. This vision of creation also comes close, as Valliere notes, to Anglo-American process theology, and even, as Rowan Williams notes, to Karl Barth. What joins

---

123. Cited in ibid., 273.

124. Valliere, MRT, 273.

125. Ibid., 276. Moreover, a theology that is truly "living" both in method and content will always be an unfinished business, resisting "systematization"—a point we shall revisit in the conclusion.

126. Ibid., 331, citing *The Lamb of God*.

these wildly diverse theologies is the conviction, over against an impersonal, Hegelian, or monistic vision of creation-in-process, that the world is neither necessary nor arbitrary: "God *chooses* not to be God without the world"; indeed, Bulgakov employs Sophia precisely as "a way of speaking about the non-arbitrariness" of God's relation to the universe.[127] Likewise, from our side, as it were, the Son's incarnation respects "the *independence* of human nature in its freedom. Christ's humanity does not take the place of our natural humanity but co-lives, co-suffers, co-abides with it."[128] The Spirit "'does not force human freedom but persuades it,' winning it over with patience and humility in an 'ongoing Pentecost' or 'final kenosis' which will continue until the end of the age."[129]

The most significant refinement Bulgakov brings to Orthodox trinitarianism follows from his distinction between the monarchy of the Father and "the Dyad" of Son and Spirit, the latter relationship comprising "the revelatory or 'sophianic' hypostases, emptying themselves into the world to manifest the will of the Father."[130] For Bulgakov, Sophia is the transcendental subject of God's *oikonomia*, or entrance into history. Neither a hypostasis nor simply identifiable with one of the Persons of the Trinity, Sophia is God's self-emptying *ousia*, the Father's self-revelation in the dyadic *unity* of the Son and Holy Spirit.[131] Again, notwithstanding the technical terminology, we must not lose sight of the soteriological thrust or eros that underlies sophianic metaphysics. Bulgakov wants us to see the creation of world "as specifically a revelation of *trinitarian* life, so that the world's life is shown to be established on the same (sophianic) foundation as God's. There is the sheer impulse of self-giving, the life of God as 'Father,' emptying himself in letting the Other be."[132] Humanity is "the crown of creation because it is the

---

127. Williams, *Sergeii Bulgakov*, 169, and 169n24; cf. Valliere, MRT, 300n23, on how Bulgakov handles the doctrine of *creatio ex nihilo*—"a favorite locus of apophatic theology because of the sharp distinction between God and the world which it implies."

128. Cited in Valliere, MRT, 333.

129. Valliere, MRT, 332, citing Bulgakov. Recall Merton's first journal entry on the Russians (April 25, 1957), in which he invokes the image of "a powerful Pentecost" to describe the human vocation in history (SFS, 86).

130. Valliere, MRT, 330.

131. See ibid. 330–34. Bulgakov acknowledges the difficulty for many in affirming that Sophia "is at one and the same time the revelation of both the Son and the Holy Spirit or, more exactly, of Son *and* Holy Spirit. People want a simple, rationalistic *identification* of Sophia with *one* of the hypostases of the Holy Trinity, although Sophia is in fact not a hypostasis at all; and they are amazed when one says that the Wisdom of God, as the self-revelation of the Father, is the dyadic unity of the revelation of the *Two* revelatory hypostasis" (cited in ibid., 334).

132. Williams, *Sergeii Bulgakov*, 169. Despite the complaints of Lossky and other critics that sophiology too freely absorbs German idealism, Williams observes that Bulgakov's two

place where the world becomes personal,"[133] where divine and creaturely Sophia are joined in participation.

What all of this means is that the prominence Bulgakov eventually gives to Sophia in his mature dogmatics implies neither a fourth person in the Godhead nor a unitarian Godhead in which the Persons are merely modes. In fact, neither heresy is to be found in his trinitarianism. What we find, rather, is "Orthodox theology in a new key, a creative reconstruction of dogma in a modern idiom, unprecedented but not ungrounded in anteced-ent tradition."[134] At the same time, "a more complex theology of creation thereby emerges, since the cosmos is viewed as being governed not just by the condescension of the divine in creation and salvation but by the heaven-wards aspiration of all creatures."[135] This "two-way energeticism," as Valliere describes it, is one of the most distinctive features of Bulgakov's sophiology in *The Unfading Light*.[136]

More freely and poetically, then, Sophia is the "love of Love" and its eternal object in the world, God's pleasure, joy, and play. She enters the world of dark chaos, of inert matter, bridging all subject-object dualisms and illumining the world with the light of the transfigured Logos/Christ. Sophia is the active and dynamic pivot or force within nature, *natura naturans*, the *anima mundi*; her rays activate and energize human beings.[137] Sophia is the cloak between God and the world, neither reducible to one nor the other, but something that both unites and separates God and the world. She is revealed above all as *beauty*; indeed, mining the iconographic roots of Byzantine spirituality, Bulgakov says that art, rather than philosophy, is the direct way to know her.[138]

At this point we have to ask what distinguishes the sophiological world-view from the immanentism that Bulgakov so stringently opposed. With its language of "eternal" humanity and vision of a world "in God," how does sophiology avoid pantheism or monism, on the one hand (i.e., identifying the divine world with the visible universe), and gnosticism, on the other (i.e., conceiving the divine world as radically discontinuous with the visible uni-verse; only a privileged few rise to participate in divinity)? It is easy enough,

---

theological trilogies are "far more dominated by biblical and liturgical allusion than by any extraneous intellectualism" (ibid., 177).

133. Ibid., 169.

134. Valliere, MRT, 329.

135. Ibid., 270.

136. Ibid. Thus the patristic theme of *communicatio idiomatum* is "rightly interpreted," insists Bulgakov, "only if it is also made to show the influence of human nature on the divine. But here we see a total lack of clarity [in patristic theology]" (cited in ibid., 298).

137. Rosenthal, "The Nature and Function of Sophia," 161–62.

138. For a rich discussion of this theme, see Andrew Louth, "'Beauty Will Save the World': The Formation of Byzantine Spirituality," *Theology Today* 61 (2004): 67–77.

as Valliere notes, to grasp why the latter worldview repelled Bulgakov: the "anti-cosmic dualism of gnosticism solves no problems for the Orthodox seeker of dialogue with the world." Indeed, "by disconnecting God from the world gnosticism undermines the God-givenness of creation and the possibility of a real incarnation." Pantheism, on the other hand, "was a view for which Bulgakov confessed a deep affinity."[139] While he saw that absolute pantheism leads to "the impious deification of the world," he was honest enough to admit that his sophiological vision "is *also* pantheism, only of a thoroughly pious kind."[140] What, then, distinguishes Bulgakov's "pious" pantheism from the "pagan" kind?

One approach to the question is through the theme of humanity itself and human creativity as *unfinished*, that is, a function of growth and process. In short, the world is still *becoming* Sophia.[141] A still better response, however, to the question of pantheism is framed in terms of the core dogmatic issue, namely, the humanity of God. Valliere's lucid analysis of this issue merits citation here, for it goes far in explaining the thoroughgoing Christian humanism of Merton's last decade, so much influenced by Russian theology and literature. It also pinpoints what distinguishes Merton's sophianic worldview finally, perhaps radically, from Zen:

> When Bulgakov postulates a world in God, he does not mean a world with the human or personal element filtered out. On the contrary, the point of the postulate in the first place is to make it possible to speak about *bogochelovechestvo*, the eternal humanity of God. The profound link between divinity and humanity manifested in the creation of human beings and in the incarnation "signifies not just the divinity of human beings but also a kind of humanness in God." God's world, or Sophia, is a humanized world. . . . If this is so, then no doctrine which suppresses the human element or assigns it a secondary role in the cosmos can be acceptable to a Christian theologian. Yet this is precisely what absolute pantheism does: it dehumanizes the world in order to deify it, for it cannot imagine the humanity of God. So doing, pantheism falls short of its goal, for the world it deifies is no longer the actual world, which always contains a human or personal dimension, but a "world" of its own devising, an intellectual abstraction. This is its impiety: not the

139. Valliere, MRT, 334–35.
140. Cited in ibid. As Valliere rightly notes, one can attenuate the difficulty by using the term "panentheism" (all-in-God-ism), but the deeper issue "is not one of terminology." Bulgakov describes pantheism as "a dialectically indispensable moment in sophiological cosmogony," in other words, as Valliere explains, "something the Christian theologian should not try to avoid" (ibid., 335).
141. See Rosenthal, 165; again, the resonances here with Teilhard de Chardin and North American process theology are many.

deification of the world, which the gospel itself promises at the end of the age, but the replacement of the divinely grounded, living world by a depersonalized abstraction. By means of sophiology Bulgakov seeks a middle way between the extremes of abstract pantheism (a deified world lacking humanity) and abstract trinitarianism (a super-essential Trinity disconnected from the world).[142]

No doctrine "which suppresses the human element or assigns it a secondary role in the cosmos can be acceptable to a Christian theologian."[143] Valliere's analysis is clear: If sophiology risks any impiety, it is not absolute pantheism so much as an absolute anthropocentricism, a too-realized vision of humankind, one that precludes, for example, a serious enough gaze on historical injustice and evil, or a sense of revelation as radical *interruption*. In other words, a more dialectical (e.g., Barthian) imagination will object that sophiology thinks too highly of the humanized world and its potency for divinization. Yet the sticking point here, it would seem, is not with sophiology as such but with the doctrines of incarnation and deification. In any case, there is no question that once the robustly analogical imagination of sophiology moves from a focus on Christmas (i.e., incarnation) to Holy Week, it must eventually ask what place the crucifixion of Jesus can have in a positive theology of the world and of history. We shall revisit this question below under the theme of apocalyptic.

III. Mother Earth: The Silent Memoria of God

The sophianic perspective envisions the entire world as "one corporeality and one body," though it is not always clear whether this body "is that of Sophia, or of Christ, or of both united at the end of time."[144] For Bulgakov the sanctification of the world, including the "transfiguration of the flesh," is heralded clearly and unambiguously in the Bible: "God saw everything that he had made, and indeed, it was very good" (Gen 1:31). "From the earth," says Bulgakov, "from Great Mother Earth, was created everything that exists."[145] Bulgakov's hymnic celebration of the mutuality between the "holy flesh" of humanity (Adam) and "matter-mother" (the earth) is anything but abstract:

> Great mother, grey earth! In you we are born, you feed us, we touch you with our feet, to you we return. Children of the earth love their mother, kiss her, wipe her tears, because they are her flesh and blood. For nothing

---

142. Valliere, MRT, 335–36.
143. Cf. SFS, 381.
144. Rosenthal, "The Nature and Function of Sophia," 167.
145. Cited in ibid.

perishes in her; she preserves everything in herself, the silent memory of the world that gives life and fruit to all. He who does not love the earth, does not feel her maternity, is a slave and an alien, a pitiful rebel against the mother, a fiend of nonexistence. . . . You silently preserve in yourself the fullness and all the beauty of creation.[146]

"The silent memory of the world that gives life and fruit to all"—these words call to mind not only Pasternak and Dostoyevsky but also the Native and Latin American spiritualities that were so compelling to Merton.[147] The invocation of the silent *memoria* of God, seeded in the soil and rock of the earth, makes it clear that Bulgakov's conception of sacred corporeality has little to do with a bourgeois or bucolic sentimentalism, and goes well beyond a literary or romantic aestheticization of nature.

In the first place, one hardly has to be a poet to acknowledge that the earth "gives life and fruit to all," or to lament the degree to which modern society threatens the environmental matrix of life and being. "The fate of nature," asserts Bulgakov, "suffering and awaiting its liberation, is henceforth connected with the fate of man, who 'subdues' it; the new heaven and new earth now enter as a necessary element into the composition of Christian eschatology."[148] This is an astounding insight. Long before the emergence of environmental theologies in the West, Bulgakov was not only advancing a theological "justification of the world to the guardians of divine truth" but observing further that the natural world suffers and groans for final "liberation."

Second, Bulgakov's approach to sacred corporeality displays a radical seriousness and breadth of application. "Is it possible," he asked early in his career, "to have a worldview on whose basis one might be a materialist—that is, conceive oneself as in real unity with nature and humankind—yet at the same time affirm the independence of the human spirit with its particular needs, its postulates about supernatural, divine being, illuminating and making sense of natural life?"[149] Bulgakov would spend two decades working out the implications of Soloviev's view of nature in the rather mundane realms of economics, agriculture, and social and political theory. In its open engagement with the natural and human sciences, the sophiological tradition, as Rowan Williams observes, "dissolves crude oppositions between spirit and body, and allows us to imagine a world that is not only self-aware but *sensually* aware of

---

146. Cited in ibid.

147. Cf. Bartolome de Las Casas: "God has a very fresh and living memory of the smallest and most forgotten" (cited in Gustavo Gutierrez, *Las Casas: In Search of the Poor of Jesus Christ*, trans. Robert Barr [Eugene: Wipf and Stock, 2003], 194).

148. Cited in Evtuhov, *The Cross and the Sickle*, 138–39.

149. Cited in ibid., 138.

itself. . . . Bulgakov sees the basis of ethics in the call to active co-operation with the sophianic transfiguration of the world . . . [a world] in which the characteristic *human* business is the transforming of an environment."[150]

Third, we should not overlook the strong tenor of protest in the passage above against those who do not love the earth or "feel her maternity." It is an intra-ecclesial protest, on the one hand, reflecting Bulgakov's rejection of the disdain for the world and the flesh that he saw in many of his fellow Orthodox "guardians of divine truth"—in Berdyaev's statement, for example, that in the eschaton "womanliness will be confirmed in the aspect of virginity rather than motherhood."[151] But it also reflects his protest against the unyielding masculinity he saw ravaging the world around him, especially during World War I. "In effect," as Rosenthal suggests, "he was invoking Mother Russia against the German Fatherland, and 'feminine' qualities against 'masculine' ones—love rather than force, mediation rather than conflict, and selflessness rather than self-assertion, aggressiveness, and war. The abstract rationalism he hated is conventionally linked with a 'masculine' style of thought, and war has always been a 'masculine' affair."[152]

Without question Merton's invocation of Sophia during the 1960s is cut from much the same cloth, that is, the cloth of *protest*. First, he protests against the "flight from woman" crippling his own past, and perhaps even crippling the prospects for renewal in the Catholic Church: "One wonders if our theological cautiousness is not after all the sign of a fatal coldness of heart, an awful sterility born of fear, or of despair?"[153] But there is also his protest against the deadly "seriousness" of American power, its Promethean grasping for life that plays out tragically, in fact, as an addiction to death. Life under the shadow of war and endless preparation for war wavers more and more desperately and unfreely between heroism and despair. "Eschatology" in such a culture becomes little more than "the last gasp of exhausted possibilities,"[154] humankind's secret desire to get it all over with. The poem "Seven Archaic Images" appears with *Hagia Sophia* in *Emblems of a Season of Fury*:

> Feathered images
> Of kings and heroes
> Monsters in pursuit.

150. Williams, *Sergeii Bulgakov*, 128–29.

151. Cited in Rosenthal, "The Nature and Function of Sophia," 167; Berdyaev further maintained that "the new man would be a 'youth-maiden,' 'an androgynous new Adam-Christ, in whom 'there cannot be the differentiated and decadent life of sex,'" a view that Bulgakov attacked as anti-biblical and gnostic (ibid., 170).

152. Rosenthal, "The Nature and Function of Sophia," 167.

153. SFS, 86.

154. RU, 75.

Man-eating war
Shakes the land with drums:
The sacred enclosure
The house of omens and weapons.

Bring coins, jewels, women and victims,
Bring sacred whores
To the hieratic city.

O great dishonorable beast, War,
Cockroach and millionaire,
Snake-eyed cousin of pestilence
Why do we dance for you,
Why do we dance to exhaustion?[155]

The poem brings to light one of the great problems confronting the sophiological perspective: the Anti-Christ. Bulgakov, to be sure, saw how easily "the creative power of human beings 'can be darkened by the spirit of satanism, can lose the awareness of its true character and lead to human satanism, to Anti-Christ.'"[156] "In a world where Anti-Christ is at large," Valliere notes, "this ambiguity is a dangerous thing, for the Adversary is, among other things, the supreme manipulator of divine things."[157] Bulgakov had the candor to admit that the crucial question—how to bridge the gulf between heavenly and earthly Sophia—remains largely unanswered in his speculative sophiology.[158] But in the meantime, if he and Merton could be accused of seeking consolation in a somewhat idealized "Mother Earth"—as Czeslaw Milosz once complained to Merton[159]—perhaps they can be forgiven. Nature, with its astounding regenerative capacity, its music, its grandeur and

155. Merton, ESF, 41; strophe VI.
156. Valliere, MRT, 265, citing Bulgakov's *The Philosophy of Economy*. Bulgakov speaks of "fallen Sophia" and Evdokimov of Sophia's "night face" to refer to historical evil. There is no question here "of a myth of some heavenly power rebelling against God," but rather a lament for a world "cut off from its true focus of meaning" (Williams, *Sergeii Bulgakov*, 171). From the sophiological perspective evil is a negation of being, a privation or parody of the good, a specter (Merton's "false self"). When Christ comes again divine Sophia will reunite the world "with the frustrated potential for sophianic life" hidden in all things.
157. Valliere, MRT, 265. In Bulgakov's day, Valliere points to "the Nietzscheans, for example, and the utopian 'god-builders' on the romantic fringe of the Bolshevik party."
158. The problem, which centers on the theodicy question, is not a minor one. Bulgakov tries to address the question with the help of Schelling's ruminations on Sophia over a century earlier, but Valliere finds the attempt wanting: "Like it or not, the question does have decisive significance for what Bulgakov is trying to do. If a convincing answer cannot be found, sophiology as a speculative project must fail" (ibid., 266). It would take another generation, and students of Bulgakov like Evdokimov, to more adequately address the "night face" of Sophia, the "metaphysical fall of the world-soul."
159. See CT, 65.

wordless silence, seems the only Presence left in the world capacious enough to hear and witness the sheer horror and scope of human sufferings, to say nothing of its own.

This brings us to a fourth point, and what is most striking in Bulgakov's hymn to the "great mother," namely, his palpable belief in Sophia's maternal care for the children of the earth, all of whom "are her flesh and blood." No matter how small, insignificant, or forgotten, "nothing perishes in her," *the memory of not a single creature is lost.* "In you we are born, you feed us, we touch you with our feet, to you we return." (In the Russian Bible, Rosenthal notes, Genesis 3:19 reads, "for earth thou art and to earth shalt thou return."[160]) We are very far here from the anonymity of a strictly evolutionary perspective of life on the planet in which the individual remains as subject to the brute contingencies of natural selection as a cockroach; or of evolutionary time, for that matter, as an endlessly horizontal march of nothing more than more of the same.[161]

The "maternity" of the earth, finally, is anything but an idealized abstraction in an atmosphere of war, with its ideological fury, its mass mobilization of machines of destruction, its dislocation of peoples and terrorization of civilian populations. When we long for healing and silence, for solitude and replenishment, it is to the earth that we (victims and perpetrators all) must "return" and find ourselves again. It is no wonder that as a young Marxist Bulgakov had been unable to reconcile himself "to a nature without God," as the machinery and rhetoric of war gathered with ominous fury around him. For if nature is "nothing more than a dead, arid desert wearing a mask of beauty," than death and burial for human beings—even for Christ!—can be nothing more than void, darkness, suffocation. In his later years, Bulgakov, the survivor of the Bolshevik Revolution and witness to two world wars, could welcome death with peace, knowing that neither body nor soul nor the labor of his life would be lost in the void. "The flowers of paradise," as he prayed to his dead son, are "waiting to bend over you, to guard your coffin."

In all of this Bulgakov uncannily foreshadows Merton's nature writings, which usher the reader into a palpable sense of communion with all things not only in life—"There is no leaf that is not in Your care. . . . no water in

---

160. Rosenthal, "The Nature and Function of Sophia," 167; cf. Valliere, MRT, 262n25, where Bulgakov's attunement with the earth (akin to that "of a Russian peasant farmer") is contrasted with the "aristocratic" sensibilities of Berdyaev.

161. "So-called modern man," writes Metz, "stands in danger of becoming increasingly faceless and (to speak biblically) nameless . . . he is being bred back more and more into a cleverly adaptable animal, into a smoothly functioning machine" (Johann Baptist Metz, *Faith in History and Society: Toward a Practical Fundamental Theology*, trans. and ed. J. Matthew Ashley [New York: Crossroad, 2007], 80).

the shales that was not hidden there by Your wisdom"—but also in death—
"The beasts sing to You before they pass away. The solid hills vanish like a
worn-out garment. All things change, and die and disappear. Questions
arrive, assume their actuality, and also disappear. In this hour I shall cease
to ask them, and silence shall be my answer."[162] Both Bulgakov and Merton
teach us that the human vocation to solitude and contemplation is inseparable
from the rhythms and cadences of the natural world. In our free "returning"
to the earth, death paradoxically loses its sting, and life quickens again in
souls "that have been exiled from themselves and from their God."[163] The
sophianic child awakens.

   Here again, we are not far from the apocalyptic climate of the New Testament, where Jesus everywhere urges us to *stay awake*, to pay attention, as life
and hope spring forth from the most hidden and unpromising materials.
"*Consider the lilies of the field, how they grow; they neither toil nor spin, yet I
tell you, even Solomon in all his glory was not clothed like one of these*" (Matt
6:28-30). Nor are we far from the hushed splendor of liturgical *anamnesis*, and
the church's participation, body and soul, in the paschal mystery that ends and
begins in an earthen tomb. For "there is nothing lost that God cannot find
again. Nothing dead that cannot live again in the presence of His Spirit. No
heart so dark, so hopeless, that it cannot be enlightened and brought back to
itself, warmed back to the life of charity."[164] What sophiology does is to give a
positive language, that is, *a Name*, to an experience that resounds in human
beings and cultures everywhere, the intuition of nature's silent receptivity and
gratuity, its beauty, mystery, and ontological depth in God—Sophia.

IV. Eros and the Feminine in God

> Only through the body does the way, the ascent to the life of blessed-
> ness, lie open to us.[165]

   The question of whether sophiology may be regarded as a forerunner of
feminist theology is a complex one. Clearly, there is a danger of applying
contemporary questions and standards of discourse to thinkers whose social
and cultural horizons were very different from our own. On the one hand,
Bulgakov's theology is replete with gender stereotyping, a gender "essential-
ism" that "jolts feminist sensibilities"[166]; on the other hand, one cannot deny

162. SJ, 361.
163. NM, 242.
164. Ibid.
165. Bernard of Clairvaux, *Sermons on the Song of Songs* 5.I.1.
166. Rosenthal, "The Nature and Function of Sophia," 170.

that the themes of Sophia, the motherhood of God, and Great Mother Earth "effect a rather striking feminization of dogmatic categories in Bulgakov's theology."[167] Without question, sophiology is controversial partly because of its potential to reshape the religious imagination in ways that pose an explicit challenge to entrenched patterns of patriarchy, both in theological discourse and ecclesial practice.

The question of whether feminized theology necessarily leads to feminist theology would not have arisen in Bulgakov's historical context. "The concern with gender and power and the programmatics of inclusiveness are lacking in his thought."[168] Yet the core issue at play here, and the best approach to the question, as Valliere suggests, is theological: the doctrine of the humanity of God presses against any conception of the divine that would subtly or not-so-subtly preclude any aspect of the *humanum* from full participation. If "the humanity of God means not just the spiritualization of the human but the humanization of the divine, and if concrete humanity is always gendered ('male and female he created them'), then one of the things an exposition of the humanity of God will require is the feminization of categories used to speak about the divine, including those pertaining to the inner life of God, as in Bulgakov's feminized trinitarianism."[169]

The point is a subtle but crucial one and can be illumined further with the soteriological axiom of Gregory of Nazianzus: "What has not been assumed cannot be restored." Like the doctrine of the humanity of God, Gregory's axiom operates in the framework of an all-embracing incarnation Christology. "It says that, if God has not assumed the whole of humanity, the whole of humanity is not touched by God and hence not saved. . . . It is a way of saying that God has approached all humanity, wholly and integrally, in and through Jesus, and not a segment of human beings or an aspect of the human condition."[170] While Gregory used the principle to establish that Jesus must have had a rational human soul, it can be applied analogously to celebrate the assumption of womanhood into the life of God, no less integrally and dramatically than that of manhood. The alternative, of course, "that womanhood is not included in what has been assumed,"[171] is ridiculous. The name Sophia reinforces in the imagination what Christian theology claims for all:

167. Valliere, MRT, 328.

168. Ibid. For an extended discussion, see Brenda Meehan, "Wisdom/Sophia, Russian Identity, and Western Feminist Theology," *Cross Currents* 46 (1996): 149–68.

169. Valliere, MRT, 328.

170. Roger Haight, *Jesus Symbol of God* (Maryknoll, NY: Orbis, 1999), 293.

171. Ibid. "From a theological perspective, Jesus could have been a woman, and to make specific theological points from the facticity of his manhood without further warrant would seem to be fundamentally wrong."

that in and through Jesus, integral humanity is fully sanctified. The love of God in Christ and through the Holy Spirit knows no bounds (Gal 3:28).

What the feminization of dogmatics does *not* involve in the case of sophiology is a kind of physicalism or reverse genderism applied to God. That is, if God has been known as "Father" for two millennia then we must now make up the difference by naming God as "Sophia," "Mother," "Goddess," or the like. The core issue for the Russians and for Merton is, not terminology, but ontology; not identification, but identity, and the retrieval of symbols in the tradition that reinvigorate a palpable sense of that shared identity in God. This is by no means, however, to minimize the significance of naming God in feminine terms, especially in the context of our times, an era in which "oppressed women have their history inscribed on their bodies."[172] Merely to invoke the name of "Wisdom, our sister" is to reclaim forcefully, in the name of God, the full personhood and dignity of women always and everywhere.

There is yet a deeper theological issue at play here, which follows from the claim that God has approached humanity wholly and integrally in and through Jesus, a claim that draws the realm of eros and sexuality into dogmatic theology. Eros may be described broadly here as the desire or intentionality for life that reaches across distances and absences to delight in a union that enfolds ("assumes," in christological terms) the whole person. Mystical or theological eros reaches across distances to unite apparent opposite realms of being (eternity and history, divinity and humanity, heaven and earth, spirit and flesh) in an integral (bodily-spiritual) realization of love, ecstasy, or mystical union. In fact the erotic dimension of the sophiological worldview follows from the testimony to eros in the Bible itself, especially in its mystical and poetical dimensions, as touched on in chapters 2 and 3. To be sure, the biblical testimony to eros as a dimension in the life *of God* has been more or less hidden from the mainstream view of divine power, agency, or presence taken from the Bible. Perhaps it is best described, as Walter Brueggemann describes the Wisdom tradition, as Israel's "countertestimony" to a different way of speaking and experiencing YHWH.[173]

---

172. Kwok Pui-lan, "Mending of Creation: Women, Nature, and Eschatological Hope," in *Liberating Eschatology: Essays in Honor of Letty M. Russell*, ed. Margaret Farley and Serene Jones (Louisville, KY: Westminster John Knox, 1999), 144–55, at 150. Pui-lan's discussion of the sex trade throws the whole discussion of Sophia into an urgent and darkly apocalyptic light.

173. Walter Brueggemann, *Theology of the Old Testament: Testimony, Dispute, Advocacy* (Minneapolis: Fortress, 1997), 346. Brueggemann distinguishes Israel's "core testimony" to Yahweh's action in the world—"highly visible, evoking terror in the enemy and praise in the beneficiaries of that 'action'"—from Israel's "countertestimony," which emerges in three facets: *hiddenness, ambiguity* (or *instability*), and *negativity* (318); he associates Wisdom especially with the first. On this point it is fascinating to mediate on Merton's mysterious ink drawing,

While the Song of Songs clearly stands out in this tradition, let us consider Proverbs 8:22-31, the text of central importance to this study. The "theological adventuresomeness" of the passage, Brueggemann suggests, may have "served to create theological room inside the house of 'covenantal nomism,' which at times was surely constrictive": "That is, Proverbs 8 imagines and articulates a way of God relating with the world that is not intrusive and occasional, but that is constant in its nurturing, sustaining propensity. It does indeed do 'God-talk' in a different tone, which witnesses to the mystery that can only be expressed as intuitive, playful, suggestive, doxological language, and which therefore necessarily opens the way for speculation about the precise relationship between the world and God." This sense in Proverbs 8 of the "nurturing, sustaining propensity" of God, of God's "play" and "delight" in creation—such language "dares to expand and intensify the scope and depth of the claim made for Yahweh; even before creation, with this delighting agent, Yahweh assured that the world would be fully permeated with an intentionality for life."[174]

To be fully permeated with an intentionality for life—such a theme certainly suggests the metaphor of God (and Earth) as Mother, as we have already seen: maternity as giving and receiving life from the other, as opening a space in oneself for and delighting in the other. But it also vividly evokes the metaphor of God as Lover or Spouse, as in the dance of sexual love. Indeed, the theme of love as eros brings together the content of theology, anthropology, and cosmology along the dew-draped strands of a single umbilicus (or helix!); whether it does so more "intelligibly," for example, in the conversation with the sciences, than divine love conceived as kenosis (St. Paul), pathos (Heschel), or agape (King) is not at issue here. The point is that neither the Russians nor Merton, who was thoroughly steeped in bridal mysticism, would shy away from daring "to expand and intensify the scope and depth of the claim made for Yahweh" in the Wisdom literature of the Bible: namely, in Merton's words, that we are "saved by love, yes, even by eros."[175]

"Christ Unveils the Meaning of the Old Testament" (see p. 130). In her penetrating study of the image, Margaret Bridget Betz describes it, alongside several of his other drawings, as indicative of "Merton's intuitive grasp of a God more inclusive than the traditional patriarchal God, and, like the God of the Psalms, all-encompassing" ("Merton's Images of Elias, Wisdom, and the Inclusive God," in *The Merton Annual* [2000]: 190–207, at 195). Even more compelling is her suggestion that the drawing, of uncertain date, may have been created as early as 1952.

174. Brueggemann, *Theology of the Old Testament*, 346.

175. CGB, 11. Cf. Bulgakov, on the Song of Songs: "The presence of this book in the canon, so questionable and incomprehensible for people of anti-erotic spirit past and present, is a true miracle revealed by the Holy Spirit; [the Song is] 'the Holy of Holies' of the Bible" (cited in Valliere, MRT, 368). Of course if eros were confined solely to passages pertaining to sex, eroticism would have a deeply ambiguous legacy in the Bible.

While Bulgakov had an essentialist view of women, he was not a misogynist. There is a remarkable account, for example, of his horrified reaction to the dismembered and distorted female bodies of Picasso's paintings at a Moscow exhibition in 1914. He attacked the artist for blasphemy against Mother Earth, the divine Sophia, the human body, and "the eternal feminine in all its gradations"; Picasso's work "reflects the horror of a world without God, its disintegration, decomposition, and inevitable death."[176] Rosenthal continues: "[Bulgakov] did not use the 'eternal feminine' to depersonalize real women, as is sometimes the case, or to deny female sexuality by exalting the Madonna over the Whore. We do know that he had an unusually happy marriage. He had a positive attitude to women and to sex, and supported his views with biblical texts. . . . 'Be fruitful, and multiply, and replenish the earth, and subdue it' (Genesis 1:28)."[177] Against the despairing (but fashionable) objectification of women and the flesh, Bulgakov expanded Soloviev's vision of sacred corporeality into every realm of concrete humanity, suffused with and sanctified by the erotic, perhaps inclusive of the eschaton.[178]

The fact that Bulgakov had a "happy marriage" and a "positive attitude to women and to sex" is not incidental, but it is *theologically* significant to the logic of this study. Whether consciously or not, every theologian operates with a "canon within a canon"; one theologian's "testimony" is another's "countertestimony." For Bulgakov, the eroticism of the Song of Songs and the playfulness of Proverbs were not peripheral to the truth of God, much less the *humanity of God*, in part because such texts resonated (we may presume) with his own experiences of grace as a husband and father in the "general dance" of the marital relationship. So also for Evdokimov, whose life as a married layman surely contributed to his affirmation of sexual union as having an analogue in Sophia, the divine Eros that "brings forth the cosmos from chaos."[179]

This begs the question, of course, about Merton's relationship with M., the woman he loved "in the depths of my heart [who] *is not symbolic*,"[180] and whose love stirred the deepest wellsprings of sacred *memoria* and imagination. "Strange connection in my deepest heart—between M. and the

---

176. Rosenthal, "The Nature and Function of Sophia," 171–72.

177. Ibid., 169.

178. Ibid. Bulgakov's reflections on the sanctification of eros, the erotic dimension of friendship in the church and so on, are not without significant cautionary notes, tensions, and ambiguities, as Valliere notes. He understood that "a good deal of eroticisim deals in sin and death" and that human experience reflects a certain "antinomy between eros and sex" (see Valliere, MRT, 366–71).

179. Evdokimov, *Woman and the Salvation of the World*, 67.

180. LTL, 328.

'Wisdom' figure—and Mary—and the Feminine in the Bible—Eve, etc.—Paradise—Most mysterious, haunting, deep, lovely, moving, transforming!"[181] Of course, as in other areas of his life, the relationship with M. exposed serious blind spots in Merton, moments of recklessness and blatant disregard for the feelings of others—not just M., but friends who watched anxiously (and were sometimes forced to cover for him) as he plunged into love. To the degree Merton failed or simply refused to see things clearly at the time, his later reflections convey no small remorse for the sinful and less flattering aspects of his behavior. But most important, to my mind, far from writing off the relationship as "just an episode," Merton recognized with humility and gratitude that in M. he had "found something, someone, that I had been looking for all my life," that she had "entered deeply into my heart to alter and transform my whole climate of thought and experience."[182] Hardly more really needs to be said than this, save to recognize (and honor) that the relationship belongs to a deeper and more mysterious narrative that transcends what even Merton himself, the consummate wordsmith, could find language to adequately describe.

The discussion of eros in the Bible, finally, raises the inevitable question of Jesus and the "climate" of Christian revelation, namely, whether the eroticism of the Hebrew Scriptures is lost to the New Testament. This is not the place to attempt a study of eros in the Christian Scriptures, but the question is not so difficult to open up briefly if we keep our heads clear of speculation about the sexuality of Jesus and frame it, rather, in terms of the humanity of God that has already been laid out here. Two formulations can serve as our guide: first, eros as "the desire for life that reaches across absences and distances to delight in the whole person"; and second, Williams's observation that the sophiological perspective "dissolves crude oppositions between spirit and body, and allows us to imagine a world that is not only self-aware but *sensually* aware of itself."[183] Along the lines of these two sophiological principles, the presence and scope of eros in the New Testament may be brought vividly to the surface with a series of rhetorical questions.

On the first principle, to what degree do the gospels reflect a God who desires fullness of life for persons not only in their spiritual context but also in their bodily and social reality; a God who crosses great distances and absences to enter into intimate relationship with persons across all social boundaries, seeking out especially those marginalized from the community; a God who delights in the company of all kinds of people, enjoys the fruits

---

181. Ibid., 131.
182. Ibid., 328.
183. Williams, *Sergeii Bulgakov*, 128.

of the earth, and attends to the rhythms and cadences of the natural world? On the second principle, to what degree is Jesus "sensually aware" in his particular encounters with others—with diseased persons, with women, with children? Who does Jesus touch, why, and in what circumstances? When Jesus heals, does he heal the body alone, the spirit alone, or the whole person? Does the faith (i.e., the receptivity) of the person (or community) play a role in his capacity to work wonders? Even more, *by whom* is Jesus himself touched—from birth, in ministry, in death—and what are the social dynamics of the situation? How does Jesus interact with nature? When does the stuff of the earth touch, enter, or surround his body? For most Christians such questions will likely evoke a host of images and stories from the gospels—not to mention a range of memories near and far from the liturgy, in which we have experienced in word, sacrament, and silence the intimate touch and presence of Jesus.[184]

The inner poetry of the New Testament reverberates with what Bulgakov calls "synergy" and Merton calls "the General Dance": that hidden play between the human community and the Spirit of the risen Christ, the wisdom and power of God. And here it seems that whether we formulate our theology in largely poetical terms, with Merton, or in intricate philosophical terms, with Bulgakov, the metaphysical inquiry itself *pulses with eros*, that is, it flows from the desire to reach across distances and absences between ourselves and the hidden God, ourselves and one another, ourselves and peoples and geographies near and far. More than this, it is the *experience of Jesus* beneath the question that propels us across the distances and absences. Here again we come to the heart of Merton's *person*-centered Christology: "We read the Gospels not merely to get a picture or an idea of Christ but to enter in and pass through the words of revelation to establish, by faith, a vital contact with the Christ Who dwells in our souls as God."[185]

The whole climate of the New Testament witnesses to "the flowering of ordinary possibilities" that are "hidden in everyday life." It remains for us to harvest the "fruits of hope that have never been seen before."[186] This is the wonder, and the risk, of God's incarnation in creatures who are free.

---

184. The usual scholastic question, "How conscious was Jesus of his divinity?" implies an immediate *distancing* in Jesus' self-consciousness from other human beings. It asks, in other words, "How conscious was Jesus that he was *not like the rest of us*?" (recall CGB, 141–42). These kinds of "sapiential" questions, by contrast, invite the whole person, through the imagination and senses, into an encounter with Jesus. Not unlike the Spiritual Exercises of St. Ignatius, the sophiological tradition engenders a compelling "countertestimony" to Christology in a strictly rational, discursive, or scholastic mode.

185. NSC, 156.

186. RU, 159–60.

Christology in the Key of Presence

> We want to be present to each other and then trust what happens. . . .
> Presence is what counts. It's important to realize that the Church itself
> is a presence, and so is contemplative life. Community is presence, not
> an institution.[187]

In his mature survey of sophiology, *Sophia: The Wisdom of God* (1937),
Bulgakov insists that "the doctrine of divine Sophia has nothing to do with
putting forward any new dogma, and certainly cannot be described as a new
heresy within Christianity, although such is the attitude adopted by certain
'guardians' of the faith."[188] Rather, "the real point at issue is . . . the problem
of dogmatic *metanoia*, nothing less than a change and a renewal of human
hearts." The sophiological perspective "brings a special interpretation to
bear upon *all* Christian teaching and dogma, beginning with the doctrine
of the Holy Trinity and the Incarnation and ending with questions of practical everyday Christianity in our time."[189] And again: "All the dogmatic and
practical problems of modern Christian dogmatics and ascetics seem to form
a kind of knot, the unraveling of which inevitably leads to sophiology. For
this reason, in the true sense of the word, sophiology is a theology of *crisis*,
not of disintegration, but of salvation."[190]

The central theological problem in this "crisis" for Bulgakov is the "never-
ending struggle" within Christianity itself "between the two extreme positions of dualism and monism," two opposite poles "in the Christian attitude
to life, which are both equally untrue in their one-sidedness. These are,
firstly, world-denying Manicheism, which separates God from the world by
an impassable gulf and thus makes the existence of Divine-humanity out of
the question; and, secondly, an acceptance of the world as it is, combined
with submission to its values, which is termed 'secularization.'"[191] The first
attitude, notes Bulgakov, confronts human beings with an "either/or": *either*
God, *or* the world—thus, in choosing God, "humans are forced to turn away

---

187. Thomas Merton, *The Springs of Contemplation: A Retreat at the Abbey of Gethsemani*,
ed. Jane Marie Richardson (New York: Farrar, Straus and Giroux, 1992), 3.

188. Sergei Bulgakov, *Sophia: The Wisdom of God: An Outline of Sophiology*, 13. Merton
read this work in the original French.

189. Ibid.

190. Ibid., 21. The description of sophiology as a "theology of crisis" is significant not only
because it frames the book that introduced Merton to sophiology but also because it sets "Bulgakov the theologian apart from the Silver Age youth." In short, it represents the (apocalyptic)
Sophia of Bulgakov's mature period: "no longer the half-Romantic *ewig Weibliche*; she had
been replaced by the ecumenical, spiritual Divine Wisdom of the mosque in Constantinople"
(Evtuhov, *The Cross and the Sickle*, 239–40).

191. Bulgakov, *Sophia: The Wisdom of God*, 14–15.

from the world . . . to leave the world to itself and to its own creativity in a state of alienation from God." The second and opposing tendency, "the secularization of life," "submits to the existing order of things," acquiescing to the widespread suspicion (pervasive in Christians themselves) that Christianity "has no answer to the problems of life." In its extreme form of modern atheism, such a worldview "represents a deification of the world and of human beings . . . a special form of paganism. It is not, as it frequently claims to be, the *zero* of religion, but a *minus* of Christianity."[192]

The prescience of this statement illumines one of the great theological concerns unifying the career of Joseph Ratzinger, now Pope Benedict XVI, not only with the Russian theologians but also with Thomas Merton. Merton too lamented the "minus" of radical atheism, not, however, as the result of secularization per se, but rather as the last Promethean gasp of existential despair. Even more, he described it as a poverty (and captivity) of imagination. Over against the despair and creeping nihilism of modern protest atheism and the "death of God" theologies, Merton too grasped the inner thrust of sophiology as a theology of crisis. In *Hagia Sophia* he counters the overwhelming "minus" of an age of radical doubt with the equally radical (but softly spoken) "plus" of biblical *memoria* and imagination. To say it another way, the sophiological tradition responds to the modern gospel of absence with a positive Christology of presence.[193]

The theme of presence has been central throughout this book, most notably in Merton's trenchant response to the anti-metaphysical bent of modern theology and his sacramental approach to language as a vessel of *theoria*, or "real presence" (chap. 3). Over and again we have seen Merton discerning the presence of Christ not only in the vitality of nature but also in the stranger, and especially in history's victims (chaps. 4–5). For Merton, the dead, like Christ, are *still present* to the living through *memoria* and prayer;

192. Ibid., 15.
193. In "The Contemplative and the Atheist" (CWA, 180–94), Merton makes an explicit case for God as "Presence," going so far as to draw analogies between the atheist's denial of God and the contemplative experience of God's "absence" in the dark night of faith; it is also significant that he ties the language of Presence in this late essay explicitly to the Trinity. Gerald O'Collins dedicates the final chapter of his christological survey (see n. 22 above) to an exploration of a "christology of presence," an image of Christ proceeding from the symbol of Lady Wisdom "who is present and active in all creation" (*Christology*, 319). Thomas O'Meara also favors the language of Presence in his important study, "Toward a Subjective Theology of Revelation," *Theological Studies* 36 (1975): 401–27. The scriptural foundations of a Wisdom theology of presence are made explicit in Roland Murphy, *The Tree of Life: An Exploration of Biblical Wisdom Literature* (New York: Doubleday, 1990); idem, "Israel's Wisdom: A Biblical Model of Salvation," *Studia Missionalia* 30 (1981); idem, "Wisdom Literature," in *The New Jerome Biblical Commentary* (Prentice Hall, 1990), 447–52.

they are the "cloud of witnesses," the communion of saints. While the theme of presence saturates Merton's theology of contemplation and nature writings, it also describes well his own crossing over to others in dialogue and interfaith friendship. Indeed, the term "presence" itself evokes both spatial and temporal meaning, suggesting: "*I am with you*, here, now, in the present moment." Nowhere, to my mind, does Merton narrate God's presence in a "sinful but hallowed world" more lyrically than in those passages invoking the Wisdom-child of Proverbs 8, "playing in the world, playing before Him at all times."[194]

We must finally confront, however, the question that confronts any robustly incarnational or sacramental theology of presence: How do we account for the perceived *absence* of God in history, the ambiguity and fallenness of human freedom, the painfully unrealized sophianic aspect of a world stricken by evil and innocent suffering? Here we might be inclined to concur with Bulgakov's own reservations under the dome of Hagia Sophia: Is not the time for such visions of "pan-unity," for "launching new schemes" and speculative "houses of cards" long since past? In the face of escalating inter-religious violence and the seemingly unstoppable desecration of nature, is not the sophiological vision of reality mere "dreaminess"?

The question of sophiology's relevance in an age of crisis hinges on its concern not only with the things of space but also with God's movement in the realm of time, that is, in *history*, the domain of human freedom. "Never before," Bulgakov wrote in 1937, "has the Christian conscience been so pressingly confronted with questions concerning humanity's destiny in history and beyond its limits, humanity's creativity and its responsibility to its own Divine-humanity."[195] The question of history and its limits, of course, is the question of eschatology. When voiced from the vantage point of history's vanquished and suffering peoples—those whose eschatology remains, as it were, radically unrealized—abstract speculation on the end times quickly gives way to the piercing cry of abandonment, and the echo of Psalm 22 from the cross: "*What is God waiting for?*"[196]

Against what he calls the "unresolved contradictions" and "bad dialectic" of modern secularizing thought, Bulgakov argues for (if the phrase is admissible) a *positively* kenotic way of being in time and space, "a true Christian

---

194. NSC, 290; Valliere too links Sophia with presence: "Bulgakov proceeds as a biblical and church theologian, proclaiming the God in whose presence human beings and the cosmos already stand. Sophiology is a means of inscribing this point in categorical terms" (MRT, 304–5).

195. Bulgakov, *Sophia: The Wisdom of God*, 19.

196. Johannes Baptist Metz, *A Passion for God: The Mystical-Political Dimension of Christianity*, trans. J. Matthew Ashley (New York: Paulist, 1998), 58, 71.

ascesis in relation to the world, which consists in a struggle with the world out of love for the world."[197] But this requires an elemental "change in our conception of the world," a "renewal of our faith in the sophianic, or theandric, meaning of the historical process. As the dome of St. Sophia in Constantinople with prophetic symbolism portrays heaven bending down to earth, so the Wisdom of God itself is spread like a canopy over our sinful though still hallowed world."[198] Here is the crucial tension: the world is *both* sinful *and* hallowed. The problem that sophiology confronts is how to account for this "both/and" without taking refuge in abstract, negative (apophatic), or even dialectical theology. As Gerald O'Collins puts it, "The choice cannot be seen as simply that between Christ's presence and his absence."[199] To come again to the cross, the ultimate limit-situation in the life of Jesus, how can we account for the passion narrative in positive theological terms, that is, as somehow integral, not accidental or arbitrary, in the life story of God?

Presence in an Apocalyptic Key: "The Time of the End"

In September of 1959, Merton noted with approval in his journal the following line from Evdokimov's book *Woman and the Salvation of the World*: "To recognize Christ in those who by appearance struggle against Him, when in reality they struggle against ideas and values which are falsely called Christian, is that not an urgent Christian task?"[200] The notation comes from a chapter titled "The Church in the World and the Last Things," a theology of history in which Evdokimov counters the apparent victory of evil in the twentieth century ("the human Anti-Christ") with the "positive goal" of history set down at the Council of Chalcedon, namely, "to actualize humanity in the form of 'the fullness of Christ.'"[201] Citing Jesus' parable of the wheat and tares (Matt 13:24-30), Evdokimov notes "how appearances can be confused with the hidden truth" of Christ's presence in the world. In fact through the eyes of faith, one can discern "a double process in history . . . a more and more intense dehumanization, on the one hand; and, on the other, the preaching of the Gospel to the entire world, and new forms of holiness."[202]

---

197. Bulgakov, *Sophia: The Wisdom of God*, 20.

198. Ibid., 21.

199. O'Collins, *Christology*, 322.

200. Cited in SFS, 330; see Evdokimov, *Woman and the Salvation of the World*, 129.

201. Evdokimov, *Woman and the Salvation of the World*, 120.

202. Ibid., 121. Reinhold Niebuhr, also writing in 1949, cites the same parable to describe a kind of "double-process" in history: "The perils of freedom rise with its promises, and the perils and promises are inextricably interwoven. . . . Christian faith expects some of the most explicit forms of evil at the end of history" (*Faith and History* [New York: Scribner's, 1949], 233).

Evdokimov wades into the problem of evil through a poetical interplay of biblical and Jungian archetypes, weaving a narrative of divine tragedy (i.e., a positive theology) centered on the figures of Job and divine Sophia: "The key to the story of Job lies in the remembrance of Sophia."[203] As in Proverbs 8, Sophia cries out at the crossroads, but we seal our ears. Finding few among "the children of men" who will listen, she turns directly to Yahweh. "The image of God in man calls to the image of man in God; it demands the Incarnation. This is the demand of the human heart, and it is Sophia who transposes this demand within God; she wrestles against Yahweh for God, and wins the victory, the only valid answer for Job."[204] The "demand" of which Evdokimov speaks here is precisely the theodicy question, reverberating directly (and eternally, as it were) into the heart of God. God's "answer" to Job, and Sophia's "victory," is God's unreserved self-emptying into, and solidarity with, creation.

Thus "'the Lamb slain since the beginning of the world' is the human image of the eternal divine birth in love. God Himself lies on Job's pallet to bring Job His answer." Christ is the Eros of God crucified. Mary is "the Gate of Paradise"; her *Fiat* opens the way to God's *kenosis* on earth, and to the human form in heaven.[205] Despite much evidence to the contrary, the love of God enters (and hides) in the world "behind a veil of humility," in and through the seeds of life itself, in sexual loving, the beauty of nature, and above all, in simple acts of solidarity, sacrifice, and holiness.

In October of 1959, Merton cites Evdokimov again, describing his theology as "arresting," noting these lines in particular: "Monasticism, apocalypse already realized, shows forth the Christian conscience burning with impatience. . . . Prayer praises God but it is also an apocalyptic manifestation. It hastens events, confronts that which is essential, embraces all times. . . . Its entire destiny is none other than to bear witness to the Last Things."[206] Two years later, in the pivotal spring of 1961, Merton will interject in his lecture notes on mystical theology a litany of similarly arresting insights from Georges Florovsky: "Already we have reached a point where theological silence . . . [is] equal to temptation, to flight before the enemy. . . . *It is precisely because we are thrown into the apocalyptic battle that we are called*

---

203. Evdokimov, *Woman and the Salvation of the World*, 207.
204. Ibid., 204.
205. Ibid., 207. "The Apocalyptic 'woman robed with the sun' 'brought forth a male child' (Rev. 12:5). Here we must try to decipher the play of archetypes. We are in the eschatological events" (ibid., 209). Recall *Hagia Sophia*: "Through her wise answer . . . God enters without publicity into the city of rapacious men" (ESF, 68).
206. Cited in SFS, 334; see Evdokimov, *Woman and the Salvation of the World*, 245.

*upon to do the job of theologians. . . . *Theology is called not only to judge but to heal.*["207]

The Time of No Room

Evdokimov's theology of history clearly struck a deep chord in Merton, an influence that comes to bear in essays throughout the 1960s, as the tenor of his writing more and more reflects a conscience "burning with impatience." Indeed, many of Merton's most penetrating social essays reflect "an apocalyptic feeling for time," the sense that God's presence is constantly "breaking out in unexpected places and, like the resurrection, bringing life from death."[208] In the pattern of William Blake and Flannery O'Connor, Merton employs striking ironic contrasts to unmask or *subvert from within* the "pseudo-apocalyptic" noise of the times, the parade of idols and "pseudo-events" that threatens in fact "to carry out point by point the harlotries of the Apocalypse."[209] Above all, Merton sets the poverty and humility of Christ, from nativity to the cross, against the Promethean climate of the times. In one of his most haunting late essays, "The Time of the End is the Time of No Room,"[210] Merton counterposes "The Great Joy" of the incarnation with a world that cannot perceive it, a world that has "no room" left for Joy, precisely because it has *no room left for humanity*:

> Into this world, this demented inn, in which there is absolutely no room for Him at all, Christ has come uninvited. But because He cannot be at home in it, because He is out of place in it, and yet He must be in it, His place is with those others for whom there is no room. His place is with those who do not belong, who are rejected by power because they are regarded as weak, those who are discredited, who are denied the

207. ICM, 37. David Tracy describes apocalyptic as a "*corrective* genre signalized by principles of intensification and negations"; it is evoked "in times of crisis" as a challenge "of the sheer intensity of the 'pain of the negative' in the cross needed as an intrinsic moment in any adequate theology of incarnation" (David Tracy, *The Analogical Imagination: Christian Theology and the Culture of Pluralism* [New York: Crossroad, 1981], 265–66).

208. J. Matthew Ashley, "Apocalypticism in Political and Liberation Theology: Toward an Historical *Docta Ignorantia*," *Horizons* 27, no. 1 (2000): 22–43, at 33; cf. Lieven Boeve, "God Interrupts History: Apocalypticism as an Indispensable Theological Conceptual Strategy," *Louvain Studies* 26 (2001): 195–216.

209. FV, 153. Texts such as "Rain and the Rhinoceros," "Events and Pseudo-Events: Letter to a Southern Churchman," "Day of a Stranger," "Original Child Bomb," and much of the poetry in *Emblems of a Season of Fury* exemplify what I am calling, following James Alison, Merton's ironic "subversion" of "pseudo-apocalyptic" events "from within." See James Alison, *On Being Liked* (New York: Crossroad, 2003), 12–13.

210. RU, 65–75.

status of persons, tortured, exterminated. With those for whom there is no room, Christ is present in this world. . . .

For those who are stubborn enough, devoted enough to power, there remains this last apocalyptic myth of machinery propagating its own kind in the eschatological wilderness of space—while on earth the bombs make room!

But the others: they remain imprisoned in other hopes, and in more pedestrian despairs, despairs and hopes which are held down to earth, down to street level, and to the pavement only: desire to be at least half-human, to taste a little human joy, to do a fairly decent job of productive work, to come home to the family . . . desires for which there is no room. It is in these that He hides himself, for whom there is no room.[211]

Merton gives us nothing here if not a positive (cataphatic) theology of divine presence, though, to be sure, a positively disarming one. Unmasking appearances, Merton draws our attention to Christ's presence in all those who simply yearn for life in its barest ("held down to earth") dimensions, all those who have been structured out of the divine-human hierarchy, the privileged festival of earthly and heavenly communion. Surely the identification Merton suggests here *is no mistake*, nor merely a rhetorical construct—unless of course Jesus himself was mistaken, or merely playing with words, in his disarming "Judgment of the Nations" (Matt 25:31-46), or the command to "Love your enemies" (Matt 5:43-48). Through an ironic intensification of the nativity, ever shadowed in his writings by the looming cross, Merton reclaims the sacramental dignity of not only history's most forgotten ones but also the vilified *enemy* (the "discredited," the "tortured," the "exterminated"), even those persons and nations whose actions appear to merit the full onslaught of our "justice."[212]

Throughout the 1960s Merton rebelled against the "cold saints of the new age," whose conception of "justice" left no room for the "higher unity" of mercy, reconciliation, and authentic peace. As he wrote in the Cold War essay, "Atlas and the Fatman," in the nuclear age, the reign of numbers, they "count with their machine the bitter, methodical sacrifices they are making in the Fatman's memory, and stand in line before his tomb. Sacrifice is counted in

211. Ibid., 73; cf. Evdokimov: "Our overcrowded cities have become frightening deserts of loneliness where Christ and Satan continue their devastating dialogue; more than ever, it is here that the preaching of St. John must continue 'with its power' (Lk. 1:17)" (*Woman and the Salvation of the World*, 245).

212. For an expanded discussion of irony and apocalypticism in Merton's late writings, see Christopher Pramuk, "Apocalypticism in a Catholic Key: Lessons from Thomas Merton," [forthcoming, *Horizons* (Fall, 2009)]; on the "irony of Christ," see William Lynch, *Images of Faith: An Exploration of the Ironic Imagination* (Notre Dame, IN: University of Notre Dame Press, 1973).

drops of blood, [and] minutes are counted like Aztecs walking a man to his death with his heart out on top of a bad pyramid: such is order and justice. Such is the beauty of system."[213] Here, a thousand present-day images parade darkly through the mind: human "pyramids" and cages at Abu Ghraib and Guantanamo Bay, the bullet-riddled tenements of the South Bronx, deteriorating public schools and health care facilities, the inhumanity of the federal prison system, untold miles of fence raised at the Mexican border. Yet we remain, as Merton implies, tragically asleep, even while images of horror multiply across our TV screens, and catastrophes, as Metz observes, "are reported on the radio in between pieces of music."[214] Such is the beauty of order and justice, the beauty of anonymity, in the reign of numbers.

Yet there is, Merton insists, "another kind of justice than the justice of number. . . . There is another kind of mercy than the mercy of Law which knows no absolution." And here his voice gives over to the clear music of Wisdom-Sophia, sounding not a little like Jesus on the plains, urging us to open our eyes and *see* the glory of God in the beauty of the world, and in one another:

> There is a justice of newborn worlds which cannot be counted. There is a mercy of individual things that spring into being without reason. They are just without reason, and their mercy is without explanation. . . . Every plant that stands in the light of the sun is a saint and an outlaw. Every tree that brings forth blossoms without the command of man is powerful in the sight of God. Every star that man has not counted is a world of sanity and perfection. Every blade of grass is an angel singing in a shower of glory. . . . You fool, it is life that makes you dance: have you forgotten? Come out of the smoke, the world is tossing in its sleep, the sun is up, the land is bursting in the silence of dawn.[215]

The point to emphasize here is that Merton's heightened temporal concern is not for himself or his "own kind" but for the sufferings of others, all those whose hope remains radically unrealized, "held down to street level."[216] Anticipating themes from liberation and political theologies, Mer-

213. RU, 105.

214. Metz, *Faith in History and Society*, 157; cf. BT, 51–64, where Merton implicitly indicts himself as an "innocent bystander," one of the intellectual class who are "paid to keep quiet" and "nourished in order that we may continue to sleep" (60).

215. RU, 106–7. The passage recalls Herakleitos: "The sun is new every day. You cannot step twice into the same stream; for fresh waters are ever flowing upon you."

216. Ibid., 73. Biblical *memoria*, writes Metz, "always takes into account the suffering of others, the suffering of strangers." Respecting and articulating the suffering of others "is the presupposition of all claims to truth. Even those made by theology" (*A Passion for God*, 134).

ton's apocalypticism is driven by an urgent sense of solidarity, intensifying our awareness of the critical present moment for those whose need is most desperate, who have no name, and thus no presence whatsoever on the world stage—"empty forms, human specters, swirling aimlessly through their cities, *all wishing they had never been born*."[217] Even the earth, "suffering and awaiting its liberation,"[218] now merits an urgent place in Christian eschatology. The irony of God's incarnation in Christ, and Christ crucified, teaches us that these striking juxtapositions joining God with the suffering world, even to the point of identity, are no mistake.

Mercy: The Cross as *Axis Mundi*

Love cannot come of emptiness. It is full of reality.[219]

Here, finally, we must acknowledge that it is not the memory of Sophia so much as the memory of Jesus—who has a concrete history, who *can be killed*—that ultimately centers Merton's experience of the "mystery of personality in God."[220] In short, Merton holds close to the psalms, John's gospel, and St. Paul in anchoring his metaphysics of presence to the memory of a God who enters a history stricken by guilt and suffering through the "Word of the Cross," the paradise tree, the *axis mundi*.[221] At the foot of the cross, "the 'absence' of the transcendent God is also, paradoxically, his presence as immanent."[222] In other words, the passion of Jesus enfleshes a mystery that can be approached only in the realm of paradox, as a reality that is, as Merton puts it, "*negatively* positive." Thus the Christian (and Christian theologian) must approach the cross "humbly and resolutely, following the call of God and obedient to the divine Spirit, like Moses approaching the burning bush, removing the 'shoes' of opinion and rationalization."[223] Neither theories nor platitudes can really account for the crucifixion in positive terms.

Yet if we approach the cross in silence and humility, and keep in view the life of Jesus that led to it, then God may become known to us not only as Absolute "Unknown," enshrouded in darkness and distance, but even more,

---

217. RU, 71.
218. Cited in Evtuhov, *The Cross and the Sickle*, 138.
219. ESF, 73.
220. DWL, 259; see also NSC, 294.
221. "Freedom is found under the dark tree that springs up in the center of night and of silence, the paradise tree, the *axis mundi*, which is also the Cross" (Thomas Merton, *Day of a Stranger* [Salt Lake City: Gibbs M. Smith, 1981], 19; from his first draft of the essay).
222. CWA, 186.
223. Ibid., 187; cf. ZBA, 51, on suffering as "contradiction and confusion"; and CWA, 174–76, on the apophatic dimension of the cross.

perhaps, as suffering Love and Presence, as unfathomable solidarity, Emmanuel, God with us. To the sacramental imagination, the cross reveals "in material and visible form" the *content* of divine presence as Being-for-others, as radical judgment, and finally, as mercy. For those who hear their music, the passion narratives are not just human theology but divine anthropology, paradoxically unveiling the life story of God as a Life and a Love that is unconditionally given, despite our tragic inclination, as St. Augustine put it, to "love the Gift more than we love the Giver." Neither the fury of religious fundamentalisms nor the "logic" of quid pro quo and retributive violence can obscure that which the Gospel reveals to be the divine-human heart of reality: "*Mercy within mercy within mercy.*"[224]

For those whose lives are held *without mercy* "down to street level" by systemic injustice and poverty, the paschal mystery potentially breaks through searing hopelessness with a word of divine solidarity ("I am with you, here, now") and promise ("*life*, not death, is my plan for you"). But what about those whose ears are closed to the cry of the poor, whose power turns on their subjugation? The cross confronts these, first of all, as a word of judgment and warning: "*You killed him*" (see Acts 5:30). Under the shadow of the cross, Merton says, whether by what we have done or what we have failed to do, "we find ourselves eviscerated by our own ingratitude."[225] Yet even here the cross is potentially the "Tree of Life," the "center of the new creation,"[226] because it is here that the false self, the self that is "captured by others," can finally be renounced.

Herein lay the fertile paradox of the cross, the potentially *creative* role of contrition, self-sacrifice, and asceticism in which "God himself, the creator, works in and through us." Though we know ourselves to be deeply implicated in the sins of the world, we no longer have to be afraid, since the judgment hanging over our lives is prompted by love and crowned by mercy:

> To "receive" the word of the Cross means much more than simple assent to the dogmatic proposition that Christ died for our sins. It means to be "nailed to the Cross with Christ," so that the ego-self is no longer the principle of our deepest actions, which now proceed from Christ living in us. "I live, now not I, but Christ lives in me." . . . To receive the word of the Cross means the acceptance of a complete self-emptying, a *Kenosis*, in union with the self-emptying of Christ "obedient unto death" (Phil. 2:5-11).[227]

224. SJ, 362.
225. BW, 120.
226. LE, 370.
227. ZBA, 55–56; cf. Niebuhr, *Faith and History*, 140–44.

Here Merton intimates that what distinguishes the *Christian* way of wisdom from all others is that Christianity stakes its hopes on a scandalously *kenotic* conception of power and presence, rooted in the historical memory of *God's own* "passing over" in Jesus, an event "inscaped with paradox and contradiction, yet centered, in its very heart, on divine mercy."[228] "Far from killing the man who seeks the divine fire, the Living God will Himself pass through death in order that man may have what is destined for him."[229] Christ crucified is God's consummate irony, perceived by few.

Merton acknowledges that this reading of the human vocation under the light (light-in-darkness) of Christ crucified and risen distinguishes Christian experience from Zen and every other religion with which he was engaged in dialogue. Neither does the "reconciliation" of judgment and mercy in the cross have anything to do with the "fuzzy romanticism" of a Hegelian dialectic. It is "an epiphany of God . . . *communicating and sharing himself,*" the restoration of a "higher unity" in "mercy, pity, peace," the work of "the epiphany of God in Man."[230] For Bulgakov too the crucifixion reveals (and hides) both the kenosis of the Trinity and the human victory (*podvig*) of Jesus in suffering love. Jesus is not a passive victim. His whole ministry and sacrifice is an active "cooperation" with God, "the synergism of God and the human being."[231] Just as God's kenosis in the ongoing act of creation is self-emptying *and* life-giving, so is Jesus actively nonviolent to the end, reconciling persons with God and the community, calling the unjust to repentance, and asking forgiveness for those who killed him (Luke 23:34). Such a love, as Merton notes, "cannot come of emptiness. It is full of reality."

Following Jesus himself, of course, St. Paul is the first of Christian poets to articulate a positive (and Wisdom-infused) theology of the cross, a metaphysics of mercy in which life springs forth paradoxically from the way of love and sacrifice. But we must never forget that Paul's sublime hymns to the love of God poured out in Jesus were also hymns to the human community that bears Jesus' name (Phil 2:1-11). The "same mind," the "same love," the same "compassion and mercy," the same "reconciliation" of "mind" and "fleshly body" that we have come to know in Jesus, and which reveal the very glory

228. Thomas Merton, "First and Last Thoughts: An Author's Preface," in *A Thomas Merton Reader*, 17. Nowhere are these themes in Merton treated more clearly and beautifully than in Anne Carr's *A Search for Wisdom and Spirit: Thomas Merton's Theology of the Self* (Notre Dame, IN: University of Notre Dame Press, 1988), especially chaps. 4 and 5.

229. BT, 22.

230. LE, 10, 7; cf. LE, 514, where Merton comments on "ransom" soteriologies of the cross: "Nowhere in the four Gospels do you find anything about God sitting up in heaven and waiting for [a] blood debt to be paid off."

231. Valliere, MRT, 341.

of God, are also fully given to us—to *all* human beings, we must not shrink from believing—in his name: Sophia. For "She is the mercy of God in us. She is the tenderness with which the infinitely mysterious power of pardon turns the darkness of our sins into the light of grace."[232]

The alternative, of course, is no mystery at all, as Merton makes clear: "[The] great men of the earth would not talk of peace so much if they did not secretly believe it possible, with *one more war*, to annihilate their enemies forever. Always, 'after just one more war' it will dawn, the new era of love: but first everybody who is hated must be eliminated. For hate, you see, is the mother of their kind of love."[233]

In sum, from the perspective of an authentically Catholic, sacramental, and (we may now add) sophiological eschatology, history remains radically *open*, hinging on the critical present moment of human freedom and its receptivity (or lack thereof) to the horizon of grace. Far from every nationalist, tribal, or otherwise dialectical conception of God's relationship to the world, the Catholic analogical imagination insists that the offer of grace and spiritual freedom is always and everywhere present, even, we must dare to believe, in the most desolate of places, where all light, love, and hope—where all *humanity*—appears to be utterly extinguished. To say it more precisely, and with deepest respect for the theodicy question, it is at the point where the analogical imagination ruptures, as in Auschwitz, or present-day Darfur—where all analogy between God and the world is rendered horrific and absurd—that the irony of Christ and Christ crucified *intervenes from within*, as it were, to mediate and intensify (I do not say "answer") faith's most difficult question: whether we have the eyes to see, the faith to shoulder, the contradictions of hope in a sinful, though still hallowed, world.[234]

Concluding Remarks

The problem confronting theology today is not merely an epistemological crisis of images, symbols, or grand narratives that no longer find a foothold in

232. ESF, 67.

233. From "A Letter to Pablo Antonio Cuadra Concerning Giants," ESF, 72.

234. The theodicy question clearly represents the greatest challenge to the intelligibility of a thoroughgoing incarnational (Wisdom) theology, and its correlative in a robust doctrine of divinization or theosis. Hence the insistence of political and liberation theologies on the corrective role of the *memoria passionis*, "the sheer intensity of the 'pain of the negative' . . . needed as an intrinsic moment in any adequate theology of incarnation" (Tracy, n. 207 above). Or, as Ashley writes, citing Bonaventure and summing up the inner "logic" of a spirituality of liberation: "There is no other path but through the burning love of the Crucified," where reason must finally be surrendered "by an act of reason" itself (Ashley, "Apocalypticism in Political and Liberation Theology," 41); cf. Merton, BW, 117–24.

the post-Christian imagination. The problem is also ontological, addressing the reigning intellectual conviction that "there is, not only no God, but no metaphysical order of any kind."[235] Beginning with Soloviev's free theosophy, Russian sophiology is an attempt to bring together truths of nature, reason, and revelation into a unified but living and multiform picture. "Living," of course, means ever changing—or to recall Newman's illative sense, *growing into the truth about the mystery of God*—and this is undoubtedly one aspect of sophiology that has always made the "guardians of the faith" nervous. The sophiological tradition views revelation not as the disclosure of once-for-all truth so much as the invitation to participate in the ongoing *event* of drawing the created order into communion with the Father, Son, and Holy Spirit. Wisdom is not simply knowledge but participation, the graced effort to make every dimension of human and natural life transparent to God's glory.

Thus the primary concern of sophiology, as Valliere has shown, is pragmatic and *soteriological*, namely, the salvation of human beings in history, the eternal tangent or sophianic aspect latent in every sphere of life and culture. In this respect, it can be said to more or less anticipate the shift in Western transcendental theologies (Blondel, Lonergan, Rahner, *Gaudium et spes*, Teilhard de Chardin) from a classicist worldview to a more historical but still mystically infused consciousness, where the human person takes center stage as an embodied historical, cultural, economic, political, and sexual being.[236] Above all, sophiology begins and ends in the experience of love, of *being loved* gratuitously by God; herein lay the *metaxu* (the "inbetween") of the sophiological worldview, which takes its cues from the erotic countertestimony of the whole Bible.

Any satisfactory assessment of Russian sophiology must take seriously its emergence not in some speculative, ivory-tower vacuum but in and from a context of "inescapable" war, ideological polarization, and mass dislocation and exile. It is not incidental that "Bulgakov discovered Soloviev's concept of 'positive all-unity' at the very time that Russia lost its *axis mundi* and was coming apart,"[237] or that Merton's *Hagia Sophia* was penned during a "season of fury" in the United States marked by race riots, the Vietnam War, and nuclear standoff with Russia. It is also important to note the striking degree to which Bulgakov's trinitarian metaphysics takes its cues from the "all-embracing humanity of the gospel": "uninterrupted humanity in the

---

235. Michael Perry, "The Morality of Human Rights: A Problem for Nonbelievers?" *Commonweal* 133, no. 13 (2006): 16–18, at 17.

236. Myroslaw Tataryn draws strong parallels between Bulgakov and twentieth-century Roman Catholic theology in his article, "History Matters: Bulgakov's Sophianic Key" (n. 86 above).

237. Rosenthal, "The Nature and Function of Sophia," 172.

God-human is the basic fact and basic premise of the gospel narrative."[238] Central to this basic premise is the "synergy" or "two-way energeticism" that comes into play everywhere in the gospels, and not only in Jesus. Clearly, the image of a God who does not merely tolerate but delights in humanity and in the dance of human freedom holds far-reaching implications for spirituality in every dimension.

One must also wonder at sophiology's remarkable catholicity, its celebration of the *multiformis sapientia* that comes to birth in the world not only through the creativity of the scientist and the artist but also in the world's diverse religions and cultures, as in the piety of Muslims at prayer. Soloviev foreshadowed the conciliar debates of Vatican II by eight decades when he insisted that "the so-called Jewish question is 'a question not about the Jews but about the Christian world.'"[239] Christians forget that "the apostles and early leaders of the church were Jews. Most of all, they forget Jesus Christ, the humanity of God in person, 'was body and soul a purest Jew.'"[240] The degree to which Bulgakov translates this historical and theological fact into dogmatic theology is striking. The human "victory" (*podvig*) of Jesus, no less than that of Mary and the apostolic church, must be seen in continuity with their "forefathers and fathers in faith as well."[241] Merton was not far behind, once describing in a letter to Abraham Joshua Heschel during the height of the council debates his "latent ambitions to be a true Jew under my Catholic skin."[242]

If anything stands out in this chapter, perhaps it is the striking similarities between the life and thought of Sergius Bulgakov and Thomas Merton. In the midst of great social and ecclesial upheavals, both men sought "'a middle way' between the extremes of anti-Christian secularism and Christian hatred of the secular world"[243]; for both thinkers, the struggle of the church had to proceed "along two fronts: unmasking the anti-Christianity of those [believers] who have Christ's name on their lips but crucify Him by the way they live, and of those [secularists] who serve him in deed but disclaim all thought of Him."[244] Perhaps Bulgakov sums up their commonalities best when

238. Cited in Valliere, MRT, 309, 338.

239. Valliere, MRT, 193, citing Soloviev's "The Jews and the Christian Question."

240. Ibid., 195, citing Soloviev's "The Jews and the Christian Question."

241. Ibid., 323. In 1941 and 1942 Bulgakov published two important essays on the persecution of the Jews in which he condemns racism as anti-Christian "and shifts the focus of anti-racist apologetics from affirming the humanity of the Jews—as if that were open to question!—to affirming the Jewishness of humanity, a counter-intuitive dogmatic truth that overturns racism at an ontological level" (Valliere, MRT, 286–87).

242. HGL, 434.

243. Valliere, MRT, 239.

244. Cited in ibid.

he stated: "To the end of my days I wish to remain faithful to the principles of freedom and the protection of human dignity, intransigent toward every sort of 'totalitarianism.'"[245] The totalitarianism against which both he and Merton rebelled included that which shadows historical Christianity, that is, the "servility and enslavement"[246] that too often cripples religious devotion and poses a very real threat to those *outside the church.* The point here is that deeds follow thought. What kind of theology would not just permit but engender hatred of those different from ourselves?

For if indeed "the horsemen of the Apocalypse cover the entire world," it must not be forgotten that they have often swept into history bearing the cross of Christ as their standard. "Not only are we idolaters," as Merton wrote in 1966, "but we are likely to carry out point by point the harlotries of the Apocalypse. And if we do, we will do so innocently, decently, with clean hands, for the blood of the victims is always shed somewhere else!"[247] Merton's acerbic reference to the mythos of American innocence and decency highlights the dangers of a communal and liturgical imagination gone terribly bad. Nationalism, war, and cultural hubris are always justified through appeals to religious imagery and great humane ideals. "We have killed the Innocents . . . and Christ flees from us into Egypt. Have we ever yet become Christians?"[248]

It is this darker legacy of a Christianity bound up with political power and majority cultural status, a legacy far indeed from the climate of mercy surrounding Jesus of Nazareth, that so troubled June Yungblut when Merton described his Christ as "the Christ of the Byzantine icons," prompting Merton to quickly clarify that he did *not* mean "Christ as ruler of a history in which the Basileus has a central and decisive 'Christian' role."[249] So also his letter to Suzuki, in which he complains of a Christian world "enslaved by images and ideas of Christ that are creations and projections of men and stand in the way of God's freedom."[250] What Merton found in Russian literature and theology was something rather strikingly to the contrary: God, in Christ, hidden "behind a veil of humility," who offers no escape from the responsibilities of stewardship in history, or still less a zone of mystical communion "beyond good and evil." The Russian diaspora had come to understand,

245. Cited in ibid., 243.

246. The phrase the elder Bulgakov uses to describe Russian life in general, "and church life in particular," during the Silver Age of his youth. "In this respect I wish to remain in the ranks of Russian 'progressive' society (I do not even want to disclaim this word)" (cited in ibid., 244).

247. FV, 153.

248. SFS, 197.

249. HGL, 637, and the follow-up letter, 642–43.

250. Ibid., 564.

body and soul, the terrible whisper of Anti-Christ, the constant danger of elevating systems and ideals—even the ideal of "Christ" and "his Bride," the church—over persons.

What could be gained, after all, by restoring a cross to Hagia Sophia? Bulgakov saw that the soul of Christianity was at stake; much more would be lost by filling the mosque with the "bloody boots" of the Russian army. St. Sophia had become for him a prophetic symbol of "universal humanity"[251]: "[The] self is gone . . . I am in the world and the world is in me. And this sense of the weight on one's heart melting away, of *liberation* from the pull of gravity . . . is the bliss of some final knowledge of the all in all . . . of infinite fullness in multiplicity, and of the world in unity."[252] Like Merton in Asia, Bulgakov too had seen "the other side of the mountain—the side that has never been photographed and turned into postcards," the "only side worth seeing."[253] Perhaps the true Apocalypse, as Northrop Frye writes, "is the way the world looks after the ego has disappeared."[254]

The journal of March 25, 1960, serves once more to underscore the influence of the Russian theologians on Merton's far-reaching embrace of the mosaic humanity of God: "In emptying Himself to come into the world, God has not simply kept in reserve, in a safe place, His reality and manifested a kind of shadow or symbol of Himself. . . . God has acted and given Himself totally, without division, in the Incarnation. He has become not only one of us but even our very selves."[255] Beautiful words, to be sure, but the question is, *can we believe it*? And how do we come not only to believe, but above all, *to live* such an impenetrable mystery?

One by one we are called, through the medium of the tradition's positive forms—Scripture, liturgy, iconography, sacred music, poetry, theology—to "come out of the confused primordial dark night into consciousness," to express "the clear silence of Sophia" in our hearts, to "become eternal."[256] In such moments the falcon once again hears the falconer, and the center holds, in the silent tremor of faith's consent.

This is the art of apocalyptic times. We remember what is to come.

---

251. Cited in Valliere, MRT, 283.
252. Cited in Louth, "Wisdom and the Russians," 178.
253. AJ, 153.
254. Northrop Frye, *The Great Code*, cited in Tina Pippen, "Wisdom and Apocalyptic in the Apocalypse of John: Desiring Sophia" (see *In Search of Wisdom*, 285–95, at 285). Frye, like Merton, was a close reader of William Blake.
255. SFS, 381.
256. *Hagia Sophia*, ESF, 64.

Drawing by Thomas Merton. Used with permission of the Merton Legacy Trust and the Thomas Merton Center, Bellarmine University.

Conclusion:
Theology and the General Dance

[And to them] I will give, in my house and within my walls,
a monument and a name better than sons and daughters,
an everlasting name that shall not be cut off. (Isa 56:5)

No road, no path, / No land marks / Show the way there. / You must go
by the stars.[1]

As early as 1953, Thomas Merton diagnosed the spiritual void or crisis of meaning in Western society as a crisis of imagination. "[The] trend
of modern thought away from symbolism has frustrated the basic human
need for symbol and metaphor to the point of perversion: we have become
instinctively suspicious of that for which we are starved. A world without
imagination, which is no longer able to cope with the immaterial and which
is incapable of the simplest efforts to link two terms of an analogy, condemns
all symbolism as mystification."[2] It would be easy enough to dismiss these
lines as the quaint ravings of a pious Catholic monk hidden away in the
hills of Kentucky, for whom the church's mystical tradition somehow held
the keys to reality, and the Bible, our "bread in the wilderness." Yet a decade
later Merton was sounding the same theme and pressing it to the limit. The
spiritual crisis of humanity in our age is inextricably linked to a widespread
poverty, even more, a *captivity*, of imagination: "The 'desecration' of man
begins when symbols are emptied of meaning and are allowed to survive
precisely insofar as they are patronizingly admitted to be misleading but still
'necessary for the ignorant.' The symbol is then regarded only as a politically
or religiously 'useful lie,' insofar as it seems to communicate information on
a childish level, information which is inadequate but acceptable to those to
whom 'objective truth' is not yet clear."[3]

1. ESF, 17.
2. BW, 30.
3. LL, 68–69.

In two important late essays, Merton links "the parade of idols" in American life and public discourse—"political and scientific idols, idols of the nation, the party, the race," "the idol of national military strength"—directly to the degradation and commodification of symbolism, not least religious symbolism, utilized as the currency of persuasion in the political theater of "wordplay."[4] It is significant that Merton reserves his harshest criticism in these essays for Western Christians, Catholics, and their pastoral leaders whose "mental snake-handling"[5] permitted them to justify everything from the Vietnam War to nuclear proliferation, race discrimination, and even race riots on the basis of good "Christian principles." Everywhere, he observes, "from extreme right to extreme left," we find people who by means of slogans, images, and symbols, move "step by step, taking the nation with them, into realms of commitment and of absurdity" where "*one is quarantined from the ordinary world of right and wrong.*" Through this "liturgy of pseudo-events," society enters "into the realm of the gods," a realm "beyond good and evil," where "the whole meaning of truth and falsity" takes on an entirely new logic: "one must follow on from one irrationality to the next in a demonic consistency dictated by machines."[6]

When the religious symbol is called upon in such an atmosphere (as it always is) to function as a mere sign, that is, to communicate "information," in the same manner that scientific discourse seeks to communicate information—these are simply the "facts"—the symbol "is then reduced to the *trademark* or the *political badge*, a mere sign of identification."[7] The problem with this, says Merton, is that identification is not *identity*. In a sharply polarized and media-saturated society, where it matters very much "whom you are with, whom you are against . . . what button you wear, whom you vote for,"[8] the sacred identity of the person is buried beneath a dangerously impenetrable heap of social judgments, wounded histories, and a priori expectations, all aimed at identification and separation: tell me, are you with *us*, or are you with *them*? This toxic kind of "rubber stamp identification," Merton argues, "is actually a diminution or loss of identity, a submersion of identity," in which "the mass man loses his individual self in the false, indeed the demonic void, the general pseudoself of the Mass Society. The symbols of the Mass Society are crude and barbaric rallying points for emotion, fanaticism, and exalted

4. See "Symbolism: Communication or Communion?" (1966), LL, 54–79, at 76–77; also "Events and Pseudo-Events: Letter to a Southern Churchman" (1966), FV, 145–64.

5. FV, 156.

6. Ibid., 160.

7. LL, 58.

8. ZBA, 29.

forms of hatred masking as moral indignation. The symbols of Mass Society are ciphers on the face of a moral and spiritual void."[9]

The dignity and sanctity of the person is eroded further by the ubiquitous presence of technology and communications media in our everyday lives. Where religion, art, literature, and poetry have, at their sapiential best, used the power of creative symbols to bring together humanity, divine mystery, and the natural world "in a living and sacred synthesis," technological rationality tends to enclose the individual in an "artificial synthesis," which "is not a knowledge of reality but a knowledge of knowledge. That is to say—man is no longer 'in contact with nature' but is only well situated in the context of his own experiments," cut off from any reality "except that of his own processes . . . his own inner chaos—and that of the extraordinary new world of his machines."[10]

Merton here cites the arresting observation of physicist Werner Heisenberg that the human community now finds itself "in the position of a captain whose ship has been so securely built of iron and steel that his compass no longer points to the north but only towards the ship's mass of iron."[11] The moral and spiritual peril of the "ship's captain" can be allayed, says Heisenberg, only "if he recognizes what has gone wrong and tries to navigate by some other means—for instance, by the stars."[12] To "navigate by the stars," concludes Merton, is to go beyond the limitation of a scientific worldview and recover our sense of symbol. "Obviously," he adds, "the direction that symbolism must take is that of expressing union, understanding, and love among men—what Paul Tillich has called a 'communal eros.'"[13]

Clearly, by the late 1960s Merton was about as far from a naive or sentimental conception of love or eros as a Christian intellectual could reasonably be. "[The] crude symbolism of violence has gained its power precisely from the fact that the symbolism of love has been so terribly debased, cheapened, and dehumanized."[14] And yet we should not underestimate the hold that the Bible had on Merton's imagination or the hope that he invested in biblical revelation to the end of his life. The power and pregnancy of biblical symbols lay precisely in their capacity to recover human identity, to "[open] the believer's inner eye, the eye of the heart, to the realization that he must come to be centered in God because that, in fact, is where his center is. . . . But the symbol also speaks to many believers in one: it awakens them to their

9. LL, 58.
10. Ibid., 60.
11. Cited in ibid.
12. LL, 61.
13. Ibid., 64.
14. Ibid.

communion with one another in God."[15] For those in whom the desire and willingness to believe still stirs, biblical and liturgical *anamnesis* tells us "not merely what we ought to be," says Merton, "but the unbelievable thing that we already *are*. It will tell us over and over again that we are Christ in this world, and that He lives in us, and that what was said of Him has been and is being fulfilled in us."[16] Such an awakening is "a matter not of knowledge, but of love."[17] Identity, in other words, is a *response*—"a response *to a name you already have!* You are given a name: *the name to which you will respond, when it is called out!*"[18] As the African American spiritual goes, "If anybody asks you who I am, tell them that I'm a child of God."

This book has explored the emergence of Sophia in Merton's life and theology as a vivid symbol both of deepest human identity and the "communal eros" that is the very life of God, eternally emptying itself in creativity, mercy, and love for creation. From God's side, Sophia is the "mystery of social love" in the Trinity, "refracted and multiplied in the many subsisting natures of men united with one another in society."[19] She is the presence of God at the crossroads of a world in crisis, calling not only Christians but all peoples to a "sense of community with things in the work of salvation."[20] From our side, from the side of all creation, she is "the protest of life itself, of humanity itself, of love"[21] in the reign of numbers. "She is life as communion, life as thanksgiving, life as praise, life as festival, life as glory."[22]

How, then, does one rise from saying the word "Sophia" to sensing her realness? It is precisely in *saying the Name*, by entering bodily into the tensive act of speech and sacrament making—that is, by entering into prayer—that we are drawn into Sophia's "more than literal" presence. Understanding is both "fixed and freed"[23] through symbols. In the moment we invoke Sophia's name truly *as Name*, we are freed from language into reality, from the act of vocalizing a word into participating, body and soul, in the breakthrough of

15. Ibid., 75.

16. BW, 38.

17. Ibid. 134.

18. LE, 504. From a remarkable conference Merton gave in March of 1967 to the young monks at Gethsemani on Faulkner's *The Sound and the Fury*, which climaxes in his ecstatic analysis of an Easter service "in the black church" portrayed in the novel, and the implicit spirituality and ecclesiology he finds there—"an absolutely beautiful thing. Really beautiful!"

19. NM, 91.

20. ICM, 110.

21. DQ, 11.

22. ESF, 66–67.

23. Marie-Dominique Chenu, *Nature, Man, and Society in the Twelfth Century*, ed. Jerome Taylor and Lester Little (Chicago: University of Chicago Press, 1957), 140; see chap. 3, n. 132.

Love and merciful Presence. "It is the spiritual power of the praying person that makes manifest what is dormant in the text."[24]

"The Name of God," writes Kallistos Ware, "is *numen praesens*, God with us, Emmanuel. Attentively and deliberately to invoke God's Name is to place oneself in His presence, to open oneself to His energy, to offer oneself as an instrument and a living sacrifice in His hands."[25] For Merton, to invoke the name of Sophia is to remember both the Name of God and our own deepest identity; it is to be drawn intimately into the realm of eschatology realized, sanctified time, the intensified apocalyptic moment. It is to place oneself in God's presence—"I am with you, now, in the present moment"—to open oneself to God's energy, and to offer oneself as an instrument and a living sacrifice in God's hands. Like a star breaking into view from the revelatory firmament of the Bible, Wisdom arises in our consciousness like the remembrance of "the forgotten mother tongue," inviting us to "forget ourselves on purpose" and join in "the general dance" of Sophia, at play in the garden of the Lord.[26] Sophiology is a theological response to a name we already have, a name to which we will respond, when it is called out, when it is remembered.

A Brief Recounting

The first half of this book was taken up largely with building a case for the validity of Merton's mystical and poetical approach to theology through an analysis of the central role of the imagination in epistemology and theological method. The argument reached a critical point late in chapter 3, where the practice of theology infused by a sacramental imagination was described in terms of *memoria*, presence (*theoria*), and hope—terms that imply a formal relationship between biblical symbols and the deep revelatory structure of reality, the "hidden ground of Love." Emphasizing the degree to which epistemological commitments implicate anthropological and theological ones, a key claim or first principle staked out early in this study is that the human person is not tabula rasa, but in the deepest recesses of the human mind and heart, indeed, in the fabric of corporeality and Being itself, there lives a hidden memory and experience of God that, whether or not we are conscious of it, binds everything together across all distances, cultures, physical landscapes, and times.

Such a radical metaphysical claim—the claim of nondualism, or Soloviev's "pan-unity"—is rendered epistemologically credible, however, only to the degree our lives and traditions cultivate the experiential consciousness of it.

---

24. Abraham Joshua Heschel, *Man's Quest for God* (New York: Scribner's, 1954), 27.
25. Kallistos Ware, "The Power of the Name: The Jesus Prayer in Orthodox Spirituality," in MHPH, 41–74, at 51.
26. NSC, 290.

Contemplation has been described in these pages as a loving, confessional, ascetic, and self-critical way of life that engages the whole person, shaping our personal and corporate discernment of "the real" at every turn. The practice of living in the presence of God breaks through all opaque and self-enclosed worldviews, becoming the "true key" for grasping truths that are "really to be found in the world, though they are not upon the surface."[27] Indeed, for Merton, a recovery of the contemplative path is the way to peace, without which it will be impossible to approach the stranger as neighbor, still less as the very one in whom Christ comes to meet us. It is not mere hyperbole, then, when Merton suggests that "the spiritual anguish of man has no cure but mysticism."[28]

Indeed, as emphasized at the end of chapter 3, Merton's willingness to give himself over to the *memoria* of strangers, to the wisdom of traditions well beyond his own religious comfort zone, poses an explicit challenge to every self-enclosed epistemology or exclusivist view of revelation: "to communicate with these pasts and these distances . . . to live them and combine them in myself, to absorb, to digest, to 'remember.' *Memoria*. Have not yet begun."[29] To repeat perhaps the pivotal epistemological question posed by the first half of this study: if Merton had "not yet begun" to allow his religious imagination to be broken open by the boundless *memoria* of God, how far is Christian theology today from beginning to do so? The point here is that deeds follow thought: How far are we from a commitment "to remember" the world and its peoples, both existentially and theologically, from the divine perspective? How willing is Christian theology to envision other peoples and traditions, and indeed the natural world, as integral in the life story of God?

While the first half of the book centered on questions of epistemology and theological method, chapters 4 and 5 sought to draw out the contours of Merton's mature Christology in terms of his awakening to Sophia. Beginning in the late 1950s and catalyzed by his concurrent study of Zen and Russian sophiology, Merton's turning to the world beyond the monastery found its highest positive theological realization in the prose poem *Hagia Sophia*, the culmination of a theology construed "under the light of Wisdom," a bold rendering of the Catholic sacramental imagination, and a classic marriage of Eastern and Western spirituality. Against a century of unspeakable violence

---

27. John Henry Newman, GA, 106.

28. NM, 114. Cf. Rahner's famous statement: "Tomorrow's devout person will either be a mystic—someone who has 'experienced' something—or else they will no longer be devout at all" (cited in *Karl Rahner: Spiritual Writings*, ed. Phillip Endean [Maryknoll, NY: Orbis, 2004], 24). As Endean cautions, we misinterpret Rahner, and here we may add Merton, if we take such statements to mean "that future Christians must be like John of the Cross." For both Merton and Rahner "we need to lose the sense of elitism associated with talk of the mystical" (ibid.).

29. TTW, 42.

and dehumanization, *Hagia Sophia* is Merton's consummate hymn to the theological dignity of humankind and of all creation. It is a hymn of peace.

The final chapter sought to frame Merton's mature theology as a piece of a much larger historical and theological fabric, drawing out the strong, sometimes uncanny, resonances between Merton's experience of God/Christ/ Sophia and those of the Russian theologians from whom he drew inspiration. What I have broadly called the "sophiological tradition" crossing boundaries of text, culture, and time—indeed, reaching into ancient wellsprings of Jewish *memoria*—gestures toward a compelling theology of Presence, with the potential for invigorating fundamental theology and Christian spirituality in diverse areas such as theology of religions, feminist and environmental theologies, liturgical theology, theologies of vocation, art, and sexuality, and surely others. Although what follows here will be somewhat more schematic, our final task is crucial, and that is to broadly assess the shape of the whole: to consider how the sophiological perspective casts new light on some of the most pressing theological and spiritual questions of our time.

The Mosaic Humanity of God

In emphasizing the "uninterrupted humanity" of the gospels, Bulgakov reminds us that Jesus was not only the son of Mary and Joseph, or only a son of Israel, just as no person is simply the son or daughter of their biological parents or the religion of their birth. Jesus was also a "son of Adam" (lit.: "son of the earth") and a "son of God," which is to say, a human being. If his question to the disciples—"Who do you say that I am?" (Mark 8:29)—is first of all "a Christian problem," that is, a question of *Christian* identity, nevertheless the living encounter with Jesus reverberates across all distances and absences to become the ontological question, the question of humanity as such: what does it mean to be a human being, to live in communion with God, the earth, and with all things?

The positive metaphysical claim at the heart of sophiology's far-reaching christocentric inclusivism is that which is already implied in the name Emmanuel, God with us: that God, humanity, and the earth belong essentially together and not apart. The point to emphasize here, recalling chapter 3, is that "there are many ways"[30] to express this central mystery of divine-humanity and sacred corporeality, many ways of "growing into the truth" of the incarnation. Just as the New Testament reflects not just one but a pluralism of christologies, so we can expect and welcome today a certain flourishing of constructive efforts to name the mystery of God in ways that

30. ZBA, 24.

are both faithful to the tradition's memory of Jesus and also responsive to the Spirit's groaning for expression in light of wondrously diverse cultures and the particular signs of our times.

If indeed there are many legitimate ways to name the mystery of God's love in Christ, then why Sophia, rather than a reinvigoration of the more familiar terms of christological or trinitarian discourse? Perhaps the most substantive criticism put to sophiology by conservative Orthodox commentators, as Paul Valliere notes, is that it is superfluous; that in treating the "spiritualization of humanity" the theologian can get along well enough with the doctrines of the incarnation and the indwelling of the Holy Spirit.[31] Acknowledging the validity of this critique, Valliere frames the question in this way: "Would anything essential be lost if the sophiological aspect [of Bulgakov's dogmatics] were discarded?"[32] His own response is twofold, beginning with a spirited defense of sophiology's distinctive method.

Sophia functions in theological method, Valliere suggests, as a kind of "benevolent fairy,"[33] making old things new in dialogue with the richness of human culture: "Sophia is the Lilac Fairy, not the Sleeping Beauty of dogmatic theology. She energizes dogma in all sorts of enchanting ways—galvanizing, crystallizing, illuminating, extending, elaborating; but she does not discard received dogmas or fashion new ones. Only the church can do that. The mission of sophiology is to foster conversation, not dominate it; to catalyze relationships between dogma and culture, not abolish the distinction. Sophia guides theologians over new terrain, mostly uncharted, where dogma meets experience, church meets world, Christianity meets culture, Orthodoxy meets modernity."[34] How does the sophiological tradition "energize dogma" and "catalyze relationships" between Christianity and the world? Perhaps above all by showing as much concern for the dynamics of reception and creative participation (from our side) as for God's initiative in the drama of salvation history. As Bulgakov puts it, "we must not forget the *humanity*"[35] of the good news which is the church's privilege to bear. Sophia invokes a method—a "method of catholicity," a "free theosophy"—for inscribing this point in theological terms, in the very life of God.[36]

---

31. Valliere, MRT, 306, citing Frederick Copleston; idem, "Sophiology as the Dialogue of Orthodoxy with the Modern World," in *Russian Religious Thought*, ed. Judith Kornblatt and Richard Gustafson (Madison, WI: University of Wisconsin Press, 1996), 188.

32. Valliere, "Sophiology as the Dialogue," 188.

33. Ibid.

34. Valliere, MRT, 306.

35. Cited in Valliere, MRT, 340.

36. Whereas "church dogmatics" as generally practiced is concerned with "the vindication of tradition," a "church-and-world dogmatics" (e.g., sophiology, Vatican II's *Gaudium et spes*)

To say it another way, unlike the conservative or defensive impulse in church-world discourse, Valliere notes, sophiology has never been an either/or proposition. In dogmatics, for example, it has never been either sophiology or patristic theology; in the conversation with the sciences and with art it has never been either sophiology or the secular world. To the contrary, sophiology has always been a "mediating discipline," a "both/and conceptuality envisioning Orthodoxy and modern civilization speaking to each other . . . walking through history together, confronting the eschatological horizon together."[37] This "both/and," of course, makes unprecedented demands on every discipline in the conversation, not least theology, since the "positive religious synthesis" it seeks is not merely a synthesis but a "living unity." "This means first of all," Valliere observes, "that there can be no final 'system' of sophiology, since new content is at all times being produced by the world process. A system of sophiology would inevitably turn Sophia into an abstract ideal."[38] Sophia is the "Lilac Fairy" because, "by interjecting testimony from nature, history, and human experience,"[39] sophiology refuses to regard dogma as a finished thing; at the same time, it challenges the secular disciplines to take seriously not just humanity but *God-filled* humanity.

Thus far the conservative critique still stands. It is still not clear why theology, in treating the doctrine of theosis or entering into dialogue with the world cannot get by with a revitalized trinitarianism or a robust pneumatology. The second part of Valliere's reply to the conservative critique hinges on sophiology's generation of new content, that is, its positive Chalcedonianism, which centers on the humanity of God. Unlike traditional approaches, sophiology goes beyond the doctrine of theosis to articulate the fully human dimension of trinitarian theology:

> As the thematizer of the humanity of God Bulgakov deals not just with the spiritualization of humanity but with the *humanization of the spiritual*, the humanization of the divine. Seriousness about this dimension of the humanity of God is what distinguishes his dogmatics from patristic dogmatics. The dogmatics of the humanity of God expresses the Word of God, but it speaks human words as well—fully human words. A fully human word is a free act, a task imagined and projected by an autonomous self, an expression of creativity (*tvorchestvo*, a key

---

must be just as concerned with "the vindication of reception, the justification of a God-seeking, God-interrogating, God-intoxicated humanity" (Valliere, MRT, 308).

37. Valliere, "Sophiology as the Dialogue," 187.

38. Ibid., 190. It is interesting that Merton describes Buddhism in similar terms: "[It] demands *not to be a system* (while at the same time, like other religions, presenting a peculiar temptation to systematizers)" (ZBA, 4).

39. Valliere, "Sophiology as the Dialogue," 188.

sophiological term for which no real equivalent exists in the vocabulary of patristic theology). One may call the fairy of creativity by another name if Sophia is disliked for some reason; but then the quarrel is about names, not substance. Bulgakov's point stands.[40]

As Valliere's analysis makes clear, sophiology is not "an accidental feature" of Bulgakov's theology, but gets to the very "heart of the matter."[41] As a "sustained metaphor"[42] for the humanity of God, Sophia is more, after all, than a methodological catalyst ("the Lilac Fairy"), and sophiology is more than a distinctive form of otherwise traditional trinitarian discourse. Indeed, to recall David Tracy's point from chapter 1, theological form is not merely "some extra aesthetic addition to content" but is "that which renders the content so that the search for the right theological form is at the very same time the search for the right theological content."[43] Thus while Valliere is right to conclude that sophiology does not and should not conspire to "invent dogma" or stabilize itself into a "system," he is also right to conclude that sophiology, as a kind of dogmatic searching (for both form and content), involves the development or "transposition" of doctrine into a dramatically "new key."[44] Throughout this book, Tracy's insight has borne out clearly, especially when we consider Merton's transposition of Russian sophiology into mystical-poetical form in *Hagia Sophia*.

The metaphor of a musical key is an apt one. On a first reading of *Hagia Sophia*, one may legitimately ask: in what sense, if any, is this Christology? The term, with its usual scholastic connotations, does not quite fit the musicality and fluidity of the text. And yet, I hazard to suggest that many Western Catholic readers who enter meditatively into the text will find its music strangely familiar, not wholly discordant. In *Hagia Sophia*, Merton has transposed the Christology of his largely Western inheritance into a wondrous sophiological key. He has done so, however, not by a chain of discursive propositions but

40. Valliere, MRT, 307. Bulgakov "reveres the formula" of Chalcedon, "but as surely as a cornerstone is not a finished house the Chalcedonian formula is not, for Bulgakov, a finished christology" (Valliere, "Sophiology as the Dialogue," 188).

41. Valliere, "Sophiology as the Dialogue," 191. Valliere adds that insofar as the Moscow Patriarchate and conservative theologians abroad were not interested in a dialogue with modern liberal civilization, "they were right to attack it" (ibid., 190).

42. Rowan Williams characterizes Bulgakov's sophiology as "far more a sustained metaphor than a theory" ("Eastern Orthodox Theology," in *The Modern Theologians*, ed. David F. Ford [Cambridge, MA: Blackwell, 1997], 499–513, at 503); similarly Valliere calls sophiology "a representation, virtually a dramatization, of Orthodoxy's struggle to engage with the modern world" (MRT, 271).

43. Cited in Younhee Kim, "David Tracy's Postmodern Reflection on God," *Louvain Studies* 30, no. 3 (2005): 159–79, at 168.

44. Valliere, MRT, 329.

rather in a mystical-poetical form that invites our active attunement, our participation in the experience of God within and behind the language. In a word, the music remains—an inner musicality that reverberates from within every New Testament Christology, and which ought to be at least vaguely discernible in christological discourse today.

Another simple metaphor will help to illumine the sometimes dramatic way in which form renders content. If all theology operates within and appeals to an imaginative framework of understanding, then it might be said that what sophiology does for our way of conceiving God is akin to putting an old picture into a new frame.[45] As a new frame draws out all sorts of colors, contrasts, and hues that were once hidden, so does the sophiological framework evoke a conception and experience of God that may seem strange and new to Christians today, especially to Western believers. Indeed, to the degree *Hagia Sophia* presses against the imaginative framework of one's assumed or inherited theology, it may strike the ear (and trouble the mind) not only as strange and discordant but, frankly, dangerous. Not everyone, to be sure, will welcome the poem's plenitude of affirmation, its invocation of unity-in-difference, its invitation into a mosaic experience of God that positively spills over traditional theological and dogmatic containers.

The point brings us back to the horizon of religious pluralism with which we began this study. If sophiology begins with the doctrines of the Trinity and the incarnation in the very center of the picture frame, its profound exposition of the humanity of God has the effect of pulling into the foreground of the picture what in patristic theology tends to remain (conspicuously) in the murky background, namely, the diversity of peoples, cultures, and natural landscapes that render the world and its history, in Bulgakov's words, "the *common task* of humanity, a single and connected action having the incarnation as its center." Sophiology, in other words, draws into the foreground not only "the whole human side of the preparation for the Incarnation"[46] but also the whole human (and cosmic) side of its saving implications for all peoples, cultures, and the earth: Christ/Sophia "is the 'world' which God experiences from all eternity, the world which he begets for himself."[47]

One can see how such a vision presses against the traditionally conceived boundaries between the world's religions. On the one hand, for the Christian imagination, Sophia, "spread like a canopy over our sinful though still

---

45. The metaphor is borrowed from Roger Haight, who uses it to illustrate how the meaning of traditional theological language changes when placed within a new spatial or imaginative context. See his *The Future of Christology* (New York: Continuum, 2005), 182.

46. Cited in Valliere, MRT, 322.

47. Valliere, MRT, 159.

hallowed world,"[48] finds her deepest identity in Jesus Christ, the inbreaking Wisdom of God, who by his incarnation not only joins heaven with earth but gives humanity a place in God from the beginning. On the other hand, the sophiological perspective reaches behind the narrative of Jesus Christ (and a strong tendency toward christomonism in the tradition) to consider the divine nature itself, the conditions for the possibility of God's revelation in Jesus. As Rowan Williams writes, "Sophia *is* the divine nature, God's own life considered under the aspect of God's freedom to live the divine life in what is not God. God as Trinity is an eternal movement of 'giving away,' displacement, so that God's very Godhead presupposes the possibility of there being an object of love and gift beyond itself."[49]

Thus while sophiology takes its starting point in Chalcedon and the divine-humanity of the gospels, the biblical Wisdom figure of Jewish memory that it draws vividly into the foreground *is not uniquely christocentric.* Insofar as the Wisdom of God is not strictly identified with the Second Person but rather with the very nature (*ousia*) and universal presence of God, sophiology has the "inestimable advantage in bringing us back upstream of the Trinitarian discourse as it was elaborated in a so to speak 'pre-Christian' universe."[50] In other words, the remembrance of Sophia has the effect of reframing the theology of God in a way that breaks open the imagination and invites us to reconsider, as Williams puts it, "God's freedom to live the divine life in what is not God."

This thrust toward the universal translates in Bulgakov and certainly in Merton not merely into a begrudging "justification" of the whole world and its diversity of peoples before the guardians of divine truth but into a positively theological celebration of natural and human diversity as a "reflection" or "epiphany" of Sophia, the world to which God eternally gives Godself away. Here, to be sure, we are no longer dealing with a modest change of the picture frame but rather getting into the real (ontological) heart of the matter, breaking open our elemental assumptions about God's relationship to humanity, history, and the diverse cultural and physical landscapes of the earth. Method and form spill over into content to the degree we are willing to open ourselves to Wisdom wherever it (she) may be found. As Merton noted four decades ago, the restoration of sanity and spiritual balance in our time will require a convergence too often presumed to be impossible, namely, "a

48. Sergius Bulgakov, *Sophia: The Wisdom of God: An Outline of Sophiology* (Hudson, NY: Lindisfarne, 1993), 21.

49. Williams, "Eastern Orthodox Theology," 503; cf. Valliere, MRT, 333–34, on the way "the concept of *ousia* enhances trinitarianism" in Bulgakov's dogmatics, but also how "the concreteness Bulgakov ascribes to Sophia" lays his theology of God open to misinterpretation.

50. Antoine Arjakovsky, "The Sophiology of Father Sergius Bulgakov and Contemporary Western Theology," in *St. Vladimir's Theological Quarterly* 49 (2005): 219–35, at 230–31.

renewal of communion between the traditional, contemplative disciplines and those of science, between the poet and the physicist, the priest and the depth psychologist, the monk and the politician."[51]

Certainly there are reasons to be wary of religious "grand narratives," of universalisms that, as Karl Plank cautions in his critique of Merton's approach to Judaism, "reduce human identities to their least common denominator or abstract persons from their history."[52] While Plank, for example, credits Merton for his sincere *desire* to appreciate Judaism, which was indeed laudable in the context of the times, he questions "the value of his actual approach to Jews," finding in Merton (and in Vatican II) a less than laudable tendency "to efface the integrity of Jewish difference."[53] The critique is an important one, for it highlights the dangers of any discourse that would too quickly appropriate (and thus effectively silence) the other's reality into one's own frame of reference. Yet, as Plank also indicates, Merton's too-facile leap toward kinship, unity, and even "identity" with the Jewish other, at the expense of appreciating and learning from real difference, "is not so much wrong as partial."[54]

At stake here is not simply the question of Christian proselytizing of (or war-making against) the religious or nonreligious other but, much more deeply, the vindication of difference itself as God-given, God-inscribed, inscribed *in* God. What is needed is a method and a language that does not efface difference right out of the gate but is committed to listening to the other receptively, contemplatively, as "an other with words to speak—words of his or her own that may challenge from difference and may love with freedom."[55] The sophiological tradition, with its commitment to an ever greater understanding of the mosaic humanity of God, exemplifies just such a method and

---

51. LL, 79.

52. Karl Plank, "The Eclipse of Difference: Merton's Encounter with Judaism," in *Merton and Judaism: Recognition, Repentance, and Renewal: Holiness in Words*, ed. Beatrice Bruteau (Louisville, KY: Fons Vitae, 2003), 67–82, at 73.

53. Ibid., 69. Among numerous examples, Plank cites Merton's letter to Abraham Joshua Heschel during the heated conciliar debates on "the Jewish question" in which Merton professes his "latent ambitions to be a true Jew under my Catholic skin" (HGL, 434). I agree with Plank that the letter is problematic on many levels, not least in the fact that "Jewish anguish . . . is not and cannot be [Merton's] own. . . . Nowhere in the letter . . . does he recognize the particular and more urgent situation of Heschel himself, the concrete situation of the Jew as Jew" ("The Eclipse of Difference," 75). Cf. Edward K. Kaplan, "'Under My Catholic Skin': Thomas Merton's Opening to Judaism and to the World" (ibid., 109–25).

54. Plank, "The Eclipse of Difference," 80.

55. Ibid., 81–82. Recall, for example, Merton's meetings with D. T. Suzuki, the Dalai Lama, and Chatral Rimpoche (chap. 4). It is significant that these meetings were in person, "face to face," and thus did not afford Merton the relative comfort and safety of distance, as would the writing of a letter, or still more an essay, while immersed in his familiar (Christian) surroundings at Gethsemani.

a language. Moreover, where "the postmodernist sees nothing beyond difference, no underlying metaphysical unity to ground speech and language"[56]— dangerously undermining the very possibility of establishing common ethical ground among diverse peoples—sophiology nurtures the imaginative and intellectual conditions in which the realization of unity-in-difference (i.e., justice) might actually be approximated in the concrete (spiritual, ecclesial, political) social order.[57] It does so, significantly, "not just as an act of courtesy but in the faith that these values, too [the values of human freedom, human rights, and human creativity] inhere in the gospel, coinhere in divinity."[58]

Whether or not such a framework can facilitate greater love and understanding in the broad sweep of history, at least this much is clear: not all universalist or Christ-haunted visions of reality feed dangerously into (as William Lynch calls it) the "absolutizing instinct,"[59] yielding triumphalist pretensions or suspicion of the non-Christian, secular, or scientific world; not every trinitarian theology necessarily leads to ahistorical or docetic abstractions, far removed from human experience, the natural world, or the humanity of Jesus. Indeed, the sophiological perspective reminds us that metaphysics is unintelligible when grandiose; it only "makes sense" when attuned to the smaller line, the ironic fact that persons as well as fish, trees, and skyscrapers are only as "real" as their tiniest, weakest, most hidden and uninspiring (yet irreducibly distinctive) elements. Thus Israel's countertestimony to a God whose power stirs not in the earthquake so much as in the "sheer silence" (1 Kgs 19:11-13), especially in the silence of human hearts, where the kingdom of heaven irrupts in faith the size of a mustard seed.

To Be a Witness for Life

In a stirring tribute to his teacher Karl Rahner, Johann Baptist Metz writes something that might just as well have been said of Merton, and now, we

---

56. Ibid., 73.

57. I say "might be approximated" to highlight the character of such statements as positive religious ideals and to distinguish the sophiological perspective of history, always shot through with eschatological tension, from various forms of utopianism.

58. Valliere, MRT, 308; cf. ibid., 127–37, 145–49. The implications of this point for ecclesial life and spirituality are far reaching, both ad extra and ad intra, calling us to confront and transform any form of dehumanization that cripples our lives in one another, in God, and in the Body of Christ.

59. By the "absolutizing instinct" Lynch means the instinct in human beings that tends to "make absolutes out of everything it touches and to pour floods of fantasy into the world about it. . . . [It is] a world of false hopes which counterfeits the reality of hope. . . . [It] magnifies. In its presence each thing loses its true perspective and its true edges. The good becomes tremendously good, the evil becomes the absolutely evil, the grey becomes the black or white, the complicated . . . becomes, in desperation, the completely simple" (William Lynch, *Images of Hope: Imagination as Healer of the Hopeless* [Baltimore: Helicon, 1965], 105–8).

may add, the Russian sophiologists: "[For] Rahner, God is a universal theme, a theme concerning all humanity, or it simply is no theme at all. God is never for him the private property of the church, nor of theology. And not even of faith: the lightning flash of God is to be reckoned on every human experiential and linguistic terrain."[60] Merton's turn toward the ecumenical, non-Christian, and secular horizon reflects a concurrent shift in the Catholic theology of grace, more recovery than invention, effected by theologians like Rahner, Congar, de Lubac, Murray, and the bishops at Vatican II.

Of course it is the task of Catholic theologians, and perhaps especially Catholic poets, to wrestle with dichotomies, the tension of opposites that cannot and should not be broken: sin and grace, fall and restoration, freedom and grace, death and life. If today Catholic discourse tends toward a hermeneutic of suspicion with respect to the secular world, Merton's lens was basic trust. If today we are tempted to wonder why there should be any love in the world rather than destruction, Merton seemed more determined than ever in his last years to affirm that humanity belongs to God and can attain to genuine holiness—even in "the world of the bomb, the world of race hatred, the world of technology, the world of mass media, big business, revolution, and all the rest."[61] Like Rahner, Merton never despaired that the lightning flash of God could be found on every genuinely human terrain, above all in the poverty of ordinary life. For contemporary seekers paralyzed by doubt, by the difficulty of labeling oneself a believer, or who despair of finding much hope in the fractured human community, this is no small gift.

Near the end of his life, the great Polish poet Czeslaw Milosz wrote: "To move mountains with a word is not for us, but this does not mean that it is impossible. Were not Matthew, Mark, Luke, and John miracle workers by virtue of their having written the Gospels?"[62] Some forty years earlier, his friend Thomas Merton wrote in a similarly sapiential vein: "The office of the monk or the marginal person, the meditative person or the poet is to go beyond death even in this life, to go beyond the dichotomy of life and death and to be, therefore, a witness to life."[63] To move mountains with a word, to be a witness to life—is this not also the office of the theologian?

---

60. Johann Baptist Metz, *A Passion for God: The Mystical-Political Dimension of Christianity*, trans. J. Matthew Ashley (New York: Paulist, 1998), 109.

61. CGB, 157. Merton's signature essay on the subject may be "Is the World a Problem?" (1966), CWA, 159–71.

62. Czeslaw Milosz, "If Only This Could Be Said," *CrossCurrents* 52, no. 1 (Spring 2002): 60–71, at 71.

63. AJ, 306.

Solidarity and (Apocalyptic) Hope

It would be wildly incorrect to conclude from all this that Merton failed to take the reality of sin and evil seriously. One might argue that he did not take it seriously enough. But if that is the case, one has to ask at what point the analogical imagination finally gives itself over, perhaps reluctantly but quite reasonably, to a dialectical worldview that alternates more or less chaotically between the presence and absence of God—a world that is still waiting for God's definitive breakthrough. Merton follows the Russians, rather, in retrieving with a new and sometimes terrible urgency the apocalyptic climate of the gospels, where divine absence is met with cruciform presence, where divine silence in history is answered, over and over again ("seventy times seven times"), as in a mantra, with the word *mercy*, the gift of forgiveness.

There were, of course, other apocalyptic voices already close to Merton's heart: Herakleitos, Flannery O'Connor, and William Blake, to name a few. Yet it was the Russian theologians who convinced Merton that theology must once again become, in the words of Florovsky, "*a public matter, a universal and catholic mission.*"[64] Indeed, Merton would fully embrace Florovsky's conviction that "we have reached a point where theological silence, embarrassment, incertitude, lack of articulation" is equivalent "to flight before the enemy." It is "precisely because we are thrown into the apocalyptic battle that we are called upon to do the job of theologians." Apocalypticism in a sophiological key reinforces what Catholic social teaching today calls the "preferential option for the poor," intensifying our awareness of the critical present moment for those who have no name, no presence, no value whatsoever on the world stage; the earth too now merits an urgent place in Christian eschatology. "Theology is called not only to judge . . . *but to heal.*"[65]

The point to emphasize is that Merton refused to drive a wedge between the mystical and the political, solitude and solidarity, contemplation and action. Certainly there will always be a temptation for believers to use the positive stuff of the tradition as a refuge from the world, a place to hide in a community of like-minded people. That danger should not, however, delude us into the opposite and arguably greater danger of believing we can go it heroically alone. Without regular immersion in the tradition, without a commitment to the community of believers, how can we come to really know Jesus as the Christ, the one who educates us in the possibilities of presence, and who helps us see the world—precisely in and through the many—limned in life, grace, and resurrection hope? It is good to remember that Merton's education in solidarity came not only in his life as a hermit but for the much

64. ICM, 37.
65. Ibid.

greater part of his years as a sojourner in the secular world, and as a priest in a community of brother monks.

Idolatry, Intelligibility, and Theological Development

The most serious challenge to Merton's mature Christology today may not be the question of relevance so much as intelligibility. Can we reasonably expect the image of Christ as Wisdom or Sophia to find a foothold in the imagination of ordinary Christians in our time, perhaps especially in the West? More broadly, can Russian sophiology stand up to the intelligibility requirement of historical consciousness? While Bulgakov's theology has certainly been scrutinized up and down through the decades, Merton has generally escaped such critique, since, to the degree he has been studied seriously as a theologian, he is often characterized as an apophatic thinker, and not without reason; when one worries about theological positivism or conceptual idolatry, Merton is not the first Catholic thinker to come to mind.[66]

In a recent landmark work in Christology, Jesuit scholar Roger Haight lays down a serious challenge to the patristic hermeneutic: "The world is pluralistic and polycentric in its horizons of interpretation. It is impossible in postmodern culture to think that one group of people is a chosen people. Or that one religion can claim to inhabit the center into which all others are to be drawn. These myths or meta-narratives are simply gone."[67] In his lucid critique of metaphysical theology, Haight raises important questions that will not simply go away. In a word, can any thoroughly trinitarian, metaphysical, or cosmic narrative withstand the skepticism of historical consciousness? Is Merton's lack of interest in the historical Jesus fatal to the credibility of his Christology?

While Merton himself often resisted such debates, such "special problems which the world may have formulated for itself,"[68] he was far from indifferent

---

66. Here I am thinking, for example, of Hans Urs von Balthasar, whose three-volume *Theodramatik* has had an enormous, if much-debated, impact on contemporary Catholic theology (for a brief comparison with Merton, see chap. 1). From the other side, one way to avoid a comparison of Merton's Christology with contemporary historical-critical approaches is to claim that what Merton does is, in fact, *not theology*; it is spiritual writing, poetry, autobiography, edifying literature, and so on. I hope this study has helped put to rest such claims. But here Tracy's nuanced perspective also intervenes: namely, "that the search for the right theological form is at the very same time the search for the right theological content" (see chap. 1, n. 85).

67. Roger Haight, *Jesus Symbol of God* (Maryknoll, NY: Orbis, 1999), 333. For an interpretation (and defense) of Haight's Christology, see Christopher Pramuk, "Returning the Mystery to God: The Theocentric Horizon of Roger Haight's Christology," *New Theology Review* 15, no. 4 (Nov 2002): 50–66; idem, "Who Do People Say That I Am?: A Discussion of Roger Haight's *Jesus Symbol of God.*" *Chicago Studies* 41, no. 1 (Spring 2002): 80–91.

68. MHPH, 483.

to the gulf separating mystical sensibilities from the modern mind. "We are not used to the perspectives which enabled the Fathers and the New Testament writers to see the mysterious com-penetration of all these realities in the one great reality of the Person of Christ."[69] Indeed, throughout the 1960s, especially under the influence of interfaith dialogue, Merton wrestled not only personally but theologically with some of the most difficult issues of epistemology, ontology, and method, and wrote a great deal on these problems with as much acuity as many historical, philosophical, or contextual theologians today. In short, Merton was taken from us tragically too soon. Had he lived another ten or twenty (or forty!) years, no doubt he would have had a great deal more to say about these matters, even under the pretense of contemplative indifference. We always "have more thinking to do, and perhaps some revising. Certainly some revising."[70]

Let me make my own position clear. There is certainly a point beyond which highly speculative (philosophical) or imaginative (aesthetic) theologies can and should be rejected as excessively speculative or imaginative. A critical tipping point occurs in Christology when a particular approach loses touch with the humanity of Jesus, and more generally the contours of human history and experience. Imaginative frameworks tending toward docetism or gnosticism, for example, are not only likely to be unintelligible to the *sensus fidei* today, they are also dangerous to the degree that they tend to sanction a self-referential kind of mystery cult within the faithful, a hierarchical model of participation in the divine that (subtly or not so subtly) excludes all those outside its purview. These, of course, are the marks of idolatry, arguably the central concern of the Bible.[71] Without question, the concern to avoid conceptual and dogmatic idolatry is legitimate and may explain the reflexive aversion among many theologians (especially those, like myself, schooled under Rahner) to ornate or speculative trinitarian theologies that seem far removed from Jesus of Nazareth, from discipleship, or ordinary human experience.

At first glance, Russian sophiology appeared to me to cross this line. Today I no longer believe this to be the case. In my judgment, the sophiological tradition represents a compelling and trustworthy case of dogmatic searching—trustworthy because it remains true to the best instincts of doctrinal development: "make the center strong, the symbols large, the words of Christ clear, and make that center accessible, the circle large, the periphery

---

69. NM, 134.

70. HGL, 644.

71. "Religion in this sense is gradually revealed in the Bible to be under judgment. It is questioned not so much by man *as by God himself*" (OB, 88).

permeable."[72] Here I am inclined to believe, I want to believe, with James D. G. Dunn, that Christianity "at its historic heart" is "an openness to the unexpectedness of divine grace, to the new thing which God may wish to do, even when it breaks through and leaves behind the familiar paths and forms."[73] At the same time, the sophiological tradition clearly requires sensitive and skillful "translation," especially in the West. Because its reception by the church and theological community is still very much an open question, it is probably best to characterize sophiology as a *theologoumenon*, that is, "a non-binding theological thesis which is neither found clearly in scripture nor in the definitive teaching of the *magisterium*."[74]

It would, of course, be a serious category mistake to suggest that Merton attempted anything like Bulgakov's magisterial effort to recast the theology of God in the modern era. Merton was not a systematician but a mystical theologian, a poet of the presence of God, and *Hagia Sophia* is by far the most realized expression of the sophiological vision he had imbibed from the Russians. As suggested in chapter 5, if Merton judged the poem's theology in need of "revision and reformulation," it is fair to conclude that he left it for others in the West to carry the reception of sophiology forward. Some four decades after his death, it is a task that seems to be gathering some momentum, thanks considerably to the studies of Paul Valliere, Catherine Evtuhov, and Rowan Williams, to name a few. Yet we should not overlook the degree to which Merton himself effected this reception. Some of his best work comes to us in a sophianic key.

In view of Christology today, Merton's *Hagia Sophia* is trustworthy not least because the poem (like Bulgakov's dogmatics) never loses sight of the humanity of Jesus; still less does it offer a kind of aesthetic or mystical flight from the poverty of human experience. To the contrary, the poem is an implicit rejection of every opaque or self-referential mystery cult surrounding Jesus Christ, every triumphal or hierarchical model of communion in the divine that would exclude the "little," the "poor," or nonbelievers. Its symbols are drawn from the Scriptures and resonate deeply in the tradition from East to West, even while the poem stretches, challenges, and purifies the tradition and the familiar categories of Christian theology. The poem's dance of saying and unsaying is characteristic of the mystical tradition at its best, finally shattering idols not in the pure silence of negation but in the plenitude of

---

72. Gordon Laycock, *Holy Things: A Liturgical Theology* (Minneapolis: Fortress, 1993), 192.

73. James D. G. Dunn, *The Partings of the Ways: Between Christianity and Judaism and their Significance for the Character of Christianity* (London: SCM, 1991), 259.

74. Gerald O'Collins and Edward G. Farrugia, eds., *A Concise Dictionary of Theology* (New York/Mahwah, NJ: Paulist, 1991), 239.

affirmation, unity-in-difference, and praise. "The Diffuse Shining of God is Hagia Sophia. We call her His 'glory.' . . . She is the Bride and the Feast and the Wedding."[75]

With respect to potential idolatry or aesthetic fancy, the heart of the problem is not representation as such, which is an integral component of the sacramental imagination, but its *misuse*. The biblical concern for idolatry pits the transcendence and freedom of God over against the hubris and amnesia of human beings. It does not, however, undermine the very idea of revelation or of positive religion, and neither should it reduce all theology to apophatic silence. So long as theology views its task within the biblical call to constant self-examination, purification, and renewal, it need not be inclined to jettison the capacious symbols of that very tradition, whether in deference to the first principles of science or a too-facile judgment of what will or will not be intelligible to contemporary believers. While Kantian or otherwise apophatic sensibilities aim (rightly) to protect the mystery of God from religious and rationalist hubris, pressed too far or invoked too prematurely in theological discourse they also risk foreclosing the capaciousness of the Catholic sacramental imagination—not least its capacity for holding in fruitful and credible tension seemingly disparate experiences (and discourses) from the realms of both religion and science.

What makes Haight's approach so compelling, along with others who advance a starting point in the Jesus of history, is that it takes with utter seriousness the situation of a Western, secular, postmodern audience for whom historical consciousness is the common intellectual currency. Merton, by contrast, questions the epistemological assumptions of historical consciousness itself, especially where it operates as the primary or decisive lens for Christology. And he too raises questions that will not simply go away: "Is the long tradition of Christian mysticism, from the post-Apostolic age, the Alexandrian and Cappadocian Fathers, down to Eckhart, Tauler, the Spanish mystics and the modern mystics, simply a deviation? When people who cannot entrust themselves to the Church as she now is, nevertheless look with interest and sympathy into the writings of the mystics, are they to be reproved by Christians and admonished to seek rather a more limited and more communal experience of fellowship with progressive believers on the latter's terms? Is this the only true way to understand Christian experience?"[76]

---

75. ESF, 65, 67.

76. ZBA, 21. Elsewhere Merton frames the problem less polemically, with greater attention to the aberrations of "mystical" religion: "We must realize that we are emerging from a long period of combined *anti-mysticism* and *false mysticism*, one aiding and abetting the other. [The] strongly rationalist character of our culture has affected even theologians, and they have

If we have learned anything from Merton, perhaps it is this: the best way forward, the way of wisdom, will allow ample room for both theological trajectories, both sides of the mosaic tapestry that makes up the communal memory and experience of Jesus Christ in the global fellowship of faith. What recommends the sophiological tradition precisely in such an "either/or" ecclesial climate is its role as a "mediating discipline," a "both/and" conceptuality that respects both the "high" and "low" elements of the gospels, that takes Chalcedon as a crucial starting point but also refuses to regard christological dogma as a finished thing. It should be clear by now that this refusal is neither an act of rebellion nor an embrace of "creativity" and "daring" for its own sake; rather, it is an act of faith in the Spirit's guidance of the church, whose vitality as a living tradition depends on the fruitful attunement of unity and plurality, the peaceful realization of similarities-in-difference.[77]

A final defense I would offer on the question of intelligibility pertains to Merton's artistic sensibilities, a gift, perhaps, from his parents Owen and Ruth. Even Merton's most formal theological texts are generally saved from abstraction or aesthetic fancy by his appreciation for the concrete and particular—the inscape, the suchness, *le point vierge*[78]—of things. Like his photography and poetry, his calligraphy and sketches, Merton's theology directs our attention to God's presence in the ordinary, where Love hides "behind a veil of humility." "Getting it" implies no "word-magic," but it does require that we open our eyes to possibilities already "hidden in everyday life." All of this is to reiterate that the question of intelligibility must be asked with the whole person in mind, and not by a measure of rationality too narrowly conceived. In the final analysis, the inner truth of revelation is not subordinate to our capacity to find it intelligible by modern rationalist standards, or beautiful by purely aesthetic ones.

To Live Our Theology

As much as any systematic evaluation, perhaps what most recommends a sympathetic hearing of Russian sophiology in the West is its role in Merton's transformation, his awakening to the world beyond the monastery. The fact

---

become shy of mysticism as 'unscientific.' On the other hand [there has been a] flowering of irresponsibility and illuminism, [a] multiplication of visionaries, etc." (ICM, 16).

77. Athanasius put the matter this way, in his defense of a fellow theologian's (opposing) position in the Arian controversy: "concerning subjects that are obscure, and which require advancement toward understanding, often not only different but even contradictory demonstrations can become clarifications of the things sought for" (*De Sententia Dionysii* 18).

78. Christine M. Bochen's discussion of the term *le point vierge* wonderfully evokes the meaning of all of these terms, which function nearly as synonyms for Merton. See TME, 363.

that a Trappist monk who passed his days in the hills of Kentucky would have died in Asia, that he had gone there as a spiritual pilgrim, desiring especially to meet with the Dalai Lama, that just days before his death he would experience a kind of mystical breakthrough at the Buddhist shrine of Polonnaruwa—all of these seeming contradictions no longer seem as contradictions in light of the eschatological trajectory joining Merton's breathlessness before Mount Kanchenjunga, to the young Bulgakov's wonder before the Caucasus mountains, and still further, to Soloviev's visions of Sophia in the Egyptian desert.

If Merton recognized that his contact with the non-Christian world was "dangerous" in 1959—and could still "thank God for it"[79]—surely the putative "clash of civilizations" in a post–9/11 world begs an obvious question: what will be our part? The term "presence" as Merton used it refers not only to the agency or grace of Christ, hidden but dynamically present in the lives of people everywhere. It also refers to the agency of God-filled human beings, the vocation of every Christian to be the presence of Christ for others in love, mercy, and friendship. It is "a call not only to love but to *be loved*"[80] by others. Both aspects of presence—to (actively) love others and to (receptively) allow oneself be loved—were crucial lessons Merton learned in the last decade of his life. "What we must really do," as he said to his brother monks at Gethsemani, "is *live our theology.*"[81] This is substantively the same message (and theandric affirmation) with which St. Paul exhorted the early Christian community: "Let the same mind be in you that was in Christ Jesus" (Phil 2:5).

Merton's life witnesses to the constitutive link between the *ad intra* grasp of God's presence (Sophia) in the depths of one's own heart and the *ad extra* discovery of God's presence in creation and in the whole of the human family. "The inner and outer world of prayer and faith are indissolubly bound up together."[82] If we really believe (not just notionally) that Christ "plays in ten thousand places," that God's Spirit is hidden in the mystery of the stranger, it is only *because we love,* because *we have first been loved* by Christ in the center of our inmost being. This intense personalism at the heart of New Testament faith in Jesus places prayer, contemplation, and some measure of solitude at the center of the Christian vocation to peace. To the degree we desire to live in peace with others and in sustainable harmony with "Mother

79. SFS, 288.

80. NM, 91; see also Plank, "The Eclipse of Difference," 81, where he comments on this crucial passage in *The New Man.*

81. ICM, 16.

82. A. M. Allchin, "The Prayer of the Heart and Natural Contemplation," in MHPH, 419–29, at 419.

Earth," we, too, will have to "live our theology," and all such living begins with prayer.[83]

It is crucial to remember that the sophiological perspective is alive to God's presence in the world never as "abstract essence," or "merely" symbolically, but concretely, sacramentally, more than literally. But this sacramental grasp of reality depends in turn on the liberation of the image of God in our selves, what Merton calls the recovery of the "true self," or, as in *Hagia Sophia*, poverty of spirit. With its foundation in the Beatitudes of Jesus, poverty of spirit is none other than the cultivation of humility and love, crucial for the attunement of the spiritual senses, for grasping God's presence in all things. It implies not the embrace of an elaborate theology so much as a way of life: a commitment to prayer, community, simplicity, solitude, asceticism—all means of "clearing" or "tilling" the body, spirit, mind, and (to be sure) the imagination of inordinate attachments. "When a man has been purified and humbled, when his eye is single, and he is his own real self, then the *logoi* of things jump out at him spontaneously."[84] The way of sacrifice and contemplation is integral to the vocation of every Christian, not only the monk. In other words, it is both our orthodoxy and our orthopraxy that "saves" us, that day in and day out builds in us, and in those with whom we live and work, "a sense of community with things in the work of salvation." "Without love," Merton insists, "this is completely impossible."[85]

Making Old Things New

Paul Valliere concludes his magisterial study of modern Russian theology with words that could well describe Thomas Merton's last decade: "The Russian school is honored not by imitation, much less by canonization, but by new theological projects inspired by the same theological eros which animated its own."[86] Both in life and in theology, Merton succeeded in his desire to unite in himself "the thought of the East and the West, of the Greek and Latin Fathers."[87] If Christology in the West finds itself at a critical crossroads, Merton's witness goes some distance in suggesting that we might look to the East for positive direction—not only the East of Zen, with which Merton

83. In "Notes for a Philosophy of Solitude" (DQ, 177–207), an essay he considered one of his most important, Merton describes solitude as an indispensable element of healing and peace not only for the monk but for all human beings—solitude as *kenosis*, as ascetic disengagement from captivity to the noise, the violence, the glitter of idols; cf. "Love for God and Mutual Charity" (MHPH, 447–72), a wonderfully informal treatise on prayer given to the novices.

84. ICM, 132.

85. Ibid., 128.

86. Valliere, MRT, 401–2.

87. SFS, 87; CGB, 21.

is most often associated, but also the wisdom of Eastern Orthodoxy, from which the Catholic West has been too long estranged. Indeed, we might say that it was the marriage of both Zen and Sophia in Merton's life and theology that points us today toward something altogether new, yet also wordlessly ancient, in the silent *memoria* of God. Aloysius Pieris suggests as much: "It was really not in Asia that Merton discovered the East; there he only recognized and named what he had already sought and found in his own monastic cell. . . . The West can recover its *Eastern sense* by dialoguing with its own monks."[88]

When I began researching this project, the question that haunted me was not strictly theological so much as existential: *why Sophia* in a century of such unspeakable violence? Certainly I am not the first to wonder what Merton would have to say about the human condition at the turn of the twenty-first century. Perhaps his "anti-poetry" would take the form of dissonant elegies, laments for the "night face" of Sophia. He might continue to describe the world as he did in 1966, as "*the nest of the Unspeakable*." But I think he would also urge us to look deeply at reality, to take the time to open ourselves to ordinary experience, its extraordinary "suchness." "The presence of God is like walking out of a door into the fresh air. You don't concentrate on the fresh air, you breathe it. And you don't concentrate on the sunlight, you just enjoy it. It is all around."[89]

As simple (or quaint) as the contemplative path may sound to our coarsened postmodern sensibilities, it should not blind us to the radical demands the Gospel places on the Christian who stands before another human being, *any* human being, face-to-face. "If we believe in the Incarnation of the Son of God, there should be no one on earth in whom we are not prepared to see, in mystery, the presence of Christ."[90] Is this not after all the deepest mystery of our faith that "has to break through a little" if we are going to live as children of God, companions of Jesus, bearers of presence, peace, and hope in the twenty-first century? And every time this grace enfolds us, even just a little, it will be "like the first morning of the world (when Adam, at the sweet voice of Wisdom awoke from nonentity and knew her), and like the Last Morning of the world when all the fragments of Adam will return from death at the voice of Hagia Sophia, and will know where they stand."[91]

"It might be good," Merton suggests, "to open our eyes and *see*."[92]

88. Aloysius Pieris, *Love Meets Wisdom: A Christian Experience of Buddhism* (Maryknoll, NY: Orbis, 1988), 12.
89. MHPH, 454.
90. NSC, 296.
91. ESF, 62.
92. ZBA, 141.

«Wisdom will honor you if you embrace her/she will place on your head a fair garland/she will bestow on you a crown of glory.» (Proverbs 4: 8–9)

HAGIA SOPHIA

¶ . . . One day/Father Louis (Thomas Merton) our friend/came from his monastery at Trappist/Kentucky/to bring an ill novice to the hospital in Lexington. (I had known Father Louis since 1955 when I visited him for the first time. Later we printed several of his books.) We had prepared a simple luncheon and I welcomed him to sit with us at table. From where he sat he had a good view of the triptych on the chest and he often looked at it. After a while he asked quite abruptly/«And who is the woman behind Christ?» I said/«I do not know yet.» Without further question he gave his own answer. «She is Hagia Sophia/Holy Wisdom/who crowns Christ.» And this she was — and is.

— Victor Hammer

"Hagia Sophia Crowning the Young Christ." A line-cut of Victor Hammer's triptych painting of the same title. Courtesy of the Estate of Victor and Carolyn Hammer, and the King Library Press, University of Kentucky.

Hagia Sophia[1]

Thomas Merton

I. Dawn. The Hour of Lauds.

There is in all visible things an invisible fecundity, a dimmed light, a meek namelessness, a hidden wholeness. This mysterious Unity and Integrity is Wisdom, the Mother of all, *Natura naturans*. There is in all things an inexhaustible sweetness and purity, a silence that is a fount of action and joy. It rises up in wordless gentleness and flows out to me from the unseen roots of all created being, welcoming me tenderly, saluting me with indescribable humility. This is at once my own being, my own nature, and the Gift of my Creator's Thought and Art within me, speaking as Hagia Sophia, speaking as my sister, Wisdom.

I am awakened, I am born again at the voice of this my Sister, sent to me from the depths of divine fecundity.

Let us suppose I am a man lying asleep in a hospital. I am indeed this man lying asleep. It is July the second, the Feast of Our Lady's Visitation. A Feast of Wisdom.

At five-thirty in the morning I am dreaming in a very quiet room when a soft voice awakens me from my dream. I am like all mankind awakening from all the dreams that ever were dreamed in all the nights of the world. It is like the One Christ awakening in all the separate selves that ever were separate and isolated and alone in all the lands of the earth. It is like all minds coming back together into awareness from all distractions, cross-purposes and confusions, into unity of love. It is like the first morning of the world (when Adam, at the sweet voice of Wisdom awoke from nonentity and knew her), and like the Last Morning of the world when all the fragments of Adam will return from death at the voice of Hagia Sophia, and will know where they stand.

---

1. Thomas Merton, *Hagia Sophia* (Lexington, KY: Stamperia del Santuccio, 1962); here extracted in its entirety from ESF, 61–69.

Such is the awakening of one man, one morning, at the voice of a nurse in the hospital. Awakening out of languor and darkness, out of helplessness, out of sleep, newly confronting reality and finding it to be gentleness.

It is like being awakened by Eve. It is like being awakened by the Blessed Virgin. It is like coming forth from primordial nothingness and standing in clarity, in Paradise.

In the cool hand of the nurse there is the touch of all life, the touch of Spirit.

Thus Wisdom cries out to all who will hear (*Sapientia clamitat in plateis*) and she cries out particularly to the little, to the ignorant and the helpless.

Who is more little, who is more poor than the helpless man who lies asleep in his bed without awareness and without defense? Who is more trusting than he who must entrust himself each night to sleep? What is the reward of his trust? Gentleness comes to him when he is most helpless and awakens him, refreshed, beginning to be made whole. Love takes him by the hand, and opens to him the doors of another life, another day.

(But he who has defended himself, fought for himself in sickness, planned for himself, guarded himself, loved himself alone and watched over his own life all night, is killed at last by exhaustion. For him there is no newness. Everything is stale and old.)

When the helpless one awakens strong at the voice of mercy, it is as if Life his Sister, as if the Blessed Virgin, (his own flesh, his own sister), as if Nature made wise by God's Art and Incarnation were to stand over him and invite him with unutterable sweetness to be awake and to live. This is what it means to recognize Hagia Sophia.

II. Early Morning. The Hour of Prime.

O blessed, silent one, who speaks everywhere!

We do not hear the soft voice, the gentle voice, the merciful and feminine.

We do not hear mercy, or yielding love, or non-resistance, or non-reprisal. In her there are no reasons and no answers. Yet she is the candor of God's light, the expression of His simplicity.

We do not hear the uncomplaining pardon that bows down the innocent visages of flowers to the dewy earth. We do not see the Child who is prisoner in all the people, and who says nothing. She smiles, for though they have bound her, she cannot be a prisoner. Not that she is strong, or clever, but simply that she does not understand imprisonment.

The helpless one, abandoned to sweet sleep, him the gentle one will awake: Sophia.

All that is sweet in her tenderness will speak to him on all sides in everything, without ceasing, and he will never be the same again. He will have awakened not to conquest and dark pleasure but to the impeccable pure simplicity of One consciousness in all and through all: one Wisdom, one Child, one Meaning, one Sister.

The stars rejoice in their setting, and in the rising of the Sun. The heavenly lights rejoice in the going forth of one man to make a new world in the morning, because he has come out of the confused primordial dark night into consciousness. He has expressed the clear silence of Sophia in his own heart. He has become eternal.

III. High Morning. The Hour of Tierce.

The sun burns in the sky like the Face of God, but we do not know his countenance as terrible. His light is diffused in the air and the light of God is diffused by Hagia Sophia.

We do not see the Blinding One in black emptiness. He speaks to us gently in ten thousand things, in which His light is one fullness and one Wisdom.

Thus He shines not on them but from within them. Such is the loving-kindness of Wisdom.

All the perfections of created things are also in God; and therefore He is at once Father and Mother. As Father He stands in solitary might surrounded by darkness. As Mother His shining is diffused, embracing all His creatures with merciful tenderness and light. The Diffuse Shining of God is Hagia Sophia. We call her His "glory." In Sophia His power is experienced only as mercy and as love.

(When the recluses of fourteenth-century England heard their Church Bells and looked out upon the wolds and fens under a kind sky, they spoke in their hearts to "Jesus our Mother." It was Sophia that had awakened in their childlike hearts.)

Perhaps in a certain very primitive aspect Sophia is the unknown, the dark, the nameless Ousia. Perhaps she is even the Divine Nature, One in Father, Son and Holy Ghost. And perhaps she is infinite light unmanifest, not even waiting to be known as Light. This I do not know. Out of the silence Light is spoken. We do not hear it or see it until it is spoken.

In the Nameless Beginning, without Beginning, was the Light. We have not seen this Beginning. I do not know where she is, in this Beginning. I do not speak of her as a Beginning, but as a manifestation.

Now the Wisdom of God, Sophia, comes forth, reaching from "end to end mightily." She wills to be also the unseen pivot of all nature, the center and significance of all the light that is *in* all and *for* all. That which is poorest and humblest, that which is most hidden in all things is nevertheless most obvious in them, and quite manifest, for it is their own self that stands before us, naked and without care.

Sophia, the feminine child, is playing in the world, obvious and unseen, playing at all times before the Creator. Her delights are to be with the children of men. She is their sister. The core of life that exists in all things is tenderness, mercy, virginity, the Light, the Life considered as passive, as received, as given, as taken, as inexhaustibly renewed by the Gift of God. Sophia is Gift, is Spirit, *Donum Dei*. She is God-given and God Himself as Gift. God as all, and God reduced to Nothing: inexhaustible nothingness. *Exinanivit semetipsum*. Humility as the source of unfailing light.

Hagia Sophia in all things is the Divine Life reflected in them, considered as a spontaneous participation, as their invitation to the Wedding Feast.

Sophia is God's sharing of Himself with creatures. His outpouring, and the Love by which He is given, and known, held and loved.

She is in all things like the air receiving the sunlight. In her they prosper. In her they glorify God. In her they rejoice to reflect Him. In her they are united with him. She is the union between them. She is the Love that unites them. She is life as communion, life as thanksgiving, life as praise, life as festival, life as glory.

Because she receives perfectly there is in her no stain. She is love without blemish, and gratitude without self-complacency. All things praise her by being themselves and by sharing in the Wedding Feast. She is the Bride and the Feast and the Wedding.

The feminine principle in the world is the inexhaustible source of creative realizations of the Father's glory. She is His manifestation in radiant splendor! But she remains unseen, glimpsed only by a few. Sometimes there are none who know her at all.

Sophia is the mercy of God in us. She is the tenderness with which the infinitely mysterious power of pardon turns the darkness of our sins into the light of grace. She is the inexhaustible fountain of kindness, and would almost seem to be, in herself, all mercy. So she does in us a greater work than that of Creation: the work of new being in grace, the work of pardon, the work of transformation from brightness to brightness *tamquam a Domini Spiritu*. She is in us the yielding and tender counterpart of the power, justice and creative dynamism of the Father.

IV. Sunset. The Hour of Compline. Salve Regina.

Now the Blessed Virgin Mary is the one created being who enacts and shows forth in her life all that is hidden in Sophia. Because of this she can be said to be a personal manifestation of Sophia, Who in God is *Ousia* rather than Person.

Natura in Mary becomes pure Mother. In her, *Natura* is as she was from the origin from her divine birth. In Mary *Natura* is all wise and is manifested as an all-prudent, all-loving, all-pure person: not a Creator, and not a Redeemer, but perfect Creature, perfectly Redeemed, the fruit of all God's great power, the perfect expression of wisdom in mercy.

It is she, it is Mary, Sophia, who in sadness and joy, with the full awareness of what she is doing, sets upon the Second Person, the Logos, a crown which is His Human Nature. Thus her consent opens the door of created nature, of time, of history, to the Word of God.

God enters into His creation. Through her wise answer, through her obedient understanding, through the sweet yielding consent of Sophia, God enters without publicity into the city of rapacious men.

She crowns Him not with what is glorious, but with what is greater than glory: the one thing greater than glory is weakness, nothingness, poverty.

She sends the infinitely Rich and Powerful One forth as poor and helpless, in His mission of inexpressible mercy, to die for us on the Cross.

The shadows fall. The stars appear. The birds begin to sleep. Night embraces the silent half of the earth.

A vagrant, a destitute wanderer with dusty feet, finds his way down a new road. A homeless God, lost in the night, without papers, without identification, without even a number, a frail expendable exile lies down in desolation under the sweet stars of the world and entrusts Himself to sleep.

Bibliography

(Unless otherwise noted below, references in the text are to the later editions of these works.)

Thomas Merton (Chronological)

Books

Merton, Thomas. *The Seven Storey Mountain*. New York: Harcourt Brace, 1948. Reprint, New York: Harcourt Brace Jovanovich, 1999.

———. *Bread in the Wilderness*. New York: New Directions, 1953.

———. *The Sign of Jonas*. New York: Harcourt Brace, 1953. Reprint, New York: Octagon, 1983.

———. *Disputed Questions*. New York: Farrar, Straus and Cudahy, 1960. Reprint, New York: Harcourt Brace, 1985.

———. *The Behavior of Titans*. New York: New Directions, 1961.

———. *The New Man*. New York: Farrar, Straus and Cudahy, 1961. Reprint, New York: Farrar, Straus and Giroux, 1999.

———. *New Seeds of Contemplation*. New York: New Directions, 1962.

———. *Emblems of a Season of Fury*. New York: New Directions, 1963.

———. *Seeds of Destruction*. New York: Farrar, Straus and Giroux, 1964.

———. *The Way of Chuang Tzu*. New York: New Directions, 1965.

———. *Gandhi on Non-Violence: A Selection from the Writings of Mahatma Gandhi*. New York: New Directions, 1965.

———. *Raids on the Unspeakable*. New York: New Directions, 1966.

———. *Conjectures of a Guilty Bystander*. Garden City, NY: Doubleday, 1966.

———. *Mystics and Zen Masters*. New York: Farrar, Straus and Giroux, 1967.

———. *Faith and Violence: Christian Teaching and Christian Practice*. Notre Dame, IN: University of Notre Dame Press, 1968.

———. *Zen and the Birds of Appetite*. New York: New Directions, 1968.

———. *Opening the Bible*. Collegeville, MN: Liturgical Press, 1970.

———. *Contemplation in a World of Action*. New York: Doubleday, 1971. Reprint, Notre Dame, IN: University of Notre Dame, 1998.

———. *A Thomas Merton Reader: Revised Edition*. Edited by Thomas P. McDonnell. Garden City, NY: Doubleday, 1974.

———. *The Monastic Journey*. Edited by Patrick Hart. Kansas City, MO: Sheed Andrews and McMeel, 1977. Reprint, Kalamazoo, MI: Cistercian, 1992.

————. *Love and Living.* Edited by Naomi Burton Stone and Patrick Hart. New York: Farrar, Straus and Giroux, 1979. Reprint, New York: Harcourt Brace Jovanovich, 1985.

————. *Day of a Stranger.* Salt Lake City: Gibbs M. Smith, 1981.

————. *The Literary Essays of Thomas Merton.* Edited by Patrick Hart. New York: New Directions, 1981.

————. *The Springs of Contemplation: A Retreat at the Abbey of Gethsemani.* Edited by Jane Marie Richardson. New York: Farrar, Straus and Giroux, 1992.

————. *Cassian and the Fathers: Initiation into the Monastic Tradition.* Edited by Patrick F. O'Connell. Kalamazoo, MI: Cistercian, 2005.

————. *An Introduction to Christian Mysticism: Initiation into the Monastic Tradition 3.* Edited by Patrick F. O'Connell. Kalamazoo, MI: Cistercian, 2008.

Journals

————. *The Asian Journal of Thomas Merton.* Edited by Naomi Burton, Patrick Hart, and James Laughlin. New York: New Directions, 1973.

————. *A Search for Solitude: Pursuing the Monk's Life.* Vol. 3. Edited by Lawrence S. Cunningham. San Francisco: HarperSanFrancisco, 1996.

————. *Turning Toward the World: The Pivotal Years.* Vol. 4. Edited by Victor A. Kramer. San Francisco: HarperSanFrancisco, 1997.

————. *Dancing in the Water of Life: Seeking Peace in the Hermitage.* Vol. 5. Edited by Robert E. Daggy. San Francisco: HarperSanFrancisco, 1997.

————. *Learning to Love: Exploring Solitude and Freedom.* Vol. 6. Edited by Christine M. Bochen. San Francisco: HarperSanFrancisco, 1997.

————. *The Other Side of the Mountain.* Vol. 7. Edited by Patrick Hart. San Francisco: HarperSanFrancisco, 1998.

Letters

————. *The Hidden Ground of Love: The Letters of Thomas Merton on Religious Experience and Social Concerns.* Edited by William H. Shannon. New York: Farrar, Straus and Giroux, 1985.

————. *The Courage for Truth: The Letters of Thomas Merton to Writers.* Edited by Christine M. Bochen. New York: Farrar, Straus and Giroux, 1993.

————. *Witness to Freedom: The Letters of Thomas Merton in Times of Crisis.* Edited by William H. Shannon. New York: Farrar, Straus and Giroux, 1994. Reprint, New York: Harcourt Brace, 1995.

Secondary Works and Edited Volumes on Thomas Merton

Allchin, A. M. "Our Lives a Powerful Pentecost." In *Merton and Hesychasm: Prayer of the Heart: The Eastern Church.* Louisville, KY: Fons Vitae, 2003.

————. "The Prayer of the Heart and Natural Contemplation." In *Merton and Hesychasm: Prayer of the Heart: The Eastern Church.* Louisville, KY: Fons Vitae, 2003.

Betz, Margaret Bridget. "Merton's Images of Elias, Wisdom, and the Inclusive God." In *The Merton Annual: Studies in Culture, Spirituality, and Social Concerns*. Vol. 13. Edited by George A. Kilcourse. Sheffield, UK: Sheffield Academic Press, 2001.

Bruteau, Beatrice, ed. *Merton and Judaism: Recognition, Repentance, and Renewal: Holiness in Words*. Louisville, KY: Fons Vitae, 2003.

Carr, Anne E. "Merton's East-West Reflections." *Horizons* 21(1994): 239–52.

———. *A Search for Wisdom and Spirit: Thomas Merton's Theology of the Self*. Notre Dame, IN: University of Notre Dame Press, 1988.

Cunningham, Lawrence S. *Thomas Merton and the Monastic Vision*. Grand Rapids, MI: Eerdmans, 1999.

———, ed. *Thomas Merton: Spiritual Master: The Essential Writings*. New York: Paulist, 1992.

Dieker, Bernadette, and Jonathan Montaldo, eds. *Merton and Hesychasm: Prayer of the Heart: The Eastern Church*. Louisville, KY: Fons Vitae, 2003.

Forest, Jim. *Living with Wisdom: A Life of Thomas Merton*. Maryknoll, NY: Orbis, 2008.

———. "Thomas Merton and the Silence of the Icons." In *Merton and Hesychasm: Prayer of the Heart: The Eastern Church*. Louisville, KY: Fons Vitae, 2003.

Kaplan, Edward K. "'Under My Catholic Skin': Thomas Merton's Opening to Judaism and to the World." In *Merton and Judaism: Recognition, Repentance, and Renewal: Holiness in Words*. Louisville, KY: Fons Vitae, 2003.

Kilcourse, George. *Ace of Freedoms: Thomas Merton's Christ*. Notre Dame, IN: University of Notre Dame Press, 1993.

McCaslin, Susan. "Merton and 'Hagia Sophia.'" In *Merton and Hesychasm: Prayer of the Heart: The Eastern Church*. Louisville, KY: Fons Vitae, 2003.

Montaldo, Jonathan. "A Gallery of Women's Faces and Dreams of Women from the Drawings and Journals of Thomas Merton." In *The Merton Annual: Studies in Culture, Spirituality and Social Concerns*. Vol. 14. Edited by Victor A. Kramer. Sheffield, UK: Sheffield Academic Press, 2001.

Mott, Michael. *The Seven Mountains of Thomas Merton*. Boston: Houghton Mifflin, 1984.

Nugent, Christopher. "Merton, the Coincidence of Opposites and the Archeology of Catholicity." *Cistercian Studies* 26 (1991): 257–70.

———. "*Pax Heraclitus*: A Perspective on Merton's Healing Wholeness." Unpublished manuscript (2005).

O'Connell, Patrick F., ed. *The Vision of Thomas Merton*. Notre Dame, IN: Ave Maria, 2003.

Pennington, M. Basil, ed. *Toward an Integrated Humanity: Thomas Merton's Journey*. Kalamazoo, MI: Cistercian, 1988.

Plank, Karl A. "The Eclipse of Difference: Merton's Encounter with Judaism." In *Merton and Judaism: Recognition, Repentance, and Renewal: Holiness in Words*. Louisville, KY: Fons Vitae, 2003.

Shannon, William H. *Silent Lamp: The Thomas Merton Story*. New York: Crossroad, 1992.

————, Christine M. Bochen, and Patrick F. O'Connell. *The Thomas Merton Encyclopedia*. Maryknoll, NY: Orbis, 2002.

Thurston, Bonnie, ed. *Merton and Buddhism: Realizing the Self*. Louisville, KY: Fons Vitae, 2007.

Wilkes, Paul, ed. *Merton: By Those Who Knew Him Best*. Cambridge: Harper and Row, 1984.

Zyniewicz, Matthew C. "The Interreligious Dialogue Between Thomas Merton and D. T. Suzuki." PhD diss., University of Notre Dame, 2000.

Works by and about the Russian Theologians

Arjakovsky, Antoine. "The Sophiology of Father Sergius Bulgakov and Contemporary Western Theology." *St. Vladimir's Theological Quarterly* 49 (2005): 219–35.

Bulgakov, Sergei. *The Bride of the Lamb*. Translated by Boris Jakim. Grand Rapids, MI: Eerdmans, 2002.

————. *Sophia: The Wisdom of God: An Outline of Sophiology*. Hudson, NY: Lindisfarne Press, 1993. Rev. ed. of *The Wisdom of God: A Brief Summary of Sophiology*. Translated by Patrick Thompson et al. New York: Paisley, 1937.

Evdokimov, Paul. *Woman and the Salvation of the World: A Christian Anthropology on the Charisms of Women*. Translated by Anthony P. Gythiel. Crestwood, NY: St. Vladimir's Seminary Press, 1994 (originally published in 1949).

Evtuhov, Catherine. *The Cross and the Sickle: Sergei Bulgakov and the Fate of Russian Religious Philosophy*. Ithaca, NY: Cornell University Press, 1997.

Kornblatt, Judith, and Richard Gustafson, eds. *Russian Religious Thought*. Madison, WI: University of Wisconsin Press, 1996.

Louth, Andrew. "Wisdom and the Russians: The Sophiology of Fr. Sergei Bulgakov." In *Where Shall Wisdom Be Found? Wisdom in the Bible, the Church, and the Contemporary World*. Edited by Stephen C. Barton. Edinburgh: T and T Clark, 1999.

Meehan, Brenda. "Wisdom/Sophia, Russian Identity, and Western Feminist Theology." *CrossCurrents* 46 (1996): 149–68.

Rosenthal, Bernice. "The Nature and Function of Sophia in Sergei Bulgakov's Prerevolutionary Thought." In *Russian Religious Thought*. Edited by Judith Kornblatt and Richard Gustafson. Madison, WI: University of Wisconsin Press, 1996.

Soloviev, Vladimir. *Lectures on Godmanhood*. London: Dobson, 1948.

————. *The Meaning of Love*. London: Centenary, 1945.

Tataryn, Myroslaw. "History Matters: Bulgakov's Sophianic Key." *St. Vladimir's Theological Quarterly* 49 (2005): 203–18.

Valliere, Paul. *Modern Russian Theology: Bukharev, Soloviev, Bulgakov: Orthodox Theology in a New Key*. Grand Rapids, MI: Eerdmans, 2000.

Williams, Rowan. "Bread in the Wilderness: The Monastic Ideal in Thomas Merton and Paul Evdokimov." In *One Yet Two: Monastic Tradition East and West*. Edited by M. Basil Pennington. Kalamazoo, MI: Cistercian, 1976.

————. "Eastern Orthodox Theology." In *The Modern Theologians*. Edited by David F. Ford. Cambridge, MA: Blackwell, 1997.

————, ed. *Sergii Bulgakov: Towards a Russian Political Theology.* Edinburgh: T and T Clark, 1999.

Secondary Sources by General Area

Biblical Studies and Wisdom Christology

Barton, Stephen C., ed. *Where Shall Wisdom Be Found? Wisdom in the Bible, the Church, and the Contemporary World.* Edinburgh: T and T Clark, 1999.

Brueggemann, Walter. *Theology of the Old Testament: Testimony, Dispute, Advocacy.* Minneapolis: Fortress, 1997.

Dunn, James D. G. *Christology in the Making: A New Testament Inquiry into the Origins of the Doctrine of the Incarnation.* Philadelphia: Westminster Press, 1980. Second edition, Grand Rapids, MI: Eerdmans, 1996.

————. *The Partings of the Ways: Between Christianity and Judaism and their Significance for the Character of Christianity.* London, SCM, 1991.

Ford, David F., and Graham Stanton, eds. *Reading Texts, Seeking Wisdom: Scripture and Theology.* Grand Rapids, MI: Eerdmans, 2003.

Johnson, E. Elizabeth. "Wisdom and Apocalyptic in Paul." In *In Search of Wisdom: Essays in Memory of John G. Gammie,* edited by Leo G. Perdue, Bernard B. Scott, and William J. Wiseman. Louisville, KY: Westminster John Knox, 1993.

Johnson, Elizabeth A. "Jesus, the Wisdom of God: A Biblical Basis for a Non-androcentric Christology." *Ephemerides theologicae Lovanienses* 41 (1985): 261–94.

————. *She Who Is: The Mystery of God in Feminist Discourse.* New York: Crossroad, 1992.

Murphy, Roland. "Israel's Wisdom: A Biblical Model of Salvation." *Studia Missionalia* 30 (1981).

————. *The Tree of Life: An Exploration of Biblical Wisdom Literature.* Anchor Bible Reference Library. New York: Doubleday, 1990.

————. "Wisdom Literature." In *The New Jerome Biblical Commentary.* Edited by Raymond Brown, Joseph Fitzmyer, and Roland Murphy. Upper Saddle River, NJ: Prentice Hall, 1990.

————. *Wisdom Literature and Psalms.* Interpreting Biblical Texts. Nashville: Abingdon, 1983.

Perdue, Leo G., Bernard B. Scott, and William J. Wiseman, eds. *In Search of Wisdom: Essays in Memory of John G. Gammie.* Louisville, KY: Westminster John Knox, 1993.

Pippen, Tina. "Wisdom and Apocalyptic in the Apocalypse of John: Desiring Sophia." In *In Search of Wisdom: Essays in Memory of John G. Gammie.* Edited by Leo G. Perdue, Bernard B. Scott, and William J. Wiseman. Louisville, KY: Westminster John Knox, 1993.

Epistemology and Method: Imagination, Memory, Poetics

Burrows, Mark S. "Raiding the Inarticulate: Mysticism, Poetics, and the Unlanguageable." In *Minding the Spirit: The Study of Christian Spirituality.* Edited by Elizabeth A. Dreyer and Mark S. Burrows. Baltimore: Johns Hopkins, 2005.

————. "Words That Reach into the Silence: Mystical Languages of Unsaying." In *Minding the Spirit: The Study of Christian Spirituality*. Edited by Elizabeth A. Dreyer and Mark S. Burrows. Baltimore: Johns Hopkins, 2005.

Coulson, John. "Belief and Imagination." *The Downside Review* 90 (1972): 1–14.

Dreyer, Elizabeth A. and Mark S. Burrows, eds. *Minding the Spirit: The Study of Christian Spirituality*. Baltimore: Johns Hopkins, 2005.

Dulles Avery. "From Images to Truth: Newman on Revelation and Faith." *Theological Studies* 51 (1990): 252–67.

————. *Newman*. New York: Continuum, 2002.

Endean, Philip. *Karl Rahner and Ignatian Spirituality*. New York: Oxford University Press, 2001.

Greeley, Andrew. "The Apologetics of Beauty." *America* 183, no. 7 (Sep. 16, 2000): 8–12.

Heschel, Abraham Joshua. *God in Search of Man*. New York: Farrar, Straus and Cudahy, 1955.

————. *Man Is Not Alone: A Philosophy of Religion*. New York: Farrar, Straus and Young, 1951.

————. *Man's Quest for God: Studies in Prayer and Symbolism*. New York: Scribner's, 1954.

————. *Moral Grandeur and Spiritual Audacity*. Edited by Susannah Heschel. New York: Farrar, Straus and Giroux, 1996.

————. *The Prophets*. New York: Harper and Row, 1962.

Hopkins, Gerard Manley. *Gerard Manley Hopkins: The Major Works*. Edited by Catherine Phillips. New York: Oxford University Press, 1986.

Kaplan, Edward K. *Holiness in Words: Abraham Joshua Heschel's Poetics of Piety*. Albany: State University of New York Press, 1996.

————. "Language and Reality in Abraham J. Heschel's Philosophy of Religion," *Journal of the American Academy of Religion* 41, no. 1 (March 1973): 94–113.

Kim, Younhee. "David Tracy's Postmodern Reflection on God." *Louvain Studies* 30 (2005): 159–79.

Laycock, Gordon. *Holy Things: A Liturgical Theology*. Minneapolis: Fortress, 1993.

Lynch, William. *Images of Faith: An Exploration of the Ironic Imagination*. Notre Dame, IN: University of Notre Dame Press, 1973.

————. *Images of Hope: Imagination as Healer of the Hopeless*. Baltimore: Helicon, 1965.

Madden, Nicholas. "Approaching Theology with Newman." *Irish Theological Quarterly* 69 (2004): 323–36.

Magill, Gerard. "Moral Imagination in Theological Method and Church Tradition: John Henry Newman." *Theological Studies* 53 (1992): 451–75.

Markus, R. A. *Signs and Meanings: World and Text in Ancient Christianity*. Liverpool: Liverpool University Press, 1996.

Merrigan, Terrence. "The Anthropology of Conversion: Newman and the Contemporary Theology of Religions." In *Newman and Conversion*. Edited by Ian Ker. Edinburgh: T and T Clark, 1997.

————. "Newman and Theological Liberalism." *Theological Studies* 66 (2005): 605–21.

Metz, Johann Baptist. *Faith in History and Society: Toward a Practical Fundamental Theology.* Translated and edited by J. Matthew Ashley (New York: Crossroad, 2007).

———. *A Passion for God: the Mystical-Political Dimension of Christianity.* Translated by J. Matthew Ashley. New York: Paulist, 1998.

Newman, John Henry. *Apologia Pro Vita Sua.* Edited by Ian Ker. London: Penguin, 1994.

———. *An Essay in Aid of a Grammar of Assent.* Notre Dame, IN: University of Notre Dame Press, 1979.

———. *An Essay on the Development of Christian Doctrine.* Notre Dame, IN: University of Notre Dame Press, 1989.

———. *Fifteen Sermons Preached Before the University of Oxford.* Notre Dame, IN: University of Notre Dame Press, 1997.

Schneiders, Sandra. *Women and the Word: The Gender of God in the New Testament and the Spirituality of Women.* New York: Paulist, 1986.

Thiel, John. "For What May We Hope? Thoughts on the Eschatological Imagination." *Theological Studies* 67 (2006): 517–41.

———. *Senses of Tradition: Continuity and Development in Catholic Faith.* Oxford: Oxford University Press, 2000.

Tracy, David. *The Analogical Imagination: Christian Theology and the Culture of Pluralism.* New York: Crossroad, 1981.

Issues in Modern and Postmodern Christology

Ashley, J. Matthew. "Apocalypticism in Political and Liberation Theology: Toward an Historical *Docta Ignorantia*," *Horizons* 27, no.1 (2000): 22–43.

Baillie, Donald M. *God Was in Christ.* New York: Scribner's, 1948.

Boeve, Lieven. "God Interrupts History: Apocalypticism as an Indispensable Theological Conceptual Strategy," *Louvain Studies* 26 (2001): 195–216.

Clifford, Anne M. and Anthony J. Godzieba, eds. *Christology: Memory, Inquiry, Practice.* College Theology Society Annual Volume 48. Maryknoll, NY: Orbis, 2003.

Cunningham, Lawrence S. "*Christos Mystikos*: Jesus Christ and the New Millenium." In *Who Do You Say That I Am? Confessing the Mystery of Christ.* Edited by John C. Cavadini and Laura Holt. Notre Dame, IN: University of Notre Dame Press, 2004.

———. "*Extra Arcam Noe*: Criteria for Christian Spirituality." In *Minding the Spirit: The Study of Christian Spirituality.* Edited by Elizabeth A. Dreyer and Mark S. Burrows. Baltimore: Johns Hopkins, 2005.

Haight, Roger. *The Future of Christology.* New York: Continuum, 2005.

———. *Jesus, Symbol of God.* Maryknoll, NY: Orbis, 1999.

Merrigan, Terrence, and Jacques Haers, eds. *The Myriad Christ: Plurality and the Quest for Unity in Contemporary Christology.* Leuven: Leuven University Press, 2000.

O'Collins, Gerald. *Christology: A Biblical, Historical, and Systematic Study of Jesus.* New York: Oxford University Press, 1995.

O'Meara, Thomas F. "Toward a Subjective Theology of Revelation." *Theological Studies* 36 (1975): 401–27.

Pieris, Aloysius. *Fire and Water: Basic Issues in Asian Buddhism and Christianity.* Maryknoll, NY: Orbis, 1996.

———. *Love Meets Wisdom: A Christian Experience of Buddhism.* Maryknoll, NY: Orbis, 1988.

Pui-lan, Kwok. "Mending of Creation: Women, Nature, and Eschatological Hope." In *Liberating Eschatology: Essays in Honor of Letty M. Russell.* Edited by Margaret Farley and Serene Jones. Louisville, KY: Westminster John Knox, 1999.

Rahner, Karl. *Foundations of Christian Faith: An Introduction to the Idea of Christianity.* Translated by William Dych. New York: Crossroad, 1978. Reprint, 1989.

Sobrino, Jon. *Spirituality of Liberation.* Translated by Robert Barr. Maryknoll, NY: Orbis, 1988.

Zizioulas, John D. *Being as Communion: Studies in Personhood and the Church.* Crestwood, NY: St. Vladimir's Seminary Press, 2002.

Monastic History and Spirituality

Bouyer, Louis. *The Cistercian Heritage.* Westminster, MD: Newman Press, 1958.

Cassian, John. *Conferences.* Translated by Colm Luibheid. New York: Paulist, 1985.

Chenu, Marie-Dominique. *Nature, Man, and Society in the Twelfth Century.* Translated by Jerome Taylor and Lester Little. Chicago: University of Chicago Press, 1957.

Griffiths, Bede. *The Marriage of East and West: A Sequel to the Golden String.* Springfield, IL: Templegate, 1982.

Harmless, William. *Desert Christians: An Introduction to the Literature of Early Monasticism.* New York: Oxford University Press, 2004.

Leclercq, Jean. *The Love of Learning and the Desire for God: A Study of Monastic Culture.* Translated by Catharine Misrahi. New York: Fordham University Press, 1961.

Louth, Andrew. "'Beauty Will Save the World': The Formation of Byzantine Spirituality." *Theology Today* 61 (2004): 67–77.

Pennington, M. Basil, ed. *One Yet Two: Monastic Tradition East and West.* Kalamazoo, MI: Cistercian, 1976.

Index

aesthetic theology, 26–27, 40, 58, 292–95. *See also* beauty

Allchin, A. M., xxix, 1, 21n68, 24, 129, 143n51, 145, 187n52

anamnesis, 26, 65n164, 84, 106, 112, 115n155, 160n128, 250, 278. *See also* memory

anthropology, theological, xxvii–xxviii, 32, 34–35, 104, 116n160, 141, 153, 179, 233–40, 281–88. *See also* humanity of God; incarnation

apocalypticism, xxv–xxvi, 23, 25–27, 77, 86, 212, 215–18, 225–28, 239–40, 250, 252n172, 257n190, 260–65, 272, 290. *See also* eschatology; Tracy, David

apophasis. *See* negative theology

Aquinas, St. Thomas, 35, 40n39, 49n80, 86n45, 121, 136, 180n15, 205, 229

art, as theological form, 100n100, 104, 117n164, 145, 193–96, 223–24, 243, 277, 283, 295

asceticism, xxvi, 84, 146, 192n67, 199, 237–38, 266, 297

Asian Journal, The, 3, 165, 171–73, 201, 227–28, 272, 289

Athanasius, St., 185–86, 236, 298n77. *See also* divinization

atheism, 222, 231, 258. *See also* "death of God" theology

Augustine, St., 19, 24n82, 35n14, 42n46, 49, 66, 69, 109n138, 117, 179, 191, 266

Auschwitz, xxv, 31, 54, 66, 123, 212, 215, 268

Baillie, Donald, 178–79, 191

Balthasar, Hans Urs von, 2n6, 22, 25–27, 143, 147, 291n66

Barth, Karl, 25, 92, 201–2, 216n9, 229n63

Beatitudes, the, 146, 197, 297

beauty, 56, 71, 158, 200, 204, 216, 222, 250, 264. *See also* aesthetic theology

Behavior of Titans, The, 137–42, 177n1, 196n82, 217n15, 264n214, 267n229

Benedict XVI, Pope, 34n12, 258

Berdyaev, Nicholas, 11–13, 28n95, 127, 144, 153–55, 247, 249n160

Bernard of Clairvaux, St., 8, 24n82, 179, 180n15, 250n165

Bible

   as *memoria*, 65n164, 111–14, 127, 140, 171n169, 197, 203, 258, 264n216

   eros in, 72, 252–53, 255–56, 269

   Heschel on, 56–66, 80, 147

   Merton on, xxvii, 17–18, 34, 79–80, 85, 106, 112–14, 125, 147–48, 277–78

   role of in theology, 9, 28, 108–112, 121, 208–9, 292

   See also imagination, biblical; monastic theology; prophecy; revelation

Blake, William, 34, 85–86, 116n160, 121, 182n26, 262, 272n254, 290